AND I FROM BOHEMIA

A MEMOIR

MARTIN S. GOLDMAN

PublishAmerica
Baltimore

First printing

PublishAmerica has allowed this work to remain exactly as the author intended, verbatim,
without editorial input.

Softcover 9781456030049
PUBLISHED BY PUBLISHAMERICA, LLLP
www.publishamerica.com
Baltimore

Printed in the United States of America

To the blessed memory of my Mother and Father
Louis and Ruth M. Goldman
who always supported me on this brief trip

Acknowledgements

I am well aware that it is the height of *chutzpah* to write a memoir. Why is one life more important than another? Why is my story more important than yours? Actually, it isn't.

But, as a trained historian, I think I have seen and done some things that deserve to be on the record. So, no apologies from me for setting this record straight.

I know that some readers will say, "This book can't be true. All this crammed into one life? Not possible!" Well, I definitely won't be making Oprah's book club but you will just have to trust me: I kept a journal in the 1950s. Every word in this memoir is true to the best of my memory and my written records.

Also, I have written this memoir because a number of Boston newspapers and magazines once accused me of fabricating certain articles I had written. And then *Boston Magazine* named me the worst political writer in Boston in 1989. I didn't fabricate then; I am not fabricating now. So yes, this memoir is a form of payback. Like Nancy Reagan once wrote with my old pal Bill Novak, it's "My Turn."

I owe some people more than I could ever repay. The experiences I have had are the sum total of having these people in my life at various junctures.

So here goes:

To my late beloved parents, Louis and Ruth M. Goldman: for putting up with an impossible teenager for years and for never giving up on him while supporting and encouraging him as an adult well into his 60s. I miss my Mom and Dad every day.

To my brother Ken Goldman: a talented, creative and scary writer in his own right who is well on his way to becoming the Poe-Lovecraft of our time. Ken was "the good son." Arrgh indeed!

To the boys at Harry's (the Spoon) who shared those crazy years shooting pool or playing pinball late into many nights in Jack Feldman's backroom while roaming the streets of Philly with me; the Spoon Boys at Harry's will forever live in my heart and memory:

Stanley "Benny" Stein, Paul Gansky, Eddie Friedman, Jerry Berger, Jerry Borkon, Irv Blank, Frankie Ash, Jack Zatz, Alan Martin, Lenny Ivker, Billy Stamps, Howard "Pretzel" Shander, Howie Gleit, Eddie Landay, Paul Rabinowitz (now Robins), Stan Halbert, Larry Laster, Bob Axelrod, the late Alfred Cohen, and the late Billy "Reds" Landau. My fervent hope is that we will all meet at the Spoon as it emerges from the magical mists of time on Diamond Street some Saturday night every 400 years or so like in *Brigadoon*. And we will all be there for one more game of 8-ball, a cheese steak and a hoagie (made by Jack Feldman).

To my late Aunt Nan Goldman Praissman: my personal teacher.

To my daughters and son-in-law:

Robin Goldstein and Ed Tripp

Laurie Lewis

To my grandchildren who never cease to amaze me and make me smile:

Hallie Goldstein, Samantha (Sami) Goldstein, Max Goldstein and Derek Tripp (your Pop-Pop loves you).

To my closest friends:

In Boston:

Larry Lowenthal and Pauline Gerson

Michael and Carol Kort

In Philadelphia:

Alvin Kolchins and Eleanor Powers

In memory of my late brother-in-law, Alvin Brown

My sister-in-law Iris (Rachman) Brown

In Maine:

John Phyllis and Ellen McKenna

Marianne Principe and Cliff Facey

In Florida:

Stanley (the B) and Myrna Stein

Sid and Audrey Wechter

Jeffrey Kern

To the many Spruce Creek softball players, coaches and umpires who have allowed me to recapture my long lost 10 year-old self once again.

To the dogs that accompanied me on my journey through the good and bad times, the long lonely nights, the hot summers and the cold winters, and the many walks and runs in the old Philly neighborhood, on the Boston Common, in the lush woods of Sudbury, Massachusetts and York, Maine: Rusty (who died in 1979 in his 19th year); Ripper of Hillcrest Farm days (a big, clunky Black Lab); Wookie (the greatest dog I ever knew); Gideon (a snow-white Labrador who captured my heart from his puppyhood in March 1995 to his last day in July 2009); and the newest member of our Maine and Florida households, Chewy B, the cutest and smartest Kerry Blue Terrier on the planet (and many thanks to Carol Postley for her generosity and unyielding love for Kerry Blues on her rambling sheep farm in Ocala, Florida where she raised our precious Chewy). There should always be a dog!

And finally, to the most important person in my life—my true love from 1956 to tomorrow. My unfailingly stylish and beautiful wife Arlene (Rachman) Goldman who has made me complete and whole—and a better man than I ever thought I could possibly be. Thanks Arlo for everything. I love you LaraLeenie!

Foreword

"Forgetfulness leads to exile, while remembrance is the secret of redemption."
The Ba'al Shem Tov

"What is frightening about looking back on your life at all the stupid things you did is the revelation that you are doing stupid things today..."
David Brenner, Comedian

"...the past soaks the present like the light of a distant star. Things that are over do not end..."
Leon Wieseltier, *Kaddish*

Memories are the footprints we leave in the snows of our past. They have a nasty habit of quickly melting away with the springs of time. I have always been blessed (or cursed! take your pick!) with a very good memory. Unlike the little kid in *The Sixth Sense*, I see things from the distant past—not "dead people." Though seeing dead people wouldn't bother me. Some of the people I have admired and loved best in this life are dead.

I can't tell you what I had for dinner last night. But my memory of the past is unfailing. The Kenya-born film director Scott Hicks says, "Memory is imperfect. It sometimes gives scenes a more golden glow." Of course, Hicks is right. And wrong! Memory has come in handy for me as a teacher over many years of college history. I can still give lectures on the Kennedy presidency, African-American history or the Holocaust virtually verbatim, without lecture notes after many years of teaching these specialized courses.

My closest friends tease me about my memory of the distant and recent past. They say that the only reason I can recall so much of the past is because I dwell in it—that, in effect, I have no present.

Well...perhaps. From 1975 to 2003, after a marriage of almost twelve years that ended in divorce, I spent close to three decades mostly alone. So, until 2003, aside from a brother and aging parents, I didn't have a family or children or anything that most normal people find that roots them to the present. And whoever said that I was normal?

Ralph Ellison, author of *Invisible Man* and one of the great writers of the twentieth century wrote in 1964,

> *That which we remember is, more often than not,*
> *that which we would like to have been, or that*
> *which we hope to be. Thus our memory and our*
> *identity are ever at odds; our history ever a*
> *tall tale told by inattentive idealists.*

Although I admire Ellison immensely, I must respectfully disagree. Sometimes memories can be indelible. Sometimes memories can take you back to magic or dark places. There must always be magic places in life. Sometimes those places are even golden. Maybe memory can be slightly tarnished, but golden nevertheless.

In 1951 I was vice-president of our sixth grade class at the William B. Mann School on 54th and Berks Street in Philadelphia. I was chosen by our teacher, Miss Ethel Barnes, a character right out of that opening scene in *Annie Hall*, to play the lead that year in the class play. The play was about the founding of the United Nations and the bedrock principles based on peace and sanctuary that were implemented to guide that august institution. You have to remember that many Americans set a lot of stock in an organization like a United Nations even before 1948. Just ask Woodrow Wilson!

The second lead was assigned to Jane Golubitsky (today a professor of Sociology at the University of Pennsylvania), the smartest girl in our class. Jane was chosen to play Miss Liberty—pointed crown, torch and all. And I was set to play the part of the first president or secretary-general (whatever) of the United Nations.

I learned that part inside out. I had it really nailed. I think I was a budding method actor. I was in every scene and things were going swimmingly in rehearsals. Who knows? Maybe I was on my way to becoming a James Dean, a DiNiro or even a Pacino. But it was not to be. I either talked out of turn in class or did something else to piss the spinsterish Miss Barnes off. She took my big part away and gave it to a bright suck-up named Joel Schecter. She then reduced my part in the play to a single line; a walk-on in the third and final act.

It was a very mean thing to do to a somewhat shy and insecure eleven-year-old kid. In those days teachers did all kinds of mean things and no one ever challenged them. No one ever dared question what a teacher did in the 1950s. It has never left my memory.

Miss Barnes didn't know it but I had asked my Dad to take the day off from work to attend the play which was to begin in the early afternoon. I didn't tell him I had the biggest part in the class but I think he suspected that my role would be something special. I wanted him to be surprised: surprised and proud when he saw his son with the lead in the school play. To the day my father died, I sought his pride and approval in just about everything I ever did. So, since I never told Pop that I had a big part, I never told him that I had lost it.

The big day of the school play came and there was my mother, who had arrived early, sitting down in the front. But sitting way in the back of that small auditorium with that great big trademark shit-eating grin that I always loved was my Pop. In the third act, with a crowd of other "immigrants" standing in front of Miss Liberty, on cue, I delivered my one line."

And I from Bohemia!

I have had no desire to act ever again. Pop never said a word. And I have been from Bohemia ever since.

INTRODUCTION

There is a scene in Barry Levinson's 1982 film *Diner* that pretty much explains one of the major forces that have guided my life. Two of the protagonists are driving down a quiet country road in the early morning after spending an all-nighter at their neighborhood diner in Baltimore. I spent much of my teenage years and young adulthood in a similar place in Philadelphia. Like the urban young men in *Diner*, I am Jewish and once knew the streets.

Boogie is played by Mickey Rourke in one of his initial film roles which began a promising career that never quite blossomed after Rourke became difficult and literally blew his entire future as our generation's Bogart through his nose. Mickey Rourke could have been a contender (as his 2009 comeback role in *The Wrestler* indicated).

Boogie and Fenwick, played by Kevin Bacon, drive by a gorgeous blonde astride a large horse cantering across a spectacular field in the Maryland countryside. The field turns out to be her backyard. Boogie, the leader of the diner gang, asks the girl her name: "Jane Chisholm. As in the Chisholm trail," the girl replies. "What fucking Chisholm trail?" Boogie exclaims. Then Fenwick asks his friend Boogie that all-important, heartrending question: "Ever get the feeling there's something going on we don't know about?"

For me, that has always been a key question in my life. I moved to York, Maine from Sudbury, Massachusetts twelve years ago last June. York lies on the rocky southern Maine seacoast. The town boasts some incredible beaches, the famous Nubble Lighthouse and, as only the second coastal town "downeast" from Kittery and five miles south of Ogonquit, lures a great many summer people who haven't the money or the stomach for the heavily trafficked Cape or the posh star-crossed Vineyard.

York's physical land mass, which most tourists drive past on their way to trendy Ogonquit, has a land mass equal to the size of Boston.

Many of the year-round residents are senior citizen retirees and many of the younger, newer people are refugees from Massachusetts attracted by the slower seacoast life, new homes and the cheaper prices. I traded a leaky, small home in Sudbury, Massachusetts for a new spacious, three-floor, rambling colonial with a two-car garage and a farmer's porch for lazy summers of watching the world go past.

I am a city mouse who has moved to the country. I am now a country mouse. The move, gradual though it has been, actually began in early 1967 when my then-wife and I rented a small ranch house in the hills of Auburn, Massachusetts on a large dairy farm about sixty miles outside of Boston and a few miles west of Worcester. We lived on that farm happily for almost eight years. Although we both were teachers, in that time I learned to farm. Every summer I planted a few acres of every kind of vegetable from corn, broccoli, squash, eggplant, melon and pumpkins to all varieties of tomatoes, cucumbers and string-beans. I made soups for the winter, froze some and gave away much of my vast harvest every year. It was a simple life—the simplest I have ever known.

There were eventually over sixty head of cattle on the farm by the time we were forced to leave after our landlord died. Our notoriously low rent of around $100 a month—low even back then did not suit his surviving family and after eight years we were asked unceremoniously to vacate the premises. There were also some sheep and horses. One of the sheep I liked was called Daisy. Her lamb was Pansy. I have always loved being around animals. I have had dogs since my early twenties—mostly Labrador Retrievers. I loved my last Lab like a member of the family. Gideon was a large, mostly white, yellow Lab who accepted me as his alpha male. Gideon died in 2009 in his fifteenth year. But the best dog I ever had was Wookie, a precious little terrier who looked like Benjie's (the movie dog) twin. He entered my life in March of 1982 and he died on December 4, 1994. He was as smart as any human I have ever known and loved me unconditionally. It may have been in a dream but I think one dark and mystery-laden New England night, Wookie actually told me he loved me. For me, December has always been my cruelest month. More about Wookie, named after Chewbacca the Wookie from Star Wars, later.

In Maine, in the thick woods behind my new house, I have already seen moose, deer, fox, wild turkey, coyote, turkey vultures, red-tail hawks, many skunks, chipmunks, red to gray squirrels and a variety of birds that would be a watcher's delight. I am told there are lynx, bobcat and even bear (a black bear foraged in my neighbor's bird feeder three years ago!). I'm not too keen on running into any of those.

I moved to Maine in '99 to fish and to write. I love the ocean. I once turned down a tenure track appointment at the University of Michigan, Dearborn to teach for a year at Rutgers. When the chair of the history department queried me about why I wasn't coming to live in Ann Arbor, I told him, "It's too far from the ocean." I don't think he understood what I meant. Most landlocked mid-westerners don't have a thing about the ocean.

I haven't written much lately although I did complete a novel that I had begun to write ten years ago. All of which means the fishing has been pretty damn good. Fishing season lasts from around the beginning of April to early October. And the catch can be as varied as flounder, stripers (bass), blues, crab and lobster. Just a few seasons ago I hauled two three-foot sharks out of the mouth of the York River just as it turns to run into the vast ocean. And, a few days later one of the guys I fish with pulled in a four-foot shark. Before September 11, 2001 was the summer of the shark. A best selling book, *Close to Shore*, about a Great White Shark eating people off the coast of New Jersey in 1916 was the most exciting fish story of the summer until the terrorists made real life in these United States more like the fiction I try to write. Until then I thought it interesting that sharks were apparently coming up the York River to feed in large numbers. Even a few of the old timers at Rick's Diner in York Village seemed interested in my shark stories—until September 11.

It wasn't just the fishing that has gotten in the way of my writing. Six months after I moved to Maine my father died. The death of a parent, at any point in life, is traumatic. But there is something about the death of a father who has been around your life for over sixty years that, as Samuel Johnson said about hanging a man, "concentrates his mind wonderfully." My Dad's death clearly concentrated my mind. I have thought about him every day since.

My father died on December 21, 1999 ten days before the end of the Millennium. He was 91 years old and had lived in every decade of the twentieth century, the bloodiest century in the history of the world. He had rarely been sick and although the doctors told me that he died from something called "Wegner's Disease," I am still not quite sure that some doctor didn't screw up. My brother says I should let it go. But I am not one, like my Dad, to ever let anything go. On the last day of his life, as they put my father on life support, in the haze of signing forms about how long he should be kept on the resuscitator, my father passed me a note. The handwriting is very scratchy and although most of the words are illegible I could make out the following sentence: "What is going on?" my father wrote in our last earthly communication. I looked at my father with the greatest sadness I have ever felt on this planet. How does a son tell the father he loves and worships that he is dying? The answer: he doesn't!

I didn't know what to tell him as he seemed to slip in and out of consciousness. "Dad," I whispered hoarsely at one point, "how long? I don't know what to do." He couldn't talk and squeezed my hand weakly. "Do you want me to keep you going as long as I can?" I asked.

He squeezed my hand again. That meant, I thought then, that we would dance to the end. My father wanted to stay around, it seemed to me, as long as he could. And since he was in no pain—he told us throughout that entire week that nothing actually hurt—I would honor his going the distance. After all, miracles do happen. We (my brother Ken and my mother) stayed with my father until they told us to leave around six or seven in the evening. Louis Goldman died a little after midnight. A doctor he was quite fond of was with him when he died. Or so I have been told. My Dad, who had been through his first dialysis the previous Friday, didn't want to go through that for the rest of his life. So I have always felt he finally decided to leave.

Should I have stayed until the end? Guilt is a useless emotion after the fact. It was my brother who woke me up the next morning and chokingly blurted out, "Dad died last night." He had known all night but saw no point in awakening us to pass on the terrible news. It was left to me to tell our mother. I had to first gather my wits. I decided to feed and exercise Gideon. When I returned from that interminable walk with Gideon my Mom was just answering the phone. It was one of the doctors who had worked on my Dad's kidney problems that week calling to say he was sorry. I think it was the doctor who had put him on dialysis that Friday when his kidneys were failing. I grabbed the phone from my mother's hand and managed to convey that my mother had not yet been told about our Dad's death. The poor doctor, unaware that my Mom hadn't yet been told, apologized profusely, told me how sorry he was and beat a hasty retreat. It wasn't an easy task telling a woman, in her 86th year with all her wits about her that her marriage of 62 plus years had come to an end. I sat my mother down on the couch, blurted it out and we cried together. It occurred to me that day that all marriages end. Some sooner, like mine; some later. Time, in its inimitable fashion, beats us all in one way or another.

The rabbi at the assisted care facility where my parents had just moved in October 1998 knocked on the door. I recall Gideon barking and, as usual, jumping. The next hours and days are mostly blurred. Making arrangements for any funeral is an onerous task. Making final arrangements for a parent is one of the most onerous things I have ever done. The guy at the funeral home grew up in my old neighborhood and although we didn't know each other well, he was very kind and did his best to make the thing somewhat palatable. Still, the whole process, as the kids today might say, sucks!

I can remember lots of friends, people I didn't know, people I did know, and others telling me how lucky I was: to have had my Dad for as long as we did. Funny, I didn't feel very lucky. Let me give you some advice. It will be the only advice I give out in this book: never tell anyone how lucky they are to have had a loved one who has died. No matter how old that loved one might happen to be or how long they were so "lucky" to have had them. I have a friend who lost her mother shortly after she turned 100. My friend grieved just as much as if she had lost her mother at 50.

Not that my father was an easy man to know. In fact, damn few people really knew Louis Goldman. He was a very private person. I recall the first thing I ever had published in the early 1960s when I was about twenty-one. I wrote a letter to *Life* about the capture and trial of Adolf Eichmann. Instead of congratulating me, I recall my father telling me that Nazis all over the world would now know who I was and where I lived.

It is perhaps a man thing. Until very recently, when too many American men have been under the heel of politically correct feminism by certain vociferous segments of the women's movement, men have been difficult to know. Tell me one movie where any woman ever really got to know John Wayne!

Anyway, this book is not one of those exercises about my getting in touch with my inner feminine side. You want that crap, go read some chic-lit.

Although I actually like some of their work, it is my contention that very few women writers get to the meat and potatoes of men or being a male in America today. Susan Faludi tried but I kind of lost her in Cleveland when she seemed to say that football was a defining factor for most males in that city. I like football. Rarely watch it on Monday night unless the Pats or the Eagles are playing. And I could easily, unlike those doofuses in Cleveland, live without it.

This memoir is about one American guy's journey. It begins on the streets of Philadelphia and it ends in a corner of Maine. As a teenager I got into the normal run of trouble, was a worse than lousy student and found my way to Dick Clark's American Bandstand where things were not exactly the way the ageless Mr. Clark might recall. I joined the pre-Vietnam army in 1956 and then went to college and fell bass ackwards into teaching. American college campuses were really very different in the fifties (although people did get laid!) and sixties—especially in New England.

Eventually I joined the Nixon administration (even though I had campaigned vigorously for George McGovern!), watched Watergate close-up and found my way, fortunately, back up to Massachusetts—the land of politics and Kennedys (and yes, there will be a few Kennedys in this book!)—where I served for eight years in the wealthiest Jewish defense agency, the Anti-Defamation League, press secretaried the beginnings of a successful Boston mayoral race, traded in politics for talk radio and then journalism and, finally, returned to my original love: teaching history in a small New England college.

The last course I taught in the fall semester of 1998 was, ironically enough, "The History of Terrorism." I've had a lot of bumps along the road. Who doesn't? Some of my friends have been pretty famous. People you would know. I once had a date with Susan Estrich, that loud-mouthed blonde that you see on the TV talking head shows all the time. It was before she mismanaged and helped sink the Dukakis presidential effort in 1988. She was a professor at Harvard Law School at the time and my pal Harvard professor Alan Dershowitz fixed us up.

The date, of course, was a disaster ending in a haze of her Marlboro smoke with me hardly getting a word in. I have been fortunate enough to interview and know and even work for some of the important politicians of our region: Boston Mayors Kevin White and Ray Flynn; State Senate President (former President of U-Mass and brother of the second most wanted felon on the FBI's top ten hit list in America) Billy Bulger; Teddy and Joe Kennedy; I worked in the Nixon administration for Secretary of the Navy John Warner (formerly Mr.Elizabeth Taylor and now a retired multi-term U.S. senator from Virginia) and in the first campaigns of Boston Mayor Raymond Leo Flynn and Senator John Forbes Kerry, erstwhile candidate for the presidency in 2004; as a journalist I have interviewed major Hollywood show business celebrities: Roddy McDowell, Jane Russell and folk singer Judy Collins were among my more interesting interviewees; and I had two long all-nighters, one in London, with Maureen Starkey (the first Mrs. Ringo Starr), where she regaled me with endless Beatle stories as she inhaled gallons of white wine into the wee hours of the English morning (sadly Maureen died much too soon of brain cancer).

America is indeed a great country. It is the only place on God's green earth that you can fail dismally and still get on TV with Larry King or Geraldo. Like Susan Estrich who kept the Dukakis campaign of 1988 in dissarray and her black counterpart, Donna Brazile, who badly mismanaged the Al Gore presidential race. They both prove my point. Nothing succeeds like some people dismally failing or even worse. Fame and failure, I have learned, are completely unrelated. It has helped make America a nation of jerks. OK, you don't agree! Then just turn on your TV to the networks every night. In the 1950s we had Milton Berle, Sid Caeser, Ed Sullivan, Lucy, Hoss and Little Joe. Now we have *Survivor* or *American Idol* which offers every jerk in America that fifteen minutes Andy Warhol was talking about.

This book will be about what I have seen: mostly jerks. "Jerk" was my father's favorite word. He often alternated it with "jerko" and "jerkoff." I have seen and met a lot of jerks. How did America become such a nation of jerks? Stick with me. I think I have some answers.

I've done some TV myself. A three-day stint on Good Morning America in the eighties on, God help me, single men in America. For a brief time I did a weekly political commentary in the late 1980s on Boston's UHF station, Channel 38. And I was an early guest on the O'Reilly Factor when he was doing his Bill Clinton-Monica Lewinsky shtick in early 1998. My fourth book, *Richard Nixon: The Complex President*, had just been published and I predicted on O'Reilly, when I could get a word in edgewise, that Clinton would be impeached (note, I didn't say convicted!) if he didn't stop lying—especially under oath. He didn't and he was!

Alan Dershowitz wrote a best-selling book saying the Clinton impeachment was all about sex. Not that it matters now but my friend Dershowitz was wrong. It was about lying under oath. In case you've forgotten, Presidents are not supposed to lie under oath—even about sex. I guess it all boils down to what one means by "supposed."

Judge Susan Webber Wright fined President Clinton over $90,000. Not for sex! For perjury during legal depositions in the Paula Jones case. And then she referred the Clinton case for disbarment to the Arkansas Bar Association where they eventually punched his law ticket. And not one of Clinton's high-priced legal suits appealed. Sex, my ass! So much for my pal Dershowitz and a Harvard legal education! By the way I always preferred History to Law!

You won't be getting the kind of history you'll find in the late Howard Zinn's *A People's History of the United States*. For example, you won't be reading me bad mouthing Abraham Lincoln as both a bigot and a racist as Howard Zinn did. You may recall, Zinn's book came up large in the Matt Damon-Ben Affleck film *Good Will Hunting*. To Hollywood's mini-minded, Howard Zinn is an intellectual hero. I can well understand that point of view. He used to be a hero of mine too way back when. And then I got to teach at Boston University where Zinn spent much of his misguided academic career. I met Zinn, interviewed him for an article and actually attended one of his so-called lectures. John Silber, Boston University's tough but fair President, gave Zinn a very hard time in the years Silber presided over the college.

Unfortunately, Zinn deserved every minute of it. Ben Affleck and Matt Damon, I hear, have purchased the rights to Zinn's *People's History*. The kindest thing that can be said about Howard Zinn's take on American history is that it is pure and unadulterated bullshit.

That is not just my opinion. The well-respected Harvard University historian Oscar Handlin reviewed it and trashed Zinn's take on the history of our country. I'll take Handlin over Zinn anytime. I suppose Ben-Matt (or is it Matt-Ben?) intend to make a bad film out of a very bad book. And another sorry generation of young American elites will be propagandized by the likes of Zinn and his myopic acolytes in Hollywood. I have never been able to understand how success as a film star or musician gives anyone the bona fide to spout off about anything political. To understand the politics and history of the United States takes many years of intensive reading and study; not years of making movies or albums. And there is not, as far as I know, a single book or a single historian who has the magic bullet to answer all the key questions. It seems to be a way of life in our popular culture. Make a go of it in Hollywood and then tell America how to conduct its business.

Of course, the sad thing is that the opposing point of view is too often represented by a poltroon like Rush Limbaugh, the loudest conservative voice of pompous political bombast these days. On one side, the besieged campuses, you've got Howard Zinn and his ilk talking to the kids. On the other, you've got Limbaugh, a loud-mouthed, ego-centric buffoon talking to everybody else.

Like I said before: a nation of jerks!

CHAPTER 1

I was born on November 7, 1939 at around noon in Jefferson Hospital in downtown Philadelphia. My Mom always said it was Election Day. But I'm not sure. I have been fascinated by history and politics ever since.

It was exactly two years and one month before Pearl Harbor. America was at peace. Poland had just been invaded and quickly overrun by the Nazis the previous September. The Jews of Europe were all still alive and well. But it didn't look good. I knew none of it at the time.

As I write, America commemorates the 60th anniversary of Pearl Harbor. Many political pundits including the *Boston Globe* are comparing September 11, 2001 to December 7, 1941. All of which demonstrates that Howard Zinn's historical analysis is winning the day. Because we lost almost 4,000 souls on September 11, far more than the 2,500 lost at Pearl Harbor, many don't understand that World War II was life or death for the democratic way.

Afghanistan's mullahs and Osama Bin Laden are punks compared to Hitler, Mussolini and Tojo. They can't destroy America no matter how many towers they take down. And let's face it…we are doing a pretty good job of destroying America ourselves. See any university in any large urban setting and their current crop of undereducated graduates for proof.

If Hitler and his brand of totalitarianism had prevailed, the American way of life would have ceased to exist. You don't need *A People's History* to comprehend that basic fact. Too bad they don't teach that kind of history anymore at Harvard.

For the first two years of my life we lived in West Philly on the corner of 57th and Catherine. I have a few nice memories of that period. I recall a neighbor had two small dogs: Ming and Pacita. My father did not like dogs at the time. He thought they were dirty. But I was permitted, a bit grudgingly, to play with Ming and Pacita. Thus began my lifelong affection for virtually every breed of canine. It took me well over twenty years. But I did it. In the latter years of his life my Dad came to love dogs too. I converted my father with a little reddish colored terrier named Rusty. I brought Rusty home in 1962 when I graduated from college. When I was married in 1965 my father would not allow me to take Rusty. Rusty lived in our house for the next seventeen years. He became my parent's third son.

In 1941 we moved to 5443 Diamond Street in the Wynnefield section of West Philadelphia. Wynnefield, on a large tract of acreage had been bequested to Dr. Thomas Wynne, physician to William Penn. William Penn, the famous Quaker whose statue still sits atop Philadelphia's City Hall, conned the Lenni Lenape Indians out of the land for the King of England. I still recall the mural of Penn and the Indians at the front of our assembly hall at the Mann School at 54th and Berks Street.

For my mother, moving back to Wynnefield was a homecoming of sorts. She had grown up there and spent a very happy, somewhat affluent childhood on Gainor Road. For my Dad who worked in the Philadelphia Post Office at 30th and Market, moving to Wynnefield was a major triumph. He was born and raised in South Philadelphia; one of twelve children; to an orthodox Jewish family. The Goldmans were dirt poor and lived without indoor plumbing when Dad was a kid. His father, a Russian immigrant from a village near Kiev in the Ukraine, was a tailor. Many of Pop's brothers and sisters were born in the old country. His mother, whose maiden name was Yetta Bitters, died when my Dad was just fourteen. Wynnefield was Pop's entry into the good life that was soon to characterize so much of postwar America: the much-vaunted American middle class.

At the age of five I was enrolled in the William B. Mann public school. The Philadelphia School System was an interesting sociological study. Most of the schools were named after upper-class WASPs (eliteWhite Anglo-Saxon Protestants) who had made their great fortunes in the years before and during the Civil War era. The late

E. Digby Baltzell, a University of Pennsylvania sociologist, spent his entire career writing about these Union League-type creeps in *The Protestant Elite* and *Philadelphia Gentlemen.* The schools were basically run by Protestants, staffed by proper stiff-necked Christian ladies and, in my time, attended by lower middle class Jews, Italians and poorer Blacks. The Irish kids in my old neighborhood mostly attended Saint Barbara's Catholic School where bat-winged ancient nuns in black habit from head to toe terrorized them and, at times when we came to play on their turf, us. St. Barbara's was just up the street from our house.

Nuns had always scared the shit out of me; until I taught at a Catholic college. Our teachers were mostly old maid biddies who hated kids—especially Jewish and Black kids. They wouldn't hesitate to pull hair, pinch skin or even rap your knuckles. I was the kid who, when the teacher left the room, jumped up on the desk, tap danced and waved my arms. As a result, I had a lot of pinching, hair-pulling and knuckle raps. The class clown, or as the teachers constantly wrote on my report card for about six years, "immature in social growth."

I can still recall our teacher's names: Miss Frye, Miss Giltnan, Miss Pyfron, Miss Seltzer, Miss Weinstein (uh oh! a Jew!), Miss Stinson and Miss Barnes. The best teacher was Elizabeth Stinson, a kindly, gentle woman and a great teacher. She quickly recognized the latent genius in this humble writer. She gave me special attention and great affection and I stayed in touch with her after I left the Mann School in 1951 for many years until she died. Miss Stinson never touched us abusively in any way. She did give lots of warm hugs and that much needed encouragement to youngsters like me who, by the 5th grade, had begun to hate school.

The worst was Miss Pyfron. Ada Pyfron was a mean, fat-ass arm pincher who always wore print dresses with her hair tied in an old fashioned bun right out of Woody Allen's worst childhood fantasy. She was, also, a thief.

In the late 1940s the Kellogg Company put out a perfectly horrible cereal product called Kellogg Pep. To entice kids to beg their mothers to buy what tasted like ground up rope, Kellogg would put a button of well-known comic characters in each box of their horrid cereal. The character button valued by most kids and seemingly hardest to get was the Man of Steel himself, Superman. I had to eat a lot of Pep to get my precious and sought-after Superman button.

My poor mother purchased a ton of Pep. After a year or so of eating that crap I had the entire collection. My mother, apparently proud of my initiative, bought me a beanie to display my cherished collection of buttons. I fastened the small comic buttons to my beanie and ran the three blocks up 54th to Berks Street and the PM session of the second grade at Mann School. I still recall being so proud to show off my entire comic button collection to my classmates. In just one short year I had progressed remarkably from the first grade where, for only a penny, I had showed my penis to Brenda Nax.

When Miss Pyfron saw me wearing my comic button beanie she snatched the hat from my head and told me in no uncertain terms that real gentlemen never wear hats to class. She would have a well deserved stroke today with all the kids and their baseball caps. Or she would probably open a Lids store at the mall. Miss Pyfron never returned my beanie or my comic button collection.

In those days we never told our parents if something bad happened at school. So, convinced I had done something really bad, I never told my parents. And they never asked about the disappearance of my treasured comic button collection. To our parents then, teachers were always right no matter what they did or said. My father was a firm believer in authority. Today, teachers would be fired for just the simple physical abuse we used to suffer. I did ask Miss Pyfron from time to time about my stolen beanie and comic buttons. She pretended not to know what I was talking about. I've always had this vision of her appearing at some family function and giving a niece or nephew my stolen collection as a gift. A few years ago I was at the famous Brimfield Flea Market in Brimfield, Massachusetts. A guy was selling Kellogg's Pep comic buttons for between $15 and $100 a piece. The most expensive was Superman. He went for $100. Maybe he was my old Superman button. I looked but I didn't see my beanie.

I learned two important things about the adult world from losing my treasured comic button collection to Miss Pyfron: public school teachers are rarely right about anything and that, like most Massachusetts politicians, they even steal. Also, I raised my price for Brenda Nax to a nickel. Sadly, a few years ago I read in the *Jewish Exponent* that Brenda Nax had passed away. I hope she enjoyed seeing my business.

Today, you have got to pay a hell of a lot more than a nickel if you want to see my willy.

CHAPTER 2

I don't recall much about what I learned at the Mann School. By the Fifth grade I had begun to show leadership qualities. In a grade-wide essay contest all the students submitted about animals in books, I won first place. Maybe Miss Stinson fixed the contest in my favor but the prize was extraordinary. A number of Philly schools sent their top budding writers to meet the world famous children's author Marguerite Henry. I know, you probably never heard of her.

But back in the late forties Marguerite Henry's work was legendary among kids who haunted public school library shelves. Even though my grades never reflected it until grad school, I was always a voracious reader. Still am!

Marguerite Henry was the author of the well-known and beloved Misty of Chincoteague stories. Misty was a little black and white dappled pony that lived on Chincoteague Island off the coast of Virginia. Miss Henry told us the stories were based on fact and that there actually was a real Misty. The stories were wonderfully warm and as well written as the Harry Potter phenomenon. Of course, I don't think Marguerite Henry ever got as rich as J.D. Rawlins.

Anyway, the Philadelphia city schools bussed many of its budding young writers downtown to a meeting with the famous Miss Henry who had just published another in her series of Misty books.

I remember her as a tall (to me anyone over 5 feet was tall!), stately woman with proper old Southern charm. I enjoyed meeting her although I can't recall a thing she said that day. A few years ago I read in *The New York Times* that Miss Henry died. The *Times* obit writer gave her a nice send-off. All I can say is that it was much deserved. Marguerite Henry gave a lot of children of my generation hours and hours of pleasure. I can still see Misty swimming in the sea her towards her beloved islands.

In the Sixth grade I was elected Vice-President of the class much to the chagrin of my spinster teacher, Miss Barnes. Miss Barnes always called me "Tony" whenever she called on me and some of the kids began teasing and calling me "Tony Alechi." I was dark and I looked more Italian than Jewish and Miss Barnes clearly did not like Italians. I always corrected her but finally gave up. For whatever reason, I was always "Tony" to old Miss Ethel Barnes.

Anyway, my rising political star flamed out quickly. As Kramer used to say on *Seinfeld*, "There was an incident!" One of the Vice-President's more important duties each and every Friday was to read the notes left in the class Suggestion Box, a progressive exercise I suppose in democratic values. One Friday one of my classmates, also a friend, Lance Zeaman, put a note in the box. The note read, "Kiss my balls." Being a scrupulously honest Vice-President, I handed the note in to Miss Barnes to be read aloud to the class. Miss Barnes just didn't have a sense of humor. I must admit here that my pal Lance was probably not seeking that kind of notoriety. The note was obviously directed to his newly-elected Vice-President. But in those days Vice-Presidents of the Sixth grade class at the William B. Mann School did not come under the protective aegis of the Secret Service.

Unlike Vice-President Dick Cheney or Joe Biden, no one rushed me off to Thunder Mountain for my own protection. So much for the democratic process at the William B. Mann School! Poor Lance was suspended while I was summarily dismissed from the Vice-Presidency for "exercising poor judgment" in my operation of the Suggestion Box and replaced by Barbara Pincus. Miss Barnes did not even permit the class to vote. Unlike Bill Clinton, I wasn't even impeached. Talk about unfair. I didn't even have my own Monica Lewinsky. Barbara Pincus, I must admit, was much prettier. And since she had just begun to sprout two lovely little pointed twillies that stuck out profusely from under her pink cashmeres, as I recall Barbara had a very successful term in office. My political Jones was sated and I have not re-entered the political fray as a candidate for high office ever since.

My brother Kenneth Carl Goldman was born on October 20, 1945 when I was almost six. Six years is an immense wall of time in the lives of youngsters. And so I have few memories of my baby brother's presence in my life until both our teens. I can still recall my mother bringing Kenny home from the hospital when he was born and I can recall taunting him relentlessly as an adolescent. I was Charlie Harper to Ken's Alan Harper. My brother Kenny was always the "good son," the antithesis of his older brother. He only gave my parents *naches*. But I was happy to have a little brother and my memories of our early years together are only good ones. Ken's, however, are a bit different. *Cest la vie!*

My early life was taken up with card collecting (Bowman baseball cards, KEMS plastic playing cards, Wild West and Red Menace), playing baseball at St. Barbara's in the schoolyard, riding my bike and meeting new friends at school. My grades were mostly mediocre and rarely reflected, much to my father's ongoing consternation, my capacity or intelligence. After bringing home a poor report card Pop always used to say, "Don't you know how important education is? It is the key to success in this country. What is it you think you want to do with your life?" My Pop was always asking me what I was going to do with my life. The last time Pop asked me that question, I think I was in my mid-fifties. I didn't have an answer. I still don't.

What I most recall about daily life at the Mann School were the assemblies. We had a great many assemblies in those days. The kids didn't complain because it took us out of those hated classes with those ancient prune-faced teachers. Most of the assemblies were about patriotism.

Since September 11, 2001 there has been a tidal wave of patriotism in the United States. Everyone has a flag on their car and in my little neighborhood in southern Maine very few houses do not display a large American flag. It is interesting to me that patriotism is back in vogue. Since Viet Nam there has not been much overt patriotism. The legacy of Lyndon Johnson will ultimately be that too many Americans came to distrust, if not dislike their government. That is not how it was at the William B. Mann School in the 1940s and 1950s.

The nation had just emerged from war and the Cold War was in full swing when I was a. student. Our assemblies always began with the Pledge of Allegiance. Then we sang "You're a Grand Old Flag" and "Here Comes the Flag." We sang those songs so many times I can still recite those words:

> *Here comes the flag,*
> *Cheer it!*
> *Valley and crag,*
> *Will hear it!*
> *Children respect it,*
> *Old folks reflect it,*
> *No one neglects it,*
> *All will protect it.*

That old song still brings a lump to my throat and tears to my eyes.

We'd finish off our assemblies singing "God Bless America" and "The Star Spangled Banner." All of this must seem somewhat hokey in these far more sophisticated times, especially to younger people. Call me sentimental! But I was patriotic long before 9/11.

I must honestly report that it all somehow remained with me into my young adulthood. I was not the best soldier there ever was. But wherever I was on any army post, and I served on many bases, every afternoon when they brought the colors down, I always stopped and proudly saluted our flag and listened intently to the post bugler playing "The Star Spangled Banner."

Those old Mann School biddies probably never knew it but the patriotism they so patiently drilled into our unformed adolescent heads has remained with me for a lifetime. Even when I was present at those vast anti-Viet Nam War demonstrations back in the sixties and seventies, when we marched around the White House and the crowd began to chant "Fuck Nixon! Fuck the war! Fuck the United States!" I did not join in. Well, at least not in the United States part.

To me the American flag is the most beautiful flag on the face of the earth. It can't be an accident that the stars and stripes are so striking. Or that so many average Americans of every generation have sacrificed their lives to keep those colors and the great idea behind those colors flying high.

Our lives in the old neighborhood were remarkably free from violence. At nine or ten years of age most of us were allowed to roam from 54th and Oxford all the way to 54th and City Line. While our parents always regaled us with stories about gentile kids catching us, beating us up and calling us Christ-Killers, such incidents were very rare. Some Irish kids from the Fairmount section of Philly caught six or seven of us once on a hike in Fairmount Park in the hills above the Schuykill River. They punched Joey Gittelman in the face, took all our canteens and sent us on our way. But they never called us dirty Jews or anything like that. They were just tough kids who knew they could easily intimidate some younger Jewish kids hiking alone in the park. My father fared far worse in the South Philly of his boyhood.

The Irish-Catholic kids at St. Barbara's couldn't have been nicer and the few Irish boys who challenged us when we played on their turf were really afraid that there were too many of us. Two brothers named Kelly once tried to intimidate us on the St. Barbara's field and when I punched the younger Kelly in the nose, they backed right down.

By the 1950's Wynnefield was largely Jewish. Most of the kids at the Mann School were Jewish. In fact, in my graduating class of June 1951 there were only three Christian kids: Joan O'Neil, Joanne Brooks and Johnny Whetstone. Johnny was a wonderful kid who came from a large family. In the fracas with the Kelly brothers, Johnny was on our side. I always kind of felt sorry for those three kids and their ongoing minority status for the first six years of their educational experience. I didn't really understand what it was to be a minority until high school and the army.

The other public school in the neighborhood was called Samuel A. Gompers, after the famous Jewish labor leader. It opened in the 1950's and the border for Gompers was Woodcrest Avenue. All the kids past Woodcrest Avenue went to Gompers. They were mostly Jewish kids too.

As the 1940's gave way to the mythical 1950's, growing up in Philly was idyllic and untroubled. We felt safe because we were safe. The rest of the century stretched out before us like a beacon and we proceeded with our young lives protected and untrammeled. Wynnefield was like a cocoon and although very few of our parents were wealthy, the creature comforts of postwar America extended to all of us. There were cars, air conditioning and, wonder of all wonders, television would soon replace radio.

Except in my house where my father sold his 1937 Oldsmobile during the war. We were not to get our next car until May of 1956 when Pop purchased a four door '55 green and white Olds 88. We were also the last family to get a TV on the block—a 16 inch RCA in 1948 or 1949. And my Pop never believed in air conditioning. The steamy Philly summers were, he told us, mind over matter. Often, when I was passing out from the stifling Philly heat in my tiny middle room with one blocked window over the alley on Diamond Street, Pop would tell me to think cool, to think January. He did, finally, put in a large fan. But it didn't help very much.

Still, our lives were safe and, except for July and August in my house, happy and comfortable. Every day, before TV, we'd come home and listen to the radio from around 4 P.M. to just before dinner. The programs were like the cliffhangers we'd see at the Wynne movie theater every Saturday afternoon. Radio programs of the 1940's were parodied so well in Woody Allen's classic film *Radio Days.*

My best childhood friend Howard "the Pretzel" Shander (who lived at 5463 Diamond right on the corner over his father's hardware store, "Feldman's Hardware"—his mother's maiden name, like my mother's maiden name), would come over and we'd sit in front of this gigantic radio my father had from the 1930s. We'd listen to Superman, Captain Midnight, Jack Armstrong, Straight Arrow and Tom Mix (brought to you by Ralston Purina with his wonder horse Tony!). On Saturday mornings it would be Smilin' Ed McConnell with Froggy the Gremlin and Let's Pretend (brought to you by "Cream of Wheat which is so good to eat that we have it every day!").

Then by noon we'd go to the Wynne Theater on 54th Street where for a quarter you could get into the movie ($.10), buy a box of JuJy Fruit ($.05) and a large box of popcorn ($.10). If you didn't like the movie you would throw the green JuJy fruits at the screen saving, of course, the reds, oranges and blacks.

The best thing about the Saturday matinees at the Wynne were cartoons; usually Looney Tunes and Merry Melodies; the Three Stooges shorts and the chapters which is what Philly kids called the cliffhangers. The chapters usually ran between 12 and 15 weeks and starred all the superheroes of the day: Buster Crabbe as Flash Gordon on Mars, Ralph Byrd as Dick Tracy versus Gruesome and a host of other Chester Gould crooks, Clyde Beatty, the famous circus animal trainer in darkest Africa fighting the dreaded flying batmen, Don Winslow of the Navy fighting the Japs (they were called "the Japs" back then!), Rocketman and the caped Zorro fighting just about everybody left. The scariest chapter I recall was called *The Purple Monster* where a guy from Mars comes down and enters other earthling's bodies and takes them over (an early version of the classic *Invasion of the Body Snatchers)*. Each week the hero would find himself in an increasingly precarious position facing certain doom and a horrible death. And each week, on our way home, all the kids would argue about how the hero would get out of his predicament on the following Saturday. We'd climb trees and leap over hedges to show off our super prowess and our own agile powers of escape from the villains.

Every superhero had a funny sidekick who was always getting into trouble. It made life even more real for me because I too had a funny sidekick, Howard "the Pretzel." Howie Shander had spiked blonde hair cut into what they called a "fritz" in those days with a tiny tuft sticking straight up in the front. He wore bottle thick eyeglasses and couldn't see past his nose without them. He was overweight but I wouldn't call him fat and was always picked last on every team. But the Pretzel had a heart of pure gold, collected cards and comics like me, and always lost at Checkers, Monopoly and Parcheesi with amazing regularity. That is when he didn't tip the game board over, quit and run home. Sometimes "the Pretz" was a bit of a sore loser. Nobody likes to lose in life with consistency. Pretz was my best friend and sidekick through Junior High and he was my loyal companion for years of Saturday matinees at the old Wynne Theater on 54th Street. And though our childhood friendship eventually flickered in the confusing candle of high school, the army, college and life's adventure in general, I can still see the Pretzel in the haze of far away memory puffing his way up Diamond Street, holding his glasses which snapped in half at regular intervals on his nose, with a quarter in his other hand, getting ready for a Saturday afternoon of buttered popcorn joy and untold adventures at the old Wynne movie house by shouting out his familiar alley war cry: "Diyup, diyoo!".

All, however, was not JuJy Fruit and popcorn in the West Philadelphia of the late 1940's and early 1950's. We West Philly kids were to learn far too soon that there was real evil in the world—in our world. Just going to the movies, we found out, could be dangerous and life threatening.

Up until the Seymour Levin murder case, evil was mostly an abstraction for us. Evil had been relegated early on to the Nazis and Japanese: Hitler and Tojo. And then to the Commie Reds (whatever or whoever the hell they were. We didn't know. We just knew they were very bad!). "Red Menace" trading cards had Stalin and Mao as our chosen villains after World War II.

Seymour Levin happened in January, 1949. I was in the fourth grade, and not yet old enough to take the trolley by myself to the Nixon or State Theaters located between 52nd and Market and Chestnut Streets where the films that had opened downtown sometimes previewed simultaneously with Captain Marvel and Batman serials. In those days Captain Marvel and the Marvel family were giving Superman a serious run for his money. We shouted, "Shazam!" as often as we yelled, "Up, up and away."

In the late 1940s and early 1950s first-run films didn't open at every mall multi-Cineplex in the country. First, because there were no such thing as malls or Cineplex; not such a bad thing in retrospect! And second, because they usually opened downtown way before they hit the neighborhoods.

52nd and Market was not a long way from our neighborhood (about three miles) but it was not considered "downtown." It was in the heart of West Philly, a place where I had been born but which was, by my adolescence, a foreign country. You had to be at least in Junior High to take the Number 70 trolley to 52nd and Market Streets where you had your choice of four movie theaters: The Nixon, The State, The Belmont or The Locust in a four-block radius. There was also H & H (Horn and Hardart's) automat on the corner of 52nd and Market where for less than half a buck you could still get a great full course lunch.

Seymour Levin was sixteen years of age. He was old enough to take the 70 trolley. On the day Seymour Levin went to the movies, he met an eleven-year-old West Philly boy named Ellis Simons. Somehow he convinced Ellis to take the trolley with him back to Wynnefield to his house on 56th Street, about a half a block from Saint Joseph's College on Overbrook Avenue. Wynnefield had an ongoing mystery: there was a 54th Street and a 56th Street; but no 55th Street. No one knew why but the next street down from 54th was 56th. That street, just about four city blocks from my house, a short, five-minute walk, was where Seymour Levin lived.

Seymour's parents were away in New Jersey—"down the shore" we called it. Seymour Levin's house was unlike most other homes in our neighborhood. For one thing, it was a single home and not a row home like the one in which I and most of my friends grew up. To us, if you lived in a single, unattached home, your family had money. For another, the big lime-green stucco Tudor was set way back framed privately behind a very large hedge row far from the street. (I know the house well because a few years later I was the paperboy on that winding street. Also, two of my classmates, Marilyn Bailis and the adorable Binnie Schuman, lived directly across the street).

The Levin house was somewhat cut off from the houses on either side by two rows of thick hedges. So, it is highly unlikely that anyone would have heard anything on that particular tragic day; like screaming.

Seymour Levin's parents and younger brother came home on Sunday night and didn't suspect that anything unusual had taken place in their weekend absence. Of course, they didn't check out their trash cans. Because there in their trash cans were the cut up body parts of poor Ellis Simons. They were found a day or so later by the trash-men who naturally called the Philly cops who had been looking for the Simons kid after his parents had reported him missing earlier that Sunday when he didn't come back from the movie.

Murder most foul had entered our young lives with a resonance that still reverberates across the haze of memory well over a half-century later. The savage killing of Ellis Simons not only rocked the tranquility of a placid urban neighborhood. It cleaved the consciousness of thousands of little kids whose world would never again be the same. It is not a little bit disconcerting to learn of a scary evil in your midst during the first decade of life. Remember, evil as a concept was something we only dealt with on Saturday afternoons at the movies when Johnny Weissmuller as Tarzan beat the Nazis or William Boyd as Hopalong Cassidy shot the rustlers and always triumphed. The utterly unbelievable tales of Hitler and Tojo were really little more than comic book villains in our unformed childish minds.

The lesson of 16-year-old Seymour Levin was indelibly chiseled into our adolescent minds: as Dustin Hoffman might have told Sir Laurence Olivier when asked, "Is it safe?" in *Marathon Man*, Dustin would have replied, "It isn't safe."

With the Columbines and the myriad high school disasters Americans regularly face these troubled days, the Seymour Levin murder story does not have legs. Today. But back then it was as if a man from outer space had landed in Wynnefield and zapped everyone like Klaatu and Gort from *The Day the Earth Stood Still*. That week, for us kids, the earth stood still. And life in placid Wynnefield was never the same.

I can remember sitting in our breakfast room eating my usual bowl of Cheerios. My mother lowered the shade on the window that looked out on our back porch which was above the alley. She looked at me strangely. Although it was morning, the room grew dark.

"Do you know a boy named Seymour Levin?" my mother whispered.

"No," I answered. "Should I?"

"Well," Mom said, "he is sixteen."

I was only nine. I didn't know anyone sixteen. To me sixteen was ancient. The few sixteen-year-olds on Diamond Street wanted nothing, unlike Seymour Levin, to do with little kids. There was a pretty girl on Diamond Street named Sybil. She was three or four years older than me and every time she walked by my heart would skip a beat. I think, if Sybil ever actually spoke to me, I would have fainted dead away. But aside from Sybil and a wonderfully creative neighbor, sixteen-year-old Irv Gottenberg, who showed me how to make model planes as he built and crafted interesting mechanical contraptions in his garage, my world of older kids was very narrow.

"They think that this Seymour Levin," my mother continued, "murdered a little boy; a little Jewish boy just a few blocks from here." (Both my parents were always acutely aware of any crime victim's ethnicity. Somehow, if the poor victim was Jewish, it was much worse in my parents' outlook. Of course, in this case both victim and killer were Jewish. To my parents, this murder was a double header and thus an even worse tragedy. When Jewish people did bad things, Pop always thought it was bad for all Jews. I wonder what he would have said about Bernie Madoff. I don't know if that had anything to do with the Holocaust. He never said.)

"Why?" I asked. If somebody killed somebody else, in my young mind, there always had to be a reason. To this day, I still have difficulty comprehending random acts of violence. I can understand revenge and self defense. I can understand violence in the heat of a moment. But killing for killing's sake with no rhyme or reason has always been a very foreign concept.

"Never mind," Mom said. "Go to school."

At school, where the gaunt and bespectacled Seymour Levin was apparently well-known because he was often seen hanging around the schoolyard and bothering the little kids, the brutal murder of Ellis Simons was the topic of the day. The problem was that no one, including our teachers, seemed to know very much. It wasn't until around 4:30 that afternoon, when the first copies of the late edition of the *Philadelphia Bulletin* came out.

Seymour Levin's picture and a nice photo of young Ellis Simons were on the front page of the Three Star edition. Levin had a vague stare but didn't look very scary as the cops took him into custody.

Murder, so rare in our peaceful community, was the headlined story of the day in the *Bulletin* and *Inquirer*. By the 1960s and 1970s, sadly, that was no longer the case.

I actually knew a number of people murdered right in their homes in Wynnefield. Unless it was particularly brutal, it rarely even made the front pages after the sixties.

It wasn't all that complicated. Seymour Levin had befriended the Simons kid while at the movie. They learned that they had some kind of hobby (model cars or chemistry sets?) in common and Levin enticed the boy to return with him to his house. No one knows for sure what happened after they got there. Did Seymour Levin attempt to sexually assault the boy? Some reports had it that Seymour had raped the Simons boy. In those days the newspapers didn't report very much about sexually based crimes. At any rate, after interrogating Seymour Levin the cops learned that the kid had started screaming and that Seymour Levin responded brutally with a pair of sharp scissors. According to the autopsy reports the boy had completely bled out. Levin then cut the kid up and hid the body parts in the trash. Not a very bright killer, what? For his part, even at his trial, Seymour Levin claimed no memory of the lurid events whatsoever.

It turned out that Seymour Levin was no stranger to the local constabulary. According to neighbors he had had a history of torturing kids and little animals. Seymour was a prime candidate to be a serial killer when he grew up. The cops had been alerted to his neighborhood cruelties on a number of occasions. Obviously, not much was done even though his parents must have known he was a few quarts low in the milk of human kindness. I don't know if a shrink's intervention could have prevented Seymour Levin from carving up Ellis Simons. I do know that back then nobody I knew went to shrinks and if you did you sure as hell didn't talk about it. Seymour Levin was a prime candidate for some definite head shrinkage.

In those days, the death penalty wasn't on the table for sixteen-year-old murderers. When a sixteen-year-old did what Seymour Levin admitted to doing, he was considered just plain crazy. There was some kind of a trial a few months later. And Seymour Levin ended up in the custody of some youth facility until he turned twenty-one.

According to one scholar at Haverford College, Seymour Levin was released in the 1970's and lives today with his father somewhere in New Jersey. After first-hand experience with the Massachusetts prison system, where under the aegis of Boston University for four years, I taught a number of history courses to rapists, murderers, thieves and assorted bank robbers I learned one thing about most crime no matter how heinous: sooner or later the perp gets out.

With most murderers in the permissive Massachusetts atmosphere, it was usually after fifteen years. Life without parole in Massachusetts never meant absolutely. I think Pennsylvania is just as permissive. So, old Seymour Levin is out there living next door to somebody. I hope it isn't you.

CHAPTER 3

Aside from the Seymour Levin saga, life went on as quietly in the 1950s as some pundits recall. Mann School gave way in 1951 to Beeber Junior High School. Named after a WASP judge, Dimner Beeber Junior High was a school that had opened in 1932 and, like the Mann School, was within walking distance of my house at 59th and Malvern Avenue. In my entire public school experience in Philadelphia, from grade school through high school, I never once took a bus. I was one of those legendary kids who walked through snow and rain to get to school every day. Try telling that to kids in the suburbs today!

Actually, the 59th Street Bridge was a major bitch to walk across on a windy cold day or in a snowstorm.

Beeber Junior High was great fun. We didn't learn much but we did have a good time.

My best friends from Mann School never forgave me for passing the "Kiss my balls" note on to Miss Barnes. So my grade school pals like Ronnie "Sly Ron" Bluestein (today a very successful Philadelphia attorney), Joey Zuritsky (a parking lot mogul and a major developer in downtown Philly and a well-known fish hobbyist and Jewish philanthropist), Barry "Big Bar" Cohen and Aaron "Weasel" Green, from the ZAP boys club, fell by the wayside.

Another good friend, Steve Cozen, whose father was coach of the Overbrook High basketball team (yes, the very team that fronted Wilt "the Stilt" Chamberlain!), was pulled from the public schools altogether and sent off to one of those ritzy private Quaker schools like Friends Central or Friends Select. Sam Cozen was a very wise man and probably saved his son from becoming just another hustling Philly lawyer. Today Steve Cozen is the leading partner in one of the most powerful law firms in the United States. Somebody recently told me that Cozen/O'Connor has over 500 lawyers working for the firm. I saw Cozen a few years ago. To me he hadn't changed much at all.

It was in the 6th or 7th grade that we all discovered girls. Up until that time girls were mostly those skinny little things that sat next to you and stuck their tongues out.

It was in the sixth grade that we found out that girls could also shove their tongues down your throat, a not altogether unpleasant experience.

There were a great many girls who were extremely popular when we discovered the opposite sex. At my twelfth birthday party, where my Mom and Dad discretely retired to their upstairs bedroom, I recall playing spin the bottle with Lynn Goldberg, Diane Dorfman and Carol Rosen. Ah, the sensual pleasures of being a twelve-year-old birthday boy!

The girl of the hour in our youth was Carol Rosen. She lived at 5347 Oxford Street with her grandparents and parents. Oxford Street was the very first street as you came up the hill into Wynnefield. It was considered the poorest street in the neighborhood. Wynnefield had a very stratified class system. It was by street. The closer your street was to Oxford, the poorer you were thought to be; the closer to City Line and Lower Merion Township, the richer.

Carol Rosen was a beautiful child who became a very beautiful woman. The prettiest girl at Mann School, Carol Rosen was also really very nice. I'll never forget the times she invited me to her house to eat dinner with her family. Most of the boys who competed with me for Carol's attention and affection didn't believe me when I told them that, after weeks of pursuit, Carol had actually invited me into her house. But she did. She always called me "Martin." Not Marty or my hated nickname. In 1992 when I ran into her in Philly, still as beautiful as ever, Carol said "Martin S. Goldman! Hello, Martin!"

Carol was my first love. And although that love was never reciprocated, a piece of me will always love that little girl. By the eighth grade Carol Rosen discovered older boys. When I saw her making out with Jay Kauffman, a red-headed ninth grader, in back of the Wynne movie, my heart was broken; the first of many such life experiences. Carol's mother Florence was also very beautiful. According to my mother, who knew Florence Rosen as a teenager in the neighborhood, Florence was, like her daughter, one of the most popular girls. Carol's father Joe Rosen, a cab driver when they lived on Oxford Street, was also a great looking guy. It is hard to believe that such a handsome, strapping guy could have died at a very young age. But he did. Anyway, Carol had great genes.

By the sixth or seventh grade Carol was a genuine star in Philly. Every Sunday morning she appeared on WCAU-Channel 10's well-known show, "The Children's Hour," sponsored by that great chain of local restaurants, Horn and Hardart's. Horn and Hardart's actually had the greatest tasting food of any restaurant I have ever experienced. Their key advertising slogan, "Less work for mother dear!" drew generations of Philadelphians through their doors and to those fun automats. I can still recall the terrific taste of H & H coffee, a bargain at ten to fifteen cents a cup. Philly lost a treasure when Horn & Hardart's finally shut its doors sometime in the 1970s. Somebody told me that the chain had been badly mismanaged.

Hosted by a big bald guy named Stan Lee Broza, "The Children's Hour" featured the most talented young people in the Philadelphia area. And the station, Philly's first modern TV outlet, was located in the area, at Monument Road and City Line just across the line from the city in Bala Cynwyd.

At first, Carol danced only ballet. I don't know much about the ballet, but our Carol sure could dance. As she grew older and filled out a little bit, Esther Broza, the wife of Stan Lee and the show's producer wisely chose to feature Carol in skits and in some singing. Soon everybody in Philly knew who Carol Rose was—dropping the n for her stage name.

Most of the kid stars from "The Children's Hour" went on to normal lives. But one kid, Tucker Smith, with whom Carol was often paired up, went on to Hollywood. If you ever watch the film *West Side Story* with Natalie Wood and Richard Beymer, you will see Tucker Smith.

He played the part of "Ice", one of the tougher guys in the Jets. He is featured front and center in the ensemble opening song with Russ Tamblyn called "When you're a Jet." Later in the film he sings a solo, "Cool." But that was it for old Tucker Smith. Not much happened after his big break in *West Side Story*. I read a tiny newspaper obit, sometime in the 1980's, that he got cancer, dying unknown and relatively unsung in Hollywood in his forties. All of which goes to show that even looks and talent, with which Tucker Smith was abundantly blessed, didn't and still doesn't count for much in Hollywood or the game of life.

As for Carol Rosen, her show biz star reached its zenith during her stint on "The Children's Hour." I often saw her around Temple University in the early sixties and we talked from time to time. She was still a heart-stopper. I heard that she married, had a family and then got divorced. But Carol was never a girl to let a little thing like divorce screw up her life and when she remarried she made sure to hook a bigger fish the second time around. Carol's second husband was D. Herbert Lipson, a very prosperous and prominent Philadelphian who also happens to be the Napoleonic owner-publisher of *Philadelphia* and *Boston Magazine*, two of the better known city magazines in the country.

My Dad always warned me about trusting guys with initials in front of their names. Pop believed that they were hiding something about themselves. Are you listening Jerry Salinger?

I never met Lipson, although I have had my own issues with *Boston Magazine*. People I know who worked for him in both towns over the years, including three of his best editors, disliked him intensely.

Anyway, according to my old friends in Philly, Carol and Lipson are no longer man and wife. Lipson's most distinguishing characteristic is that he has rarely been able to hold on to an editor or a wife and has single-handedly turned what was once a fairly good investigative urban magazine in Boston into a glossy slick featuring only the trendiest, upscale restaurants, fur salons and the most expensive place to buy a watch or other jewelry that is out of reach for the common man and woman. I only read *Boston* when I go to the dentist or the proctologist.

I saw Carol Rosen again at our 50th Philly class reunion in 2007. She kissed me gingerly on the cheek once again saying, "Hello Martin," announced that she was a recent newlywed and, when I couldn't help teasing her during the course of dinner, Carol shouted across the room, "Martin! Get a life!"

I got one Carol! Read on!

CHAPTER 4

The most powerful thing about the years we spent at Beeber Junior High in Philly was the presence of Negroes in large numbers. A note here: I am going to use the terminology of the time. If the reader finds that offensive, or as they say, "politically incorrect," I can only respond, "Too bad!"

In the 1950s Black people were called "Negroes" and "colored." My Negro friends actually preferred colored. Nobody got too bent out of shape about it in those simpler times. We all knew the word "Nigger." My Negro friends didn't like it and didn't use it the way Rappers do today. If our Negro friends didn't like it, that was good enough for us.

We didn't use the word. By the way, they didn't much like the word "Black" then either.

The "Black Experience" has always featured large in my life. I taught the very first "Negro History" courses at Holy Cross College and Clark University in the 1960s. I concentrated on the black experience in my graduate work and doctoral dissertation and later taught "Black History,…Afro-American History," "The History of Black America, Black Political Thought, The History of the South, Race: An Idea in American History," and some other creative titles that I've largely forgotten. Later, I taught Black History at Rutgers and Boston University and my first published book is titled *Nat Turner and the Southampton Revolt of 1831.* That I was never hired or even considered for a tenure track job at any college or university where I taught is part of the scandal of late twentieth century academia in this country. I'll get to that sad story in due time. Last year (2010) I taught African American history at the College of Central Florida in Ocala.

By the time I got to Beeber Jr. High I had not read *The Philadelphia Negro* by W.E.B. DuBois. Actually, I never heard of it or him until many years later. I was still in my Boogie/*Diner* stage.

There were no Negroes at the Mann School. At Beeber, a conservative estimate was about fifteen per cent. As I recall, a lot of the kids made big fusses about the black students at Beeber; always in a positive sense. There was a kid named Harry Hilliard in one of the seventh grade sections who was an extraordinary box-ball player. Box-ball was the major competitive sport at Beeber. Every class had a team, there were standings and we'd have regularly scheduled games, weather permitting, every day at lunch period. Harry Hilliard could hit and field. He played third base. Although he wasn't in my book (or section), all the boys made a big fuss about Harry. Not so much because he was black but because he was a hell of a box-ball player. Box-ball was like baseball except without outfielders. You had to hit a pitched "pinkie" ball in a square, boxed boundary. The toughest positions were always third, short and second because anything hit by those positions would usually go all the way for a home run and every class had a list naming the team players on the blackboard and what their teams were hitting in regard to singles, doubles, triples and homers. It was seen as a major way to impress girls in our classes who, we all couldn't help but notice, were beginning to sprout tits.

I played first base and third for 7A-1 and 7B-1. Our second baseman was a Negro kid who became one of my best friends in Junior High, Raymond Lee. Ray Lee was an all-A student who could hit the stuffing out of a "pinkie" or a tennis ball. He lived with his parents and a younger brother on 57th and Master Street in West Philly. I invited Ray Lee to my house for lunch a couple of times and he reciprocated. My mother was nice to him. His mother was nice to me. I recall a couple of the neighbors peering through their curtains when we walked up the street together. But other than that the world didn't end and Ray and I traveled back and forth to one another's neighborhoods in relative safety and absolute innocence.

Don't get me wrong! I knew that Negroes were different than Whites. And that they were forced to live in relative poverty compared to the rest of us. But to me Ray Lee was just another kid in my class and I suppose we might still be friends today if he had gone on to Overbrook High School. His parents just wanted more for him and from him. By the ninth grade Ray Lee had left Beeber and gone on to Central High, the best public school in the city of Philadelphia.

I wouldn't have gone to Central on a bet. First of all, with my lousy grades I could never have gotten in. And more important, there were no girls at Central High.

My old friend, Julius Lester, one of the great writers of my generation, once wrote that he never met or spoke to a white person until he was past fourteen. While the racial divide wasn't that bad in Philadelphia, it was still pretty bad. Until I got to Beeber, I had never spoken to a Black person who wasn't providing a service. Much like Julie Lester, to whom Whites were a vague, and perhaps negative abstraction, my experiences with Negroes were severely limited until past the age of twelve or thirteen.

The only Blacks in our immediate neighborhood were service people like maids, delivery "boys" and boot-blacks (someone who gave a shoeshine for around fifteen cents in those days). Our role models for Black people were extremely limited and although most of us were painfully aware of what Jackie Robinson had done for baseball and the Brooklyn Dodgers at the expense of our beloved Philadelphia Phillies (who had no black players), the Black people we saw from day to day did not enhance our understanding in any sense of the Negro plight in America.

On the plus side was our mailman, Norris, a very tall, handsome, polite and gentle man.

Norris delivered our mail until I was almost twenty and he watched the kids on our street grow up. He knew every kid on the block by name and would often intervene if two kids on the street got into a fistfight. Norris would often break up fights and chase kids who were bullies. My Dad, who was also a U.S. postal employee, made sure to give Norris a gift every Christmas and constantly drummed it into our heads that he was a man to be respected. I recall somebody telling me in the Sixties that Norris had died. But Norris was about the only positive Black role model in our neighborhood.

Happy was a bootblack at Gilbert Cohen's barber shop on 56th Street. He had a big, round, shiny dark face. He was friendly to all the kids. Happy was always laughing about something (hence his nickname). Except when he snuck off to the alley where he could be seen drinking something from a brown paper bag.

When Happy left he was replaced by another Negro named Garrie. Unlike Happy, Garrie was an alcoholic and often toddled down the alley to the shop in his cups, worked all day, drank in the cellar of the shop on his breaks and staggered back up the alley to catch the trolley to God knows where every afternoon. Gearrie (we called him Gearrie, I don't know why) would often stumble right through piles of horseshit left by horse-drawn milk wagons and other peddlers as he made his way through the back alleys. The horseshit started to disappear by the mid-fifties along with the horse carts but Gearrie remained a fixture in the neighborhood for as many years as we lived on Diamond Street.

There was a delivery boy named Alvin at Charlie Squires's Grocery Store (formerly known as Muchnick's Grocery) on the southwest corner of 56th and Diamond who always appeared pleasant and courteous. But Alvin must have resented the Jewish shprintzers who would have him pedal a quarter pound of lox and a couple bagels all the way past Wynnefield Avenue in his wire delivery basket on the front of his bike.

Every year my father hired a black local handyman named Curtis to help him "lift the rugs." We had winter rugs and summer rugs in our house. I have no idea why.

At any rate, it was heavy work and always took a couple of hours after applying camphor to the rugs, rolling them up and storing them down in our cellar. I have always despised the smell of camphor. To the day she died my mother still applied camphor to all her closets! She never told me why.

Over the years, Curtis would often show up for work drunk as a skunk. After some hours of heavy lifting he would sober up a little. For years I can remember Curtis coming to our house twice a year to help my father's biennial ritual to "lift the rugs."

The fact that we did not know the last names of the Negroes we met seemed to make little impression on us. It wasn't until I read Ralph Ellison's classic novel *Invisible Man* that I came to understand what was happening to Black Americans. That was the world we saw and we did not ask questions. We did not learn much about slavery or the Civil War in grade school or even in Junior High where the presence of Blacks in the classroom seemed to cause some of our Social Studies teachers to shy away from such painful topics. It wasn't until high school that we received some real instruction in those events. My first memory of being taught about slavery and the Civil War was in the eleventh grade. By that time I was sixteen. That is a long time to live without exposure to the very real evils of racism and its twisted history in the United States.

When I myself was teaching high school in the mid-1960s I recall one of my colleagues reporting at a history department meeting that he generally skipped over slavery and the Civil War because he felt it made the students uncomfortable. By that time all his students were Black! It was, however, in Junior High where we came to see Black kids close up and found that in many respects they were a lot like us. That is because they were like us—mostly lower middle class from two parent families. I suppose the Negro students at junior high schools like Sayre and Shoemaker, deeper in the boughs of West Philadelphia, were somewhat different than the students we met at Beeber. By the early 1950s, West Philadelphia, once predominantly Jewish, had begun to turn predominantly Black. Poor southern Negroes and Negroes from other cities had begun the second wave, initially begun after World War I, of the Great Migration where rural, southern Negroes migrated to the burgeoning urban areas along the East Coast. The prosperity that rode on the heels of postwar America after 1945 hit cities like Washington, Baltimore, Philadelphia and New York. And, like my own grandfather Max Goldman on my father's side, a rural villager in the Pale who emigrated to seek a better life for himself and his family at the turn of the century while escaping a hostile Tsarist Russian regime that did not exactly embrace its impoverished Jews, rural southern Negroes completed the trek to seek a better life that led them to become an urban underclass in large East Coast cities like Philadelphia.

Because of districting most of the Negro kids we met at Beeber came from two-parent, lower middle class families who had moved up to the affordable row housing in West Philly after the war. We rarely got into fights, we got along, and although I can't say there was extensive interracial dating during Junior High, I can recall a number of Negro kids invited to our parties and dances. It wasn't exactly Brigadoon or Walden Two, but race was not a big issue in those Wonder Years. Of course, all of that was to change drastically in high school. In high school race was not only an issue, it was the issue.

CHAPTER 5

The years between seventh and ninth grade are the only ones in my life I would not want back. They were much too painful. I sometimes think it would have been better to have remained in a state of suspended animation from age thirteen until the age of fifteen or sixteen. Something terrible happens to adolescent boys in terms of their raging hormones and their metabolism. Whatever it is, it isn't good. There ought to be a pill you can take to get you through those difficult years. By now, there probably is one.

For one thing, youngsters at that age are remarkably cruel. It doesn't take a Columbine to empathize with the victims of unrelenting bullying, meanness of spirit and the enervating feelings of absolute powerlessness that those teenage years produce. As an adult, I have usually said and done what I wanted to say and do. Not that such a luxury comes without a heavy price. Even as adults we don't enjoy the freedom we'd like to think we have.

For a year or so I had a talk radio show in Boston. I said what I wanted to say every week for eight to twelve hours a week. I pissed a lot of people off. And some people liked me. After that I latched on to a political column as editor of a weekly Boston newspaper. At the same time, I was hired as a bi-monthly columnist for a new Boston slick that went national for a time called *Bostonia Magazine*. Again, I pissed a great many people off. Some of them were very powerful people. They complained to my publishers and station manager incessantly about what I wrote or said on the air. My publisher loved it. That meant that powerful people were reading his paper and his flagship columnist. So, most of the time, he left me alone. In five years of writing columns, only two were ever pulled.

But between age twelve and sixteen, you really care what people think about you—especially your peers. Cruelty just seems endemic in teenage souls during these difficult years.

Early on in the seventh grade I became deeply enamored with a cute little girl named Harriet Katzin. She couldn't have stood over five feet, and soaking wet weighed maybe 75 pounds. Harriet lived on 57th and Wyndale Avenue with her older sister Judy and her parents. Every time I'd see Harriet walking in the hall between classes my poor love-struck heart would skip a beat. I got some of my friends to invite Harriet to our various parties. I'll never forget a Friday night party at Richard Traiman's house on Gulf Road. We all played two new and exciting games: Post Office and Spin the Bottle. I even got to kiss Harriet. The fact that she had a mouthful of wire and steel made no difference to me whatsoever. A kiss, as Dooley Wilson sang in *Casablanca,* was still a kiss! Or as Stephen King pointed out so poignantly in *Hearts in Atlantis,*

"It would be the kiss you will always remember."

Sadly, Harriet Katzin barely knew I was alive. On Saturdays, I'd follow her to the Wynne Movie with her best friend Toby Shupak. When she came into Cosmo's, the pharmacy where I dished out ice cream, milk shakes and cokes for fifty cents an hour, I made sure, to the consternation of my ever-so-patient boss Ben Weintraub, to always give Harriet a double scoop for a lousy dime.

When her friend Toby threw a surprise party for George Lubeck in the spring of 1952, I was devastated not to have been invited. For one thing, at the time Lubeck was one of my closest friends in the seventh and eighth grade. He played shortstop on our class box-ball team. And like me, Lubeck loved Paul Arizen, the great power forward for the Philadelphia Warriors.

I'll never forget the sad and empty feeling I felt that terrible Saturday night in 1952 as I sat out George's party at home while just two blocks away all my closest friends from 7A-1 were having such a wonderful time playing Post Office and Spin the Bottle. And, of course, little Harriet was there. I found out two things later from George: Toby Shupak, for some reason I could never fathom, didn't like me. Perhaps she once saw me jerking off under my desk in Mrs. Dougherty's Social Studies class. Pulling my pudding, I learned early on, was always much more productive than Social Studies. I still feel that way. I wasn't a Catholic and nobody ever told me that something that felt so good was a venal sin. And since I never really took "It out," as Elaine Benes complained to Seinfeld, it wasn't Toby Shupak's damn business anyway. I was always careful just to rub my pants very quietly under my desk. Besides, what was Toby Shupak doing watching me when she should have been focused on tin production in Bolivia? What I did under my desk during sixth period was none of her affair.

As it turned out, Harriet Katzin liked another boy—a kid from Conshohocken (the Philly neighborhood not the town) named Norman Greenberg. Norman Greenberg was one of those Ivy League types who wore button down shirts with chinos that had a belt in the back. Norman was so Ivy League that I think he may have had a belt sewn on the back of his head.

At the time, my fashion icons were the tough Italian guys who wore pegged pants, double belt loops with three inch high risers and box-toe shoes. My favorite pants had saddle stitched sides and were gold, rust and powder blue with a twelve to thirteen inch peg. If you need to ask what a peg or a rise was…well, just don't. I also wore my dark hair long with a duck's-ass (a DA it was called) in the back, heavily pomaded with a greasy, green, foul smelling substance called Olivo.

Sometimes I would switch from Olivo to the better smelling but greasier concoction called "Dixie Peach." Again, don't ask.

The really cool girls in the seventh grade at Beeber Junior High belonged to the Yellow Ribbon Club. Every spring the Yellow Ribbons threw a dance. For many of us it was the biggest event of the year. Harriet Katzin, being the first girl who ever made my pants move, was naturally my chosen date for the Yellow Ribbon Club dance. Although I knew she liked someone else, I called her on the phone and asked her to the big dance that spring.

Calling a girl on the phone was one of the most challenging things I can recall about those adolescent years. I would dial (no touch-tones in the 1950s kiddies) and then hang up before it even rang. Often, I would dial a number and hang up a dozen times before I finally allowed the phone to finally ring. If a parent answered, I often hung up again. It would always take quite a while to bolster my courage and finally complete a call to a girl on the phone. To this day, as my closest friends will tell you, I do not enjoy talking on the phone. When the phone rings, ever since I lost my parents, I rarely answer it. As my ex girl-friend Ann Marchette once complained, "You give very bad phone." I am a telemarketer's worst nightmare. Aside from most phone conversations being a colossal waste of time, I guess I am too often reminded of the excruciating self-inflicted torture from my adolescent attempts to reach the opposite sex by phone in the early 1950s. The last time I recall phoning a girl for a real date must have been circa 1964. And I married that girl! I have always placed Alexander Graham Bell in the same historical category as Adolf Hitler.

That time Harriet answered the phone. I always tried to say something very cool besides just "hello" in an initial phone encounter. Something like, "Were you studying? Am I bothering you?" or, "Hi. This is Marty." After the usual response, "Marty who?," I always knew I was in deep trouble. For reasons I'll never be able to comprehend, Harriet accepted my offer to escort her to the Yellow Ribbon Club dance in that spring of 1952 even though I wasn't Norman Greenberg. Maybe I begged. Maybe Norman was busy shopping for belts.

But, I had a major league problem. I couldn't stand to wear itchy wool pants and I knew my high-rise pegged pants would never do. I may well have been headed for my thug stage, but in the seventh grade that stage had not yet arrived. Even though at twelve little Harriet was mostly braces and hair, she still did it for me. I would never have embarrassed her by dressing like one of my hoodlum pals from Hungry Town or Little Italy. Nobody wore jeans or chinos in those prehistoric days. Except for hoods and bikers, of which I was neither. Of course, in 1955 James Dean helped to change all that.

My Dad was always very good at solving problems; especially since he always seemed to buy me the itchiest pants on God's green earth. He suggested that I resolve my itchy pants problem by wearing my pajama bottoms under my wooly pants. We would fasten them with rubber bands before I left for the dance. Nobody would ever be the wiser. Or so my Pop said. Pop kept envelopes filled with dozens of rubber bands. He was the rubber band king. I think if you asked my father to name the greatest invention in all of human history, he would answer without hesitation, "The rubber band!" When my Pop died in 1999, I found one of his dresser drawers crammed with envelopes filled with rubber bands.

Unfortunately, the rubber bands Dad used to solve my itchy pants problem must have been manufactured sometime before the Civil War. Because when I was fast dancing with my lovely Harriet Katzin, the rubber bands snapped and my PJs tumbled down from my itchy pants hanging all the way down almost past my shoes. My pajamas, like most of my other clothes, were two sizes too large. Dad always believed in buying us clothes that my brother and I would eventually "grow into."

Poor Harriet Katzin was mortified. A crowd of kids pointed at us and were laughing. I just wanted to curl up in a fetal position and return to the womb. Any womb would have been fine at that painful moment. If there is one thing that sticks in my mind about that period in my life it is how relentlessly cruel teenagers can be. It ain't *The Wonder Years* or *Leave It to Beaver*. I wanted to disappear in a big puff of smoke like the Rocketman did every Saturday in the cliffhangers at the Wynne.

Harriet Katzin would never go out with me again. But we remained friends over the years and we both attended the same university. Curiously, I fictionalized this event in my first novel with a few embellishments for maximum literary effect. I thought Harriet would hate the story but never thought she would read it. (In the fall of 2010 I received a phone call in Maine almost sixty years after this incident. The caller was Harriet Katzin. She had read my novel and called to tell me that even though she had no memory whatsoever of the incident she was flattered to have been remembered. We had a wonderful chat and reminisced about those amazing days. Harriet is still just as sweet as she was as a twelve-year-old. But I never knew she was in love with Big Barry Cohen back in high school!)

As for me, I have never again owned a pair of itchy wool pants. To this day, I rarely wear anything but blue jeans or cotton khaki pants. I have saved a shit-load of money for pants over the years.

In 1992 I ran into Harriet Katzin at our 35th high school reunion in Philadelphia. She was on her second marriage, still short and kind of cute. The only thing really different about Harriet was that she didn't have braces anymore. It was actually kind of funny. She barely remembered my lifelong nightmare that was the Yellow Ribbon Dance. My most painful teenage memory and old Harriet Katzin didn't have a clue. I remember looking around for Norman Greenberg. I don't think he was there; although I did see a bent-over, bald guy with a belt on the back of his pants. Toby Shupak even hugged me at the reunion that night. But she didn't offer to shake my hand. As the late Kurt Vonnegut coined the phrase, "And so it goes.

CHAPTER 6

I once thought that life would be perfect after reaching the age of thirteen. Thirteen, for a Jewish male, is a major and magic milestone. It is the year of your Bar Mitzvah. I studied hard that year putting aside all the many childish shenanigans I pulled at Har Zion Hebrew School on 54th Street where I attended classes three times a week. For example, when poor Oscar Davinsky, the harried and overworked school principal who we nicknamed "Doc Popcigar," would visit our class a few of us would jump up, hold our noses and scream that the poor kid still sitting in the front, targeted by us way beforehand, had let go a big, old, ugly gasser—our fart word for cutting the cheese.

But thirteen was serious business. I luxuriated in my Bar Mitzvah lessons with Cantor Isaac Wall, a gentle and beloved teacher. For the first time, I began to feel an attachment to Judaism that went far beyond the little blue cans we used to shake for contributions to the Jewish National Fund and the miraculous new Jewish state of Israel. Cantor Wall's teaching, for the first time, linked me to Judaism in a way that had never happened in the boring Hebrew classes we were forced to take at Har Zion Temple. Studying *Torah* actually began to make sense.

Israel, a faraway place, had little real meaning to most of us then. Although we well understood that the survival of Israel was actually an insurance policy to all the Jews of the world who had escaped the evils of Hitler and Nazism, we shook those blue cans on cold wintry days because our Hebrew school teachers told us it was good for the Jews. And who were we to argue about what was good for the Jews?

My Bar Mitzvah came and went on November 15, 1952. My two partners were my friends in the Cub Scouts: David Perilstein, whose Dad, Paul Perilstein, was our Cub-master; and Herb "Erky" Ehrlichman. Herbie's later claim to major fame came in high school when he would breathlessly relate the tale of how he would come home from school to find milk and cookies waiting every day, put out by a faithful family retainer, his Negro maid. I can't recall her name, but Erky got a lot more than milk and cookies from her. Or, so he said.

My pal Erky was a strong proponent of integration in those days. After finishing his milk and cookies, Herbie would repair to his bedroom where he would lie down on top of his covers stark naked with a big, old boner. His maid would walk by his room and when she saw him that way, according to Erky, she would come in and do things to him that fifteen and sixteen year-olds could only dream about in those sexually repressed days. Sadly, I heard that Herb Ehrlichman died in his early fifties. He probably had a heart attack because the last time I saw Erky, he was smoking a couple packs a day. Erky told he was trying to cut down to two-and-a-half packs a day. Erky was only in his twenties when we last ran into one another in Philly. He looked over fifty, coughing, bent over and rail thin. I hope that he was thinking about his old maid and those milk and cookie boners when he died. Then I would know that Erky at least died a very happy man!

My Bar Mitzvah party was held at the Golden Slipper night club in South Philly, in the heart of my Dad's old neighborhood. I don't recall too much about the evening. I received many nice gifts, a lot of money which Pop used to pay for the party and at the end of the evening to top off the day's events my grandfather (on my mother's side) got drunk and punched his son-in-law in the nose. His son-in-law, married to my mother's youngest sister, much younger and stronger than little Herman B. Feldman, knocked my grandfather on his ass. I remember hysterically crying as chairs and people went flying. I begged the two of them to stop screwing up the biggest night of my life. But they were both too damn drunk to pay much attention to a weepy Bar Mitzvah boy. Besides, I was thirteen, in our tradition, a man. And men were not supposed to cry! The sad thing is that I don't even know what they were fighting about.

After my Bar Mitzvah I tried to stay in Hebrew school. But it was never really the same.

The teachers clearly didn't give a shit. And Cantor Wall was still teaching the younger Bar Mitzvah boys. One interesting thing from those days is that girls did not figure very large in the plans of our Hebrew school. Sure, some of the girls were Bat Mitzvah, but there was hardly the fuss that was made over the coming of age of the boys. Today, girls are treated with the same fuss at age thirteen as the boys. I suppose that is progress; of a sort. After a last year at Har Zion, I dropped out of Hebrew school after I turned fourteen. Pop, whose own upbringing was forced orthodoxy, never said a word. When it came to rabbis and organized religion, my father never possessed a great depth of faith. He loved the Jewish people and, I think, the traditions. Pop just never trusted the business or political end of Judaism which he always viewed as catering to the wealthiest members of the congregation. After many years of working in and for the Jewish community, I must sadly report that Pop wasn't far off the mark.

However, all was not lost as a result of the six years I spent in Hebrew school. I can still read and write Hebrew to this day. Just don't ask me to translate. That they never taught us!

After my Bar Mitzvah, life in Wynnefield settled into a routine of sports, making new friends and my first real job—a paper route where I delivered the early afternoon edition of *The Philadelphia Bulletin*. There was a saying in those days: "In Philadelphia, nearly everybody reads *The Bulletin*." That slogan was apparently not wholly accurate since sometime in the 1970s, *The Bulletin* went belly up. An avid reader of newspapers, I always knew *The Bulletin* to be far superior to *The Philadelphia Inquirer*. But *The Inquirer* also owned the tabloid *Daily News* and was eventually able to drive *The Bulletin* which came out in the late afternoon out of business. Beware of a one-newspaper town. Its citizens are inevitably destined, with all the inherent bias residing in a solo paper, to be terminally ill-informed.

By the ninth grade the major oppression of adolescence finally began to lift. After years of delivering the paper all over the neighborhood, I finally got my choice two-street paper route: on my own street, 54th and Diamond and the next street down, 56th and Diamond.

As an added bonus, there were two incredibly cute girls who lived almost next-door to one another. And wonder of wonders, their parents read *The Philadelphia Bulletin*.

Charlotte Cutler lived at 5629 Diamond Street and Gloria Langnas, who lived at 5633 Diamond, were best friends. I would usually collect my route on Saturday mornings and Charlotte, praise the Gods, would often answer the door in a loose fitting bathrobe over an even looser fitting nightgown. Charlotte had a wonderful laugh—actually a little giggle—and she had other wonderful points as well. Or should I say pointers! The girl, even at twelve, had great tits!

I would come to collect for the newspaper, Charlotte would answer the door, giggle and call her mother: "Mom, the paperboy's here! You know, that boy who lives up the street! He wants forty-five cents for the paper. Now, mother!"

Her mother, probably in her thirties or forties and almost as cute as Charlotte, would never fail to give me the forty-five cents and a fifteen cent tip each week.

Gloria Langnas, her neighbor two doors down, seemed a lot more serious than Charlotte Cutler. Gloria had a very pretty face if you didn't mind braces. But it was really her older sister Marlene who drew the neighborhood boys to the Langnas house over and over for the next couple of years.

Marlene Langnas was what they called *zaftig* in those days. *Zaftig* is Yiddish for stacked.

Gloria had a younger brother, Rodney, who was about nine or ten. He was a little pain-in-the-ass who always demanded money to leave us all alone. Later, Rodney would try to hang out in the backroom of Harry's, our local diner. Since he was much younger, we would often toss his ass out since there was a pool table and a couple of pinball machines. Like Claude Rains in *Casablanca* you may be shocked. But serious gambling was always taking place in that dark backroom at Harry's. Stakes were often in the hundreds of dollars at the pool table when the older guys played.

At the age of nineteen, Rodney Langnas was arrested and charged with homicide in one of the most brutal murders to ever hit the old neighborhood. He pleaded guilty and got twenty years to life from a tough old Irishman, Judge Vincent A. Carroll. I should know because I was there in the courtroom when Rodney pleaded out and was sentenced; but more about all that later.

I owe a great deal to Charlotte Cutler. As time passed we became friends. I would visit her house and we would play records, and dance and talk and talk and dance and talk. Charlotte had a vast network of girlfriends who also came into our Diamond Street orbit. Her girlfriends were Ruthie Bayer, a tall, pretty curly-haired blonde; Rozzie Rubin, a hyper, freckle-faced dumpling who always appeared to be worried that something terrible was about to happen. Of all the girls, I liked her best but Rozzie Rubin wanted none of my business.

She viewed me as a budding hoodlum and, like Harriet Katzin, preferred more Ivy League types. She liked a kid from 53rd and Diamond named Carl Soifer. Soif was good looking, a very nice boy. His parents were card-playing friends of my parents but Carl was much too straight-laced to ever hang around with the likes of me and my gang.

I can't report that anything sexual ever took place in those days; because it didn't. But just slow dancing with Charlotte and Gloria as we watched Bandstand or spun 45s on the turntable was a memorable experience. For a twelve-year-old in the seventh grade, Charlotte was, as I said, remarkably developed. And when she danced close you couldn't help but feel that remarkable development through her pajamas or, if she was dressed, through the tight pink and gray sweaters she always wore. Sadly, no touching was ever permitted by Charlotte.

As I said, I owe Charlotte Cutler large. It was through her that I met the neighborhood guys who were to become my lifelong friends. I stayed friends with this group of guys through high school, college and young adulthood. And although we have all gone our separate and mostly successful ways, from time to time I still see some of my old pals from those days.

In those days our neighborhood friendships were divided very much by street. With a few exceptions most of my closest friends lived on Diamond Street or on streets adjoined by a connecting network of wide alleys—on Gainor Road or Lebanon Avenue.

One Saturday night early on in the ninth grade I knocked on Charlotte's door. Charlotte answered the door, sheepishly said that she had company and that I couldn't come in. It was obvious to me that some other guys were in her house. But I couldn't make out who they were. So I went up the street to Harry's where the locals were hanging in the backroom shooting pool.

"There's a party down Diamond Street," I lied. "Anybody up for crashing?"

In a few minutes I was leading half the neighborhood down Diamond Street to knock on poor Charlotte's door and scare the couple of guys who were inside her house. There must have been fifteen or twenty of us. This time I knocked in force. Charlotte came to the door and though she saw it was me again, this time she threatened to call "the Red Car." In those days the Philly cops drove very identifiable cruisers painted apple red.

A couple of the boys in the house peered out the window. All they could see was an angry mob, stirred up largely by yours truly. These were guys who could handle themselves in a fight.

But they were not about to take on all of Diamond Street, Gainor Road and Lebanon Avenue. A lot of my Diamond street pals were cursing and threatening dire consequences if the guys inside the house would come out to fight. So those guys inside held on to discretion as the better part of valor. Charlotte never did call the cops. What with all the noise we were making, somebody else on the street did. The cops arrived quickly, threatened to arrest all the guys on the street and eventually my "gang" gave up and went back to shooting Saturday night pool up the street at Harry's.

But the guys inside the house who also ate at Harry's from time to time wanted to make sure that there would be no repercussions. So they asked for a meeting. Their leader was Paul Gansky, a kid who wore a black leather motorcycle jacket—even though he had no motorcycle at the time. These guys came from Wanamaker Street, Hobart Street and Melvin Street—all side streets off Malvern Avenue, about a half-mile from Diamond Street. As it turned out, they were pretty good guys and had a large network of their own: soon Irv "Pigsby" Blank, Stanley "Benny" Stein, Alan "the Thief" Martin, Eddie "Zeke" Friedman, Howie "Tire" Gleit, Jack P. Zatz (aka "Zatzmo"), Jerry "Bergano or Yogi" Berger, Frankie "Oval" Ash and a few others became very close friends as we merged some of the Diamond Street guys into Harry's—

the toughest and most visible group of our generation, taking over Harry's shrouded backroom in the ensuing years for our social life and other nefarious teenage activities. To this day, I am still friends and in touch with some of these guys.

Sadly, some of our guys never grew up.

Jack Zatz, the last time I heard, was doing a twenty-five-to-life stretch in the Florida state prison at Tallahasee. Zatzmo shot-gunned a guy in Cincinnati after a drug deal he was fronting went from bad to worse. The guy had apparently ratted out Zatz, who was making his living fishing for shrimp, grouper and snapper. Drugs obviously paid much more than snapper.

As a well-respected Florida maritime captain, Zatz became familiar with the inland waterway and its many winding channels through the Everglades. Zatzmo was nabbed by the feds running a haul of marijuana worth $10 million. The pot was seized off the seacoast near Pearlington, Mississippi. Zatz should have stuck to the waters off Florida. The Feds charged that Zatz and his confederates had smuggled some 15 tons of marijuana from Columbia into the Mississippi port. Zatz was alleged to be the skipper of a 73 foot shrimp trawler, Gulf Stream, from which he intended to unload the dope. Apparently, Zatz caught up to the guy who informed on him in Cincinnati where he aced him. Busted at his home in North Lauderdale by the Feds who traced the shotgun, the brazen shooter had unwisely left at the scene of the crime, Zatz waived extradition to Ohio. Even though he had been the past president of the Biscayne Chapter of Organized Fisherman of Florida, Zatz was sent up for murder, did some hard time, got paroled and then went back to his fishing in Everglades City.

Poor Zatzmo! He was always a slow learner in high school. Once again, another informant traded him up the federal food chain. Zatz got caught running drugs up through the inland waterways near Everglades City in 1989 or 1990. This time the feds threw the key away. Zatzmo had violated the terms of his parole on the Cincinnatti murder beef. Zatzmo was one of our guys who, when he rowed, rarely had both oars in the water. Like the time he stole his uncle's Plymouth and then dumped it in a quarry after we took a long joy ride.

Teenage life in Wynnefield was very territorial. I often attempt to explain that strange, almost tribal territoriality to my students. For the most part, the students I have taught over the course of my academic career come from small New England towns. The tribalism that existed on an urban frontier like West Philly over half a century ago is very foreign to youngsters who grow up in fairly homogeneous settings.

For example, we did not have parents who constantly ferried us to baseball, tennis, soccer, dance or guitar lessons. We walked everywhere. Because, for the most part, our streets were safe and because there was little need to rely on our busy parents to get us to Hebrew school or to the movies or to anywhere. If we wanted to play baseball, basketball or touch football all we had to do was walk out of our houses and there were dozens of other kids out there on the street. Girls played jump-rope or hopscotch and boys played sports. If we didn't have a basketball net, somebody would pinch a peach basket from the corner grocery store, punch it through and nail it to a telephone poll. And we had a basketball court! If we wanted to play stick-ball all we had to do was to find an old broom handle and ante twenty-five cents up a piece for a couple of "pinky" hi-bounce balls.

Although we didn't have well manicured baseball diamonds or even a grassy field, we always had enough kids to make up two teams for a baseball game on the tarred lot of Saint Barbara's Church at the top of our block across 54th Street. Sometimes the priests and nuns would chase us. Sometimes they would leave us alone. Their policies were never very clear.

One Sunday my Dad wanted to hit some out to me on the paved St. Barbara's lot. On my first pitch Pop hit the baseball right through the church's stained glass window. It was a pretty good clout. Then, to my surprise, Pop ran away leaving me to face the music when a young priest came running out of the rectory. I'll never forget that angry priest with my baseball in one hand, chasing me down, grabbing me by the collar and hauling me down the street where he banged on our front door and asked my sheepish father to keep his kid off the church's private lot. My father gave me hell, winked and told the priest that he'd see that the window was paid for by docking my allowance. What allowance? Of course, I never finked out Pop. For which, at the time, he seemed very grateful. In later years Pop would argue that he had no memory of the incident. It is one of those precious memories—a special footprint in the snows of my past—that I cherish to this day.

CHAPTER 7

"It was the past that defined us. We were arrogant enough to ignore the future. And young enough to be certain that the present was something that would never change."
Barry Levinson
Sixty-Six

A word about Harry's (or as we called it, "The Greasy Spoon"): The old-fashioned diner where the guys used to hang out is rapidly disappearing in America as kids today spend the bulk of their leisure time heading for the sterility of vast complexes with the same cookie-cutter stores from coast to coast we call shopping malls. You could be in a mall in Atlanta, Georgia, San Diego, California or Boston, Massachusetts. It would all be the same. As if you were trapped in a Ray Bradbury short story or Rod Serling's *Twilight Zone*. Welcome to the Stepford-GAPing of America.

The diner had a brief nostalgic rebirth with the 1982 film *Diner*. But the diner as we knew it in the forties and fifties has really become somewhat of a dinosaur caught among the butcher block and jungle fauna that prevails in the culinary badlands of urban yuppiedom.

The *New York Times* columnist David Brooks, who grew up in suburban Wayne outside of Philadelphia, describes much of this upward sterility brilliantly in his book *Bobos in Paradise*.

The diner or neighborhood luncheonette was a place that most American kids today will never know. For there was a time when a boy coming of age in an American city could experience the exhilarating lifestyle of, with all apologies to Mark Twain, an urban Huck Finn.

No parents were allowed as the diner became your home away from home.

In Wynnefield we called the place "the Greasy Spoon," or just "the Spoon." The Spoon was located on the northwest corner of 56th and Diamond right down the street from my house. I could walk out my door and be in the back room in about sixty seconds. The real name of the place was Harry's even though the original owner, old Harry Wapner, was long dead. Harry had sold the place to Jacob "Jack" Feldman shortly after the war. Jack, did not want to spring for a new sign; so he kept the old one fronted by big bold letters, "Harry's Luncheonette." Harry's wasn't exactly a diner. And it wasn't exactly a luncheonette. It had a darkened private back room with a pool table, two pinball machines and a bowling game where the "nice" girls in the neighborhood would never dare to venture. Harry's was where my friends and I spent the bulk of our lives between the age of 13 and our early twenties.

When he died in 2001 at age 85 a Philly newspaper called Jacob Feldman, "the Godfather of Wynnefield." That was a little misleading. First of all, I'd bet a week's pay that few of the Harry's regulars in those years knew that Jack was Jacob. I didn't know until I read the obit.

Jack Feldman was hardly connected to the Mob. Although gangsters did, from time to time, frequent his eating establishment because his food was really good. Jack was among the first to introduce real pizza to West Philly. His hoagies were endless feasts. (A Philly Hoagie is a Sub or a Grinder to New Englanders who wouldn't know a real Italian hoagie if it bit them in the ass! Forget genuine Philly cheese steaks in New England!) Jack's cheese steaks could only be matched if you went to Pat's in South Philly or Jim's in deep West Philly for a cheese steak or all the way to the Super Sub in Atlantic City for a great hoagie. We called Jack Feldman "the Innkeeper."

The worst that can be said about Jack Feldman is that if you wanted to place a bet on a horse or a sporting event, then Jack was the man to see. One of the Philly papers wrote, "Mr. Feldman was considered a friend, confidant, banker, disciplinarian and surrogate father to generations of teens who grew up in Wynnefield. His luncheonette, which he operated for 24 years, until 1971, was the usual place to meet in that neighborhood."

I can live with that description. At times, Jack could be very tough on us. If we acted up, Jack would throw us out. If we were too noisy and a customer complained, Jack would throw us out. But when we showed up on school days and repaired to the back room to shoot 8-Ball Jack rarely asked us why we were not in school. I spent the better part of my eleventh year of high school in Jack's dark backroom. I paid for my cutting school with three sessions of summer school over my high school years and a great many flunks on my report card. Since we usually forged our parent's signatures or had duplicate report cards that we could pass by our parents most of the Spoon boys lived under the same dark academic cloud.

The back room was small and usually as many as fifteen or twenty of us would be packed in like sardines shooting some stick, playing pinball while discussing the deeper meaning of life or the dangerous possibility of visitors among us from outer space.

I can't recall a single conversation in Harry's that ever had anything to do with what any of us were going to do in life, or a book that somehow influenced us, beyond EC Comics, or the fact that most of us were doing very poorly in school.

Of course, since we were all paying customers, Jack was always careful to extend us the courtesy of a return visit. Unless we did something so outlandish—like curse in front of customers or get into an ugly fistfight, which were not infrequent occurrences—and then Jack would ban us from the Spoon for a length of time that usually matched our infraction. I was only banned from Harry's once and I can't recall the incident that led up to my brief exile. My sin could not have been too egregious since I have no memory of it whatsoever.

The cops were always being called if we were congregated on the street corner and I can remember many a Saturday night when the cops would either herd us outside for instant dispersal to our homes or even pack us in the back of what we called "the meat wagon," a large red truck that Philly cops used to haul miscreants to the local jail. On more than one late-night occasion I had to wake my father up to come get me and my pals out of the police station at 63rd and Thompson in West Philly. My father rarely handled these occasions well.

Jack worked very hard. Sometimes we would forget that Harry's was Jack Feldman's major livelihood. As I recall, he had a very large family—rare in the fifties. For many years Jack drove a battered old blue Plymouth—and those were the days when a new car listed for around $2,000. He would arrive by 11 A.M. and often would still be making sandwiches after 9 or 10 P.M. He had some counter help—a very nice Black woman we all liked, Thelma; once in a while his eldest son, Norman and his nephew Nelson, who constantly antagonized whoever was in the back room. I got along with everyone except for Nelson and saw Jack as a surrogate parent.

You knew you were accepted into Harry's inner circle when Jack put you in the book. That meant you could run a tab. Jack kept a book on all his regulars. One of his endearing qualities was the fact that Jack seemed to always know if one of us was down on his luck. He trusted those of us on the book to eventually pay up and most of did. Jack had been in World War II but he never spoke of what he saw or did; at least not to the younger guys.

Most of us had jobs, but Jack rarely dunned any of us for the monthly tabs. Most of the older guys honored their debts although I doubt Jack ever really collected all that he was owed since the book he kept was substantial. And he was allowing three to four generations of young men to eat on his cuff at the same time. The ages of the young men who hung out at Harry's went from the early teens well into the mid-twenties.

Jack, we all knew, loved us. And the affection was reciprocated. Few of the guys who hung out at Harry's stole from Jack. Yes, we used a file from time to time on the pinball machines to play for free. But the pinball machines were contracted into the store (probably by the Mob), so none of us felt very guilty about getting free games by using a nail file from the tough guys who came to collect nickels, dimes and quarters once a week. Few of us were above stealing, but stealing from Jack Feldman was a real no-no. That was a way to get your ass kicked. We usually didn't take that kind of a problem to Jack. He took care of us and we, in turn, took care of him.

Like the returning World War II vets in *The Best Years of Our Lives,* Jack had come back to get his slice of pie that encompassed so much of the American dream after the war. Work hard, treat people decently and life will all work out. For many years, it did.

Generations of young men came through Harry's doors. And no matter how tough he was on them, I never met one who didn't really love the guy. A stocky man, who wore his slicked dark hair close-cropped, Jack's uniform after he put away his army air corps greens, was a white apron. What finally drove Jack out of Wynnefield was the changing racial climate of the old neighborhood. By the late 1960s, Wynnefield was becoming largely black. To survive, sometime in the early sixties, Jack moved Harry's to 54th Street. But it was never the same. For one thing, there was no back room. And, as the years went by, the Harry's regulars all drifted apart. Most of them left the streets, found their way to college, jail, Vietnam, the suburbs, jobs, families and the promise of American life.

Today, there is no evidence at 56th and Diamond Streets that Jack Feldman or Harry's ever even existed. Maybe, like *Brigadoon,* we'll all be back on that corner every 400 years.

That would be nice. I am definitely looking forward to it.

A beauty salon replaced Harry's and when that disappeared in the haze of rising urban street crime and neighborhood degeneration, nothing followed. If you visit 56th and Diamond today, the streets are usually deserted. There are no kids hanging on the corner, no touch football games in the street and no little girls jumping rope. Although people live there, there is usually no visible sign of life and like Margaret Mitchell's fictional Tara, Harry's is *Gone with the Wind* and 56th and Diamond is a far cry from a Philly street that was teeming with teenage urban life in the 1950s and 1960s: Too many drive-by shootings perhaps.

CHAPTER 8

For the young guys who hung out at Harry's the days were easy and the weekends full. We hated school, galloped rented horses like the Wild Bunch through neighborhood streets, shot eight-ball and bathed in the warmth of steamy spring and summer Philly nights on the corner.

We would pick up horses at Jack's Stable in Fairmount Park for $2.00 an hour and even though we were never supposed to leave the winding park trails, at Parkside Avenue we'd take off into the city like a posse of urban cowboys. Most of us could ride well and it was quite a sight to see eight to ten guys galloping horses down the black asphalt of Diamond and 56th Streets. How many times do you get to see an actual Jewish posse?

My poor mother would get angry phone calls from neighbors: "Do you know that your Marty and those thugs he hangs with on the corner have horses tied up outside of Harry's?

You'd better get down there before they arrest your son." To her great credit, Mom left me alone and never embarrassed me in front of my friends. And she never told my father.

Unlike Ida Laster, my old friend Larry's mother, who once, when we came galloping down Oxford Street, almost fainted dead away when I trotted up to her front porch to ask if Larry, whose equestrian skills were severely limited, had gotten out of bed that morning.

I had learned to ride one magic summer when I spent the entire time working with some Negro kids who gave pony rides at the beach on Boston Avenue in Atlantic City. This was way before Atlantic City became Las Vegas east. With the exception of the ancient Ostend Hotel, which catered to aging Jews, there were no hotels on the Boston Avenue beach. An Irish guy named Pat Callahan owned the ponies and horses and he would get poor black kids from the impoverished

Atlantic City ghetto to operate his absentee pony concession for mostly tips.

The only time we ever saw Pat was when he came around once a day in the late afternoon to collect his cash. Like the black kids, I loved horses. Unlike them, in 1953 I didn't know how to ride a horse.

I didn't make much money and it bothered my parents that I was the only white kid working the pony rides. They had not taken their son down the shore to work on the hot beach under the Boardwalk to shovel piles of horse pucky. Instead of joining my family on the beach every day, I would spend my time shoveling manure while tending to the horses and ponies. A *yente* from our rooming house named Rosenberger told my mother that it was a shame to bring a kid all the way to Atlantic City for a vacation and watch him spending time with the *"schvartzahs."* My parents would have obviously preferred me not spending my summer days with Negro kids and young Negro men. But they never said a word.

That summer of 1953, two Black guys, Harold and Calvin, taught me to ride. Harold and Calvin could ride horse-back like the Cisco Kid and his sidekick Pancho. When things were slow we were permitted to take the horses for a gallop around the ring. Most of our time was spent sitting out of the hot sun under the Boardwalk playing mumbly peg with an ice-pick or cards. I got to be pretty good with that ice pick. I rarely won at poker.

For a quarter you could buy your kid a pony ride or, if he or she was a little more adventuresome, a ride on a big white stallion called Biscuit or a chestnut mare named Queenie. Both horses were very gentle. We'd take the kids around the big rink a couple of times; once in a while if the kid wanted we'd run by their side while they were permitted to trot. We always held firmly to the reins and then their parents would often tip us a dime.

Harold became my closest friend that summer. He was a year or so older and on lazy hot August days as we sat in the shade under the boards, he would often speak of his hopes and dreams for the future. Harold was very bright but in the early 1950's dreaming and hoping in America was largely reserved for White kids. I think Harold always knew this but dreaming was always free.

I often wonder what happened in life to my summer friend Harold, who loved when I would call him by his Hebrew name, *Chara*. For many years I have been a strong opponent of affirmative action. I have written about it in many newspapers, been quoted in *Time* magazine, and debated the issue on numerous TV and radio shows. In 1973, for all the good it did, I even testified against affirmative action before the House Sub-Committee on Education. I have been convinced for many years that the worst thing to ever happen to Black America, aside from their betrayal by so many of their corrupt leaders, has been affirmative action.

However, I hope that my summer friend Harold, whose own dreams were so severely limited in the America of the 1950s, has benefited from the societal changes we have all witnessed and that he has achieved, in one degree or another, his long ago summer dreams.

It was always quite a sight to see those black kids proudly galloping a dozen or so horses and ponies every day up Boston Avenue past Pacific Avenue on their way to the beach. These young Black kids didn't have much. You could always see their pride as they galloped up that street, posting in their western saddles and looking straight ahead as they clip-clopped by early every July and August morning.

At the age of fourteen three of the guys who hung out at Harry's Luncheonette signed a pact in blood. We swore in writing that one day, we would buy land, horses and start a ranch. Alfred Cohen sold booze on St. Thomas for many years after returning in one piece from Vietnam. I've heard that Al Cohen's was the biggest retail liquor operation on that island for many years. I went to St. Thomas during my honeymoon in 1965 but I don't think Al had arrived there yet. The last time we spoke, Big Al was retired and living comfortably near Monticello outside of Charlottesville, Virginia. Al Cohen was one of my closest friends since the third grade. Sadly, my friend Alfred died in October of 2009. I called and wrote to let him know that a few of us wanted to see him. But Al, always proud and always somewhat recalcitrant, obviously didn't want his old friends to see him when he was sick. He was married with children so I have to assume that Big Al was surrounded by those who knew and loved him at the end.

When Al got out of the army in the late 60's he headed for St. Thomas where he made a successful life and a name for himself. Everyone in St. Thomas knew Al Cohen.

The other member of our blood pact made tens of millions in the insurance industry, owns a boat almost as long as a city block and recently sold one farmhouse for five to six million while moving into one of the largest farms nearby in Pennsylvania horse country where, of course, he owns a great many expensive horses. This guy would vote Republican if Donald Duck were nominated.

A few years ago I visited his farm for a week. We caught up on our many lost years, went skeet shooting and spent an entire afternoon riding my friend's very well-bred horses. My old pal was impressed when I followed his lead in a jump we both took at a full gallop along the trail with apparent ease. I guess riding a horse is like riding a bike. Even for a Philly kid closing in on 60 at the time. It is peculiar that although none of the three of us ever lived up to our pact, all of us ended up living at one time or another in rural areas with horses. Unlike my old friends, my horses were always borrowed.

CHAPTER 9

Life in Harry's backroom was a daily adventure. Many of the other guys in the neighborhood envied us the camaraderie that our backroom always provided. Saturday nights were usually exciting because you just never knew what was in store for the evening. We'd meet at Harry's and, when there were about a dozen of us, decide where in Philly to head. The whole city was ours for the taking. By the age of fifteen many of us had cars. Although it was illegal to drive before the age of sixteen, some of our parents signed statements that their sons had come of age or needed to drive for the family business. Not Lou Goldman, of course.

My father insisted that I pass a driving course at the high school before I was permitted to get a license. It didn't matter much at the time since my father had just purchased a brand new 1955 Olds 88, our family's first car since I had been a toddler. He wasn't about to let me drive it anyway. Passing driver's education also meant a substantial reduction in the insurance premium and Pop was always into that key word: "reduction."

Al Cohen's father needed his son to help in the family wallpaper business at 5th and Federal Streets in South Philly. So Big Al always had Phil's '52 Dodge panel truck or, on special occasions, the family's '51 Buick Roadmaster with power-glide for a Saturday night cruise around Philly. The green truck had large lettering that said "FEDERAL WALLPAPER" on the side panels. It was known throughout the neighborhood.

We'd pile into the back of Al's old truck and then, like a small army platoon on the move in a Humvee, we'd take off for our intended destination. Al was a talented driver but at times he took some chances on the road. One late summer night, coming back from the shore, Al either fell asleep at the wheel or thought a car's headlight in the other lane was coming straight at us.

Doing over 65, Al spun the wheel a full ninety-degrees and the truck skidded around on two wheels, almost turning over. Sitting in the "death seat" without even a moment to say my prayers, I watched the world spin around. I thought the end was at hand. But Al skillfully brought the vehicle to a stop even though it had crossed the highway, completely reversing direction. Larry Laster, the third member of our triumvirate, and I staggered out of the truck to kiss the ground fully aware that we had narrowly escaped serious injury or much worse. When we recovered enough from the scare to discuss what had happened, we all agreed that there must have been a bigger plan in store for one or all of us. That is about as philosophical as we ever got in our "Spoon" days.

A few years later, while racing through South Philly on a delivery for his father, Big Al hit an old woman crossing the street between two parked cars. She flew thirty feet into the air and was probably dead when she hit the ground. Although I've seen my friend Al since that tragic event, I never brought it up. Al Cohen was not in any way an insensitive guy. He had worked hard from the age of fourteen and, instead of going to college with the gang, went right to work in his father's wallpaper business after high school. Phil Cohen was an immigrant from the old country and he didn't know from education or college. Like many Jews from the old country, Phil's whole world consisted of work. He would come home, eat a big meal and go to bed. Six days a week and sometimes a half a day on Sunday. He thought work would be just as good for his son. In a way old Phil Cohen stole some of his son's childhood. Not that Phil didn't love his son "Butchie"—he rarely called him Al, Alfie or Alfred.

In the early 1980s I was walking with my parents near Wolfie's deli in Miami Beach when we ran into Phil Cohen. He recognized me almost immediately and *kvelled* about his "Butchie who, he told us, was "the King of St. Thomas." I had flown to Florida to visit with my Mom and Dad who were vacationing. Pop didn't like the hotel. "Too many old Jews," Pop complained. "Yeah," I laughed saying, "and you're one of them!" Pop was almost 75 at the time. Then we both laughed.

I told Phil Cohen that I hadn't heard from his son in many years and we reminisced about Federal wallpaper and other things from the old neighborhood. When I said that Phil must have been very proud of Al, the old man's eyes filled with tears and he said, "Proud? I always knew my Butchie was special; very special!" A few years later I read in *The Jewish Exponent* (Philadelphia Jewry's newspaper of record) that old Phil Cohen had died.

It just seemed to me that working a serious job at fourteen or fifteen wasn't what a young man should be doing. There was plenty of time in this life for work. Being young, to me, meant having fun. Going to college, even in the city, was fun. Growing up would come soon enough.

To be sure, Alfred Cohen had some perks that I envied. At twelve or thirteen Al had a Schwinn Black Phantom—the Cadillac of bikes. I always wanted a Black Phantom more than anything, but my parents made me settle for a J.C. Higgins model, a much cheaper bike put out in those days by Sears. In the end, though he always had material things, I think Al paid a terrible price for growing up so quickly and going right to work out of high school. To me, he missed a great deal in life.

I was always sad that Al didn't go on to college with the gang because he was certainly smart enough. I used to see him from time to time when I was a young teacher. I always had a sense that Big Al felt some shame that we were out getting educations while he worked in his father's wallpaper store. Maybe shame is the wrong word. But on those infrequent occasions when we bumped into one another in Philadelphia as young men, it was never the same. We would struggle to make conversation and to tell one another about where our lives were heading.

The old warmth between two close friends who had known one another since the third grade and that feeling of camaraderie was missing. Gone forever and never to return. I am not ashamed to say that I loved Al Cohen and that I missed him and his green Federal truck to the day he died. I am not a big sit-com fan but I often watch "Everybody Loves Raymond." Comedian Ray Romano is a dead ringer in both voice and demeanor for my old buddy, Big Al Cohen. They even look alike.

Of course, there was a plus side. Al always had more money than those of us in school.

He was able to buy a boat and a silver Corvette convertible before he turned twenty. But those luxurious gizmos could never replace an education that eventually opened up the future and the world to lower middle class kids whose perspectives were so damn narrow. It was inevitable I suppose that, as time passed, we would drift apart and go our separate ways in life. Al went off to the world of work while most of the rest of us went to school.

Al must have really suffered emotionally after running that old woman down. Although he was a kibbitzer, he could be very serious. Al's mother died when he was nine or ten. And although Phil remarried, Al rarely got along with his stepmother and his home life was not very happy. Somehow, he got out of the legal jam resulting from the accident. Soon after that Al was drafted and ended up in Vietnam. A consummate survivor, Al Cohen, unsurprisingly, beat that silly war in Southeast Asia, returned to Philly, opened up a few businesses and then found his way to fame and fortune on the Caribbean island of St. Thomas.

Since Al was tall, we never got stopped by the cops; almost never anyway. Since I was one of Al's best friends, I usually rode in the front—the only other seat in the truck while the other guys would be content to sit like soldiers about to jump from a plane in the darkened rear. I got my first French kiss, touched my first bare female breast and other dark places in the back of that old wallpaper truck. The girl—a nice Catholic girl who attended St. Barbara's with a little green jumper uniform from that parochial school. She always complained about how strict the nuns at Saint Barbara's were about things like sex. I used to wonder what they would do if they ever knew she was letting a Jewish boy feel her titties and other parts. But touching and French kissing was as far as this girl, about fourteen at the time, would allow me to go; a good thing too since I would hardly have known what to do anyway.

We could be heading to a dance at the OCJC (Oxford Circle Jewish Center) all the way up at the end of Roosevelt Boulevard; or crashing a frat party at Penn in West Philly; or sneaking into a Har Zion dance;

or going to a movie downtown with pizza at Fonzo's (our favorite Italian restaurant) at 48th and Chestnut in West Philly. At the end of the night, around twelve or one in the morning, we'd reconvene in the backroom of Harry's to discuss our sexual conquests—we lied a lot—while Jack made some late-night hoagies and cheese steaks. Needless to say, our discussions about sex were extremely limited; as were our sexual conquests.

One of our guys, Alan Martin, had a saying. Every week he'd lament, "Well boys, another Saturday night down the drain." I wonder, as our Saturday nights are now running to terminal, if old Alan Martin still thinks those magic nights were "down the drain."

Nobody, not even the tough Italian kids from across the bridge in Hungry Town would challenge the guys who hung at Harry's. Harry's was like insurance. If you were identified with the place in any way, most kids in Wynnefield knew you had massive retaliatory force to generally back any play. The various youngsters who could be found in Harry's watched out for one another and even took care of some seamy neighborhood business from time to time.

The young men who hung out at Harry's from their mid-teens through their early twenties made up a strange assortment of urban street types. They were mostly lower-middle class Jewish kids who were not uncomfortable roaming the various neighborhood streets of West Philadelphia.

Although they pretended to be tough, they were not. There was an accompanying cast of neighborhood characters who would have made Damon Runyon jealous. Harry the Goon was a street person before people talked about the homeless living on our city streets. He split his time between a wooden milk crate on 54th Street in front of a drugstore and a milk crate in front of Harry's where he skimmed nickels and dimes from passersby.

Two mountain sized brothers, the Ochrochs, were known for their tendency toward practical joking by their ability to lift small cars from the streets onto the sidewalk.

One kid, Gene Liebman, was nicknamed "the Alley Man." The nickname was very appropriate because Gene would leave his house off the corner of 54th and Wyndale and head to Harry's every night through the labyrinthine back alleys. It wasn't long before Gene knew every window where you could see a naked girl or, even better, a naked lady. Gene would often brag how he had seen Betty Ruth Schwartz, the far better half of the Schwartz twins, buck naked. For some reason Betty Ruth would often go to bed early. And to accommodate "the Alley Man," she'd undress right in front of her window which overlooked the alley on Gainor Road. In the beginning nobody believed the Alley Man that he had seen Betty Ruth Schwartz in the altogether. But, as they say, the eyes don't lie.

One dark night Gene offered to prove it and I accompanied him on one of his alley jaunts. Sure enough, there was Betty Ruth Schwartz, standing stark naked in front of her bedroom window. But the icing on the cake was when Gene took me through an alley where you could look in the first floor bedroom window of the local owner of a millinery shop on 56th Street. Thankfully, that lady too retired early and it was great fun to go on his rounds with the Alley Man. I suppose we would be called creepy "Peeping Toms" today. But, believe me, the fun was more in the creeping than in the peeping. Of course, seeing Betty Ruth Schwartz naked was a lot more fun than seeing her twin brother Norman.

One close friend in those days was Larry Laster, known as "Larunsky Jewsy Bumski," a slightly built drink of water. Larry usually walked the streets of the neighborhood with an army-surplus hand grenade strapped to his belt. Until one day, angered by everyone's constant teasing, he calmly pulled the grenade from his belt, yanked the pin, tossed it into an old abandoned house at 53rd and Wynnefield and blew part of the second floor to smithereens. I dug a piece of shrapnel out of the wall that day with my penknife to prove that he really did it to show the guys back at Harry's. I still have that piece of shattered shrapnel (just in case you don't believe me!).

Today Larunsky has no need for hand grenades on his belt. He retired as a tenured professor of bio-statistics at the University of Pennsylvania where he also earned a Ph.D. Doctor Larry Laster has received international recognition for his many contributions to veterinary and dental research.

One of the early leaders in our gang was Paul Gansky—the Gansk as we called him. The Gansk was the Fonzi of our crew, with his multi-zippered black leather jacket, greasy, pomaded hair topped with a high pompadour and very quick fists. In a fight the Gansk always had the advantage over his opponents. Most guys in the neighborhood would spar around, feeling out their opponent or even wrestle. The Gansk would hit you right in the mouth; hard. There were other guys in Wynnefield who could take the Gansk. But he was widely respected and in any fight, you'd always want the Gansk on your side.

Ironically, the Gansk hooked up (not the way the kids mean it today!) with Charlotte Cutler who became his first girlfriend. Once, Charlotte told the Gansk that I had felt her up at a party. The Gansk didn't even ask me if it was true (it wasn't!). He walked up to me, hit me right in the mouth and knocked me on my ass. After I swore to him that I would never feel up his girlfriend (also, not exactly true, since given the opportunity and considering the size of Charlotte's well-developed breasts, I would most definitely have had to think about it), the Gansk apologized. He became one of my closest friends all the way through college.

In the ninth grade, I introduced the Gansk to his second girlfriend, Sally Ann Heisman who lived in Overbook on Lancaster Avenue. Sally Ann was one great looking girl. She was so great looking that the Gansk married her.

Even though he lived on Wanamaker Street, the Gansk was the only member of our crowd whose family had real money. His father, who owned an insurance agency, kept an apartment in the Warwick, a new and posh building in Ventnor, the first town above Atlantic City.

Gansk would spend most of his summers down the shore. Although my grandfather had two summer homes on the water in Margate, the most I ever got out of Gramps was a weekend or so every summer. My mother had grown up in Atlantic City where her mother ran a rooming house on Rhode Island Avenue after the family lost everything in the Depression. She usually rented a small apartment or took rooms for us in a Boston Avenue boarding house where we would spend some of August and the first week of September. She had little or nothing to do with her father who had remarried after my grandmother's death at age 44 in 1934 from a botched abortion. My Dad would come down the shore on weekends, from Friday to Sunday.

For his sixteenth birthday, the Gansk got a black, '55 Chevy Bel Air convertible. In 1960, his Dad got him a new Thunderbird. After he graduated college, the Gansk went into his Dad's business. He retired in his forties, lives in a Main Line farmhouse in horse country with his second wife where they have over a half-dozen very fine looking horses and a large indoor riding rink that easily cost a small fortune to build. The Gansk has a boat that is over 110 feet long that is more luxurious than any house I have ever owned. In the summers, the Gansk's boat is parked gratis in front of Trump Plaza in Atlantic City where the Gansk and Mrs. Gansk II both like to gamble. In the winter, the boat is taken by Gansk's fulltime captain down to Florida. I am told it costs over $300,000 a year just to keep the Gansk's big boat afloat. I have only been on the boat twice. On both occasions a fulltime steward served an excellent lunch with a delicate white wine. The Gansk no longer wears his black-zippered leather motorcycle jacket and, sadly, his greasy trademark pompadour has gone south with much of the rest of his hair. Gansk's once muscular build has given way to middle age portliness as the good life has taken its terrible toll on our crowd's Arthur Fonzarelli. But underneath all the fine trappings, the Fonz lives. He is still the Gansk. And, as Stanley "Benny" Stein always says, "It's the Gansk and he will be calling us soon!" We are both patiently waiting.

CHAPTER 10

September 10, 1954: my first day at Overbrook High School. My journal entry reads:
"I went to Overbrook. Lots of schvas (Negroes)."

In retrospect, that journal entry appears racist. Jews who call blacks *schvartzahs* today are shunned as bigots. The word is now pejorative. In essence, it is only an old Yiddish expression bastardized from German for the word black—*schvarz*. Today blacks who understand the word are offended. I can't say for certain, but I don't think we meant any disrespect back then. Anyway, it was true. Overbrook High School *was* filled with Black kids.

The salient feature of Overbrook High School was the presence of Negroes in very large numbers. Not quite half the 4,000 kids at Overbrook in 1954 were Black. For the first time in our urban adolescent life we came into contact with kids whose experience, background and home life were much different than our own. Overbrook High wasn't the Blackboard Jungle. But it came damn close.

Although we were very aware of the unfair dichotomy between Whites and Blacks in American society, I can't report that it was predominant in our daily thoughts. We knew it was not good to be Black in American society and that Black people were unfairly treated—especially in the South where lynching was still going on. Slavery, we knew from our Social Studies courses, had been evil, brutal and wrong. But Lincoln and the Civil War had taken care of that problem. And none of our grandparents or great-grandparents ever owned a single slave. They were, for the most part, too busy running away from raping and pillaging, Jew-hating Cossacks. They didn't teach much about Jewish history or pogroms in our Social Studies classes but still…we knew.

Civil rights, and wrongs, were just not high on our hit parade. Not yet. We had Nazis, the Bomb, Commies and girls to worry about. Besides, if most of us were not exactly poor, our families still struggled too. Most of the guys I was friendly with did not go to private camp in the Pocono Mountains during the hot Philly summers. My own parents would send me to the YMCA on 52nd and Sansom Street in West Philadelphia for three summers for four bucks a summer session. It was at the YMCA that I learned to swim and hit a baseball.

If you drove down South Street, Bainbridge Street or Lombard Street in South Philly, the streets were often teeming with Negro streetcorner men drinking out of brown paper bags congregated on the corners. Any time, night or day, you could see them. They were always there. What were they doing? Why didn't they work? Like our fathers? Who were they? Where were their families? Nobody ever told us and, of course, I can't recall any of us ever asking.

Most Negro kids at Overbrook High School initially kept to themselves. They had their own music, dress, language (which we often copied) and their own way of doing things. They ate lunch at separate tables (by choice), kept together in gym hogging the ball courts largely unchallenged and walked the halls in between classes in loud, aggressive packs.

At first, it seemed, they didn't want any part of us. Unlike Beeber where strong and lasting interracial friendships were formed, there was little initial camaraderie between Whites and Blacks at Overbrook. The Negro kids at the Brook were a lot tougher than the ones we knew at Beeber. In some cases, the girls were just as tough as the guys. And, in some cases even tougher. The toughest black girl in my graduating class went on to a long career as a Philly cop.

We all knew about the South and the evil of forced segregation. We knew about the problem of lynching—the terrible Emmett Till lynching in Mississippi was brought home to us in the summer of 1955 as pictures of the poor kid's bruised and battered body made their way into many magazines and newspapers. Till, a Chicago Negro kid, was visiting his relatives for the summer. Some assholes claimed that he had whistled at a white woman. What was the problem? We were always whistling at women and couldn't fathom getting iced for it.

But believe me: Negro kids at Overbrook High School took no shit from White kids in the year 1954. If there was any shit being shoveled out, it was the Negro kids who usually did the shoveling. There was a great deal of intimidation. And it is not an exaggeration to say that just getting through a day in one piece at Overbrook High School was an accomplishment. Negro kids beat up White kids a lot more than White kids beat up Negro kids. Anyone who was there in those years could easily corroborate that fact.

Although we were not afraid of the Negro kids, we did our best to avoid trouble with them. We knew that many of them carried knives and although some of us had knives too, some even with switchblades (I still have mine!), we did not relish a fight where real weapons might be put into play instead of fists. None of us wanted to get hurt badly.

A kid I knew from my paperboy days, David Batalsky, carried a knife. One day he actually got into a knife fight with a black kid. David, a tough kid from Malvern Avenue, pulled his blade and stabbed the Negro kid, cutting an artery. There was blood and cops everywhere. There were two fulltime cops, one in uniform and one in plainclothes, on duty throughout our school day in these years.

By the time I returned to Overbrook High School as a teacher in the early sixties, there was a cop on every floor. These were tough kids and tough times to go to school in a big city. If the Negro kids knew you were afraid of them, you were doomed. Even if you didn't want to fight, it was better to take a good beating in defense of your lunch, which was something you always had to protect, than to let a kid take it. Then you were his forever. And so was your lunch.

On one occasion a black kid pulled a knife on me and, in a rapid move that I think he later regretted, inflicted a deep cut on my arm when I tried to grab the knife. It took a while to quell the bleeding and I still carry a five-inch scar on my forearm to this day. I never reported the kid and he never bothered me again. It got around that I didn't rat. And, for the most part, after that incident, I was rarely bothered.

The lunchrooms were segregated at the Brook by sex. The building was divided into two lunch rooms. Boys were not permitted to eat lunch with girls. You would be suspended if they ever caught you on the girl's side. And, to me one of the silliest rules, you were not ever permitted to leave the building. You had to eat the shitty cafeteria school food. Once you walked into the building, you were a virtual prisoner. That is how it felt too.

In the three years between 1954 and 1957, I was suspended from school on many occasions. Most of my suspensions came as a result of eating out. Although fighting and cutting classes were also among my numerous high school infractions.

I remember one time when the plainclothes cop, a heavyset Irishman, stopped a Negro kid in front of the school and asked for his identification. The kid gave the cop some mouth and the cop pulled out his blackjack to go upside the kid's head. The kid, much faster than the fat Philly cop, grabbed the sap and beat the cop's head into a bloodied jelly mass. I wasn't told about this. I saw it happen. After beating the hell out of the cop, the kid took off and that night our school cop made the local papers. It took him some weeks to recover from that severe beating. I don't know if they ever caught the kid.

I met my first close Negro friend at Overbrook in gym class. He was a great looking kid, about five foot ten, Denzel handsome with a deep caramel color. For the first couple weeks in class we didn't say much more than nod to one another. But Ellis "Butch" Small was unlike most of the other Negro kids. He wore his hair long, slicked (and "processed") on the sides with a big James Dean pompadour in front. He also wore jeans, a black leather jacket and heavy motorcycle boots, the standard uniform of the urban tough guy back in the fifties. Most Black kids didn't dress with jeans and leather jackets. Most Black kids at Overbrook High were far more stylish.

I can't recall who approached who first, but after a couple of weeks of playing some pickup basketball in gym class, we kind of bonded and became close friends.

Ellis 'Butch' Small was a big, good natured, tough looking kid who wasn't tough. If anything, he was a very gentle guy. But I noticed in gym class that few of the tougher Negro kids ever messed with him. What was really cool about Butch is that he looked tough. So, I initially figured, if I hung close to Butch, they wouldn't mess with me either. Turned out I was right.

Butch lived down near 57th and Race near or in the projects. He was built well, loved to dance, dated mostly white girls and was into rock 'n roll and great looking street clothes. We became very close and before the tenth grade was well underway, we were sneaking cigarettes together under the terrace overlooking the athletic field. Of course, smoking in school was forbidden. I got suspended for smoking once too.

Butch's father and mother both worked. His father operated an elevator in Gimbels department store and he had a younger brother, Harry, who worked at the local cleaner on the corner of 57th Street and Wyndale Avenue delivering clothes in the afternoons. But, unlike my Beeber friend Raymond Lee, Butch was dirt poor.

I'd often grab the G bus down to 56th and Market, meet Butch in front of the projects and then, with some of his project friends, we would all go to the State or Nixon to see a movie. At first, I must honestly admit, I was uneasy. By that time, very few Wynnefield kids ventured down deep into the heart of the West Philly ghetto where I had been born.

A lone white kid walking around West Philly in those days could get hurt; but, as time went by, my newfound Negro pals led by Butch Small all accepted me without question. Most of Butch's friends went to Bartram High and, by some bad luck of neighborhood districting, he had ended up at Overbrook. Butch hated Overbrook more than I did. He would often say that "the colored kids" at the Brook were not like his "colored" friends at Bartram. He often referred to the Negro kids at the Brook as "thugs."

After tenth grade Butch wrangled a transfer to Bartram and although we tried to stay in touch, we lost track of one another. Butch used to tell me that Bartram, in southwest Philly, was a lot less intimidating than Overbrook and that the Black and White kids got along a lot better. I visited him there once or twice and noticed that most of the White kids at Bartram were not Jewish. However, Butch and I did have two major adventures that year: the "gang fight;" and our attempt to integrate American Bandstand; an attempt which ultimately failed.

Overbrook's major claim to fame in 1954 was the dominating presence of a seven-foot basketball player from West Philly by the name of Wilt Chamberlain. There are a great many myths surrounding Wilt Chamberlain. Most of them have little basis in fact. Here are some that do:

1. Wilt Chamberlain hated being called "Wilt the Stilt," "the Big Dipper" or "Dippy." Wilt or Wilton was fine with him. He rarely allowed anybody to call him "Dipper" and often sternly corrected anyone misusing his name.

2. Wilt Chamberlain was a very difficult player to coach. Sam Cozen, my friend Steve's father, was his first coach at the Brook. Sam, who was my homeroom teacher in the tenth grade, had a great many problems coaching Wilt Chamberlain who had been getting national press attention since the 10th grade. Coach Cozen's decision to leave Overbrook to coach basketball at Drexel University, I think, had a lot to do with his negative experiences trying to deal with a budding and legendary superstar.

3. His next coach at the Brook was a young phys-ed teacher, Cecil Mosenson. Cecil was still teaching and coaching when I arrived back as a young teacher in 1962. He often confirmed how difficult it was to coach Chamberlain although he stayed on good terms with the superstar until Wilt's untimely death at age 62.

4. Chamberlain was not an ego-centric spoiled star. In fact, he was a pretty nice kid off the court. Once in a while he'd come to play pick-up at Tustin (the playground across the street from Overbrook) and at the Gompers schoolyard where my friends and I often played pickup games. Although he didn't know me from Adam's rib, because he had seen me a few times at Tustin or Gompers, when we passed by in the halls, he'd always say, "Hey man! How ya doin'?" As far as I could see he dealt with his celebrity in high school as well as could be expected.

5. I once saw Chamberlain score 115 points. It was a home game against Dobbins Tech (where I also taught and coached in 1964) sometime in the winter of 1954-55. It was spectacular to see. Chamberlain was on fire. I've never seen a basketball game like this one again in my life.

6. Wilt Chamberlain was not a freak athlete nor was he a one-sport player. He also excelled at track and field. He was one of the most talented athletes to play any American sport and ranks with Joe Montana, Joe DiMaggio and Babe Ruth in the annals of American superstardom.

7. Wilt Chamberlain was a good student. He read books and enjoyed learning all of his life. You want proof? He usually voted Republican.

Overbrook High had many other claims to fame. It produced some other major NBA stars: Wayne Hightower, Bobby Jones and Ralph Heyward. The Brook's singers and singing groups became legendary: Dee Dee Sharp of *Mashed Potato* fame and Len Barry (Borisoff) whose *One, Two, Three* is still played on every oldies station in America. Len Barry was also the lead singer of the Dovells who's *Bristol Stomp* was one of the hottest chart busters of the early sixties. It is no wonder that when fifties teen heartthrob Tab Hunter visited Philly that he chose Overbrook High as the school he would visit. He came to a senior assembly in 1957 and the girls, Black and White, swooned and cheered. Back then nobody knew Tab Hunter's long kept secret—that he was gay. Nobody would have believed it in those days anyway!

By the time we arrived in the tenth grade at Overbrook High School our romance with education had been long over. We didn't just hate school. We despised school. In retrospect, there was a good reason for all of this. With few exceptions, the teachers we were forced to endure were terminally dull. Instead of making learning the exciting adventure it could be, these dullards did everything they could to make it an enduring drag. Math, Science, History, English—it didn't matter.

Most of the people who taught us did their level best to crush any spirit of initiative, individuality or spontaneity. I am not talking sour grapes here even though my career as a student was an unmitigated disaster. Years later I returned to Overbrook High as a young teacher myself. If I had had to spend my career with those people—many of the same drones who taught me were still teaching—I might have put a gun to my head. With only a few exceptions, I liked them even less as colleagues!

In 1954 Overbook High School was a little less than fifty per cent Negro. The White kids were mostly Jewish and Italian. The Italians lived in Hungry Town and Little Italy, near the school. The Jews lived across the 59th Street Bridge in Wynnefield and in Overbrook Park, a somewhat newer neighborhood down City Line toward Upper Darby on Route 1.

The Negro kids came from deeper into West Philly past Lancaster, Lansdowne and Girard Avenue. The Italian and Jewish kids were lower middle class. Some of the Negro kids were middle class but most of them were very poor. One of the first things our older friends at Harry's warned us about at Overbrook was to watch our lunches, jackets and sneakers. I didn't know a single kid who got through Overbrook High School without, at the very least, losing a lunch or a pair of sneakers.

One of my closest friends, Stanley "Benny" Stein had a reversible blue and checkered jacket that one day disappeared from his locker during gym class. Stanley was deeply upset when that jacket disappeared. A few weeks later Stanley, who we all called "Benny" after his great hero Benjamin Franklin, was walking across the 59th Street Bridge with me after school when we saw his blue-checkered jacket coming towards us. It was on a Negro kid from our gym class. It helped that we didn't like this kid very much. The way Overbrook High School Phys-Ed teachers conducted their gym classes was remarkable. They would open the doors to the gym for hundreds of kids, throw in a half dozen basketballs and leave everyone to fend for themselves. The bigger Negro kids would, of course, grab the balls and play pick-up while the rest of us, mostly White kids, watched along the sidelines. But this particular Negro kid, the kid with Benny's blue-checkered jacket, wasn't very big. He was our size. And Benny and I both remembered that he was particularly mean-spirited on the basketball court. Benny, one of the best athletes in our crowd, had an amazing jump shot for a little guy. He was deadly from any spot on the court.

I pretty much stunk at basketball. My sport was baseball. But I liked to play and this mean-spirited Negro kid had always been giving us a hard time in gym class on the court. He would often grab the ball away from us, push us off the court and, with all his bigger buddies around, there wasn't much we could do about it.

But here he was coming toward us, all alone; and with Benny's jacket. No question about it. It was definitely Benny's jacket. Benny had a habit of chewing his collar and the collar on this jacket was frayed. Benny and I surrounded the kid. "Where did you get this jacket?" Benny asked. "None of your mother-fuckin' business," the kid replied. That was all we needed to hear. We knocked the kid on his ass, pulled the jacket off him and ran away.

When we got back to the sanctuary of Harry's, Benny took a closer look at his stolen jacket. It was his jacket all right. Except one of the sleeves was now torn. And the jacket was so God-awful filthy that Benny couldn't wear it. He threw it away. But the next time we saw that kid in our gym class, he did his best to avoid us and he never pushed us off the court again. He could easily have gotten his pals to kick our ass. But then he never knew when we would catch him alone again on the 59th Street Bridge.

CHAPTER 11

My friends were able to handle themselves in any neighborhood fight. But they were much more at home playing pickup basketball at Gompers schoolyard, riding horse-back in the streets or shooting eight-ball in Harry's dark backroom. We were not tough guys although, like that actor-doctor on TV, we did our level best to play one.

We had few heroes; maybe James Dean and later, the early Elvis. We knew little about Eisenhower, Kennedy or the Cold War. We loved Marilyn Monroe and Jayne Mansfield. Once, when Jayne Mansfield was making a bad film called *The Burglar* in Philly, she stopped at my next-door neighbor's to get some clothes fitted and sewn for the film. My neighbor was apparently a very talented seamstress and somehow the tall, blonde actress ended up driving her silver Cadillac Eldorado convertible right up to our house on Diamond Street.

Mansfield was spectacular looking with spectacular assets which she obviously had no qualms about sharing with the world. She may have been a Marilyn wannabe, but she was a very beautiful woman. Mansfield died tragically in a terrible automobile accident in 1967.

Few people knew that Vera Jane Palmer was born in Bryn Mawr, just outside of Philly, so coming back to make that movie in 1956 must have been sort of a homecoming.

Mansfield's daughter, Mariska Hargitay, has one of the leads in TV's *Law and Order: Special Victims Unit.* She is actually a good actress and, as an added bonus, she inherited some of her mother's sultry good looks—especially that sexy pout. I'll never forget that day La Mansfield drove right up to our door, slid out of her Caddie and talked to us. She wore form-fitting white pedal pushers that looked as if she had been shoehorned into, stiletto heels and a tight white top that amply displayed deep cleavage and huge tits. My little brother Kenny came up with the best line that day as Mansfield walked by: "That lady got some mighty big apples!" Jayne Mansfield giggled, patted my brother on the head and went into our neighbor's house for her fitting. Sadly, *The Burglar,* even with Mansfield and the famous film noir star Dan Duryea did not do big box office.

There were two major events during the tenth grade that affected my life in a major way: the gang fight and the (American) Bandstand time. Back in the ninth grade, in the spring of 1954, I had caused a minor disaster. About a dozen of us from Harry's were hiking in Fairmount Park not far from the stables where we rented our horses. It was a warm April day and had been a mild winter. The leaves from the previous fall were brittle and dry. We had built a campfire and were cooking some lunch—hot dogs and soup. Some of the guys left to rent horses; some went for a hike. I stayed put with a few of the guys to eat our meager lunch. Then, instead of going to a nearby stream to get water to douse the campfire, I lazily kicked it out. Some of the burning sticks hit some nearby leaves. I watched it for a few seconds too long and, in a matter of minutes, the surrounding brush turned into a raging inferno far too powerful for a few kids to put out.

My friends were angry at me; and why not? It was stupid of me to have kicked the campfire. The acreage that was burning out of control was my fault. I felt terrible and I was afraid. The fire grew. It looked dangerous. I ran away. I always excelled at running.

Now it just so happened that a rival gang from the 54th and Berks Streets area of Wynnefield was also camping out and cooking nearby. When they came by to watch the fire, they asked my friends what had happened. I don't know who, but one of my pals said, "Mutzy set the fire.

It was Mutzy Goldman!" "Mutzy" was my nickname. I didn't mind it, but I didn't really like it either. It came from Har Zion Hebrew School when our teacher, Jeremy Goldstein, the rabbi's son, asked us our Hebrew names and when I said I didn't know, he "christened" me *Mottel Zimmel*—which the other kids soon translated into "Mutzy." Unfortunately, the nickname stuck all the way through high school and college.

Even my girlfriends called me "Mutzy." Sometimes when I call an old friend today, I hear their wives still shout, "Benny, its Mutzy!" or "Paul, its Mutt." It's something you learn to live with. For some unfathomable reason, kids who grew up in cities gave all their friends nicknames. Everybody in our neighborhood had a nickname. Besides, a lot of the guys had worse names than Mutzy. There was Tire, Erfel Tweed, the Smelly Man, Sucky, Greasy, the Thief, the Ferd, the Rodent, Zeke, Pretzel and Pigsby, for example. The worst nickname I ever heard in West Philly was Freddy Hitler. It belonged to a guy named Fred Klinghoffer, an older Harry's boy who was killed in a drag race with a spoiled rich kid named Steve "Monk" Robinson in the early hours of a Philly morning in the mid-fifties at 57th and Wynnefield. I didn't know Freddy Hitler well because he was so much older, but he had always treated me kindly.

Meanwhile, the fire I had stupidly failed to put down burned out of control and soon a large section of Fairmount Park was engulfed in flames.

Police hit the scene along with a Philadelphia fire truck or two. When it was all over, I was later told, a dozen or so acres of wooded parkland had burned to the ground.

The rival group of guys from Berks Street set out to find the asshole responsible for the fire: namely Mutzy Goldman. Not that anybody had deputized them or that the Philly cops were even looking for me. These Berks Street assholes just believed strongly in a measure of vigilante justice and, as card-carrying neighborhood bullies, they relished the chance to dish it out.

These were big guys, all of whom were close to six-feet and outweighed little me by a mile.

Among my many problems was the fact that I wasn't very big. Puberty had somehow taken a major detour in my life and even at fifteen I still looked twelve or thirteen. My friend Benny Stein always teased me when we went to the beach because I didn't have hair under my armpits. Of course, neither did Benny! He always claimed it was because he was six months younger. I used to wear a sweat shirt in Atlantic City on the hottest days. Like I said, I'll take a pass on "the Wonder" years. Soaking wet, I weighed maybe 115 pounds. My size, weight and physique didn't change much until years later after some time in the Army.

Four of them caught up with me under a stone bridge on the horse trail, below Monument Road, still in the park. I was trying for home when they grabbed me. These four guys easily gave lie to any claim that Jews are the Chosen People: the leader, Mike Danowitz, was a lanky, tough kid from 53rd and Berks with a reputation for being a mean prick around Wynnefield; David Moses, a big bruiser who went on to play football for Overbrook, easily weighed in at over 250 pounds; there was Melvin Hunn, a terminal Lurchlike dimwit who had once been in our grade, but who had been left back so often we lost track of the grade to which he had been demoted. Mel Hunn was the kind of kid who, if you removed a thorn from his paw, would be your friend for life; and, finally, Sheldon "the Sniper" Snyder, another dimly lit bulb who would happily pummel you as long as one of his pals held your hands firmly behind your back. The Sniper was the coward of the county. He would never give anyone a fair fight. That was why they called Sheldon "the Sniper!" He was bigger than me, but in a fair fight, I could take the Sniper. I once kicked his ass in the Mann School yard and he never forgot it. This was to be payback.

To make a long and painful story short, Danowitz and his boys beat the crap out of me. Not that I didn't deserve it. From what they said, I was guiltier than Mrs. O'Leary's frigging cow!

Fairmount Park had burned to the ground. And maybe, because of me, all of Philly was soon to follow!

Wisely, I didn't fight back. Not that fighting back could have done much good. All Dave Moses had to do was sit on you and you were dead meat. So, I took the beating and even the last indignity the bastards heaped upon my tiny person—they found a steaming mound of freshly dropped horseshit on the trail, pushing me into it face first. Unlike George Costanza, I have never seen any great virtue in horse manure or manure of any kind!

I emerged from the park that day badly bruised and badly embarrassed: covered in horse poop, not to mention, smelling like the stalls in Jack's Stable. My friend Benny Stein, who came upon me under the tunnel after they left, helped me to get home. But, to this day, he has never let me forget how I looked or what I smelled like.

Some years later when Gilbert Hunn, Mel Hunn's older cousin, beat the snot out of Benny for messing with his parked jalopy, I had little sympathy for my pal who blubbered and sniffled like a baby all the way home. At least Gilbert Hunn didn't push Benny Stein face first into a pile of horseshit!

OK. Like I said, maybe I deserved the beating. And maybe even the horseshit. I could live with it. But that wasn't nearly the end. Not as far as Danowitz and his boys were concerned. In fact, for me it was only the beginning.

Over the next year or so whenever I would run into Danowitz and company they would use me for a punching bag. Whether it was the schoolyard at Gompers, coming out of the bowling alley at 54th and City Line, the movie at City Line Center, a Har Zion dance—whenever this company of cowardly bullies ran into me, they would beat the crap out of me. It got to be a major pain-in-the-ass. I could take the beatings, but it was damn embarrassing to have the Sniper or Danowitz grab me from behind in front of a girl I was trying to impress and say, "Hey look guys! It's Mootzie," (they would even purposely mispronounce my nickname!) and then proceed to push me around and pummel me. It wasn't easy impressing girls that you were a tough guy when Danowitz and his guys used you for a punching bag on a bi-weekly basis. Burning down some of Fairmount Park was one thing. But shouldn't there have been something like a statute of limitations? Apparently not with these guys from Berks Street...

One Monday morning in gym class, after the Danowitz boys had batted me about once again at the bus stop in Overbrook Park after the Friday night movie at City Line Center, I was lamenting my sad fate to my good friend Butch Small. Butch was sympathetic. "Hey man!" Butch said. "You don't have to take that shit. You want me to get some of my project boys? We'll take care of your problem. Them boys won't bother you after we get done with them; not unless they crazy!"

Project boys? Me bringing project guys into the neighborhood against Danowitz and his goon squad? It sounded pretty good to me. There was little solidarity among Jewish kids in the 1950's—especially on the streets of West Philly where divisions were simple—mostly by streets or sections of the neighborhood. Israel was still a foreign country to most of us. And if I could get some guys—any guys—to kick the crap out of the bullies who had by then tortured me for almost two years, well…it sounded like a plan.

I floated the idea with my friends at Harry's. Most were opposed. They sympathized with my plight although none of them, as I recall, offered to step up to help me stand up to these bully boys. Still, bringing Negroes into Wynnefield to kick the shit out of Jewish guys could get out of hand. Who were they? Would they bring knives or guns? Aside from Butch and one or two others, I didn't really know and couldn't offer up any assurances of how it all might go down.

So, I took my conundrum back to Butch who was very understanding.

"OK," Butch said, "You're pretty close to two or three guys from Hungry Town and Little Italy in gym class." Why not widen the scope of our offensive? Ask some of your Italian friends, Butch suggested, to join in the fight.

It was true. I had two or three very close Italian friends at school. And everybody knew, you didn't screw around with the Italians. The one group at Overbrook High who nobody messed with were the Italians. Even the Negro kids would generally steer clear of them. I always envied the Italian kids. You touched one of them and their entire neighborhood would soon be on your ass: cousins, aunts, uncles, fathers, mothers—it seemed every Italian in Philly no matter what neighborhood they came from was related. It was something the Jews never did; maybe Israelis, but not American Jews.

I'd seen it a dozen times. In West Philly, in South Philly and even in Atlantic City, no ethnic group had the solidarity that matched the Italians when it came to all out street-fighting. My closest Italian friends at the Brook were Joe Campanaro who lived near Overbrook in Hungry Town on 65th Street. Joe was a big but gentle bruiser who played on the football team and I had known him since Junior High; Anthony Micicci, who had transferred out of the Brook to St. Thomas More, was another old pal as was Joe "Moe" MacNeil. Moe was the quarterback of the football team and his mother was Italian—which made Moe, who lived on 63rd Street, as Italian as they come. I took my problem to Moe, Joe and they called Tony. We met that week. Why hadn't I come to them earlier? I was their pal from the 7th grade—a member of *la famiglia!* They were just great. Sure, they would be happy to put the word out to all their friends in Hungry Town and Little Italy. They would definitely be there for me. And no, they didn't mind the idea of a few Negro kids joining our side. It might even be interesting for Italians to team up with *the Moolunyan.*

What about my Jewish friends in the neighborhood? Would they show up? How many? When did I want it to go down? I set a date. The Danowitz boys were all still a grade behind us at Beeber. Butch and his project guys, my Italian contingent and some of my Harry's guys (damn few as it turned out!) would meet at Beeber at the appointed time when school got out, send me out as a decoy, wait until Danowitz, the Sniper and the others surrounded me and then they would strike. Sounded like a pretty good idea to me.

I remember that day well. It was warm, so it must have been in the spring. I borrowed my friend Benny's black leather jacket (just like the Gansk's!) and to make my outfit complete I put on my old battered motorcycle hat—a hat just like Marlon Brando wore in *The Wild One.*

I went to Beeber right from Overbrook. To my great surprise and terror, there were four or five carloads of Italians from Hungry Town and Little Italy. Although Joe Campanaro and Moe MacNeil were there (I don't recall seeing Tony Micicci), most of the guys in the cars were young adults—not kids in high school. I saw my pal Joe Leone and his older brother Tony (the Leone brothers were better known as lovers than fighters!) and a tough little guy I was always friendly with in my class at the Brook, Vince Savino; I also saw Butch Small and a handful of Negro guys from the projects; I saw some of my friends from Harry's—Larry Laster, the Gansk, Alan Martin and Benny Stein. But I didn't have a clue as to who the guys in the cars were. Then I saw one of the toughest Italian guys in West Philly—Johnny Trongo.

Trongo had a rep as a real gangster. While we played at it, Trongo was the real thing. He was kick-ass tough. Everybody at the Brook knew him. He was the most feared Italian guy in all of high school.

Nobody would even say hello to John Trongo. If he didn't like how you looked, he might turn around and kick the shit out of you—kick being the operative word. He wasn't a big guy, but nobody messed with Johnny Trongo.

Trongo sat in a 1949 or 1950 Ford convertible with two other guys. One of them wore the signature tough guy sleeveless undershirt so typical of South Philly guys. Trongo beckoned and I walked over to his car. I couldn't believe I was actually talking to John Trongo. I had never actually met him. He said that I should get in the car. I got in the car. Sit up on the back seat, he said. I sat up on the back seat. The guy in the undershirt was with me in the back. Trongo sat in the front passenger seat and the car took off up 59th Street toward the back gate of Beeber where the students usually congregated after school. We reached the gate just as the kids were coming out.

The driver parked in front of Dave's Candy Store. I turned around and saw that we had led a small caravan of tough looking Italian guys along with some of my friends coming up 59th Street on foot along with Butch Small and his project pals. All told, we had perhaps twenty to twenty-five guys waiting outside of Beeber that day.

"My God," I remember thinking, "what the hell have I done? Somebody could really get hurt."

"OK," Trongo said. "Walk across the street and wait till these guys come after you. We'll be right behind you. Don't worry! Nobody's gonna touch you here." He had apparently been briefed. But not by me!

A girl I knew and liked, Susan Perloff, saw me get out of the car and also saw all the Italian and Negro guys across the street from the school. "What are you doing?" she asked. For years I had tried to get Susan to go out with me. She had always turned me down. The reason: I hung out at Harry's with all the hoodlums and my friend Billy Stamps's younger sister, Ellen, had told Susan that I was a hoodlum too. I always tried to tell Susie Perloff that it was just a case of mistaken identity. Now, she would forever know the truth. I was with John Trongo! My identity as a hoodlum in Wynnefield would be forever etched in stone. I just looked at Susan and didn't respond.

I walked up to the gate of the schoolyard. The first guy I recognized was David Moses. He walked right by and began talking to some kids. Probably didn't even know who I was in my black leather jacket and stupid looking motorcycle hat. Next out was Danowitz. He joined Moses, walking right past me too. Then Sniper and Hunn came out to the street. It was the Sniper who recognized me.

"Look guys! It's the Mootsie! What the fuck you doing here!" the Sniper exclaimed surrounding me with his faithful retainer Hunn. Sniper pushed me. Hunn pushed me. Moses and Danowitz looked up and saw it was me and walked over. They were about to engage in their bi-weekly sport of "beat the shit out of Mutzy Goldman" when all hell broke loose.

Within seconds Danowitz and company were surrounded by Italians and Negroes. Even some of my Harry's boys walked across the street—more to watch than participate. Danowitz and Moses could immediately see that these guys were not from the neighborhood, but they were older. A few were even out of their teens. The Negro kids were itching to fight. One of them said, "Hey man, let's get to it!"

But John Trongo held the crowd in check walking over like a young Julius Caesar reviewing his triumphant legions in Gaul. For the first time in almost two years I was standing up to Danowitz and his gang of bully goons. It felt good; and bad. I ran on pure adrenalin.

"We hear you give our little friend here, a hard time!" Trongo said icily.

(Hold on! What 'little friend'? I thought to myself.)

"Oh, we just fool around with him," Moses said. "We're all friends! Right, Mootsie?"

Trongo kicked Moses as hard as he could right in the ass and pushed him down. David Moses could have easily crushed John Trongo in a one-on-one. But not this day! Trongo operated on pure red hot anger and few guys I knew would ever challenge him. I heard some girls twitter nearby. Moses took the kick, got up and backed away from a fight with Trongo and the others.

"Which one of these jerkoffs bothers you the most?" Trongo asked.

I pointed at Mike Danowitz. Trongo spit in his face. The spit missed and hit Danowitz's shirt. Danowitz began to backpeddle. "We don't want no trouble," the tough guy from Berks Street whined.

"Yeah, well ain't that too bad. 'Cause you got trouble," Trongo responded. He turned to me. "You wanna hit him in the mouth? Go ahead! Hit him in the mouth!"

The truth is that I wanted very much to hit Danowitz in the mouth. But not like this. I wasn't like the Sniper. I wasn't going to hit any guy in the mouth who couldn't fight back. And I knew that day, no matter what I did to Mike Danowitz, nobody would have lifted so much as a finger.

"No," I said to Trongo, "it's OK. I don't have to hit him in the mouth."

"You hear that. This kid don't want to hit you! But I do!" Trongo said shoving Danowitz into the Sniper while Mel Hunn looked on, too dumb to be afraid, but smart enough to know when to keep his yap shut. Trongo kicked Danowitz in the slats as Danowitz, surrounded by a lot of Italians he had never seen in his life, looked back in terror.

"OK," Trongo said, "here's the deal! If ever our little friend here comes back and tells us any one of you bothers him in any way, we come back. Hard! We know where you live. Got it?"

The four of them nodded. We could hear police sirens in the background.

"Good," Trongo said kicking Mel Hunn for good measure but not nearly as hard as he had kicked Danowitz or Moses. I pushed the Sniper out of my way, walked across the street, climbed back into the rear of the Ford convertible and within a matter of seconds we were all gone.

The Italian guys dropped me off at Harry's, I thanked them, they left me in the back room and then they were gone. I was all alone. I was also scared shitless. I waited for my friends. Butch Small and some of his buddies were the first to come by.

There were cops all over the place, they said. They were going to hop a bus and head back to West Philly. I thanked them all and they left.

Soon my friends arrived. For the most part, they were all incredulous. What I had done would go down in the annals of Wynnefield history. Nobody in recent memory had ever assembled such a multi-ethnic force. What about the fallout? Danowitz and company would catch me and beat the living shit out of me forever. I was as good as dead, my friends said. It was time to ask my parents to move. Maybe Texas would be far enough away from Wynnefield. Maybe!

My friends were right. It was a stupid thing to do. Mike Danowitz would catch up to me and beat me to a pulp. Texas began to sound pretty good. But there was one small problem. Pop wasn't a cowboy. The only horses my Dad liked ran at the Garden State Parkway track in Jersey. I would have to stay in Wynnefield and tough it out.

Nothing ever happened. Like the bullies in the great 1986 Rob Reiner film, *Stand By Me,* Danowitz and his boys never retaliated. Whenever they saw me, they made some "Mootsie" cracks and they may have even said some unkind things about my mother. It was always open season on mothers in my neighborhood. But they never bothered me again.

About a year later, a gang of Italian guys from over the bridge got into a fracas with some Jewish kids at a party in the neighborhood. Punches were thrown, cops were called and, from what I later heard, it was an all out melee.

Word soon got around that it was me who had called in my Italian army once again. An old friend of mine from seventh grade, Alan "Rocky" Mintz, one of the tougher Jewish guys in the neighborhood, stopped by Cosmo Pharmacy where I dished out ice cream one Friday night. Rocky jumped out of his red 1950 Ford convertible. I could see Danowitz and Moses sitting in the back seat. He walked into the pharmacy and Ben Weintraub, the owner and my boss, told him to get out, that he didn't need any trouble. Ben even threatened to call the cops. I told Ben, who was only looking out for me, that it was OK, that I would talk to Rocky outside and that he didn't have to call in any cops. Rocky Mintz, who had kicked many a guy's ass in the old neighborhood, would never give me a beating.

I walked outside with Rocky onto 56th Street. The Rock put his arm around me. Rocky Mintz was easily one of the toughest guys in the neighborhood. In Junior High we had been very close friends. I still own what may be one of the first Rock 'n Roll records in music history: *Rock the Joint* by Bill Haley and the Comets. Rocky Mintz gave me that record when we were in the 7th grade. By high school, because we had clearly decided to take different paths in life, Rocky and I had gone our separate ways. I pretended to be tough. Rocky Mintz *was* tough. But I always liked Rocky and I think he knew it. In grade school Rocky had his name changed legally from Alan to Rocky and he would never answer to any teacher who dared call him "Alan."

"Mutz," Rocky said coldly, "some Italian guys come over the bridge last week and beat up some Jewish kids real bad. These guys tell me it was you who brought them here. Is that true Mutz?"

"No, Rocky," I answered truthfully. "I didn't have a thing to do with it. Don't even know who they were."

"You swear to me?" Rocky asked.

"I swear," I answered.

Rocky jumped back in his red Ford convertible, told Danowitz and Moses that I was guiltless and they drove off into the night. And my brief days as a Philly gang-banger were over forever.

I don't know what ever became of John Trongo, Butch Small or Rocky Mintz. Wherever they are today, I hope that the wind is still at their back and that they always walk in the sun.

CHAPTER 12

After the seventh grade, I was never a very good student. My grades, although poor, were usually passing but they were nothing to write home about. My father was deeply distressed. He couldn't understand why my grades were always so low. After all, whenever he saw me my nose was always buried in a book. I read all of the Edgar Rice Burroughs Tarzan novels (and still own the entire collection in hardback) and Mars adventures. I even read some classics: Mark Twain, Charles Dickens, Victor Hugo and Alexander Dumas. I loved the Hardy Boys and the "adventure" novels about four British kids who were always getting into trouble during their summer "hols" on strange islands off Scotland and in mysterious castles in the English countryside.

Comic books back in those days were also essential reading matter: Superman, Batman, Captain Marvel, Captain Marvel Jr., Mary Marvel, Tarzan, Sheena and the EC horror-science fiction comics—I owned thousands of comics. If I still had those comics today (I do have a few!) I could retire in great comfort. I was a voracious reader; just not in school. Never in school! I hated school with a passion. To this day, I am not certain why. Maybe I was smarter than my teachers. Maybe I was from Bohemia!

Then, in the tenth grade, I began failing big time. I failed Geometry, repeated it and failed again—six straight failing grades in Geometry class. I failed easy things like Music, Hygiene and even Phys Ed. I failed Spanish. I can't easily recall what it was about school that I disliked so intensely. All I can tell you for sure is that high school for me was pure torture.

I often watched the clock during every period counting down the forty-five minutes by the seconds to the end of each class. Today, I think, they would say I had ADD. I didn't. Once in Mr. Contini's

Spanish class, Pasquale Contini caught me looking at the clock and said, "Martin S. Goldman is always watching the clock. Time will definitely pass. But he surely won't!" Old Contini flunked me and gave me a new nickname which I wore proudly: "Martin F. Goldman." My classmates were hardly impressed. Once, my old friend from the seventh grade, George Lubeck, approached me in the hall. "What has happened to you?" Lubeck asked. "You used to be a nice kid. Why are you hanging out with the wrong crowd, flunking and always getting into trouble like a hood? Look at how you dress!" I stared at Lubeck, who was in my Spanish class, dismissively as if he were nuts. I wore blue-jeans. I pretty much still do. Levis. But Lubeck was right about one thing. I was messing up in high school; big time.

Years later when I returned to the Brook as a young teacher, Pasquale A. Contini became one of my closest friends. More than anyone at the Brook, he encouraged me to go on to better things than teaching high school. He would often invite me into his Spanish classes to tell the students that I was living proof that there was always hope. I was, he told his charges, one of the worst students to ever cross his path and that I had slept through most of his classes. Of course, he would say it in Spanish and didn't think I understood what he was saying. When I left Overbrook and Philly, I went to say goodbye to Contini. The old man's eyes filled with tears. I don't think he ever had children so the kids became sort of surrogates. And he had been Phi Beta Kappa at Penn. We hugged as he wished me well. I was trying to move up the academic food chain. Probably something that Contini had always meant to do but had never gotten around to accomplishing. For a few years we sent each other cards at holiday time. Contini had been known for years as "Mr. Overbrook." I had taken six semesters of Spanish with him. That's three solid years of Spanish with not much to show for it. Contini was one of the few damn fine teachers in my high school. I was just too young and stupid at the time to appreciate that fact.

One of the things that contributed to my declining grades during the tenth grade was (American) Bandstand. You probably think you know all about Dick Clark and his vast television empire that began with American Bandstand. Let me tell you something you may not know about the ubiquitous Dick Clark.

There is an excellent book by John A. Jackson titled *American Bandstand: Dick Clark and the Making of a Rock 'N' Roll Empire*. I don't think Richard Wagstaff Clark would really want you to read it. I'm not going to rehash the Dick Clark story here. Jackson tells it all brilliantly. It is basically an American success story—about how this clean-cut guy with absolutely no visible talent one day catches a big break and takes advantage of it. Oh boy, does he ever take advantage of it!

Dick Clark has his champions. Connie Francis, the great singer from the fifties and early sixties, swears by him; and why not? When Miss Francis was in serious emotional trouble, after being raped and assaulted, with her career heading downhill, Dick Clark always stepped up to the plate for her.

And I suppose those dweebs who do that lame TV show about "real men" with Dick Clark have nice things to say about him. But don't ask Barbara Mallery Clark (the first Mrs. Dick Clark); or Loretta Martin Clark (the second Mrs. Dick Clark). Or his loyal Philly producer: the late Anthony "Tony" Mammarella; or my old friend Butch Small.

After Page 176 in the Jackson book there is a series of pictures of the Bandstand days along with the Bandstand kids. The bottom photo shows a kid in the center dancing with an unnamed girl. The captions reads "Jerry 'the Geator with the Heater' Blavat (center) is wearing a dark shirt and white jacket." Closer examination of the photo reveals two things: the kid in the picture is wearing his Overbrook High School sweater, not a jacket. And the kid in the photo is definitely not Jerry Blavat. The kid is me! Back then I was often mistaken for the Geator with the Heater. Over the years, that possibility has long since passed.

How do I know that this is true? I have a photo taken by the same photographer—a guy who used to eat at Harry's. He gave some studio photos to me that he took. I still have one. The host in the background when that particular photo was taken in early 1955 is, of course, not Dick Clark but Bob Horn, one of the original two founders of the

Bandstand concept. If Bob Horn was not so damn…well, horny…you most likely would never have heard of Dick Clark and he might still be hawking storm windows on Philly's Channel 6.

Here is the story. In late 1954 and early 1955 one of my oldest and closest friends, Larry Laster, told me he had heard of a great way to meet girls: a local TV dance show. It was on every day, five days a week, at the WFIL-TV studios at 46th and Market in West Philly.

There was, Larry pointed out, one slight drawback: the girls were mostly from nearby Catholic schools and the boys were mostly semi-tough Italian guys from South Philly. How tough, I wondered, were a bunch of guys jitterbugging with West Catholic girls in green jumpers, knee socks and plaid skirts? For some reason, Larry always did much better with Catholic girls than he did with Jewish girls.

Larry Laster was easily the best dancer in our gang. He was somewhat shy with girls but when he hit a dance floor it was like Clark Kent becoming Superman or Billy Batson yelling SHAZAM!—Larry would actually be transformed. He became a dancing superhero. There were two styles of Philly jitterbugging back in the mid-fifties: North Philly and South Philly. I had mastered neither. Larry danced a mean South Philly. And our friend Gene "the Alley Man" Liebman had mastered North Philly which consisted of a great many arm twists and turns of your partner. Unfortunately, I would always grab the wrong arm and was also the proud owner of two left feet. Every time I went to a dance, it would take me over an hour to get up enough courage just to ask a girl to slow dance—and then I still usually stepped on her toes! I was not what anyone would ever have called "a fancy dancer." The ghosts from the old Yellow Ribbon Club dances still haunted me.

After weeks of cajoling, I finally agreed to go down to 46th and Market with Larry to try to get into Bandstand. I had one caveat: that we would go down to Bandstand in force. So that none of the "tough" Italian kids from South Philly would mess with us. Larry agreed.

We asked Gene "the Alley Man" Liebman and a kid from our last period class in Geometry, Tom DiMambro, to go with us as well. Tommy knew a lot of guys from South Philly. He might be some insurance against us getting our asses kicked. That possibility never even arose. We soon found out that, as Norman Mailer once wrote, "Tough Guys Don't Dance."

Of course, the chances that we would get into Bandstand were very slim. Our last period was over at two-fifteen. Bandstand went on air at three. We didn't have a car. By the time we hopped the G bus and the El (the name of the Philly subway—it meant Elevated), the show would be well underway.

Unknown to us, admittance was fixed. There was always a long line queued outside the studio and it was supposed to be first-come, first-served. But they never told you that there was a standing committee of Bandstand regulars who walked right by the teenage peasants in that line and into the studio every day. The members of "the Committee" were the boys and girls who could dance well, looked cute on TV and who sucked up to the show's genial host Bob Horn and his producer, Tony Mammarella. How well some of those girls "sucked" up did not come out until many years later; they could probably have given Monica Lewinsky a few pointers.

Bob Horn was a robust man, with pasted-down, slick hair just like Dick Clark's and a laugh that started down in his gut that reminded you of Ed McMahon, Johnny Carson's old late-night sidekick (who happened to be announcing in those days across town at WCAU-TV and hanging out nightly at the San Marco, a posh Italian restaurant and bar on City Line owned by a tough Italian guy named Beanie. I was once having dinner with my older first cousin, Elaine Goldberg, at the San Marco when McMahon ambled over, bought us drinks and sat down with us. I know one thing: it wasn't my big tits and fiery red hair that brought McMahon to our table!).

I didn't care if we couldn't get in to Bandstand. Maybe we would hook up with some of those cute *shicksas* from West Catholic in the line. On the first day we got shut out and we didn't meet any cute Catholic girls in the line either. But the next day school let out early, we arrived in the line before 3 P.M. and to my utter dismay we were soon being ushered into the lackluster Bandstand studios.

The grandstand, where all the kids sat, was set up with tiers of long and uncomfortable wooden benches on either side of what looked like a large garage with a concrete floor, a makeshift phony podium fixed up to look like a record shop and three large not very mobile monstrous cameras spaced at various angles around the periphery. A big board to the left of the podium held bright colored pennants from virtually every high school in Philly and South Jersey.

It was only my second time in a TV studio. And when the hot lights went on and that familiar Bandstand theme song played, I was terrified. There was no way I was getting up to dance with a strange *shicksa* on TV. No way. So I sat there…and sat there…and sat there. Five o'clock soon came. Bob Horn signed off, thanking all the kids there and the viewing audience. He told the kids watching how to come down to Bandstand and get on TV. And then the show was over. Tommy, Larry and Gene had danced with a lot of girls. I never even moved my ass off the damn bench. Not even for the two lineups where you were supposed to tell the vast viewing audience what Philly high school you represented. You had to be in high school to get into Bandstand. But if you were cute enough, that silly rule was often waived.

I grabbed my coat and we took the subway and then the slow Number 70 trolley. Since it was rush hour, my father, who took the train, beat me home that night. I walked in a little after six.

Pop took one look at me and glared. In his younger days you had to watch out whenever my Pop glared. In my father's house dinner was always at five-thirty. And you had best not be late because Pop was an amazing creature of habit.

"Where is your new coat?" Pop asked with precious little affection in his voice.

"I'm wearing it, Pop!" I answered, looking down at my "new" coat.

"That is not the coat I bought you at Krass Brothers last week!" Pop said sharply.

I looked down again. Uh oh! The coat Pop bought me was beige and a single-breasted model. The coat I was wearing was a double-breasted, six-button Benny with a tattered sleeve, a big stain under the pocket and the lining hanging out. Well, at least it was beige!

I was in big trouble. I was always tearing or losing my coats. When I was ten, I went to the Philadelphia Navy Yard with the cub scouts to see a real submarine. Going down the hatch, I caught my new navy-blue pea coat on the periscope, ripping a big hole in the front. Pop had never let me forget it. Now I had traded in a brand new $75 top coat for a tattered and drab wreck. My father started to yell at me. Then he called my mother in from the kitchen.

"Ruth, this jerko lost his coat today. Tomorrow he is going right back to that studio to look for that coat. He better come home with it tomorrow night! Or that will be the last coat he ever gets!" Pop roared his face reddening. When Pop got angry, the best thing to do in those days was say nothing and get out of the way.

I said nothing. "I'll take care of it," Mom said. "Let's eat Lou!"

I don't need to tell you that there was little conversation over dinner that night about my amazing debut on local Philadelphia television.

The next day my mother called Bandstand. Somehow she got the show's producer, Tony Mammarella, on the phone. I didn't overhear the conversation, but as the saying goes she must have ripped poor Tony a new asshole. When I arrived at the studio with Larry and my other friends the next day, Mammarella was waiting at the front of the line.

"Are you Martin S. Goldman?" he asked looking askance at my beat-up six-button Benny.

"Yeah," I answered surprised that he knew who I was.

"Well, you're now on the Committee. You can come right in whenever you want. Look for your coat. If you see it, just let me know and I'll take care of it," Mammarella said.

"What about my friends?" I asked.

"Did they lose their coats too? OK. Them too," Mammarella said unhappily, ushering us all in to the studio.

I never did find my topcoat. I hope whoever swiped it enjoyed it. I rarely wore my six-button Benny. It didn't really fit anyway. But for the next eight or nine months we all went to Bandstand and never had to wait in the line. And even better, I finally got up the courage to dance. I danced with the very popular Barbara Morison, Rosalie Beltrante (Big Ro as she was known to the fans) and a cute Bandstand regular named Carmen. Barbara Morison is next to me and Carmen is sitting right beneath me next to Tommy in the eight-by-ten glossy I have kept and still treasure. Larry Laster and Gene "the Alley Man" Liebman are in the photo too.

If you watched Bandstand in the months between 1955 and spring 1956, you saw me.

In the twice daily lineup, I always appeared at least once. I was "Marty, Overbrook High, Yay!"

Bob Horn even got to know me. He once asked, "Aren't you the kid whose mother yelled at Tony about the coat?" Pop eventually recovered from me losing another coat and, after a few weeks, he stopped asking me if I found my new coat. But it remained a sore spot between us. My father had an amazing memory. I didn't get another new coat for the rest of high school.

Today, I have three closets filled with ski parkas, leather jackets, and topcoats. And my attic is crammed with jackets and coats. At last count I had around thirty-five leather jackets. And that is with fifteen of them being stolen in 1999. Pop never knew about my jacket and coat fetish. They say Jerry Seinfeld has over a hundred pair of sneakers. I guess Seinfeld's Pop yelled at him about his losing his sneakers. I have dozens of jackets and coats stuffed in my closets. No nuttier, I guess, than Jerry Seinfeld.

I continued attending Bandstand, ostensibly looking for my wayward coat, on into the spring of 1956. I was in the eleventh grade when Bob Horn got into some serious trouble.

First, there was the allegation in the Philly papers that Horny Bob was diddling one of his teenage dancers. That was bad enough. Then in June of 1956, Horn was stopped in his fancy pea-green Eldorado Cadillac after running a red light in North Philly. Horn was arrested, taken to a nearby police station and pronounced "drunk and not capable of operating a motor vehicle."

Horn's driving "drunk" arrest was the end for him. WFIL suspended him almost immediately after the Philly papers had a field day reporting on Horn's DWI. Horn might have greased by the driving under the influence charge but coming hard upon the heels of accusations that he might be sexually involved with one of the Bandstand teens, he was as good as dead. Horn was temporarily replaced on the daily show by

Tony Mammarella. It was, Mammarella must have thought, his chance of a lifetime.

But poor Tony was not really in the Bandstand loop. There was a young guy in his mid-twenties doing on-camera storm window bits for the station. He also had a local radio show.

Worried that Bandstand would be cancelled in the wake of the Bob Horn scandal, the station management quickly opted for a Mr. Clean, more All-American-Boy look. Tony Mammarella was just too damn Italian looking. As Rick Lewis, the lead singer of the famous Negro doo-wop group "the Silhouettes" (Get a Job!) once said, "People looked down on you if you were Italian. If you were Italian, shit, you were almost a nigger!" If anyone thought that anti-Italian prejudice was dead in America, all they had to do was look at how Dick Clark came to American Bandstand. Tony Mammarella was out; Dick Clark was in. They did allow Mammarella to stay on in his old job as Bandstand's producer.

In the beginning some of the kids gave Dick Clark a hard time. Led by young Jerry Blavat (one of the best dancers on the show), a group of kids protested the firing of Bob Horn. Blavat, even then skilled at drawing media attention, stood in front of the studio with a picket sign after he led a walkout from the studio with a bunch of other disgruntled kids. Blavat got his picture in all the papers. But the protest didn't last very long. Soon Blavat and the other protestors were back in the studio dancing to Crazy Otto, Jaye P. Morgan's latest disc and rating all the new records. "I'll give it a 95 Dick 'cause it's uh… duh…it's danceable."

Jerry Blavat went on to become one of the hottest disc jockeys in Philly—"the Geator with the Heater." Another well-known Philly disc jockey, Sid Mark, who made his bones with his own radio show, "The Mark of Jazz," and in later years by hosting an all-Sinatra syndicated show once told my barber Danny, "Jerry Blavat is going to be the biggest thing to ever come out of Philly."

Well, not quite. With his nightclub in Margate, New Jersey and weekly dance parties all over Philly, Blavat had his big shot in the sixties when the Twist and Chubby Checker were hot. He even got himself a brief TV teenage dance show gig. But, unlike Dick Clark, the Geator with the Heater's heater flamed out, along with other fabled fifties Philly DJs like Douglas "Jocko" Henderson, The Man with the Goods—Georgie Woods and Hy Lit—Hyski O'Rooney McFadio Zoot, as he called himself. Ask anybody in South Philly. They all know the Geator in Philly. But once you are out of 50,000 watt range of Philly and South Jersey, the half-Jewish, half-Italian Jerry Blavat, even with a good friend like the late Sammy Davis, Jr., is just another aging ex-teeny bopper like me. I often wonder what Blavat must think of Dick Clark's amazing success: a guy with little obvious talent becoming a Hollywood fixture and a multi-multi-millionaire.

I myself didn't give much of a shit about Bob Horn or Dick Clark. I didn't join Blavat's protest against Clark. I liked Tony Mammorella and continued to go to Bandstand until my friend Butch Small called to ask if he could meet me at 46th and Market Streets and maybe partake in some of that good looking West Catholic, Irish and Italian poontang. Sure. Why not? Butch was cool. And, since he had transferred to Bartram High from Overbrook we didn't see much of each other.

I met Butch at the subway stop at 56th and Market and we grabbed the El two stops to the studio. As we walked in the door Tony Mammorella took one look at Butch and held up his hand. "All filled today, fellas. Sorry!" he said. But I was a regular. What about my lost coat? No dice. Mammorella was somewhat sheepish. He just told us to come back on another day. But Butch and I understood. We understood all too well. No Negro kids were going into Bandstand. That was a standing policy for quite a long time. Years later, I would watch American Bandstand from the day room at Fort Knox, Kentucky and Fort Benjamin Harrison, Indiana. By then Dick Clark had taken the show coast to coast. There were still no Negro kids on the show as late as 1958-59. At least none that were on "the Committee."

"I was on that stupid show," I told my army buddies. "Get out! You know Kenny (Rossi) and Arlene (Sullivan) and Bob (Clayton) and Justine (Carelli)! Get out! No way!" the southern soldiers would say finding it difficult to believe that a skinny shave-tail like me could ever have actually danced alongside the celebrity teen heartthrobs of American Bandstand.

The truth is that I didn't know Kenny and Arlene or Bob and Justine. After Dick Clark took over the show, I gradually drifted away. Clark was inviting wimpy looking guys who wore white buck shoes to lip sync their records on his show. Nobody I knew in West Philly wore white buck shoes and lived to tell the tale. Besides, this guy sang mushy love songs about love letters in the sand and he stole Tutti Frutti from real doo-woppers like the great Little Richard. We all knew—for sure, this white bucked Pat Boone wasn't going anyplace.

Poor Bob Horn got nailed from all angles. The IRS hit him for income tax evasion connected to alleged payola he had been receiving from some of the record companies to spin their records on the show. Dick Clark was soon embroiled in the payola scandal as well. But somehow, though the evidence appeared strong that something was going on, Clark escaped that particular bullet. Not so Bob Horn. He had two highly publicized Philly trials for statutory rape and two trials for his arrests on drunken driving. Although Horn plea bargained the payola away, he was fined and sentenced to six months in prison. Proper Philadelphia has forever disliked any whiff of public scandal intensely. Horn would never come back. The broken-hearted Horn left Philly in disgrace and died a shattered man a few years later in relative anonymity in Texas.

By the end of the eleventh grade I was into other things. But I did see Dick Clark when he began. And I also saw that he didn't allow Negro kids into American Bandstand until his back was up against the wall. Clark rarely talks about racial issues from those days. He once stated that Bandstand was "open to anyone who wants to attend" and that he could not control the camera shots. But as late as 1959 the Negro newspaper *New York Age* asked, "Have you seen Negro kids on Dick Clark's program?…the unspoken rule operates—Negro kids simply have been quietly barred from the American Bandstand." I know, as does my old friend Butch, that this was true; which is one reason I have never been much of a Dick Clark fan.

In all fairness to Dick Clark, America was a very different place in the mid-to-late 1950s. Dick Clark hardly invented racial bias. Still, discrimination was plain wrong and Dick Clark was in a position to do something about it. I wasn't. I didn't understand much about such things then when I was only fifteen. But my pal Butch Small did.

On top of my racial gripe is the fact that Dick Clark is a greedy bastard. I have tried to think of a single instance when a Dick Clark production has added anything salutary to the popular culture. Bandstand, his quiz shows, bloopers, talk shows, selling crappy insurance or fraudulent magazine lotteries to unsuspecting senior citizens with, of all people, the late Ed MacMahon—this no-talent geezer who continues to amass millions just won't go away. I sometimes think when I see Dick Clark launching another new vapid TV project of a short story by Leo Tolstoy that I read in college: "How Much Land Does a Man Need." Tolstoy's last line has the answer and says it all: "Six feet from his head to his toes."

Whenever I see Dick Clark on his "rockin" New Year's Eve show, I am probably one of the few Americans rooting for that damn ball to come crashing down on his greasy head. But still, you have to hand it to the guy! He's outlasted Fabian, Frankie Avalon and Bobby Rydell, Philly's teen heartthrobs of the late fifties. And, despite a debilitating stroke, the Clarkster seems to be still going strong. And the guy has enough money to finance both the Iraq and Afghan war!

The fact is that Dick Clark, who was born in November 1929, is a solid decade older than I am. That picture of me on Bandstand, taken back in 1955 just months before Dick Clark came onto the scene, shows a skinny, slight teenager with slick dark hair. Today, that fifteen year-old is long gone. And so is that gorgeous dark hair! At 70 something my once dark hair is thinning and pure white. I have had white hair since my forties. Another reason I do not like Dick Clark: he is Dorian Gray. The bastard still looks exactly the same! He has hardly changed an iota. Dick Clark must have an aging portrait of himself hidden away deep in his damn closet. Or something!

CHAPTER 13

As I entered the eleventh grade, with my marks continuing to drop, I began to cut school prolifically. A bunch of us would meet up in front of school, get into a car and either wait until 10 A.M. when Jack opened the doors at Harry's or go down to a billiard parlor in West Philly to hang out. Sometimes we would head off for an adventure. Once Jack Zatz drove up to the Brook in a new '56 Ford Fairlane and six of us piled in going all the way to New York City for a happy day of Big Apple exploration. It was my first time in New York City. We hit the Village, the coffee shops, the fabled Lindy's on Broadway (known for its cheesecake), had great pasta and veal at Mama Leoni's and still made it back to Philly in time for dinner. I suppose most kids go through this stage at one time or another. I enjoyed cutting school very much and am not sorry for the education that I received on the streets of Philadelphia. But I am sorry about my poor grades and the needless aggravation I caused my beleaguered parents.

My class cutting was very costly grade-wise. I attended summer school every summer during the years I spent in high school to make up the courses I had flunked. Summer school was held for the entire city at Olney High School up the Roosevelt Boulevard near a largely Jewish neighborhood called Logan in North Philadelphia. I would come to know Logan well a few years later when I married a Logan girl.

After I turned sixteen we would car pool, so it wasn't too bad taking the twenty-minute drive up the Expressway to the Boulevard. However, in the first year I went to summer school, I took the streetcar (we called it the trolley!) and two buses. If you didn't have a car, your summer was screwed.

It took almost two hours to get to Olney without a car. That was four hours a day in a steamy Philly July to sweat it out on the crowded un-air-conditioned PTC buses with all those noxious fumes. As I recall, I had a lot of the Harry's guys for company. My old friend Pretzel was no rocket scientist either and he joined me that first excruciating summer at Olney High School.

Once summer school was over though, the rest of the summer was usually great fun. My brother always loved Atlantic City. He loves it to this very day and spends much of his time at his condo in Margate (near where our grandfather had two homes). I could take Jersey or leave it. But since many of my closest friends were down the shore, I generally looked forward to the week Mom took the bus to Atlantic City to look for a suite of rooms or an apartment for the month of August. My brother would patiently await our mother's return, standing by the window to hear the good news that she had found a place for us all to stay.

Atlantic City was divided between uptown and downtown. Uptown was the area from Steel Pier on Pennsylvania Avenue down to the Inlet. When I was young, we stayed uptown in the area where my mother grew up on Rhode Island Avenue—streets you might know from playing Monopoly: Rhode Island, Vermont and Connecticut Avenue. Then for many years we stayed on one street—Boston Avenue, downtown about a mile after Million Dollar Pier a few streets above the Chelsea, Ambassador and Ritz Carleton hotels. My mother always had a sentimental attachment to that street. She had met my Dad at a hotel there in the summer of 1936. They married the following year.

It was sometime during eleventh grade that we started to get into some bad stuff. We began robbing. Not so much for the money but for the fun of it. Writing that now sounds pretty damn dumb: "For the fun of it." Something must be dreadfully wrong with the brains or thought processes of adolescent boys because what we did was both stupid and dangerous—not to mention criminal. Sixteen is a very dangerous age for males. They are not quite men, but they are no longer little boys. They have all the natural urges of men and yet, precious little outlet for those urges. They want to be mature. The problem is that they are not. If I ever had a son, sixteen is the age where I would be most attentive and most on the alert. Just don't ask me for what!

At first, it was mostly small-time stuff. We would boost porch furniture from the fronts of people's homes in the neighborhood. Or we would break into garages looking for used aquariums or other easily sellable goods. We would stash the stuff or sell it very cheaply.

From porch furniture we got into boosting stuff from cars—mostly tires and hubcaps. There was a big market in those days for "spinners"—a special kind of hubcap that had something on it that, when the wheel went around, it flashed. A lot of guys wanted spinners on their cars. They were considered cool. So, we got into the "Midnight Auto Supply" business too. My Pop's new '55 super 88 Olds had a magnificent set of spinners on the front wheels. I won't embarrass my friends by naming them as co-conspirators. The interesting thing is that two of them are in the car business today where they both have very lucrative dealerships selling and leasing very expensive cars. And they can still get you anything on wheels: model or supplies; legitimately.

One of our guys was boosting department store vans. He always had an ample supply of one-hundred percent wool or cashmere sweaters at very reasonable prices. Another guy worked in his brother's gas station and figured out that a brand-name soda machine company was stupid enough to make one key that fit every soda machine in every gas station between Philly and South Jersey. We would drive around late at night, see closed stations with our "brand," stop for a quick soda and proceed to empty out the machine's cash box. We did a great cash and carry business in those summers. I recall one night in particular: we were emptying out a cash box when a car pulled up. One of the guys yelled, "Cops!" And the guy with the cash box dropped it; nickels, dimes and quarters rolled all over the street and we hit the road.

I was on lookout and scared out of my wits. Still, we got away safely and laughed about how the guy who had just pulled into the darkened station for a soda must have freaked when he saw hundreds of nickels, dimes and quarters on the ground in front of the machine.

Once we went into Horn & Hardart's on 54th and City Line for a cup of coffee. H & H was usually always our last stop after a busy night if we didn't head for Harry's. Coffee was about ten or fifteen cents in those days. Our bill was easily under a buck. We left the startled waitress a hundred dollar tip, climbed into Big Al's truck and made the money back in less than an hour.

In the summer of 1955 five of us decided to rob a posh yacht moored in the back bay of Ventnor the next town over from Atlantic City. The Gansk had a beautiful motor boat and another kid in our crew, Alan Martin, would often borrow a big speed boat from one of his uncles to tool around the bay. We were always fishing, crabbing or pulling up to Chelsea beach from the oceanfront to impress the dozens of Philly girls who squealed with delight when we invited them out for a breakneck beachfront tour of Atlantic City by speedboat on a warm August day.

We planned our big caper very carefully. We had hoped to steal some expensive fishing and marine equipment. The five of us were set to hit the marina right after midnight. Two of us would swim out to the boat; two of us would serve as lookouts right on the wharf; and one of us would be out on the street as a backup precaution to signal the wharf guys if anybody drove up to the marina.

The big night came. We met up at the Super Sub Shop on Ventnor Avenue and grabbed a trolley to the street with the marina. We took our spots and the two swimmers, the Gansk and Alan Martin with waterproof tool bags, hit the water. Silently, they swam through the pitch blackness to the yacht while Benny Stein and your obedient servant waited nervously on the dock. I was glad that I hadn't been chosen to make that midnight swim. I hate to swim in cold water. And, although I am a strong swimmer and still swim 50 laps almost every day when I can, long before *Jaws*, I have always had an irrational fear of being eaten by a shark. I had seen some pretty large ones off the coast of Atlantic City and I knew that the bay was filled with small sharks and skates. Although I have free dived off the coast of Maine and Massachusetts and snorkeled in the aquamarine Caribbean. I am still uncomfortable in the ocean and always on the lookout for big sharks—especially Great Whites.

Just about the time when the guys reached the boat, a car pulled up. Our backup lookout, Irv Blank, saw the car and immediately left the scene. Benny and I were frozen. We gave the signal, a high piercing whistle, but we were much too far from the Gansk and Alan for them to hear us with the chirping sounds of August crickets, lapping ocean and their own heavy breathing in the cold water.

Talk about bad luck. As it turned out it was actually the owners of the boat we had intended to rob. For some reason they decided to return to their boat for a little party. They rowed a small dingy out to the yacht, got on board and were obviously going to stay for a while. Did they catch our guys? From the shore, Benny and I couldn't see. Where were they?

We didn't know. Well, there was nothing much we could do for the Gansk and Alan Martin at that point. They had to know that the game was up. So, Benny and I took the path of least resistance. We ran like hell. No sense all of us ending up in the Atlantic City pokey.

We got on a trolley. We didn't know where our fifth guy could be; we didn't know where the Gansk and Alan Martin could be. So, we headed back to the Super Sub which usually stayed open until one in the morning during the summer months.

Later that night (actually, early the next day), the Gansk and Alan Martin ambled up to the Super Sub. They looked frazzled. They had hung over the side of the boat for over an hour freezing their asses in the cold night water while the people on the boat partied. They couldn't take the noisy chance of swimming away. And they had lost all our tools. When the people finally left, Gansk and Alan, frozen to the gills, finally swam back to shore. Where were their faithful lookouts? At the Sub Shop enjoying super subs with all the works; so much for our career as pirates!

Still, the budding hoods were undaunted. The very next day we "borrowed" a car, broke into a locker in an Atlantic City marina and boosted a 75 horsepower Johnson outboard motor. We put it in the trunk and began driving to all the adjacent seaside towns, stopping at every boat store for a quick sale.

The Johnson outboard was easily worth $1,000. We were asking $400. The best offer we got was one boat shop owner's offer to call the cops if we didn't get the hell out of his store. Frustrated after a long night and day of failed criminality, we drove to a bridge not far from Bader Field near the airport. There we dumped the almost new, expensive Johnson 75 into the bay. As far as I know, it is still there.

Looking back at the stupidity and silliness of these petty criminal acts, I plumb my mind for some good reason why kids from basically comfortable lower middle class homes would risk their futures, if not their lives, for such stupid kicks. And, for the life of me, I can't come up with a good answer. In New England where I have spent most of my life, a constant occurrence in many small towns is the sad saga of a bunch of local kids killed while speeding during a late night of joyriding.

Usually, drinking is also part of the equation. The other kids in town will often make a pilgrimage to the spot where their friends have died to place teddy bears and stuffed animals at the site which will almost guarantee that local TV crews show up to record the same dumb-ass event over and over. Whenever I hear of such a tragedy, I think back to what we used to do.

Why do teenagers think that they are invulnerable? Why do they think it is a kick to take a winding New England country road at 85 miles an hour? Why does the same, sad story play itself out on TV so many times without those lame news directors catching on? I really don't know the answer. And, I think, neither do they.

I can report that there was a book that had a tremendous influence on us. Most of my pals were not big readers but they all read *The Hoods* by Harry Grey. Harry Grey was actually a real hoodlum named David Aaronson. We all wanted to be "Noodles the Shiv" Aaronson.

The Hoods was about a bunch of tough Jewish kids who formed a New York City street gang during the Great Depression. The Hoods were made up of cool guys with nicknames just like us: Noodles, Big Maxie, Patsy, Cockeye Hymie and Jake the Goniff. They all hung out at a candy store called Gelly's. You may never have heard of this book but Sergio Leone turned it into a pretty fine film in 1984, *Once Upon a Time in America*, starring Robert de Niro as Noodles and James Woods as Big Maxie. If you rent it, get the four-hour long version. The dopey suits in Hollywood cut this excellent film to shreds and it failed dismally at the box office.

It wasn't about money either. In the summers of 1956 and 1957 I had managed to get a terrific job at the concession stand at Playhouse in the Park and later, as a waiter at the famous Philly golfer Helen Sigel Wilson's outdoor restaurant. I saw all the great plays free for two summers—Arthur Miller's *A View from the Bridge; Anastasia; and The Desperate Hours* to name a few. Often I would watch these plays five or six times to the point where I even got to know some of the lines. I also met many of the actors and actresses who would eat for the week of their run at my station.

I recall waiting on Hume Cronyn and Jessica Tandy, Gig Young, Luther Adler, Princess Grace Kelly's famous Philly family, Gale Sondergaard (just making her way off the dreaded Blacklist—her husband was one of the famous Hollywood Ten) and the well-known character actor Albert Dekker.

For some reason, I was always lucking out in the job department. My father had a friend from the Philly Post Office who was the head usher at Shibe Park (later Connie Mack Stadium) home of the Philadelphia Phillies. From 1953 to 1956 I ushered almost every home game and since the usher's locker room was right next to the clubhouse, I got to meet many of my boyhood heroes close-up: Del Ennis, Richie Ashburn, Robin Roberts, Dick Sisler, Andy Seminick and my particular favorite, Willie "Puddinhead" Jones, who played 3rd base and in 1950 hit 25 homers.

In retrospect, it would have been better for me not to have met them. They smoked, cursed like sailors and drank beer. My Phillies pass admitted me to any game whether I ushered or not. Sometimes, during the week, I would cut school and head for the ballpark. I would often see my father's older brother Sam, an unreconstructed gambler who always had at least a sawbuck riding on a game. Uncle Sam Goldman would wink at me, flip me half a buck and say, "Your father asks; you didn't see me. And I didn't see you; right kid!" So much for the cherished heroes we have from childhood. Though there will always be a soft spot in my heart for the 1950 "Whiz Kids," our own Philly Boys of Summer.

CHAPTER 14

Somehow, an angel sat on our shoulders. None of us ever got caught doing the stupid things we were doing. Nobody ever got hurt. And no permanent harm was ever done. Of course, that wasn't true for all of us in later years. But I'll get to that sorry tale later.

How we escaped getting caught stealing cars and robbing was a minor miracle we never thought to question. Shortly before turning sixteen, I sat in the back seat of a stolen car on a late-night joyride. We were three dumb Philly kids going absolutely nowhere. The driver, a kid by the name of Fred Avery, was very short and barely reached the steering wheel. Late that night he pulled up to a light at Haverford and City Line, stopping when it turned red. A dark Lower Merion patrol car pulled up beside us. The two cops took one look at the three of us and, turning their flashing light on, signaled us to pull over. An unforgettable sinking feeling went from my throat to the pit of my stomach. We were all going to jail and we were not going to pass GO!

Freddy Avery would steal cars on a regular basis from his father's service station, Max & Jacks, on 57th and Upland Way. His father, Jack, was a pretty tough working class guy and he was a card-playing friend of my father as well. His mother, Jean, a wonderful woman, was a close friend of my mother and I was always hot for his younger sister, Judy who was gorgeous (though I'm not sure Judy Avery ever knew it!). It would be Freddy's ass if we were caught. And mine as well. Not to mention the fact that swiping a car was a major felony. Three teens in a stolen Cadillac and not one wise enough to know that cops were smarter than they were.

Our pal Jack Zatz sat shaking in the front seat. He had not yet decided to become a career criminal. Freddy looked at the cops waving us over and clenching his jaw saw that nothing was coming in either direction at that late hour. With nobody in front of us, before the light turned green, Freddy pushed the accelerator to the floor. We peeled out in a loud screech that easily over-road my yelling to Freddy from the backseat to pull the hell over. Cops, after all, had guns! Guns that shoot!

The cops put on their siren and the chase began. Before that night, I thought I knew what it was like to feel real fear. After all, I had sat through *House of Wax* as well as all the Dracula and Frankenstein movies from Universal! But the stark terror of that late night chase, aside from very real family tragedies, was the worst fear I have ever known.

Instead of heading back towards the safety of the neighborhood where we might at least ditch the damn car, Freddy Avery swung a hard right onto Haverford Avenue into the winding, twisting and unfamiliar streets of Lower Merion—the home turf of the cops who had now stupidly decided to pursue us at very high speeds. Freddy kept the Caddie floored until it was easily doing over seventy-five. I looked back. The cops, like that strange posse chasing Butch and Sundance, kept coming. For fifteen or twenty minutes they were right up our high speed asses. But Freddy Avery was one hell of a driver— for a little guy who could barely see over the damn steering wheel. To make a long and frightening high-speed chase short, we finally lost them; another miracle in my brief life.

We made our way carefully back to Wynnefield, ditched the car, wisely split up and went home. I saw red Philly cop cars cruising all over the neighborhood looking for us that night.

Obviously, the Lower Merion constabulary had alerted the locals to be on the lookout for three punk kids in a big mother of a Cadillac. But since everything had happened so quickly, I doubted if they had solid descriptions of us. I lay in bed that night thinking hard. My life of crime was hardly paying off very well. I was hardly the successful hoodlum that I aspired to be. After spending a largely sleepless night, jumping up to my bedroom window in panic every time a set of car lights pulled down our dark back alley, I never again got involved in stealing cars either as a driver or a passenger. Stealing cars that you couldn't keep was for dopes and suckers! My brief criminal career was over for good.

I can't pinpoint why most of us stopped all that silliness with any certainty. I think some of it may have been due to our discovery of the opposite sex. In Wynnefield, the nicer girls were not overly impressed by boys who wanted to grow up to be Noodles the Shiv.

You may have noticed that I have not written extensively about… SEX. That is mostly because there was none to really speak about. Oh, we all bragged a good game. But, like me, most of my friends entered our senior year of high school as virgins. For me, that was not to be a terminal condition.

I did not usually do very well in the girl department through the eleventh grade. I had my share of crushes and sexual misadventures. But there was never anything to really write home about. In the summer of 1956 I met a girl from Collingswood, New Jersey in Atlantic City. Lana Meredith was a dead ringer for Natalie Wood and built even better. For the first time, Pop allowed me to take the Olds and pick up a date all on my own. Having a car in the steamy summer of your sixteenth year was the ultimate freedom. I would pick Lana up, drive out to Somers Point or Longport, park at some rocks high over the crashing ocean and steam up the car for hours. It was Lana who gave me my first real lessons in French kissing.

When that torrid summer was over my virginity, though somewhat in disarray, remained intact when Lana broke up with me on Labor Day weekend insuring that I would never get to see Collingswood, New Jersey. And I headed home for my senior year in high school still as pure as the first day of a driven Philly snow in January.

As twelfth grade got underway some of us fell by the wayside. The Gansk, who had flunked virtually every course in the tenth grade, had been taken out of Overbrook by his wise father and shipped off to Valley Forge Military Academy. The Ganskys were the only family in the gang who could afford private school for their kid; lucky Gansk! We would go up to "the Forge" on weekends to visit because during much of his first year the Gansk was not permitted to even come home. Jack Gansky wanted to break his wayward son out of the Harry's mold along with the bad influences that came with public school. And he had the money to do it.

At the Forge, the Gansk would enter a strange world none of us knew much about. It was a world of rich, spoiled kids whose families had the money to buy them out of academic or other kinds of trouble. There were other neighborhood high school flunk outs at the Forge. Two Wynnefield kids I didn't like very much, Donald Steerman and Stephen Kendall, were also sent to Valley Forge by parents who could afford the freight. The Gansk pretty much avoided these guys. Gansk's first roommate was a multi-millionaire's son from Latin America, Pedro something. He seemed all right for a strange kid with a foreign accent.

Valley Forge scared the crap out of me. I wasn't very philosophical as a teenager, but I understood a little bit about the concept of freedom. At Valley Forge there was no freedom.

Freedom is a concept that I have always cherished and I suppose it is one reason I am so enamored of our more famous Founding Fathers.

If nothing else, Jefferson, Adams, Washington, Hamilton and Madison, understood a great deal about liberty and freedom even if they didn't exactly practice what they preached. Freedom is one of the great joys in life never to be taken for granted.

At Valley Forge the Gansk lost his freedom. He might just as well have been in a damn prison. The Gansk was forced to get a haircut where they virtually shaved his head—I don't think it ever actually grew back. You may notice that whenever people attempt to make you less free one of the first things they will do is shave your head. Nazis did it in the camps. They claimed it was to rid the concentration camp victims of lice. I don't know much about bugs but I do know something about individuality. People who are forced to shave their heads don't have any. On top of that the Gansk had to wear an itchy wool uniform with a high-button tunic to all his classes. How can anybody learn anything in itchy pants? Even worse, he was forced to eat his meals in a military fashion where he squared each spoonful or forkful of food before putting it in his mouth. He also had to take a lot of shit from upperclassmen. At Overbrook High, if anyone would have talked to the Gansk the way some of those WASPY assholes at Valley Forge did, he would have punched out their lights. At the Forge, the Gansk actually adjusted. Gansk was like McMurphy in *One Flew over the Cuckoo's Nest*—after the lobotomy. It was kind of sad to see.

I didn't know much about military school beyond what Valley Forge's most famous graduate, a New York Jew named Jerome David Salinger wrote in *The Catcher in the Rye*. Valley Forge Academy in Wayne, Pennsylvania about twenty miles from Philly was the very same school old J. D. Salinger/Holden Caulfield had attended. I was probably the only guy in the crowd who read Salinger. He had obviously had mixed emotions about Valley Forge. But, like I said, we didn't trust guys with initials in front of their names.

The interesting thing about Valley Forge Academy is the fact that being Jewish was not a drawback. In the 1950s, anti-Semitism was still a powerful factor in American private education at every level. Apparently, the military men who ran the Forge could have cared less. Salinger, his daughter Margaret reported in a memoir, apparently experienced some disturbing anti-Semitism at the Forge in the 1930s. I don't recall the Gansk ever mentioning it at all.

In the end military school saved the Gansk. He rejoined the old gang at Temple University a few years later seemingly none the worse for the wear. But he was changed. I couldn't exactly say how then. In retrospect, I think that military school knocked all the spontaneity and individuality out of the Gansk. So, on one hand while he might have been saved academically, in the end Valley Forge was a costly education in more ways than one.

The Gansk we had known as teenagers never actually returned to the old neighborhood. With the Gansk very much removed from the daily scene and the end of high school looming, some life-changing decisions were in order. Since I wasn't going to make it as a hood, I had to begin thinking, like Dustin Hoffman in *The Graduate*, of my future.

Pop's boss at the Post Office, Harry Clark, was a full bird-colonel in the army reserve. Pop must have told Colonel Clark that I wasn't doing well in school and that it didn't look like college was in the cards for me either. I made it clear at home that after high school I didn't really want to go to college. Education, to me then, was pure bullshit. High school had cured me of any further use for education. I had all the answers. Of course, I didn't even know the questions. It must have broken my parent's heart to think that I was wasting my talents not to mention my life.

At any rate, Colonel Clark suggested that, on my 17th birthday, Pop sign the papers for me to become a member of the reserve outfit he commanded. In November of 1956, on the week of my seventeenth birthday, I signed up for the United States Army along with one of my closest childhood friends, Lenny Ivker, a kid I had known since kindergarten. Lenny lived up the street on 53rd and Gainor. He came from a strictly orthodox Jewish family and, as a result, was kept out of the line of Harry's backroom fire to some extent. In Abe Ivker's house there was no such thing as a dissenting opinion. While we shot pool on Saturdays, Lenny was in synagogue; most Friday nights too.

We both agreed to go off for basic training together right after high school under the military's "buddy system." Pop's idea was that if I liked the army, after my initial six months, I could re-up for a two to three-year tour and "find myself." If I didn't like it, as he hoped, maybe I would come to my senses and return to Philly for college. Colonel Clark assured my father that the service would straighten me out. He was right. The army was to be a life-altering experience; both for me, I think, and the army as well.

But it wasn't the army that really changed the path of my life. It was a girl.

CHAPTER 15

"...So far only one uncontestable truth has been stated about love: 'This is a great mystery'; everything else that has been written or said about love is not a solution, but only a statement of questions that have remained unanswered..."
Anton Pavlovich Chekhov, *About Love*, 1898

"Love means never having to say you're sorry." Erich Segal, *Love Story*, 1969

"Just make sure you can tell the difference between love and a stiff penknife!"
Louis Goldman to his eldest son, circa 1957-58

"Love decides what's wrong, what's right and all the in betweens... It's true, sometimes love decides for you."
Jane Oliver, *Love Decides*, 2001

I met Arlene Rachman on December 20, 1956, at a Har Zion Temple Hy Lit (a Philly DJ) dance. I had worked an eight-hour day at Howard Clothes, a downtown Philly men's store. Pop had been moonlighting as a salesman at Howard's on Wednesday nights and all day on Saturday. He got me the job that fall and I worked the same time schedule he did. We would meet downtown in the late afternoon, have dinner at H & H, work till nine and go home together on Wednesdays. On Saturdays Pop would haul my lazy ass out of the sack early, make us some breakfast and off we would go by trolley and subway. Pop would never drive because there was no place to park free. At noon we'd usually take lunch at Bayne's (Pop's friend Ollie Bayne owned the deli) together with a good looking Italian guy that Pop liked who worked in the haberdashery section of the store. Buddy, was younger than Pop and had been having some marital difficulties. He often used Pop as a sounding board for his domestic troubles.

I usually sat there listening. Years later Pop told me that poor Buddy had taken his own life. My job, in the Will Call section, involved me working with two attractive Negro girls about my own age. A customer would show up, give us a ticket and we would then go up to the dark third floor to retrieve the garment where the ancient tailors, mostly foreign-born Jews, endlessly labored to sew the clothing to the customer's size needs. Once, in the freight elevator, one of the girls grabbed me by the ass, pulled me to her and began to gyrate against me. I was so scared I didn't take advantage of a wonderful opportunity. The district manager of Howard's, a stately man by the name of Frank Porter, had hired Pop and me because he was almost like family. Fastidiously dressed and meticulously groomed, Frank Porter reminded me of the actor William Powell, Hollywood's first Thin Man. When I was a baby, the Porters lived next door to us on Diamond Street and our two families had kept in touch over the years.

With Pop and Mr. Porter (it was always "Mr. Porter") on the floor it would hardly do for the service elevator doors to swing open with me standing with a Negro stock-girl and my pants at half-mast around my ankles. Barely seventeen, I still had never been very intimate with the opposite sex. Beyond making out with a few girls, the closest I had ever come to real pussy was with that Catholic girl in the back of Big Al's truck. And, after gently placing my index finger into her delightful wet mystery, I wasn't quite sure what to do next.

On that particular Saturday I came home from work bone-tired. I almost didn't go out that night because I was so fatigued. A full day of work at Howard's, going up and down that hand-operated freight elevator a thousand times, was not my idea of the good life at around seventy-five cents an hour. But that night my close friend Larry Laster (the fancy dancer of Bandstand fame) called and finally convinced me to grab a shower, put on a tie and sport jacket and then take the short walk from my house to 54th and Wynnefield Avenue where the dance was being held in the old synagogue's ample auditorium.

Larry met me at the dance and we walked in. You couldn't miss Larry. He wore a hot pink jacket that set him apart from every kid at the dance. The first girl I saw was Elida Servin, a dumpy little thing I had known for about a year. Actually, we had been together on the previous New Years eve (ironic, in that my New Years date for 1999, some forty-three years later was one Elida Michels, the very same Elida Servin, no longer dumpy and, as a grown woman, boldly blonde with long cascading hair, by 1999 very well-built and in firm possession of killer legs and a killer body to boot!). Approaching sixty, the new version of Elida looked no more than forty, proving without a doubt that time is not the enemy of every woman.

Larry, as was his style, immediately jitterbugged off and left me standing by myself. Elida came over to talk as did her cute blonde girlfriend, a girl who lived on Woodcrest Avenue, Arlene Rachman. Arlene wore a gray poodle (without the poodle she tells me!) skirt, a gray sweater over a white blouse and her hair was tied back in a long ponytail. Arlene always reminded me of the young Shirley Jones in *Carousel.* She still does.

She was thin and about five-two or three. For a Jewish girl she had a great *shicksa* look. I took one look at Arlene and, as the Italians put it, I was struck by the thunderbolt. But I wasn't just struck. I was smitten by the thunderbolt! All it took was one slow dance. Wham!

A word about love, youth and all that crap: I am far from an expert on the subject of love and women. In my early seventies, the best that could be said is that I am a very slow learner. When it comes to the opposite sex as an adult, I have always had a severe case of, as the warden said in *Cool Hand Luke,* "…a failure to communicate." But never with Arlene Rachman.

At seventeen, I fell in love. Fortunately, I didn't know then what I know now. I did know that a very weird feeling I had never felt before swept over me. The feeling went deep down to the pit of my stomach and almost caused me to be short of breath. That is what it felt like during my first dance with Arlene Rachman. Like having the living breath knocked right out of you. The other thing I remember about that first dance with Arlene was the smell of her hair. It was a fragrance

I have never forgotten and have never known since. Even when she was sweaty, I loved the smell of that girl.

Bob Seeger caught it all for me in the first verse of his 1980 song *Against the Wind*:

It seems like yesterday
But it was long ago
Janey (Arlene) was lovely, she was the queen of my nights
There in the darkness with the radio playing low
And the secrets that we shared
The mountains that we moved
Caught like a wildfire out of control
Till there was nothing left to burn and nothing left to prove
And I remember what she said to me
How she swore that it would never end
I remember how she held me oh so tight
Wish I didn't know now what I didn't know then

Today, all of this is very dangerous stuff. First of all, because Arlene Rachman was only fourteen when we met anything that happened between us over the next four or five years was, strictly speaking, illegal. Sex, even between consenting teens, was and is against the law. What with all the horrid and lurid stuff coming out about the Catholic Church and their scandal-ridden pedophile priests in Boston and elsewhere lately, the less said about illicit relations, no matter how long ago and consenting, the better. So, I will say no more. Read *Splendor in the Grass*, a poem by William Wordsworth. Better yet, rent the movie.

The next six months were the happiest months I have ever spent in my life with any member of the opposite sex I have ever known. It was Romeo and Juliet. In case you were wondering, I played Romeo.

After that Saturday night dance, Arlene and I were virtually inseparable. She says I stalked her and made it impossible for her to say no to me. Whatever! For the next month or so I picked her up at Beeber Junior High and drove her home even though home was just down the block from the school. That January she graduated with honors (in those ancient times there were still mid-year graduations) and Arlene entered the tenth grade at Overbrook.

Soon I was walking or driving her to school every day. We would meet in the dark halls during study periods or lunch and we'd steal kisses in the empty stairwells. I did my best to see Arlene wherever and whenever I could. For the first time in my teenage life, something was coming between me and my time at Harry's, between me and all the guys, between me and serious trouble. Something mattered. And it was a very good something.

As I entered my last half year of high school, I suddenly had purpose. Arlene's parents, Sol and Mary Rachman were fairly strict with her. On top of that, Mrs. Rachman didn't like me very much. Somehow she had found out that I wasn't a very good student and that I hung out at Harry's with other hoodlums; and that, most important, my Pop wasn't a very rich man. Her Arlene had top grades—all A's and B's. Like her sister Iris, who went to the University of Pennsylvania on a full scholarship, Arlene was ticketed for a top-flight education. What was their pretty, little daughter doing with this bum from Diamond Street, "Mutzy" Goldman? Sol Rachman, who was foreign-born and spoke with an accent, was a quiet little man who worked as a cutter for College Hall Clothes in Philly. He usually had little to say to me past "Hello Mutzy," when I came by the house to pick up his precious daughter. Then he would disappear.

Not so Mary Rachman. She made it crystal clear that her daughter wasn't meant to be with an uneducated nobody who was clearly ticketed to nowhere in this life. And besides, her daughter was much too young at fourteen to be getting serious with any boy anyway!

Mrs. Rachman did her level best to come between us. She would schedule monthly weekend trips to New York City for clothing jaunts to make sure that we would be apart. Mary Rachman's maiden name was Chapman and her sister-in-law, who I never met, was the famous New York City designer Ceil Chapman. Arlene was always very well dressed. She still is.

In retrospect, Mrs. Rachman was absolutely right. I suppose today, if I had a pretty fourteen-year-old daughter (Arlene turned fifteen on

May 3, 1957) who brought somebody like me home, I would have a minor hemorrhage. But she was also wrong because she never took the trouble to get to know me. I had potential. It may have been locked away but it was there. And at seventeen, all I knew was that I was in love for the first time in my life, that this was the girl with whom I would be with for the rest of my life and that I would do whatever was necessary to be with her. Mary Rachman, in my young eyes, was the enemy. I hated her.

So, when Mrs. Rachman put strict limits on the time we were allowed to spend together, I simply got Arlene to agree to meet her girlfriends on the days and nights we were not permitted to date. And presto, I would show up! Mrs. Rachman never knew it, but I was actually spending more time with her daughter than I would have had she not put down any restrictions. Soon I was spending virtually every waking hour with her daughter. And thanks to Pop—I had a fine Oldsmobile that even made as much privacy as we wanted a real possibility. Arlene soon told me she loved me, that there would never be anyone else and that I only had to do two things: improve my grades and go to college. That would appease her mother. I had to make something of myself—an issue to which by 1957 I had given absolutely no thought. Overweening ambition has never been one of my stronger suits. One of the guiding forces in my life has been inertia.

Improving my grades was easy. Arlene was at school. So I went to school. And I stopped cutting classes. Since Arlene took school seriously, I would take school seriously; for the first time since kindergarten. We spent a great deal of time over the next months studying together. That Mary Rachman could never protest. And, when I showed up at the Rachman house most days after school with my books in tow, she did not.

College? Well, college was another story. College was for kids who wore Ivy League shirts and pants with a buckle in the back. I still wore blue jeans (we called them dungarees in the 1950s). College, as far as I was concerned, was out. With my lousy grades, I'd never get in anyway. But I didn't tell Arlene any of that. She knew that I was off to the Army in the summer of 1957. We'd play college by ear when I came back from the service in a few years.

That winter of my great content soon gave way to the delights of a Philly spring. Spring always arrives early in Philadelphia. By mid-April warm, balmy breezes usually waft over the many neighborhoods of the city. I was doing well in school. I was head over heels in love, and life was absolutely perfect. My wise-guy period was over. I was ready to join the human race. Seventeen and in love; you want twelfth grade to go on forever. When the future stretches out before you like a golden highway, you almost believe that it will. If only all of life was like the twelfth grade, it would be one terrific trip. There ought to be an office in Washington designed to make life like the twelfth grade. I think part of me knew then that it could never last. And it didn't. But I wouldn't trade that brief time for anything.

Although I hated high school, and was never a member of the so-called "in-crowd," the last half of my senior year was marvelous. Even some girls in my grade, who had little to do with me for many years, would see me walking hand in hand through the hallways with Arlene and they would comment how I had changed. I was even dressing differently—chino pants with belts in the back, button-down shirts and, God help me, I even traded my engineer boots in for saddle shoes. Arlene began picking out my clothes as the jeans hit the back of my closet.

There would be picnics in Fairmount Park after school and long make-out sessions in "The Glenn," an abandoned nineteenth century manor house in Bala where we could park for hours without being seen from the road by the outside world. Once some Lower Merion cops caught us at night in "the Glenn," shined their light on us and saw two basically half-naked teenagers. The two cops were both good guys. They allowed us to dress and kicked us out with just a warning. We soon found an even better spot. I'd pick Arlene up on a Saturday night and drive right back into my garage. No cops were ever going to bother anybody in their own garage. And no cops ever did. Talk about ingenuity. And saving on gas!

But as Wordsworth knew, "Splendor in the Grass" doesn't last forever.

CHAPTER 16

I graduated without distinction from Overbrook High in late June of 1957. Arlene, Mom and Pop sat dutifully through the boring ceremony. Pomp and circumstance; Christian songs about "Our Lord Who Art in Heaven," and even more boring speeches by the students most likely—most likely to fail in life that is. Shooting high school stars have a way of flaming out as adults. It is what I call "The Norman Mailer Syndrome." Norman Mailer wrote his best novel, *The Naked and the Dead*, before he turned twenty-five. It was also his first book. For the rest of his life poor Norman, with a miniscule but notable triumph here and there, has produced mostly unreadable crap. His early literary star, rising as rapidly as a gaseous comet, like many of the notables in my high school graduating class, just farted out. Moral: don't break Babe Ruth's record too early in this life.

Graduation night was very warm and I sweltered in the new suit Pop bought me at Krass Brothers on South Street—a suit that would also be my graduation suit from college and last well into my early thirties! After the ceremony we all went to Stouffer's in Ardmore for a late supper. At the bar, while we waited for our table, Pop bought me my first alcoholic drink—and we toasted with a grasshopper. I guess that was Pop's way of saying, "Congratulations kiddo, you made it! Too bad, but now you are an adult!" I remember being supremely happy that night.

With my future spread out on the road ahead…well…why not? That road looked mighty golden in 1957. My grades had improved to the point where I almost graduated with a 70 average—not quite, but almost. All of which was attributable to Arlene Rachman. I seemed to do very well in the history courses I took. All through high school I had never achieved a grade higher than C until that last half year of school when I got a number of A's and B's—in history courses.

Arlene Rachman looked perfectly ravishing that night. Wearing a new tight-fitting dark brown suit furnished by her famous New York designing aunt, with her long blonde hair pulled straight back into a glorious pony tail, I will never forget how I melted inside when I looked at her because it has happened so rarely in a lifetime of so many relationships with women.

I have always had a workable theory about beautiful women. To me, a really beautiful woman is one who can simply pull her hair straight back from her forehead and still look terrific. That option is available to very few women. If you like the pure beauty of Lynda Carter (Wonder Woman), Veronica Hamel from *Hill Street Blues* and *Thirtysomething's* Mel Harris you get my point. In my eyes, that was the kind of beauty Arlene Rachman possessed.

Arlene's lively intelligence, her beauty, her touch and her kisses are what all others have been measured against. As Stephen King understood so well in *Hearts in Atlantis,* "It was his first real kiss…and Bobby never forgot the feel of her lips pressing on his…It was the kiss by which all others of his life would be judged and found wanting."

If you apply my Norman Mailer hypothesis here, I suppose you might think this was a sad state of affairs. For my part, I do not. If that feeling occurs just once in this life, consider yourself fortunate above all other men.

After dropping my parents off that night, we drove to our spot, made passionate love and promised each other a million and one things about the rest of our lives. Then, with her mother still tormenting us, I took Arlene home and caught up with all my other friends. At the various graduation soirees we partied happily through the night into the morning of the next day. I woke up that afternoon with a slight buzz and realized that within a few weeks my Philly street days would be over. I would be off on that marvelous adventure called life.

Over that summer my Mom took a job as head girl's counselor in a camp in the Pocono Mountains called Lindenmere. It was a terrific place and Mom negotiated a camper's spot for my little brother Kenny, now almost twelve. She also got me a three-week gig as one of the camp's waiters.

During the days, after serving breakfast and lunch, we traveled around the Poconos by bus to play baseball against other camps. Lindenmere fielded a pretty fair team and won often.

I started as the team's lead-off hitter and shortstop. The only thing wrong was that Arlene remained in Philly. But she knew it was to be an attenuated summer for us anyway. On July 19, I returned to Philly, took Arlene out for the last time that year, made love at our spot and early the next day showed up with all the other Philly recruits at 30th Street Station for the exhausting train ride to Fort Knox, Kentucky.

At the train station Arlene broke down, crying uncontrollably. Mom cried too. Pop was stoic but I can guess what must have been going through his head. He was sending his oldest kid off to the Army. America was at peace in the summer of 1957 thanks to the wisdom and leadership of Dwight D. Eisenhower who knew too well about war. I imagine Pop was praying that the peace would hold over the rest of the summer. It would hardly do to send your kid off to the service and have him get his ass shot off in a far-off place you couldn't pronounce.

In the pictures Mom snapped that day, I didn't look any too happy. But I didn't cry. No matter what Larry Laster says! There is no crying allowed in the United States Army. On the way down to Kentucky a number of the older guys—and nearly everybody in the Army that summer was older than me—who noticed the gorgeous blonde weeping by my side couldn't imagine why my sister had been so upset. When I told the guys Arlene was my girlfriend they were incredulous. What could a girl who looked like Arlene see in a scrawny, pimple-faced boy? The guys just couldn't believe it—a cute chick and a skinny kid with acne. What was my *kavorka*? Look at Sinatra and Ava; the rumor was that Ava Gardner loved Sinatra because he was so well hung. No comment!

CHAPTER 17

"But if the length of the journey was all, it would be no burden…
Great things are wanted to be done."
   John Adams, 1776

Fort Knox, Kentucky, July 20, 1957-September 20, 1957: I hated the Army. That was my first emotion. I have always despised and rebelled against institutions that have made absolutely no sense. And the United States Army in July of 1957 made absolutely no sense; at least not to this soldier. Not then. Not now. It was a far cry from the all-volunteer military we are so lucky to enjoy today. Calling the Army pointless back then would be a compliment.

After a train ride through the day and the following night, on Sunday, July 21 we arrived in Louisville where we were then transported by bus to nearby Fort Knox. I had never been south of South Philly in my life. The American South was to be a major eye-opener for me.

Later, because of my fascination with the South, I would concentrate on Southern history for my M.A. degree and would introduce the first courses in Southern and Negro history at Clark University and Holy Cross College. My first book was on a well-known slave revolt in Virginia. Anyone who tells you that the South is just like the rest of the country has no idea what they are talking about. Start with Faulkner. The best non-fiction book ever written about the South is W.J. Cash's 1941 study, *The Mind of the South*. Cash thought long and hard about what the South has meant to our nation and culture. He committed suicide shortly after his book was published. I'm not saying there was any correlation to Cash's suicide and his attempt to delve into the enigma that is the American South. I'm not saying there wasn't either.

On the way to Kentucky our train stopped throughout western Pennsylvania, Ohio and then wound its way south. The first thing that struck me about the South was the greenery. Lush. I had never seen that kind of green in the north. I saw other things as well.

As I looked out the window of the train I saw an America I never even knew existed. I was, of course, keenly aware of urban poverty. But urban poverty was only a small step removed from our protective neighborhood. The poverty I watched fly past our train was astonishing to a seventeen-year-old youngster from inner-city Philadelphia. It was rural poverty—the worst and most invisible poverty in America. Three years later, campaigning through West Virginia, a young, elite presidential candidate was also struck by the rural poverty he encountered for the first time. Like me, John F. Kennedy never knew it was there. They didn't teach much about rural poverty at Harvard or in the Philly public schools.

The first thing I recall about Kentucky was the unbearable heat. It was the middle of the summer. I thought I had known steamy summer heat in Philly. The Founding Fathers often did their best to escape Philly during the First and Second Continental Congress because of the sweltering heat and the danger of disease—mostly yellow fever. Jefferson and some others would often repair to Germantown in the summer months where it was a few degrees cooler. Compared to the heat that hit us when we got off the bus at Fort Knox, Philly heat was a balmy breeze. Philly's sizzling summer heat is uncomfortable. The summer heat in the South hits you like a clenched fist, then envelops you like a smothering shroud and finally does its damn best to crush you body and soul.

We were all still wearing civvies when the young sergeants began barking loud orders as we got off the buses. I wore a long-sleeved shirt and heavy black khakis. Most of the city boys had long, slicked back hair and this didn't sit too well with these closely cropped warriors as they yelled at us: "Move, move, move!" Move? Move where? None of us knew why they were all yelling at once or what the hell they were talking about. These tough looking soldiers made no sense. Nor could we understand most of them as they slurred their words as good-old-boy deep southerners, Black as well as White, have a penchant for doing.

We queued up and soon olive-drab buses came to take us to our barracks. But the first stop was to be an air-conditioned amphitheater where the commanding officer of Fort Knox, Kentucky, General Paul Disney, addressed us en masse. General Disney, in a crisp, ribbon laden summer uniform, told us how fortunate we all were to be members of the United States Army—the best fighting army in the entire world; how we should listen and learn from our NCOs, (Non-Commissioned Officers), all tough, combat-tested veterans of World War II and Korea. He reminded us of our patriotic duty, of how tough the next nine weeks of basic training would be and how we were the last line of defense for democracy and the free world where the evil Russians and Chinese were just waiting for us to falter. I had never met a real Russian (the fact that my grandparents originated in Russia never even occurred to me) and the only Chinese person I ever spoke to besides a summer friend at the YMCA on 52nd and Sansom Street was the guy who sold takeout at Chopsticks on 54th Street.

The first thing I remember thinking: "I wonder if General Disney is related to Walt Disney. I wonder if he knows Annette!" Annette was the only Mouseketeer with tits. For some strange reason I didn't feel very fortunate. After the general's pep talk, we were taken to our barracks. In our company there were four wooden barracks. Each barrack had two floors with reddish linoleum and two-tiered bunk beds—obvious remnants of World War II. Some of our more fortunate train mates ended up in brand new concrete structures called "the Pink Palaces" because of their color.

I ended up in the second platoon, in the second building, on the second floor, in the second tier of a bunk under my assigned "buddy," a 350 pound Negro who said he had graduated from Benjamin Franklin High in North Philly. Henry Jenkins (not his real name), who had the IQ of a small brussel sprout, was not easy to sleep above. He snored like a steam engine, farted a lot, smelled like a goat because he refused to shower daily and every time he got up at night to take a leak, the iron bunk shook as if hit by a tornado. My best friend, Lenny Ivker, could have easily spared my ass from the Jenkins fate by bunking in with me, but he apparently wanted to have a genuine "army experience" and opted for a quiet little guy by the name of George Hodges as his bunkmate. It was the beginning of the end of a long friendship that had begun in kindergarten although, to this day, we have somehow managed to keep in touch. Lenny's sweet mother Francis, who died a few years before my own mother, was in the same assisted care facility outside of Philadelphia as my Mom and they had become good friends. I still shudder at that hellish summer sleeping above that formidable pile of surplus human blubber, Henry Jenkins.

Fort Knox specialized in armored (tank) warfare. General George S. Patton once trained there. Tanks are always accompanied by infantry; us. Thus, my new mailing address:

Private Martin S. Goldman

ER 13594980

9th Battalion

Company A, 2nd Platoon

USATCA (United States Army Training Center Armor)

Fort Knox, Kentucky

It seemed a long address to get my mail. Like I said, the U.S. Army always made little sense.

CHAPTER 18

It was the first day of our training. The non-coms awakened us screaming at 3:30 AM.; a quick breakfast of "shit on a shingle" (some kind of creamy chipped-ham crap on a slice of very stale toast), milk or coffee. My friend Lenny Ivker complained that the creamy ham wasn't kosher and went hungry. I ate it all. God could never want Jewish soldiers to starve.

And then the worst—to the base barbers where they literally sheared us like sheep until we were all snatched bald. We all now looked the same. Long-haired Italians from South Philly; crew-cut goobers from Ohio: All the same. I write in my journal, "I look like a goon." They obviously don't want us to retain any semblance of our individuality. My new ID card is scary looking.

Next, they took us for shots. I despise needles. I can't recall how many needles go into my arms that day; a lot. Then clothing: We are hustled to the Quartermaster where they process us through long lines: boots, shoes, socks, underwear, green fatigues, hats, helmets, an M-1 rifle, khaki-colored class-A uniforms with short sleeve shirts for the stifling summer months, long-sleeve shirts, a winter field jacket, khaki Bermuda-type shorts, white T-shirts, and two winter very wooly uniforms—a spiffy new aquamarine job with gold buttons with a matching MacArthur-style hat and the other, the WWII drab Eisenhower jacket uniform with the itchiest woolen pants ever conceived by man. I thought of Pop and that Yellow Ribbon Dance. No pajamas in the army. Everybody slept in their skivvies (underwear). Since the summer of 1957, I have never purchased pajamas. To this day I still sleep in my skivvies.

Our barracks reach a temperature above 100 degrees during the day. The temperature went so high that even at night when the temperature goes down the second floor was a damn steam bath. Even so, each of us must serve alternative "fire duty" to see that the coal-fed furnace on the side of the barracks never shuts down. These morons have the heat on in the middle of the summer!

Our sleep is never sound although we are physically exhausted after each day of training. We all sleep wet, very wet. We dressed each day for training in green fatigues, combat boots and a floppy, ill-fitting hat we called a "cunt cap" that made us all look even more ridiculous. Sometimes they tell us to wear our steel-pot helmets; often with the intense heat, our lighter helmet liners. Four hundred bald young men, all looking alike, all standing in formations for hours, waiting, waiting, waiting…for what? Godot? They never say. The first day was exhausting. Our arms ached from the volley of shots; from carrying our new army issue in heavy duffel bags; from standing around. But nothing really happened. They just marched us from one place to another. "Hup, two, three, four, I don't care if your Mama's a whore!" Nobody seems to know anything. If they do, nobody told us anything. They just kept us moving and marching. I hated the stupid marching! "Hup, two, three, four…" I hated the stupid Army!

Lines; always…lines. Every so often they gave us a "smoke break." There are many "smoke breaks" during army training. "Smoke, if you got 'em!" our Sergeants barked. The Army encouraged us to smoke. When we were in the field they handed out C-rations with a small pack of Phillip Morris cigarettes in each trooper's ration. At the PX (Post Exchange) cigarettes sold for 19 cents a pack, $1.90 a carton. I learned to become a heavy smoker in the Army. If I ever get lung cancer I plan to sue the Pentagon. I finally kicked the putrid habit in college. I still miss smoking to this day. So Michael Gideon, the anti-hero in my novels, smokes!

Our toilet facilities were a nightmare. I am not shy. I can take a piss in front of anyone; but the other. That should be a private affair. In the U. S. Army of 1957, it was not. The latrine is the worst. A long trough-like urinal lines the wall. As if the soldiers were horses, lining up to drink instead of pee. There are six toilets—all open. No stalls. You want to take a leisurely crap in the morning right after breakfast? There are a hundred guys in the second platoon in your barracks with the same human urge. And six lousy toilets! One of the worst Army things is to be sitting on the pot with about a dozen guys in line standing right in front of you yelling for you to hurry the fuck up because the First Sergeant is about to shout, "Fall out!" If you have not moved your bowels, then you are forced to hold it in through a full morning of training until you get back to the barracks for lunch. And then the long line is there again. If you have never been forced to crap in front of a large unappreciative and impatient audience, you don't know what you're missing. Showers are just as impersonal. Don't ever drop your soap in the barracks shower!

Even though they awakened us between 3:30 and 4:30 A.M. every morning, time is a major problem. They are always rushing us. Where? Why? They never say. It is no fun to awaken in the dark and watch the sun come up every day. PT (Physical Training) while it is still dark. By the end of the cycle I can do 100 pushups. I never do pushups again after 1957.

For some reason that I could never fathom the Army was hell-bent on taking every ounce of our humanity, dignity and individuality. I can easily understand that, in a tough combat situation, a well-trained soldier must put aside his individual needs to fight with his comrades as a unit. I just never understand why taking a good shit or a hot shower in private could have anything remotely to do with winning a battle...or a war.

I wrote Arlene every single day. She wrote me every single day. Mail-call was the high water mark of my day. If, somehow, the letters get backed up and there was a day I didn't receive a letter, I was sorely depressed. Of course, the next day there were two letters. The guys kidded me relentlessly because the envelope usually had a lipstick SWAK (Sealed with A Kiss) on the back. I didn't care about the ribbing. Arlene's letters were steady as clockwork. No "Dear John" for this trooper. I felt bad for some of the guys whose girls or wives back home were not as faithful. Some of these guys were married as teens. Mom wrote about once a week. Pop never writes. Not even once. Mom always says hello for Pop who, in his long life, rarely displayed any public emotion about anything. Pop doesn't have to write. For some reason, unlike my brother, I always know. My Aunt Nan Goldman (Pop's older sister) wrote every week. She also sent stamps with every letter as if I was stranded on the moon. I wrote to the folks and Nan about once a week. Letters from home became my lifeline. Do people still write letters to soldiers? I have no idea.

My brother Kenny doesn't seem to know I have left. Ken is only eleven and always wanted my room! That six-year gap between us is an ocean too wide for either of us to navigate until adulthood. I never realized until that summer how much I loved my family; with all their craziness. I missed them. I began to understand that we all take family for granted. I can't begin to imagine them no longer there. I never take my family for granted again. I rarely missed Thanksgiving or Passover for the rest of their lives. Was I finally growing up? Or, was I just like some of those crybaby fat guys who cycle out because they can't cut it.

Years later Arlene tells me that her husband (then her ex-husband) takes all my letters from the Army and throws them down a sewer in a jealous rage. So, there is no record of my day-to-day activities at Fort Knox. I stopped keeping my journal on the second day. I am too exhausted at night to record the events of the day after I do it in my daily letter to Arlene.

I have never been much of a correspondent since my Army days. I don't relish the idea of another insecure asshole destroying my love letters and ripping up my most personal and private thoughts and emotions.

During the week, we had no opportunity to make phone calls. There are no phones in or near the barracks. The only contact permitted with friends and family is on Sundays when we hiked to "The Phone Center" where we were allowed to stand in a long line for an operator, write down the number we want to call (reversing the charges, of course) and then move to a private phone where we waited for the operator to put our call through. The Phone Center was always a mob scene and, in my mind, another nonsensical obstacle that the United States Army stupidly put in the average soldier's path to come between loneliness and his ability to reach out to friends and family. In 1957 there were no videos, tape recorders or cell phones to make life easier. I think maybe it was better that those technological devices did not exist. We had to endure loneliness and…well, we did. The daily difficulties forced us to grow up. Our generation was a lot better off growing up without the intrusiveness of technology. To this day I do not carry a cell phone; except when I am out on my boat doing some off-shore fishing alone in Maine. You never know when you might need the Coast Guard!

The physical training was difficult. But at seventeen I was in the best shape of my life. I am rail thin, weigh in at maybe 130 pounds and have a 28 inch waist. I am about 5'7 inches tall. Over the next six months I put on ten to fifteen pounds and grow a couple inches. I become me.

Years of schoolyard baseball, basketball, horseback riding and running from the Philly cops through the back alleys of Wynnefield held me in good stead. When they dragged our tired asses out of the rack for a forced fifteen-mile field march with full back pack, a 9.5 pound M-1 rifle and full field gear, I marched on by some of the fatter guys who fall down in the dusty road wheezing and weeping, refusing to go on in the 95-plus degree heat of a Kentucky July and August.

A fat guy from Ohio in the Fourth Platoon who actually resembled Private "Gomer Pyle" (played brilliantly by Vincent D'Onofrio) in Stanley Kubrick's *Full Metal Jacket* is always being picked on by the drill sergeants. He can't climb the obstacle course. They deride him. He forgets to take his salt pills on a forced march and throws up. They make him stand there with the vomit running down his field shirt. This guy, we all realized, isn't going to make it. Better him than us. Nobody complained or stuck up for him. He cycled out on a Section 8 before the first three weeks were up. I made every forced march—even the ordeals up (and down) Heartbreak Hill which had achieved legendary status in Fort Knox. I took my salt pills but carefully rationed the water in my canteen. I wanted to see how far I could push myself without a drink. I can still go without water for a longer time than most people.

Don't get me wrong. I was not a good soldier. In fact, if truth be known, I was one of the worst soldiers in the Second Platoon. My bed was never taut enough; my foot locker was usually in messy disarray;

my boots rarely sparkled even when I spit-shined them; something was always wrong on my uniform; I didn't salute correctly; I couldn't break my M-1 down quickly enough or put it back together. The First-sergeant always found a dirt spot in the barrel of my rifle, a dust bunny under my locker or dirt smudges on my window sill.

I was a complete fuckup when it came to the daily bullshit of soldiering. But, when it came to the physical stuff, I was virtually unstoppable—as I became a trained killer who can march (but not in step), hike, run, climb, crawl, shoot and toss a hand grenade accurately.

Our platoon was very fortunate. We had two really terrific Non-Coms—Master Sergeant Laracuente is the Second Platoon's First-sergeant. A pint-sized Puerto Rican veteran of World War II and Korea, he had seen a great deal of action in both the European and Pacific theaters. It was only a dozen years since we kicked ass in Germany and Japan. He was a tough man but also a kind and patient drill sergeant. With me he had to be patient; very patient.

Our other Sergeant, if you can believe it, was even nicer. Percy Cochise Bassett was a small, wiry Negro and although he too was a tough, seasoned World War II and Korea combat vet, Bassett really cared about his troops—especially the wise-ass, younger city kids. Bassett was, like me, from Philadelphia. With that in common, he sort of took me under his wing and did his best to overlook my many fuckups. One night Bassett, who lived in a private room off our floor, was bullshitting with his guys about his combat adventures. He told us that he was once on patrol on an atoll in the Pacific and moving silently down a jungle trail at daybreak when he spied a single Japanese soldier cooking his morning meal. Bassett watched him eat as the grayness of dawn turned into morning. The Japanese soldier finished his breakfast and walked into the woods where Bassett watched him drop his pants to take a shit. "What did you do?" an enthralled chorus of eager young recruits asked. "Do?" Sergeant Bassett smiled cunningly, pausing for maximum effect. "I sited that little Nip in the crosshairs of my Carbine. Then, when the little bastard had his pants down, I shot his mother-fucking ass off! Is what I did. But I let him finish his breakfast. Lucky I saw him before he saw me."

But disaster befell Sergeant Percy Bassett right in the middle of our training cycle. For reasons he never explained, Bassett stole a car on post and went AWOL (Absent Without Leave). The speculation was that he had to see a lady about something. He never tells. When he returned, the MPs arrested him and he was taken to the stockade. Released until his court martial, Bassett returned to the Company. He seemed a sadder man. Bassett was tried before our cycle was completed, busted down to Private and sentenced by the military court to time in the stockade. On the day he left, we threw him a little going-away beer bash. But we were all very sad. Of all the soldiers in the Second Platoon, I missed him the most.

Bassett had kept the lion from my door. He leaves. I never saw or heard from him again. We all silently hope that Bassett is not replaced by any of the other drill sergeants in Company A. The sergeants in the other platoons are all mean, *Biloxi Blues*-type bastards. Master-Sergeant Guerett, a Korean vet, was a tall, lanky, bigoted southerner. He called the Negro soldiers "dark-faced man." He called me "pimple-faced man." Not even the good-old-boys escaped Guerett's evil wrath. Sergeant-First-Class Caufield was another mean prick. He called troopers "red faced man" or "jack-off bumps man." These guys were always harassing us by trying to scare us about the next "big war." They talked about shooting a man as if it was a sport. It is clear to one and all that they can't wait until they are back in combat. The next war, they took great joy in constantly reminding us, was "just around the corner."

Unfortunately, they were right. They bragged endlessly about all the "gooks" they killed in Korea (Koreans having had the distinction of that label long before anyone ever heard about Viet Nam). They never tired telling us how much they hate "the Commies;" it never occurred to any of us that these dullards didn't have the foggiest notion of what a "Commie" actually was. We certainly didn't. In a few years these guys would be in their heavenly glory in Southeast Asia.

They finally got their war courtesy of Kennedy, Johnson and the generals—those lying sack-of-shit generals and technocrats like Robert McNamara, JFK's and Johnson's lickspittle Secretary of Defense. Our leaders combined their overweening talent and ambition in the 1960s and 1970s to put over 50,000 American soldiers like us up on a damn wall in Washington, D.C. God only knows how many ended up in Veteran's Hospitals or broken for life on the streets of America. Forty years later McNamara and the rest tell us they made a huge mistake in Viet Nam.

But *their* names, curiously enough, are nowhere to be seen on the Wall. There are some times in life when "Sorry!" or *"mea culpa"* just doesn't cut it. Viet Nam was one of those times. I taught about that war at Boston University in my course on John F. Kennedy for many years. I went on to write two biographies of the men who led us in those years: John F. Kennedy and Richard M. Nixon.

Sergeant Laracuente, who had obviously experienced the difficulties of being a minority in the Army of the 1950's, saw the shortcomings of the other sergeants. He didn't put in to our Company Commander, a young ROTC Lieutenant by the name of William S. Schmidt, for a replacement. The Second Platoon trained for the rest of our cycle with but a single drill sergeant. There are no non-coms in the barracks after lights out. And although Sergeant Laracuente was a good man, unlike Percy Bassett, he could not keep the lion from my door.

CHAPTER 19

The soldiers in Company A were a diverse collection made up of very distinct groups: five urban types consisted of the Jewish, Irish, Italian, Polish and Negro guys from big cities; the urban blacks got along pretty well with these urban whites. But it is in the second group where some troubles arose: southern Negroes were much different than their northern brethren and the rural southern Whites are different from everybody. A large number of rural Pennsylvania and some Ohio goobers, added to the urban-rural mix, didn't help the situation.

The rural soldiers at Knox were guys who think they died and hit heaven on the way. They did not seem to mind the terrible food so aptly described in *Biloxi Blues* as something against which you are forced to defend yourself. I often watched incredulously at mess as they heaped large piles of greasy crap they called food on their silver trays. The burnt meat cannot be identified as to what the species had once been. The goobers didn't seem to care. This was gourmet dining as far as they are concerned. They are all wide smiles and "Golly gees!" Nor did they mind the rigorous physical training that was a constant source of agony to most of the rest of us; or the hours; or the bullshit. To them, this dumb-ass army was one ongoing country picnic.

Growing up in Philly I had been exposed to very few extreme forms of overt prejudice.

Nobody had ever called me a "dirty Jew," and I never heard the word "Kike" uttered in high school by any kid, Black or White, Christian or Jew. Nobody ever threw pennies at me in school. If they had, I would have put the pennies toward a big Philly soft pretzel with mustard at Joe-Ex-Soldier. My friend Larry Laster used to wear a leather jacket with a red Jewish star taped to the back. He did that, he said, to see if anyone would respond. As I recall, he had his ass kicked once or twice. But then Larry Laster was always a difficult guy who looked for trouble.

Pop often told me tales about growing up in South Philly when Jewish kids were fair game as "Christ Killers." In the 1920s, my Pop said, Jewish kids were often warned to stay away from Church yards and Christians especially around Easter. To me, they were Pop stories.

Stationed in the South at a number of army bases, I learned quickly about the evils of segregation. We could not drink in the same bars, stay in the same hotels, go to the same movie theaters or eat in the same restaurants in Louisville as the Negro soldiers with whom we lived, trained and served.

It was the same in Richmond, Virginia when I was stationed at Fort Lee in nearby Petersburg. It was also true in Indianapolis, Indiana at Fort Benjamin Harrison. Years later I learned that in the "Roaring Twenties," Indiana was a hotbed of Ku Klux Klan organization and violence.

The Armed Forces, desegregated for only a decade by the political courage of President Harry Truman in 1947, couldn't control what happened to servicemen off post. The Negro soldiers in Company A could fight and die for their country; they just couldn't get a decent burger with a bottle of cold suds or a fine room at the famous Brown Hotel in downtown Louisville where many of us went on our first weekend pass midway into Basic Training.

Although I was unaware then of the racial history behind all this, faced with segregation for the first time, I hardly needed a college professor to clue me in on its abject evil. Of course, I was aware of the Holocaust because of what I had learned in Hebrew school and seen in the movies—though the word "Holocaust" itself was not yet in vogue. I had read two excellent books: the French scholar, Leon Poliakov's *Harvest of Hate*, and a rare book entitled *Plot Against the Peace*. Both offered sufficient evidence and information about what the Nazis had done to the Jews of Europe. But Europe and the American South were a long way off from West Philly and my insulated little neighborhood. I must admit that I rarely gave American race relations or the fate of millions of European Jews more than a passing thought by the time I turned seventeen to enter the service. I was only two years away from American Bandstand.

The rural whites in Company A from western Pennsylvania, Ohio and Kentucky were an alien group to a Jewish kid from the big city in 1957. While not all of these soldiers fit the stereotype we had back then of a card-carrying Ku Kluxer, some of them were not far off the mark.

Most, although very different from soldiers like me from cities, just wanted to get through all the military tedium like the rest of us, with as little hassle as possible. At the same time, there were a handful of soldiers who were bigots to the core of their being. These characters had never lived in any proximity to Negroes and they damn sure didn't know any Jews.

Interestingly enough, their ethnic roots seemed to be German or maybe Pennsylvania Dutch. The bigots in Company A were cowards as well. Because they assiduously avoided the Negro soldiers like the plague. They avoided them for two reasons: they didn't like them; and they were wary of them. They knew if they hassled a Negro soldier in Company A, that they might have had their heads handed to them on a platter—especially from the street-savvy urban Negroes who knew how to use their fists and took no shit from anyone except our tough drill sergeants. Out of about 200 men in the company, ten soldiers were Negroes.

The Jewish soldiers in Company A were something else. Most were college graduates in their early twenties eager to get their military obligation out of the way and get on with life. They enlisted in the Army to write their own ticket and, at the same time, avoid the draft which would have held up their lives for at least two years or more. In 1957, Israel was not even a decade old and the image of Jews as gritty desert warriors depicted in Otto Preminger's 1960 film *Exodus* (from a bestseller by West Philadelphian Leon Uris) had not yet emerged from the ashes of the Great Destruction. The rural bozos stereotyped the Jewish soldiers: you can say anything you want to a Jew and he won't fight back because all Jews are "pussies" and "fairies." You can pick on a Jew and he will take it because a Jew will chicken out before ever stepping up to go behind the barracks to fight. They obviously didn't know any Jews from West Philly.

Aside from two Pennsylvania farmers, I didn't have much trouble with the guys on our floor. I stayed out of the way of the two farmers who always seemed to do their best to imitate Gomer Pyle whenever they spoke to one another. The two guys must have come into the army under the same buddy deal as my friend Lenny Ivker and me. They lived somewhere in western Pennsylvania, they were cousins (whose parents had probably married siblings!) and they bunked together. You rarely saw one of these goobers without the other. They called one another "Abner" all the time—a take-off, I imagined, of the famous Al Capp cartoon hillbilly character "Lil Abner." I was certain that they never had a clue that Al Capp was a Jew.

Their names (and this I checked) were Kermit R. Fluck and Richard W. Furst. I didn't like the Cousins "Abner" Furst-Fluck very much but they pretty much avoided me just like they avoided the Negro guys in the barracks. As long as they didn't bother me, their grating hayseed act, and I was pretty sure it was an act, didn't mean much of anything.

However, on the first floor there was a western Pennsylvania soldier by the name of Richard Hilbert. Hilbert, who hung out with the Abner twins, was always making cracks about Jews under his breath. His wisecracking bigotry seemed to delight his audience of the flunky Abners. But nobody ever called Hilbert on it. And since Hilbert weighed in easily at 200 plus pounds with his shaved bullet head and close-set eyes, resembling a highland mountain gorilla or a burly psycho from the Cuckoo's Nest, I was not about to take him on at 120 pounds soaking wet. If the older Jewish guys could take his anti-Semitic bullshit for nine weeks, I could live with it too. No hero, I did my best to avoid him. Some of the older Jewish guys noticed Hilbert's overt anti-Semitism and even discussed taking on Dick Hilbert and his two Abner stooges. But they were not heroes either.

It was just barracks talk. Nobody ever challenged Richard Hilbert.

Two of the older guys, Harry Forrest, an Irish-Catholic from Chester, Pennsylvania and Irv Green, a bookish Penn State graduate who thought J.D. Salinger was God, intervened at one point, warning the two Abners to stop hassling me. I don't recall what I did that bothered them, but it was probably something to do with my lousy soldiering and did not, as far as I can recall, have anything to do with me being Jewish. But the two Abners didn't like me. That much was clear.

And *that* had a lot to do with me being Jewish. There was bad blood between me and the two Abners almost from day one but nothing ever happened. We kept our mutual distance.

Harry Forrest and Irv Green, both over 22, kind of adopted me. They saw me as a little kid who somehow made a very bad decision that ended up in the Army. They were both at least five years older and had seen a lot more of the world than me. Rather than face the draft, Harry left a good job with Sunoco in Chester. He hoped it would be there when he got out. Irv was a recent graduate from Penn State. He seemed to be trying to figure out what to do with the rest of his life. He too, like many of the older guys in Company A, didn't want to be drafted. The President of the United States was Dwight D. Eisenhower. For five years he had kept the nation out of war.

Without a war, the army was monotonous and dull. Everybody wanted to be a short timer. As I said, I was far from a perfect soldier. I was not even a good soldier. In fact, if truth be told, when it came to real soldiering, I was a lot closer to Curly, Larry and Moe than to John Wayne or Gary Cooper. One of my friends still kids me that if they had sent me to Nam, that I would have thrown my typewriter at the Viet Cong and run.

Actually, I never had a typewriter in the Army.

The morning I remember best during Basic Training started off badly as I got myself into some difficulty in the mess hall at breakfast with a fat-ass mess Sergeant because I reached over to another table for a carton of milk when I noticed that there was no carton of milk where I was sitting. Perhaps I somehow should have known that reaching over for a milk carton was a definite firing squad offense. But I did not.

This fat-ass cook, a mess Sergeant by the name of Richburg, was a mean-spirited, nasty, pock-faced Negro with two big gold teeth in the front of his mouth. Everybody in Company A feared KP because for twenty-four hours your ass belonged solely to old Sergeant Richburg.

If Richburg wasn't 'Fatso' Judson from James Jones's *From Here to Eternity*, he was damn close.

Unfortunately Richburg saw me grab the milk carton and he proceeded to bring a case of milk over to my table. I can still recall those big gold front teeth breaking into a Cheshire cat-like grin. I smiled back.

Richburg read my shirt name and said, "You like milk Private Gold-brick-man?" I answered, "Yes Sergeant!" loud and clear. Whereby, Richburg then ordered me to drink the entire case since I obviously had this thing for milk.

As an adult looking back over this incident I can see a lot of humor. As a seventeen-year-old on a sweltering Kentucky mid-August morning, nothing is funny about it. So I began to drink the fucking milk.

By the fifth carton I gave up and Richburg now had my ass. He happily put me on KP (Kitchen Patrol) for the rest of the day—which really hurt because it was a Saturday and in the Army, Saturday was only a half-day; even during Basic Training.

After lunch I was planning to grab a bus to Louisville with some of the guys. So now I was on KP well into the evening. No half-day Saturday. No Louisville. No cold beers. No burgers.

One of the most unpleasant experiences I have ever known is KP. It was not only boring and exhausting but the kitchen non-coms were mostly all mean and stupid bastards like Richburg. It was as if they drove a bus through Fort Knox and rounded up the dumbest pricks they could find.

Then they deposited every mean prick they could find in A Company's mess hall.

KP finally ended after Saturday night dinner. Since many soldiers had taken off, the mess traffic was lighter than usual. I had been on kitchen duty for over twelve straight hours. But the mess was finally closing until early Sunday morning. It was too late to catch a bus to town and I was too damn tired anyway. But this asshole Richburg wasn't through with me.

With his two gold-plated front teeth glowing in the Kentucky sunset, Richburg walked me back to the barracks. Once there he ordered me on to LP—Latrine Patrol. By the next morning, this "goddamn latrine," Richburg warned, "better sparkle." Or it was back to KP for me on Sunday!

It was late Saturday night. I was scrubbing the open toilets, the sinks, the long urinal and the grimy shower stalls. Then I mopped down the dark cement floor. I actually got the place sparkling.

I was virtually alone in the barracks. Everybody else had taken off to Louisville. After rendering the latrine in 2nd Platoon virtually spotless, I put up a sign saying that the latrine was "off limits" to all personnel until the wet floor dried and the rest of the cleaning and scrubbing was completed. It was not out of the ordinary for anyone assigned to latrine cleanup to put up the sign. If a trooper wanted to take a leak, he had two choices—the First Platoon or the Third Platoon, a walk of just a few short yards in either direction from our barracks.

I cleaned and scrubbed. I scrubbed and cleaned. All the while I wondered whether or not I had been doomed by an unjust, wrathful and vengeful God or if my unhappy plight was a simple role of the milky dice: Shit! Snake-eyes!

Enter the Jew-hating Richard Hilbert along with his moronic sidekicks, the two Abners.

Hilbert was dressed in his class-A's. The boys must have been in town because they were obviously in good spirits. In the army good spirits are spelled a lot of B-E-E-R. The three goobers are juiced.

Richard Hilbert was a dead ringer for Hoss Cartwright from Bonanza and about just as tiny. Your first instinct on meeting Dick Hilbert was to remove a thorn from his paw. He had a deeply furrowed eyebrow that ran across his forehead in one long line giving the distinct impression that you were face to face with a pre-Paleolithic man engaged in deep but rather vacuous thought about finding raw meat. Hilbert spoke first.

"Whatcha doin', ya little Kike?" he said to me slurring his words.

The two Abners snickered. I was not, however, at a loss for words.

"What's it look like I'm doing you fat pile of shit! You guys will have to wait or go next door to use the head. I'm not finished here," I responded.

"Jewboy, you're finished when we say you're finished. And we say you're finished," Hilbert said smiling nastily.

At that Hilbert whipped out his uncircumcised pecker and squirted a long stream of piss across the room. The piss hit me in the chest, just below my chin. My first reaction was sheer amazement at Hilbert's pissing feat. I have never seen anybody piss that far. I was at least twenty-five feet from Hilbert when he pissed on me. My amazement gave way to anger. Especially as Hilbert joined by the two Abners began to empty their bladders on my newly scrubbed latrine floor. As I looked around, a cloud of anger and humiliation swept over me. My basic philosophy of life has always been that it is better to be pissed off than pissed on!

The nearest object was a bucket of filthy water that smelled like a sewer and one of those old fashioned push-string mops. I grabbed the bucket of water and hurled it at the two Abners soaking them in their spiffy uniforms. Then I took the mop and whacked Hilbert so hard over his bullet head that I broke the mop in two pieces. Hilbert looked at me and he smiled weirdly like Vincent D'Onofrio in Stanley Kubrick's *Full Metal Jacket*. "Duh," he says, "I don't believe you really did that!" He seemed to be unscathed and the mop appeared much more damaged than his fat head.

For a brief moment, the Abners in their soiled uniforms and Hilbert, who seemed oblivious to the pain of getting whacked over the head by a wooden mop, stood there in total disbelief. I was as amazed at my reaction as my antagonists. I guess it was a good thing I didn't have my M-1 out of its rack! Then maybe I really would have pulled a Private Pyle.

I threw a hard right at one of the Abners as they moved on me. It didn't come close to landing. My second swing, a left, caught Kermit Fluck right in the puss. He howled in pained surprise as the three drunks then began to take turns using me as a punching bag. When they were finished pummeling me after a few minutes, they left me in a heap on the urine-soaked latrine floor.

I never told any of the guys in the platoon what went on that night. Getting pissed on was not one of the high spots of my military experience. Fortunately, Sergeant Richburg neglected to come back to inspect the latrine. He had either forgotten the milk incident or didn't really care. He left me alone for the rest of basic and rarely even acknowledged my presence. I pulled KP on one more occasion, but Richburg didn't seem to know I was alive and KP, though still exhausting, took no further toll on my battered psyche. The lard-ass cook must have just been having a bad day when he singled me out over the milk carton and, unlike me, seemed to have forgotten the incident entirely.

Basic Training proceeded uneventfully as August mercifully gave way to September. In late September we had a pleasant graduation ceremony as the soldiers in Company A awaited reassignment. But there was one thing: Richard Hilbert, Kermit Fluck and Richard Furst stayed out of my way for the rest of the cycle. And I never heard them make another nasty crack about Jews within earshot of any soldier in our platoon for the remainder of boot camp. Sometimes getting cracked over the head with a dirty wet mop concentrates the mind and leaves lasting and indelible memories.

CHAPTER 20

In late September we received our orders. Most of the soldiers in the company opted for two weeks leave. But we (Lenny Ivker and me) were given an immediate assignment to Fort Benjamin Harrison for advanced training in—get this—Finance. Fort Harrison, just outside Indianapolis, Indiana was the headquarters for the entire army's finance operations. Why they decided to send a math-deficient seventeen-year-old to accounting classes was beyond me. Later, I learned it was the heavy hand of Louie Goldman reaching into my life to see that I do not fire weapons any more than I have to and to prepare me for the good life in my Cousin Len Glickman's CPA firm in Philly. What did I know? I might as well be an accountant as anything else. Of course, in 1957 I had no idea in the world what an accountant actually did for a living. I think if I had known what a life in accounting would be like, I may well have grabbed my M-1 and turned it toward my head. To me, accounting was spelled B-O-R-I—N-G!

Since Colonel Clark's outfit is in Finance, Lenny Ivker and I found ourselves heading to Indianapolis by Greyhound bus on September 20, 1957. The closeness with which we enlisted together in 1956 had evaporated. We had been friends since kindergarten. But in the Army Lenny became a moody bastard. We grew distant. After the next few months in Indiana, Lenny Ivker and I went our separate way for over forty years. We were finally reunited in 1998 as we turned 60 when my parents and his mother Francis ended up at the same assisted care facility on the Main Line outside Philadelphia.

Fort Ben, as we called it, was beautiful in the late summer-early autumn. The trees in the deep woods surrounding the base were turning deep reds and bright golden yellows. One amazing thing about our new post was the barracks which were more like college dorms. Instead of living on top of one another, we are billeted three men to a room in handsome three-floor brick buildings. Three men to a room in this man's Army is the Plaza Hotel. Also, the latrines are like normal bathrooms. Wonder of wonders. Enclosed toilets in the Army! No more crapping before a cheering or jeering audience!

But the best thing about Fort Ben was the mess hall. It was more like a restaurant. Instead of those long sterile wooden tables, there were tables for four with linens and glassware put out. And the food is actually palatable. Baskets of fresh fruit adorn each table with every meal, milk or a variety of juices in glasses (not cartons!) and decent chow. After nine weeks at Fort Knox, Fort Ben is heaven to the new troops. An army resort. Like the Poconos or the Catskills.

Because we arrived at our next duty assignment without taking leave, we will have the option for early release, if we choose, before Christmas. By giving up two weeks of paid leave, we may get an entire month off with pay; a pretty good deal. All in all, Fort Harrison was the most un-army-like army post I have ever seen. We still have to fall out for reveille every morning. But the bugle usually doesn't sound until five-thirty. After weeks of being jolted awake between 3:30 and 4 A.M. by shrill shouts from hard-ass drill sergeants, sleeping to five-thirty was a great luxury. And being gently awakened by the soft strains of the piped in patriotic music was an added bonus every morning.

Why the world of difference? Most of us didn't think to even ask. But looking back at Fort Ben in 1957 it occurs to me now that there were very substantive reasons that Fort Benjamin Harrison, Indiana was a galaxy removed from Kentucky. For one thing, there were a couple of WAC detachments on post. Other than the few civilian women who worked on post at Knox, I never saw a female on the base. At Fort Ben, women go to the same classes as the guys. But the reason, I always believed that Fort Ben was such a show place, was the fact that there was a full detachment of foreign officers training on the base. We rarely came into contact with these soldiers. They took mess at different hours than we did. They trained in other parts of the base. At night, in our time off, wherever we went, they did not. They wore uniforms similar to our own. Their insignia, however, were different. We would see these soldiers as we went to mess, or sometimes when we were in class, they would march by the building in close formation. They never spoke to us and the most we got was a smile or a nod when we passed them by in the company streets. They were from a place called Viet Nam. At the time, I had never heard of Viet Nam although I knew it had to be somewhere in Asia near China.

I did not know the first thing about Southeast Asia or what the hell these officers (and they were all officers) were doing in their training at Fort Harrison. I did not even know where Viet Nam was located on the map; or the difference between the North and South. I did not know of a Ho Chi Minh or a thing about the Viet Cong. I suspect that I was in good company and that very few Americans knew very much about Viet Nam or that we were training (secretly?) their burgeoning officer class. It was, after all, 1957! Years before JFK decided to send 15,000 American advisers to Southeast Asia, sinking the United States into a swampy morass from which the nation, at this writing, has yet to recover. And for which Kennedy has been largely given a pass—though not by me in my second book, *John F. Kennedy: Portrait of a President.* Centuries from now, when some future Edward Gibbon-type traces the decline and fall of the "American Empire," it is a good bet that he will start with America's misadventures in Viet Nam and the major fuckup that was the Kennedy presidency. Camelot? Just some lame bullshit concocted by Jackie Kennedy and bought hook, line and sinker by the late Theodore White!

The days at Fort Harrison are long and boring as the warmth of September gave way to the chillier days of October and November. I did not do very well in Finance School and ultimately flunk most of the exams except typing. As a result, the Army seemed to have no idea what to do with me. I was called before a board made up of majors and colonels.

They questioned me intensely about my failure to adjust to the finance coursework they offer. My IQ, they state, is high enough that my performance in the Fin-School appears deliberate.

They demanded to know if I am flunking the exams intentionally. I don't recall what I answered. I did not do poorly intentionally. My failure in Army Finance School came naturally. I remember not being at all intimidated by all the old guys with the fruit salad on their uniforms.

My attitude, like so many other classroom experiences from high school, was basically, "Fuck it!" The officer's board seemed perplexed. For my part, I could not understand what the big deal was all about. To me, Finance School and arranging endless columns of numbers in the right order by hand was a giant crock of shit. I must have really pissed these guys off because they forwarded a very negative report back to Colonel Clark and I was eventually bounced, to the consternation of my embarrassed father, out of the outfit back home and reassigned to a line infantry reserve outfit—the 79th Infantry Division.

Turns out I was right. Computers soon replaced the hand-posting crap they taught us for eight hours a day over four long months. Within a few years the Finance course was totally obsolete and irrelevant! Last I heard Fort Benjamin Harrison and the Army Finance Center had been shut down by Congress in one of their numerous base cost-cutting moves.

Meanwhile, in what appeared to be some sort of retribution, I was pulled out of all classes and assigned to the base Post Office; which turned out to be a pretty good deal. I was given a Jeep to pick up the mail on base twice a day. After delivering the mail for sorting and posting, there was very little for me to do. So I picked up a paperback at the PX, *From Here to Eternity* by James Jones, and read it cover to cover while on duty. I am struck by Robert E. Lee Pruitt and Angelo Maggio. The Army treated them like shit…and yet they still loved it as an American institution. The Army I was in was not that far removed from the 1941 Army James Jones described so brilliantly in his classic work. Since I hadn't seen the film version with Frank Sinatra and Montgomery Clift, the novel had a major impact on my thinking when it came to the military. Unlike Pru and Maggio, I wasn't going to be defeated by the Army and their attempt to stifle all individuality. I decided then and there in the waning weeks of 1957 to get out while the getting was good. I decided to do what my parents and Arlene's mother wanted me to do—go to college.

My Post Office assignment had other benefits as well. The class I started Finance School with was assigned to bivouac in the field—to the field in December! Living in tents and freezing their asses off while I was living in my cozy, warm private room by myself in the lap of military luxury.

The only downside was that I had to pull KP and guard duty. And my luck was to pull KP on Thanksgiving Day. But, wonder of wonders, you were permitted to sell your KP assignments. I found some hillbilly soldier who wasn't going home for the holidays, slipped him twenty bucks and I was off the hook. The only problem was that if you are listed for KP you could not get a legitimate pass to leave the base. No problem. I went home anyway. Thanksgiving had always been a major festivity in my family since childhood. My father and his closest boyhood friends, Frank and Esther Rudney and Joe and Lil Stein, always alternated the dinners after taking all the kids to the big Thanksgiving Day Parade along Broad Street. I had never missed one of these dinners in my life and I was not about to allow the Army to break my record. Even after the year 2000, though everybody except for my Mom was dead, we still had those annual Thanksgiving dinners at Dr. Barry and Arlene Halpern's house. Arlene was the eldest daughter of Frank and Esther Rudney. Sadly, the Rudneys died within a week of one another in 1980. My Pop lived for almost twenty years without his best pal and missed him every day of all those years.

Joe Stein, Pop's other pal, died in the late 1980s. But happily, the dinners went on until all the kids were well into adulthood. And I never missed one of them. The Halperns and the Garfinkles (Maxine Rudney married Dr. Jerry Garfinkle) and all their kids were like family to me.

I located a career army guy on base who had decided to drive to Philly from Indianapolis for the holidays. On the Wednesday before Thanksgiving 1957, I took off for Philly by car—a long seventeen-hour trip. I was what the Army would call AWOL—Absent without Leave.

But I had taken care of my KP, the Army didn't know I was gone and I sure as hell wasn't about to tell them. When I told my father he was apoplectic. Wasn't I ever going to buckle down? What if I was caught? I would end up in an Army prison. I would never be able to get a government job or even go to college or law school. Pop was always a worrier. I was not. I got a big kick out of beating the Army's stupid rules and regulations. They had a saying on most bases in those days. It was not "Hoo-aah!" It was FTA—F—the Army!

Back in Philly, I blissfully reunited with Arlene Rachman after the Thanksgiving dinner at the Rudneys who lived just around the corner from her on Woodbine Avenue. That Friday night we went bowling with all the gang at 54th and City Line and on Saturday night we headed downtown for dinner at the Pub and to see Pat Boone in his new mushy film, *April Love*. I was happier than I had felt for months. My journal entry reads, "...I feel so happy. Its (sic) great to be home with Arlene and the folks again..."

I was a soldier on leave for the first time in five months, at home with his loving family and with his girl. Like Dion sang, "A Teenager in Love." After the movie we walked hand-in-hand down Chestnut Street passing scores of West Point cadets and midshipmen from the Naval Academy in Annapolis who came to Philly for the annual Army-Navy game at Penn's Franklin Field. Dressed in civvies, with my closely cropped hair the only clue to my military status, I was silently amused that these future doofus officers didn't know they were walking by one badass AWOL. Besides brilliantly making up for five loveless months that weekend, Arlene pushed me: she wanted to know about my future plans.

What plans? I have no plans. Would I be coming back to Philly for Christmas and New Years? What about college? What about us? Where are we going? Arlene Rachman was only in the tenth grade. Today, I look at my grandkids who are just thirteen and sixteen and I get the shakes.

They are just beyond being little kids; children. What was I thinking? What was she thinking? I can't recall. But I do know that I genuinely loved her. I do know that I wanted to be with her and if that meant marriage...well then. Of course, her mother was right. Neither of us had a clue about life or responsibility. I am a seventeen year-old schmuck in an itchy army suit.

You will recall Charolotte Cutler, the well-developed girl down the block at 56th and Diamond. In the middle of basic training, Jack

Pomerantz, a guy I knew from my graduating class at Overbrook High School, was whisked out of Fort Knox and sent packing back to Philly in the middle of his basic training. Apparently, he had knocked up Charlotte Cutler. He returned home to marry her. She was fifteen; he was seventeen; they become Brenda and Eddie in the Billy Joel song, "Scenes from an Italian Restaurant." They marry. They have a baby girl. The next year they have another kid, a boy. By seventeen Charlotte Cutler, who has dropped out of school, is alone facing life with two infants. A few years ago I ran into one of her best friends in Atlantic City. I asked about Charlotte Cutler. I was told that her daughter, a young woman, had committed suicide. Charlotte, I found out, remained alone. Talk about the curse of being well developed with large breasts at twelve.

The positive results of that wonderful weekend were twofold: first, I didn't get caught being AWOL. I returned to Fort Harrison without incident and resumed my budding military career as post mailman. Second, while I was in Philly I sent in the forms for the SATs that were to be held in early December in Indianapolis at Shortridge High School, a school made famous by Boston writer Dan Wakefield in his classic coming of age first novel, *Going All the Way*. Ironically, I would get to know Wakefield, a transplanted Bostonian, decades later in my early years as a professional journalist and writer in Boston.

Nothing of great import took place during the rest of my time at Fort Harrison. My two closest friends at Fort Ben were both Negroes: Gerald LaGarde, a street-savvy guy from New Orleans. He was a tall, light-skinned Creole and very handsome. I really liked this guy as we spent many hours talking about life, love and...life. LaGarde always called me "Goldy." Gerry made the classic mistake of signing up for three or four years and was supremely unhappy under the tight constraints of military existence. He was doing his level best to get out from under his long military obligation by acting crazy and trying to convince the people in charge that he was a genuine crazy—in the Army, if the powers that be determine that you are nuts, it is called a "Section 8." Gerry gets his Section 8. I can't recall what he pulled. But he was released and returned to his hometown of New Orleans. We corresponded for a while but I never saw him again. I thought of him down there when Hurricane Katrina hit a few years back.

My other friend was Marshall B. Randall, Jr., a dark-complexioned Negro from a tiny rural town called Hardeeville, somewhere near the Great Pee Dee River in South Carolina. Randy and I became inseparable after Gerry LaGarde left the post. We took all of our meals together and, since I enjoyed a large empty single room, Randy became a bunkmate.

Randy had graduated from a small Negro college and then, to avoid the draft, he signed up for a three-year hitch. He was a first-rate soldier and he wanted much more than the Army could offer him as a Private. In 1957 the Army had only been integrated for a little more than a decade and there was not much upward mobility for Negroes beyond the ranks of the non-commissioned class of Sergeant. This was not yet the Army of Colin Powell.

But Randy would not be denied. He applied for OCS (Officer's Candidate School) somewhere in Kansas or Nebraska and was ultimately accepted. The last letter I received from Randy, about a year later in Philly, is signed "Lieutenant Marshall B. Randall, Jr." So, I am happy to report, Randy made it. If being stationed in Alaska over a three-year hitch is making it.

But life in the United States Army is definitely not for me. Somebody else will have to stop the Commies. I wanted civilian clothes, longer hair and I missed the streets of Philadelphia something terrible. Not to mention the touch, the smell and the being of my teenage golden goddess.

In early December I took the SATs with a weekend pass; then I did all the necessary paperwork to permit me to muster out of the service by Christmas. Arlene waited for me as she promised. I had decided. My days in the active service of my country would be over. The United States Army and I would soon go our separate ways. I would serve the rest of my time in the Reserves for the next seven years. I was going home to Philly to the life I had always known; and somehow, to please Arlene, her mother and Mom and Pop…to college.

CHAPTER 21

On New Year's Eve 1957-58 I went out with Arlene. After dinner it was actually in. I took her home at around 5 A.M. With my parents and younger brother Kenny in Atlantic City, it turned out to be quite a New Year at my empty house. After dropping Arlene off, I met up with Larry Laster and Al Cohen for a New Year's Day brunch at Murray's deli on 54th Street.

I had two major problems going into the New Year: where to go to college and clothes. I was never much of a clothes horse. I got through three years of high school with one coat (no topcoat, of course!), a black toggle car-coat, and maybe three or four shirts, a couple of pairs of black khakis, jeans and one pair of shoes. I used to borrow the Gansk's black leather motorcycle jacket when I wanted to put out my James Dean effect.

One of the first things Pop did when I returned from the Army was to take me down to Krass Brothers on South Street. When it came to men's clothes, Pop swore by Krass Brothers which was one of those no-frills stores with racks and racks of suits in every conceivable size. It was operated by a bunch of Jewish brothers whose reputation for quality was impeccable in Philadelphia's Jewish sartorial circles: "Good clothes cheap with a tailor on the premises." To prove the fact that Krass Brothers was the place to buy your clothing, the Krass brothers had pictures of themselves with every major show business personality plastered all around the store. If Krass's was good enough for Sammy, Frank and Dean, it was good enough for Louie Goldman's kid and his pals.

We bought jackets, pants, shirts and shoes. Pop was not sending me off to college like he did to high school. I was going to be sharp. My problem was that I had not been admitted to the college I wanted to attend. I had been accepted at Penn State but not to the main campus up in State College past Harrisburg. I would have to attend one of their branches outside of Philly in Ogontz, Pennsylvania. I drove to Ogontz in Pop's car. It was out somewhere past Abington—East Bum-fuck to me—a damn long commute from West Philly. I registered and paid the fees for my freshman semester not at all certain how I would ever make that long drive up and back every day without my own wheels. The commute would have been at least a couple of hours every day and nobody I knew except for Lenny Ivker was going to Penn State mid-semester of 1958. My friend Larry Laster was away in the Air Force and he was dead set on going to Penn State when he returned. But in early '58 it would just be me.

On January 10 I was at our family doctor, Dr. Harry Rubin in West Philly, when Pop called to tell me that a letter had arrived indicating my acceptance to Temple University. The folks at Penn State were kind enough to refund my fees and I wrote Temple back that I was accepting admission to the school as a freshman. Temple was only a twenty-five minute commute from Wynnefield through Strawberry Mansion and many of my friends had already been accepted. Getting a ride to school every day would be no problem. Billy Stamps, a close friend for years who lived directly across the street at 5446 Diamond had a car and we even scheduled many of our classes together. For the first three years of college Billy became my main source of transport to Temple. Although he majored in accounting, eventually becoming a CPA, Billy's first love was always cars.

Today the successful owner of numerous auto agencies in Philly under Fleetway Leasing Inc., he was to become one of my best friends during my college years. We were virtually inseparable and had some wonderful times. It was Billy Stamps who introduced me to the music of Frank Sinatra and for that I still owe him. We would sit in his room in the back of his house, studying accounting, English and history accompanied by Sinatra's new LP, *Come Fly With Me*. We often double-dated (a few years later I even introduced Billy to his wife, Carole Bloch, who I had briefly dated), partied and even spent our spring vacations in Florida coming of age as young adults together at the Boom-Boom Room in Fort Lauderdale in the era of *Where the*

Boys Are. Coming from very modest circumstances, Billy's goal in this life was to become very rich. I am happy to report that he fulfilled that goal; and then some. Billy was somewhat like Don Vito Corleone: everything with Billy was always "just business." His employees in the car business lovingly refer to him as "The Commander."

The reason I had to see Dr. Rubin was deeply disturbing. I always had bad skin in high school. The army's greasy cuisine did little to improve my complexion. I came out of the Army with a face covered with acne that resembled a small pepperoni pizza and there was little Dr. Rubin could do beyond recommending a changed diet and a good dermatologist, one Dr. Morris Samitz. I soon began a long regimen of weekly radiation treatments at Dr. Samitz's Center City Office. Years later *Sixty Minutes* did a segment on the fact that many young patients treated by radiation for a severe acne condition in the fifties were coming down with thyroid cancer. Naturally, I called Dr. Samitz. Of course, he didn't remember me, said that he was now retired and that the best advice he could give me was to seek out the services of a good radiologist. My records, he told me, were no longer around. Since I was close to forty at the time and worried about thyroid cancer because of the stupid treatments I was unwittingly exposed to at the age of seventeen and eighteen, I consulted a close friend in Boston who was a radiologist. He told me that if I was going to get thyroid cancer, it probably would have already appeared. Since the radiation episode, I have had little faith in most doctors. How they could have radiated thousands of teenagers in the fifties without the proper precautions or research is another one of those ongoing medical scandals that has received only passing attention by the lightweight American media. All I know is that the treatments lasted almost a year and that by the time Samitz had finished radiating me, I might as well have been at ground zero in Hiroshima. The good news is that my acne finally cleared up. The bad news is that I glow in the dark.

Aside from Dr.Harry Rubin, who treated our family from the time I was born to the time he died in the 1970s, I have always had little faith in doctors or the medical profession in general. Whether it is birth control pills, hormonal therapy like estrogen or radiation therapy, it seems to me that the doctors go ahead with the treatments and then wait until some Ivy League research team publishes its findings to demonstrate that the treatment causes cancer before they do their best Gilda Radner impersonation—"Never mind!"

College life in the late 1950s and early 1960s was not very exciting. To placate my father I majored in Accounting with a plethora of business oriented subjects. By my junior year I changed my major to Marketing because of the fact that I didn't excel in my Accounting studies and the important fact that I did not want to become an accountant. But clearly, Marketing and business was not to be my forte either.

Temple University back then, in reality, was like the 13th, 14th, 15th and 16th grade. The gang from Harry's with one or two exceptions— Al Cohen and Zatzmo, for example—was at Temple. Stanley Stein, Paul Gansky, Paul Rabinowitz, Jerry Berger, Jerry Borkon, Billy Stamps, Bobby Axelrod, Howie Gleit—all Spoon boys, we were all at Temple together. Some new guys joined the crowd—from Merion, Marty Lustgarten; from the northeast, the Glaberson cousins, Sonny and Arnie; and a guy from the neighborhood, Ellis Zakrov, who we nicknamed Elkie-Moo.

We no longer played the role of West Philly tough guys but we were never the Andy Hardy college-boy types either. We still hung out in our spare time at Harry's shooting eight-ball and we were still pretty much together when we were not with various girlfriends.

Instead of joining one of the numerous Jewish fraternities like AEPi or TEP on the Temple campus, most of us still preferred the warmth and comfort of our dimly lit cocoon in the back room of Harry's that we had known since our early adolescence. We could not imagine a late Saturday night without meeting for our weekly ingathering. Not much had really changed.

Most of us, with few exceptions like the Gansk whose father built a huge new house in Lower Merion on the Main Line, were not from wealthy families. Money for college, even an urban commuter college like Temple, was scarce for most of us. Since most of our classes were finished by early in the afternoon, we could hold part-time jobs to help pay for tuition, books and the other necessities college kids needed in those times. Billy Stamps and Stanley Stein got jobs with small accounting firms in Center City. The Gansk went to work in his father's insurance company. By our junior year the Gansk would marry sweet Sallyann Heisman, his teenage romance, and be ensconced in a spacious two-bedroom apartment in Balwynne Park, a subdivision built in the park right where we used to rent our horses to gallop back into the old neighborhood. The Gansk would never have to worry about money for the rest of his life. In the meantime Woodside Park, Crystal Pool and the ancient horse stable were history. On the same acreage where I had accidentally set that mammoth forest fire in the early 1950s, two new grotesque subdivisions were added to our neighborhood—Balwynne Park and Wynnefield Heights as well as a number of monstrously ugly high rise apartments replaced the last remnants of rural greenery—a part of my Philly boyhood that would now give way to the encroaching urban sprawl. It was the beginning of the end of our Wynnefield but we were all much too busy coming of age to take notice. Woodside Park, a large amusement park with funhouses and roller coasters like the Wildcat, had once been the destination of secure postwar suburbanites on a warm Philly summer night. It would be gone along with the trolley tracks that connected Wynnefield to Strawberry Mansion as carefree riders sat in open-air trolleys that cut through the lush forests of Fairmount Park. I watched the 1950's giving way to the 1960's; the secure world in which I grew up was rapidly disappearing as the warm summers of my lost Philly childhood innocence rapidly waned. And, like me, America would soon be losing its innocence as well.

By today's standards our college tuition was a joke. Pop was able to procure a "senatorial scholarship"—a payoff to the local state senator to put you on his list which was then handed over to Temple for a substantial reduction in tuition. My college costs per semester were never higher than $400. A thousand bucks a year easily covered my four years at Temple University as an undergraduate. After I earned my degree in 1962 I never paid another dime for tuition through a Master's and Doctorate degree.

Within a few months of the start of school most of us were working. As usual, Pop got me my first real job and it would have a pronounced influence on my life.

But Pop allowed me to slide that first semester. I had been a piss-poor student in high school and he didn't want me flunking out of college as a freshman because of money. So, backed by a few bucks I had saved from the Army, I pulled a 2.0 my first semester at Temple, a solid C average, surprising everybody including myself that I didn't flunk out. A lousy D grade in Math was balanced out by a B in history; which was a portent of things to come.

Arlene Rachman, mature beyond her years for a girl in the 11th grade, stayed solidly with and behind me that year. As it appeared that we had made up our minds, even her worried mother finally relented and we were permitted to date as often as we chose. For the first time I even felt welcome in the Rachman home and often had dinner with the family. Arlene's sister, Iris, had graduated Penn with honors and was teaching in the Philly public schools.

Weekends came and weekends went. We were virtually inseparable. We spent the carefree summer of 1958 together in between Philly and Atlantic City. For the first time since I had been a child, I did not accompany my family for our annual vacation down the shore. I remained in the city, took a job and was pretty much self-sufficient except for the weekends when, with Arlene usually in tow, I would show up at my parents rented place on Providence Avenue in Atlantic City.

For some reason I don't recall, I went to summer school and took an introductory course in Sociology. I did not do very well, barely passing. I guess I was so damned used to summer school that I just couldn't break the habit.

That July my Army reserve unit was sent off to Fort Lee not far from Richmond, Virginia. The Virginia summer heat was ungodly. But the training wasn't tough and the new guys in the outfit, mostly from Philly, were easy enough to get along with. The officers and non-Coms were people we knew from Philly and they saw to it that we got a lot of break-time as well as time off post. On July 4th weekend a bunch of us headed to Williamsburg where we rented a room at the Pocahontas Motel, took sumptuous meals at the Williamsburg Inn and toured the colonial sites.

One of the guys, an introspective soldier who had recently graduated from Penn, holed up in our room rather than swimming in the motel pool or touring the sites and, with a borrowed typewriter, wrote a story about a hangman who went from town to town in the old West performing his grisly task. He let me read it when we came back that night. I told him that I thought it was pretty good. "Pretty good!" my pal exclaimed. "I only wrote for Mask and Wig at Penn!"

"What the fuck is Mask and Wig?" I asked. He just laughed at the fact that I didn't have a clue that Mask and Wig, Penn's answer to Harvard's well-known Hasty Pudding, was the famed drama society at the University of Pennsylvania.

That soldier's name was Richard Levinson and he fancied himself a writer. Wordsmiths were not exactly plentiful in my Philly circles but Dick Levinson was an acerbic, funny and very witty fellow. And in that happy summer of 1958 he was my buddy. Dick saw the Army with all its structured rules and formality as a ridiculous absurdity. He had obvious contempt for the non-Coms and officers often using big words which they did not understand when he spoke to them. His wry sense of humor combined with a stinging intellect often flew over the heads of most of the guys not to mention the people who thrived on giving us orders. There was one particular lieutenant, an officer who Dick delighted in pissing off. This young officer was always ass-kissing anyone above the rank of Captain and seemed to have absolute disdain for the enlisted men. Levinson was constantly making fun of this unctuous ROTC schmuck and what was so hilarious about it was the fact that this putz never seemed to have a clue that he was being put on.

Since I often understood what Dick was getting at when he made sport of some of these ROTC Nazis, even though I was four or five years younger than most of the guys, it began to dawn on me that maybe I wasn't as dumb as I had always been led to believe by my high school teachers.

Richard Levinson was one of the brightest guys I ever met to that point in my life. And, if I could hold a conversation with him, well... after all, he *had* graduated from Penn.

Of course, his name may not mean much to you. But I guarantee that you have seen his work. With his lifelong writing partner, William Link, Richard Levinson went on to create a number of unforgettable characters for American television: Mike Connors in *Mannix*, Peter Falk's unique homicide detective *Columbo*, and Angela Lansbury's Jessica Fletcher in *Murder She Wrote*, to name just a few.

Richard Levinson also won a number of Emmys for his TV movies. My particular favorites were *My Sweet Charlie* with Patty Duke and Al Freeman, Jr., who played Elijah Muhammad in Spike Lee's film *Malcolm X*, and *The Execution of Private* Slovik with Martin Sheen. Some years ago I even saw a TV western about a hangman in the old West. When the writing credits came up—you guessed it!—the crawl read, "by Richard Levinson." He once used our military experiences to write a TV film with Hugh "Wyatt Earp" O'Brien about the Army. But that piece of work was not one of his best efforts. Sadly, Richard Levinson left this life much too young.

A co-writer with William Link on numerous films, in the '90s he had a sort of bio-film about him with the great actor James Woods playing a dying writer who very much resembled Richard Levinson. It is a tragicomic film about a dying writer's (non-gay!) loving relationship with his writing partner, actor John Lithgow. The dying writer still laughs in the face of life spitting into the wind of his personal tragedy. Watching that film I found myself tearing up at the end as I realized it was about Dick Levinson. It had to be William Link's homage to his late buddy and longtime creative writing partner.

I returned from Virginia in mid-July and was able to get a job waiting and busing tables at one of the most exclusive restaurants in Philly—Helen Sigel Wilson's well-known restaurant in the park. Helen Wilson was a famous golfer and she and her husband Charles owned a posh restaurant on Walnut Street. In the summers they managed the very exclusive and expensive outdoor eatery high on a hill overlooking the majestic Schuykill River next to the Playhouse in the Park. As a result, I waited on some very well-known celebrities at the time: wealthy Philadelphia builder John B. Kelly (Princess Grace Kelly's father) and his family; Hume Cronyn and Jessica Tandy; Gig Young, who always seemed to play second banana to leading men like Clark Gable, and other famous actors ate for a week at the restaurant while their various plays were scheduled that July and August for summer stock in Philadelphia. The academy award winner (*They Shoot Horses, Don't They?*, 1969) Gig Young sent me all the way up the hill to retrieve some cigars for him. It was a hot Philly night. I was sweating profusely when I returned with his cigars. The cheap prick flipped me a quarter. In 1978, the 65 year-old-actor married a 31 year-old German actress, his third wife. Three weeks after they were married he took a gun, shot her in the head and killed her. Then he turned the gun on himself. The New York cops found the dead actor still clutching his gun. Old Gig's last film was ironically called *The Game of Death*. Maybe his new young wife wouldn't go up the hill for his cigars. Or down.

Hume Cronyn and his lovely wife Jessica Tandy (who starred in Hitchcock's *The Birds)* were gracious customers and generous tippers. Many years later I was in an elevator in a Montreal Hotel. The doors opened, Hume Cronyn walked in and the doors closed. "Hume!" I exclaimed more than a little exuberantly. Terrified, poor Hume Cronyn backed against the wall and stammered, "Don't hurt me. I'll give you my money." I wasn't sure if he was kidding or not but I quickly identified myself as his waiter when he and his wife Jessica Tandy played *The Gin Game* in Philadelphia's Playhouse in the Park in 1958. It was somewhere around 1980 when I ran into Mr. Cronyn in Montreal. It hardly dawned on me that over twenty years had passed. He must have thought that I was a nut when I was only greeting him as an old and long lost friend. He laughed it off, the doors opened and off he went, convinced that there had to be a madman in his elevator. I haven't heard from him since but I never missed his or his wife's work for the rest of their long careers.

That magic summer of 1958 became the fall, and like the October leaves on Philly's oaks, my Arlene fell off the tree. I'm not sure what went wrong but when I returned to Temple that fall Arlene, once again blaming her mother, began hinting that it might be a good idea if we allowed one another to date other people. My problem remained simple: I had no "other people" to date. Since 1956 I hadn't gone near another girl. I was happy with the way things were—another defining moment in my lifelong struggle to understand what it was that women wanted from men. When it comes to women, I was like an immutable Newtonian law of physics: an inert force, without motion, tends to remain inert. Inertia with the opposite sex has been one of the guiding principles of my life. Inertia has been my religion.

Arlene, obviously devious, had already begun seeing a neighborhood guy named Richie Richman. Richman was a three-letter athlete at Overbrook, quarterbacking the Panther football team, and excelling in basketball and baseball. To compound the problem, although I did not know him very well, I liked him. Richie Richman was one of those rare and unassuming triple-threat athletic talents that come along only once in a great while. Unlike say a Dion Sanders type, Richie Richman wasn't an asshole.

He was snapped up by Villanova where he starred in three sports there as well. Eventually, he inked a lucrative minor league contract with the Philadelphia Phillies where he played with Phillies pitcher Dennis Bennett's younger brother. Like too many high school and college standouts, Richman never made it to the Bigs. The word was that he couldn't hit a hanging curve. But I think baseball was his third sport. He was actually better at football and basketball.

By early winter Arlene must have gotten tired of her superstar boyfriend because after one particular award dinner honoring her new beau, she called me and tearfully admitted she had been dreadfully wrong, that we belonged together and that I should take her back. I had been devastated by our breakup but my strategy, communicated to Arlene covertly through Larry Laster and her girlfriend Elida Servin, seemed to have worked. The idea was for Arlene to think that I did not give a shit and that if she chose to spend her social life freezing her ass off on ice cold benches at football games it would be fine with me. I too would date "other people."

Actually, I began dating a girl I had been attracted to for many years. Susan Perloff lived on 54th and Wynnefield Avenue. Like Arlene, she wore her long dark brown hair in a pony tail pulled straight back on her head. In junior high, Sue had rejected me as a hoodlum-punk in a leather jacket. Now I was a college guy wearing button-down shirts and chino pants with a belt in the back. Now she was interested. She wanted to find out, I guess, what a great looking girl like Arlene Rachman could have possibly seen in a skinny, pimpled nineteen-year-old like me.

Sue Perloff was my New Years date as 1958 became 1959. We doubled with my close friend Stanley "Benny" Stein and his girlfriend Myrna Levin. You might recall that Benny was my co-lookout in the great boat robbery caper. We stayed up all night, I slept at Sue's house that morning and I recall throwing up on the sidewalk on New Years Day as we made our way to Broad Street and the famous Philly Mummers Parade. It wasn't that I had been drunk. Actually I have never been drunk inasmuch as, beyond a beer or two, I do not enjoy drinking. Staying up all night has always upset my stomach. Staying up all night with Sue Perloff just made me more nervous than usual. Stanley Stein has never let me forget puking on that New Year's Day, 1959.

But aside from some heavy backseat breathing in Benny's green Pontiac convertible, we were on very different wavelengths by young adulthood and although I liked Sue, I was overjoyed to get back to my comfortable and loving relationship with Arlene Rachman. By the spring of 1959, as I completed the first half of my sophomore year, Arlene and I were a couple again. I never asked her about Richie Richman and she never asked me about Susan Perloff; which was fine by me since I actually had nothing of consequence to report. It was best, I thought at the time, to allow Arlene to imagine the worst. Susan was a "nice" girl in 1950's terms when we started to go out. And, although she sported the biggest pair of tits of any girl I had ever been with to that point, that "nice girl" part remained intact when I went happily back to a loving relationship with my Arlene. When it came to women, I have to admit, I have always been a forgiving schmuck!

Many years later I ran into Susan Perloff at Gansk's sister Marla's wedding. I was living in New England and had been gone from Philly for quite a while. I asked Susan to dance even though I was married at the time and her husband didn't look overjoyed to see me dancing with his lovely wife. Susan told me she had two kids, a small row house in Overbrook Park and that she loved her life. Her husband, she told me, was in insurance. Ironically, he was actually working for the Gansk! Susan certainly looked as if she loved her life. Especially the part when she sat down to eat dinner. Although she was still pretty as a picture with those humongous hooters of hers, after a couple of kids old Susy Perloff had put on a couple pounds.

CHAPTER 22

By the middle of my sophomore year at Temple my life had come down to an unexciting mix of school in the morning and work in the afternoon. Every so often I would pick Arlene up after school with Pop's '55 Olds and we would head for our secret lovers retreat on that abandoned 19th century estate in Lower Merion. Through the gate, onto the cobblestone lot in front of the carriage house, behind a large ingrown hedge, and then stolen minutes of passionate afternoon delight. We would speak almost every night on the phone but once I began working downtown after my classes, our relationship was generally relegated to weekends. College life in the fifties was a large and prolonged snore at Temple University.

With one or two exceptions, our professors were lackluster bores who went through their dull paces of English, economics, business, science, math and other subjects. One exception for me was Professor John D. Stark, a newly minted Ph.D. from Duke University who made American history come alive in his introductory classes. I always kept up with the reading assignments while looking forward to Stark's animated and knowledgeable lectures. Stark's specialty was the American South during the Civil War and Reconstruction eras.

But what could you do with history to make a living? That was always the question Pop asked me. It was, however, my job that really opened a new world for me. Pop's eldest sister, my Aunt Nan Goldman, was one of the most interesting characters I have ever known—emphasis on the word character. Nobody in the family ever knew exactly how old Aunt Nan was and she always tried to keep her age as secret as the Manhattan Project. Since my father's mother Yetta had died when he was fourteen, his sister Nan had become a surrogate mother. When he married my mother in 1937, Pop felt obligated to ask his older sister to come live with them. To my mother's everlasting consternation, Nan accepted. I remember thinking as a small boy that I was very lucky. Most kids had only one mother. I had two. In retrospect, Pop was wrong. You don't start off a healthy marriage by having in-laws close by—especially a demanding in-law like Pop's older sister. When we moved to Wynnefield from 57th and Catherine in West Philly, Aunt Nan became part of the package. I suppose families were different in the forties, but my mother deserved a medal for putting up with my old man and his sister in those early years.

Nan lived with us on Diamond Street until I was three or four. She slept in the back room of our four-bedroom row house. I don't remember much except I liked having her around. Nan always seemed to pop up with candy or other neat surprises. Eventually, I was forbidden to enter her inner sanctum; which might have resulted from my flushing all her fine bottles of expensive perfume down the toilet. It took a severe case of the croup to get her to relent and finally forgive me. But, to the day she died, she never let me forget it!

One day I awakened to find all of our downstairs furniture gone. And so was Aunt Nan.

Apparently the animosity between my mother and Nan had grown so fierce that it almost became physical. According to family legend, Nan and my mother's eldest sister, Dorothy, actually did come to blows. But as I wasn't there, I have no memory of the incident. Aunt Nan and Aunt Dorothy clearly disliked one another, never speaking for the rest of their long lives—not even in 1974 at my grandfather's funeral. The ill will between Nan and my mother lasted for the rest of Nan's life but because I adamantly refused to be drawn in, they finally reached some level of detente in the early 1960s when my mother invited Nan and her longtime "friend," "Uncle" Maurice Praissman, to a family dinner at our new house on Bryn Mawr Avenue. It had been more than fifteen years since Nan had set foot in our house.

For many years as a child, my father would put me on the number 70 trolley, instruct the conductor to hand me over to a woman waiting at 52nd and Spruce Street and pray that I would not be grabbed up by a kidnapper—Pop had an inordinate fear of strangers which my brother and I have humorously shorthanded into a single Pop warning over the years: "Watch out for drunks!"

Nan would be dutifully waiting at the trolley stop as I got off and then I could look forward to lunch at my favorite Philly eatery, Horn and Hardart's automat, a new comic book, a downtown movie at the Stanley, Earle or Goldman theater and then Chinese takeout in Nan's tiny one-room apartment. Nan never ever cooked. Our last meal together, shortly before her death, was Chinese takeout. That time I brought it to her.

For many years the Aunt Nan weekends became ritual in my life. I never failed to wonder at her "magic Murphy bed" she'd pull out from a wall closet. I would sleep over and the next day I'd make the reverse trip back to Wynnefield where Pop would be patiently waiting at the trolley stop on Gainor Road. I soon found out what had become of our downstairs furniture. It was all in Aunt Nan's new apartment.

Not to be outdone by her hated rival, my mother's older sister Dorothy vied for my affection as well. Like Nan, Dorothy also lived in West Philly with her second husband Jack Washburn. "Uncle Jack" was an ill-tempered, anti-Semitic Irishman, a retired naval commander who constantly berated "the goddamn Kikes" for every real and imagined evil in the world. The epithet "Kike" had absolutely no meaning to a little boy of five or six then. Like Nan, Aunt Dorothy would buy me toys and comic books but because I was never at ease with her prick of a husband, I always looked forward to the Aunt Nan weekends. Nan Goldman was a liberated woman decades before the neo-feminist phonies of my era.

To the day she died in 1997, unlike my mother's sister who rarely spoke to me as a teen or adult (even refusing to attend my Bar Mitzvah and wedding), Nan's love remained strong over the years without qualification. Even though we often fought bitterly in the years we worked together and also whenever she frequently badmouthed my mother, I felt deep affection for her. We spoke at least once a week, usually on Sunday mornings, to the day she died. Often, Aunt Nan could be petty, bigoted and very vicious. After one particular falling out we stopped speaking for almost a year. But I couldn't hold a grudge against a woman who worshipped my father and whose generosity to me over the years was unmatched by any other relative.

Somehow, kids, like dogs, seem able to sense genuine affection. At any rate, as a little boy, I clearly became the child in our family Aunt Nan never had. And although my mother may not have been happy about it, she wisely chose not to interfere, probably saving her marriage. The longstanding family joke was that Lou Goldman was married to two women: my mother and his sister. Over the years, Pop would talk almost every night on the phone for hours with his sister. Don't ask me what they talked about; probably money. Maybe! Pop had lost two sisters to cancer in the fifties; a kindhearted older sister, Sarah Glickman, and his youngest sister, Florence Ditlow. Florence, a very sweet woman in her early forties when she died, was the baby of the large Goldman family. At her funeral in November, 1953 Pop wept uncontrollably. It was the only time in my life I ever saw my father cry.

Mom and Pop took in Florence's youngest son Eddie who occupied the room next to mine for almost a year. Pop hoped to ultimately adopt five-year-old Eddie who adapted quickly to our family but his father, Harry Ditlow, a man who flitted aimlessly through life and was often unemployed much of the time, demanded that both his sons (Mark Ditlow was living with another relative) be returned. Pop wanted to turn to the courts, but Nan, now the matriarch of the Goldman clan, felt a court battle would be too harmful to little Mark and Eddie who were returned to live with their hapless father.

By the mid-1950's Nan, who remained single until her marriage to her longtime beau, lawyer Maurice Praissman, in the mid-1960s, had worked her way up in a downtown Philadelphia business to Comptroller. She kept the company's books by hand, a self-taught bookkeeper who could handle accounts receivable, accounts payable and payroll. As time passed Nan became the chief watchdog of the company manning its financial barricades. The only time of year Nan needed the help of a professional CPA was when it came to the quarterly trial balance needed to deal with the IRS and the complicated tax problems required of a large family-run business that fed hundreds of employees and ultimately supported four large families in a lavish style for the time.

The name of the company was Arkay Builders founded by Robert Krevolin (RK—Arkay, get it!), a dapper little man with a pencil thin mustache, the slight trace of a shtetl accent and a year-round deep tan. RK reminded me of a Mafia Don from South Philly with his pinky diamond ring, impeccably tailored shiny suits and new pink Cadillac Fleetwood. Mr. Krevolin insisted on being called "boss" and that is what we called him whenever he was around.

Aside from that trivial formality, he was like many self-made, first generation immigrant Jews, a kind and generous man who thrived on his business and loved his family. He also loved and trusted my Aunt Nan who was entrusted with all of the large Krevolin family's inner secrets and finances.

Arkay Builders was located off the corner of Walnut and Ninth Streets, at 904 Walnut Street in a long suite of ground floor offices that had been remodeled to affect the look of a city street with houses—a different house front for each separate office. Arkay's specialty was mostly kitchen and bath remodeling but they could paint a house or even rebuild it entirely from the ground up. Barry Levinson captured the crazy ambience of Arkay Builders in his quirky 1987 film *Tin Men*, a follow-up to *Diner*, about the antics of aluminum siding salesmen in 1960's Baltimore; although Arkay Builders was actually a combination of the more humorous *Tin Men* and David Mamet's harder-edged *Glengarry Glen Ross*.

At Arkay the work was subcontracted out. Every Friday afternoon various contractors—plasterers, carpenters, plumbers, painters, electricians, wallpaper hangers and others would gather at the far end of the string of offices to pick up their checks for the work they had performed that week.

It would be up to the good graces of my Aunt Nan to see that the checks were ready on time. If a contractor or salesman had a particular problem with his paycheck they might appeal to "the boss" or even to his amiable and beloved son, Jerry Krevolin. The response would invariably be the same: "Take it up with Nan!" Clearly, she controlled the company's purse-strings and the reason the old man loved her was the fact that he knew my aunt watched over his family's money like a ferocious mother nighthawk ready to swoop down to save a nickel.

Nan always had the option to hold a check or even to pay only part of a contractor's bill. It all depended on whether the contractor came across. Nan honed extortion to a fine art. She reminded me of a Mafia capo every week as she waited for her envelopes or gifts. If Nan needed a ride home and the plumber was around that night, if he didn't offer to drop Aunt Nan off, that Friday his check just might not be ready on time. Or, even worse, light.

Around Christmas, if a contractor didn't grease Nan with a nice, expensive gift—say a fifth of Cutty Sark, Jack Daniels, Canadian Club or J&B—that she usually re-gifted to her beloved brother and others in our large family—the contractor might end up on her shit list for the next 6 months. You wanted to avoid that list at all costs. Nan's shit list always translated into late or light paychecks. You'd get your money; but on Nan Goldman's timetable. Nan ran Arkay Builders accounts payable with an iron but loving fist. She watched over Bob Krevolin's money as if it was her own. And Mr. Krevolin knew it. Next to his family, Robert Krevolin entrusted my Aunt Nan with the most intimate knowledge of his most private business and personal affairs. He knew she was as honest with his money as any member of the Krevolin family and that is exactly how he treated her—like family.

At Arkay Builders, Aunt Nan knew where all the bodies were buried; literally and figuratively. When Mr. Krevolin died suddenly in the mid-sixties, he left Nan a substantial bequest. As did his loving widow Anna many years later.

When Nan died in 1997 we found dozens of still unopened gifts from many Christmases past in her overflowing "gift closet" which she used over the years to distribute her extorted largesse to her army of nieces and nephews.

By 1958 Mr. Krevolin had survived a couple of heart attacks and, like the ailing Don Vito Corleone, he turned over the day-to-day management of the family business to his beloved son Jerry and his two sons-in-law, Seymour (Sy) Rochestie and Charlie Lotman. By 1958 Arkay Builders had expanded its remodeling operation into Lit Brothers and Wanamakers, the two largest department store chains in Philadelphia, the business had become lucrative enough to support hundreds of employees and all those families in fine style. In addition to "the Boss," who still received the largest weekly salary, the family members running Arkay Builders were all paid equally. Included was the boss's brother, Harry Krevolin, who managed the company's expanding commercial contracts in a city that was about to explode economically with downtown development.

Mostly as a result of newspaper and radio ads, sales leads would pour in from the two department stores, a team of salesmen would be handed the leads at afternoon sales meetings, go out (usually at night), sell the jobs under the imprimatur of the department store or the private company and the various home remodeling tasks would then be subcontracted out. Jobs sold through the auspices of the department store would always have to be inflated to cover the percentage taken by the chain.

Jobs sold through Arkay Builders did not pay tribute, so in effect there was more than a single company that had to be kept on the books. Two sets of advertisements would be drawn up and placed in the local newspapers. I suppose the practice was somewhat shady but the public never seemed to catch on. Philly's corrupt City Hall, I suspect, was always well paid to look the other way.

As I came to know the business, I never understood why the customers didn't just hire the various contractors themselves and save half of the money they were spending for new kitchens, baths or recreation rooms. It must have occurred to other people too because that is the basis for the huge success of places like Home Depot and Lowes. You buy a new kitchen sink or enough tiles to put in a new floor and they supply the name of a reputable contractor to install it or you find your own. It was another time. Postwar America and most Americans were still innocent. And pretty fucking stupid!

In addition to the sales force, a team of company inspectors saw to it that the jobs were completed to the customer's satisfaction. The customers may have paid high prices for their new kitchens and bathrooms but since they were dealing with reputable Philly department stores, the company did its level best to see that the jobs were at least of the highest quality.

The inspectors were managed by Charlie Lotman, a Krevolin son-in-law in his late twenties, and headed by two rough-hewn, working class guys, Marty Squaresky and Harry Stein. If a complaint came in, especially on department store jobs which were guaranteed, it was up to the inspectors to rectify it.

All told the company had almost a hundred or so people on its payroll in addition to the many sub-contractors and their helpers who were also employed. Since the weekly payroll was still done by hand with handwritten checks accompanied by entry into ledgers, Aunt Nan had a lot of work to do each day. One day would be relegated to accounts receivable; one day to bank deposits (Nan had scores of bank-gift toasters and umbrellas in that closet!); one day to accounts payable; one day to payroll, generally Thursdays. In addition, Nan had to chart every single remodeling job, no matter the price, by hand as well.

Each job had a cardboard chart where the costs per contractor, the commissions paid and the dates of completion had to be meticulously recorded in order for management to see profitability at a glance by measuring whether the salesmen had estimated correctly.

The unwritten rule of thumb was 100 per cent. Thus, a job with a cost of $1,000 would have to be sold for $2,000 to be profitable to the company after expenses and commissions. The average commission was between 10 and 15 per cent depending on the size of the job and whether the job was a home or commercial operation. Arkay also renovated buildings.

And it was always Nan who figured out commissions. There were not supposed to be any draws against commissions but once in a while Mr. Krevolin would intervene on behalf of a salesman down on his luck. It was up to Nan to see that the salesman eventually made good on what he owed the company. But, because Bob Krevolin was a kind and generous man, some salesmen were carried for years. Most of the staff remained stable and turnover was negligible, especially in the sales force.

Sometime in the fall of my freshman year Aunt Nan approached Mr. Krevolin asking for permission to put her "street smart" college nephew on Arkay's payroll. I was to work directly under her supervision, assisting in keeping the complicated Arkay books. Mr. Krevolin immediately agreed and my hours were set. I would work every day from around 2 PM to closing at 5:30. I would also operate the display in Lit Brothers department store on Wednesday nights from 6 until 9PM and all day on Saturday. On the floor of Lit Brothers my responsibilities would be to develop sales leads by communicating the company's offering to anyone who stopped by the display booth, answer the phones which were patched into the department store from the company offices on Walnut Street and check out the gorgeous girls who worked or shopped in the store. Well, not exactly in that order.

If things were slow in the department store I was permitted the luxury of studying. I just had to make sure that my books were tucked away well under the display desk to avoid the wayward glances of various executives, floor walkers and store detectives who might not look kindly on a Lit Brother's employee studying college history or accounting while ostensibly working the floor. A negative report to the Lit's brass on the fifth floor could always endanger the tenuous relationship Arkay had with the large chain. In reality Arkay was a concession but as an employee of Lit Brother's, I was also given a 20% discount card on all purchases. It wasn't easy juggling a fulltime college course schedule with what was virtually a fulltime job.

I was soon pulling down between fifty and seventy-five bucks a week—not a paltry sum back then. As I grew to know the Krevolins better they began to treat me, like Aunt Nan, as part of the family. Charlie Lotman would ask me to take his new Pontiac to the car wash on a Friday afternoon. When I returned Charlie would sometimes say, "Hey, I'll catch a ride with one of the guys. I'll use Sasha's car (his wife Sondra) over the weekend. Bring the car back Monday after school." Sometimes Jerry Krevolin would ask me to make a drop or pick something up in the large Arkay flatbed truck and then tell me to keep the truck over the weekend rather than return it to the Arkay parking lot.

And more than once, Mr. Krevolin himself would ask if I could chauffer him down the shore. He would then flip me the keys to his pink Caddie Fleetwood with the big fins and tell me to drive him home and then pick him up on Sunday for the trip to Atlantic City. In the meantime, I had a big, new Cadillac to tool around the neighborhood for an entire weekend. Nan lived in constant fear that I would smash up one of the Arkay vehicles. But I was always very careful and over many years never had a mishap. Pop always appeared somewhat bemused when I drove that old truck down narrow Diamond Street and parked it in front of the house. But I guess he was happy because that truck meant he'd have the Oldsmobile to himself for the weekend.

By late 1960, thanks to the Krevolin family and a loan from Pop and Nan (which I repaid!), I was able to afford my first car—a brand new, fire-engine red Valiant with an ornamental wheel on the trunk. The selling price, stick shift without a radio, was $1800. I put up $1000, Nan came in with $300 and Pop covered the remaining $500; which I repaid in about two years. My friend Billy Stamps teased me for years that I bought a car without a radio. But Billy took care of the problem. Billy, still in the midnight auto supply business, saw to it that my new Valiant was soon fitted with an expensive portable radio which he installed under the seat, just in case the cops ever stopped me. Billy Stamps didn't enjoy the ride to Temple without the radio on. My next car, a new '65 Mustang, had a radio. But I didn't get air conditioning in a car until the mid-1990s when it finally became standard!

I relished the years spent at Arkay Builders. It became my real college. I watched men who worked with their hands and grew to know some of them well. I loved the Krevolin family—especially Sy Rochestie, Charlie Lotman and Jerry Krevolin who always treated me with respect and genuine affection. In the summers they would always make sure to include me on the company fishing trips or other outings. I was often invited to Krevolin family events and, when the company handed out bonuses every Christmas, there was always an envelope stuffed with a couple of twenties for me.

Charlie Lotman, Mr. Krevolin's son-in-law was only a few years older than me, and we would often grab lunch together or even find an excuse to take a ride down the shore. Charlie was married to Sondra, the youngest Krevolin daughter called Sasha, and they had two young kids. But he still had an eye for a well-turned skirt and would sometimes hang out with me and some of my guys on the Boardwalk in Atlantic City. Charlie had gone to work right after high school, had married quite young and I think he missed the coming of age part of life that going to college and flirting with pretty girls on Chelsea beach afforded. Charlie often commented on the fact that he envied my freedom and lack of responsibility in life. I always envied the fact that he was pulling down really big dough, drove a nice car, married a very attractive woman and had a home and a comfortable life. I guess the grass, as the saying goes, is always greener...

There was a small bedroom built into the Arkay offices, ostensibly for use by the boss for a quick catnap if he came to work—which he rarely did. But the bedroom was hardly wasted. Arkay's back door fronted the company parking lot on Locust Street, Philly's nearby red-light district of various bust-out joints and gangster bars. Often the inspectors would pick up a hooker in one of the bars and bring her back to the office late at night. Since I had a key to the office, after my work at Lit Brothers I would always return to the office to drop off any leads or complaints and grab my car which was in the back lot on Locust Street. The office was often still in use. But nobody was doing any remodeling business after 9 PM. I was trusted enough that none of the guys ever worried that I would rat them out to Nan. And I never did. Years later when I finally told Nan what used to go on late at night at the office, she just laughed: "Do you think you're telling me something I didn't know?" My aunt was one smart cookie.

Although in my early years at Arkay I was much too shy and loyal to Arlene to take advantage of the extracurricular office shenanigans, by the end of my time at the company I have to admit that I too came to enjoy the sensual pleasures of that small bedroom in our offices.

From Nan I learned the skills of bookkeeping and accounting before the age of the computer. The only machine that aided me in my work was an electric adding machine. Nan taught me how to keep the various account books. Although she was a harsh taskmaster, I must have learned well. No other member of the vast Goldman family was ever invited into the inner financial sanctum of Arkay Builders. Other cousins and my brother Ken would eventually inherit the Lit Brothers gig. But I was the only one to work side by side with Nan week after week for almost six years.

Aunt Nan was much tougher on me than she would have been on a regular employee. Intent on showing the Krevolins that I would never receive special treatment, she often came down on me much harder than I thought necessary. For years I depended on public transportation—the Broad Street subway and then the subway from Market Street, to get downtown. To get to work from my house would mean buses and subways and well over an hour of travel time. If I came in few minutes late, and I was often late because of hanging around Mitten Hall at the university after grabbing lunch at school, instead of just docking my pay, Nan chewed my ass out loudly enough for everyone to hear throughout the entire suite.

Once Jerry Krevolin's secretary, a young woman named Pat Timmins, who proudly displayed her assets whenever I passed her desk—two of the largest twillies known to modern man—whispered to me in the hall, "I don't know how you put up with all her bullshit!"

I left Philly in 1966, a few years after I stopped working for Arkay Builders. Mr. Krevolin died of a heart attack the summer I got married. Charlie Lotman finally got caught screwing around and Sasha divorced him. He tried a few things in Philly and then migrated to south Florida. Charlie was found shot to death in his car on a hot day after he had stopped to get some ice cream. His killer was never apprehended. In 1988 Charlie's son, Hank, called me in Boston. We met for lunch. He wanted to know about his father. Of course, I only had good things to say when it came to his Dad. A few years later, Nan called to tell me that Herman "Hank" Lotman had committed suicide. Why a good looking young kid decided to end his life doesn't compute. A lot of kids are children of divorced parents and they do just fine. Hank Lotman must have had inner demons that he kept concealed from the world. Those demons were certainly not apparent on the day we met in Boston.

Sy Rochestie died in 2000 of cancer. I was living in Maine when I got the news. I called his wife Reita and I called Jerry Krevolin. I had last seen Jerry and his wife Franny at Aunt Nan's funeral in 1997. Jerry and I reminisced about the happier times. We made plans to meet for lunch the next time I visited Philly. Jerry was still running the company. But the home remodeling business had changed drastically. It was, he told me, a daily struggle. Why not take the money and run, I asked. "Retire? Never! What would I do? They'll carry me out of this place," Jerry laughed.

We never made that lunch. Jerry Krevolin died in the fall of 2001, a few months after our conversation just a few weeks before my next visit to Philadelphia. He was still working and running Arkay. Jerry had been worried about his beautiful wife Franny who suffered a slight stroke the year before. He worried about a daughter who had never married. He worried about the business. But, like me, he loved Sinatra and he bragged about his son Larry who had become a doctor. You win some; you lose some. That's what Jerry used to say. His lovely wife Franny died just a few years ago. I always wondered if those people knew what they meant to me. I never did tell them.

By the time I left Arkay I knew two things: that I would never become an accountant and that the world of business was probably not for me. In my junior year, to my father's great dismay, I changed my major from accounting to marketing and advertising. I began to minor in history. What, Pop constantly asked, was I going to do with my life now that I didn't have my Cousin Lenny's accounting firm as part of my job horizon? I didn't have a clue.

CHAPTER 23

My junior year at Temple University was a combination of excruciating pain and magnificent self-discovery. The year was 1960— a watershed year for the country and for me personally.

In mid-winter Arlene Rachman graduated high school. We had been together going on five years and had made wonderful plans. I should have known better. There is a saying, "If you want to hear God laugh, tell Him you have a plan!"

Arlene entered Temple as a freshman that February. She had blossomed into an extraordinarily beautiful young woman who still wore her shoulder length blonde hair either down or straight back tied in a pony tail. Again, Goldman's first rule on women: whenever a woman can wear her hair straight back from her forehead, she is usually a beautiful woman. Like Lynda "Wonder Woman" Carter or Bo Derek.

To this day, whenever I see an attractive woman with blonde hair tied back in a pony tail, I often zone out into long buried memories that wash over me like warm water in a soft summer rain. I was still a somewhat scrawny kid with bad skin in 1960. I couldn't believe my continuing good fortune. After all that time, Arlene still loved me. Somehow, I had managed to fool her into loving for me over the years. There were many guys at Temple who were a lot better looking with more money; much more money.

I had saved up some required freshman courses which we would take together. At the same time it was a way for me to keep my mediocre grades up. Arlene was always an excellent student with honor averages throughout high school. We would take the classes and study together as well. My grades would improve along with my love life. What could possibly go wrong? Her mother could hardly complain. As long as she didn't know about the love life part.

My three years at Temple had been somewhat lackluster. I wasn't ever in danger of flunking out but, because I fell a few decimals below a 2.0 average in my sophomore year, I was placed on academic probation. I bundled up on history courses and after a couple of B grades was removed from probation. For some reason beyond my comprehension, I loved to study history. My friends would tease me about my predilection for wars, presidential administrations and my ability to memorize the kings of France and England. Once, we were walking by a bank in downtown Philly. The bank had an advertised contest in the window: come in, fill out a form by noting the names of the various American presidents with their dates in office and win an Atlas. "I could do that," I told the guys. They laughed. Impossible; nobody could name the presidents of the United States in order and, in addition, the dates they served in office. I went in to the bank, filled out the form and, to the utter amazement of my friends, walked out with the Atlas.

What was the trick? My friends wanted to know. There was no trick. I didn't memorize the presidents. I knew them; intimately. I knew who they were and what they did in office. My friends, like me, were marking time just getting through Temple. With few exceptions, they were either going into their father's businesses or, like Billy Stamps or Stanley Stein, were set on making millions in the world of business and finance on their own. Business courses bored me. Finance, marketing, statistics, whatever—I hated sitting through these terminally stifling courses. Check that! I despised sitting through these courses. For some reason, I was never attracted to money. Don't get me wrong: I liked a nice car, nice clothes and expensive restaurants. Money was just never a major factor that motivated me while in college; or later in life!

The only one to drop out in our gang was Jerry Berger. He left in his sophomore year to work with his father in the wholesale meat business. Berger's father, a tall, handsome, prematurely graying man was a taciturn presence in the neighborhood. He was called "The Cameo" by the older denizens of Harry's and known to be found often in a gas station on 54th Street. Don't ask me what the Cameo did at that gas station. Jerry Berger was soon married and lost forever to the world of work and a growing family.

Today my old pal Jerry Berger lives in New Jersey, works happily in photography and, still married, is a grandfather. Leaving college early cut his days at the Spoon short back in 1959.

I would pick Arlene up three days a week for our first class at 9 AM, Introduction to Psychology. For about six weeks things went swimmingly. Arlene and I sat in class holding hands and taking notes from the young professor who often joked, as he called the role, that the lovebirds were present. Life was good. I was in heaven.

But even heaven always has its downside. For one thing, you're dead!

Hanging out in Mitten Hall where she often waited for her ride home, Arlene soon found herself the center of attention of a number of the boys. A gregarious type who was often openly flirtatious with the opposite sex, Arlene thrived on the obvious interest of so many guys from many neighborhoods far beyond our insular urban Shangri-La. Over the years I was hardly oblivious to Arlene's touchy-feely nature. However, one of the positive qualities I have developed throughout this short life is that I am not and have never been the jealous type. I have always graciously accepted the old Woody Allen dictum that the heart is a funny little muscle that wants what it wants.

At the bowling alley on 54th Street Arlene would often sit on the lap of Temple basketball star Bernie Ivens. Bernie was an old friend. I never said a word. She would openly flirt with a good looking guy named Bobby Cherry. As long as they looked and didn't really touch, I never made a big thing out of it. Arlene was always hugging somebody and over the years I guess I just got used to it. The guys could hug her all they wanted. Arlene's most intimate parts belonged to me.

At Temple University, however, that part of my possession changed very rapidly. I was very friendly with a guy from West Philly, Maury Wolcoff. Like me, Maury majored in marketing and long before Arlene came to Temple I began hanging out with Maury, whose father owned a Jewish deli in West Philadelphia near Penn. We'd often study together and then head over to Milt's, Delicatessen. Maury was a very attractive, dapper little guy. Never one to care much about clothes, Maury turned me on to the sartorial side of being a male. He often wore a jacket and tie to classes. One day Maury showed up at Temple in a hat—the kind you saw Sinatra wearing on his album, *Come Dance with Me*. The next week Billy Stamps was wearing the same hat. Soon we were all coming to school in jackets and ties. And Sinatra-like hats!

When Arlene met Maury the attraction was immediate and obvious. I may not be the jealous type, but that doesn't mean I take stupid pills either. She was always sitting on his lap in the student lounge when I happened to come by Mitten Hall. I knew I was in deep shit when Arlene asked me if she could go with Maury to see *West Side Story*. I had no idea then what *West Side Story* actually was but I said, "Sure, go ahead." I had to work that Wednesday night anyway.

The Broadway musical drama, as everyone knows is a takeoff on Romeo and Juliet, a very romantic tragedy presaging my own romantic tragedy. The next day when I picked Arlene up for psych class she gave me that classic, "We have to talk," shit. After class Arlene laid it out in spades. She had gone to see *West Side Story* with Maury and afterwards they went out to get something to eat and then they made out. I felt dizzy and sick. It was an empty feeling deep in the pit of my stomach. I had never known that feeling before and, after a lifetime of ups and downs with the opposite sex I have rarely known it since. Even the breakup of my marriage did not produce the terrible emptiness that grasped the pit of my stomach over the next weeks and months. I mooned and moaned like AJ Soprano when he lost that cute Puerto Rican girl.

Five years of my life flashed before my eyes. I didn't ask how far their making out went but I knew Maury…and worse, I knew Arlene; too well. I envisioned the worst.

Initially, I made it clear that I was willing to forgive her. But Arlene always much wiser than me in matters of the heart gently told me that I didn't get it. She was attracted to Maury and that meant that whatever it was that we had was on shaky ground. Shaky ground my ass! She wanted out.

The next weeks were gut wrenching. I had never known existential pain of the heart and soul. I was trapped in a dark, Dostoyevsky-like nightmare. I stopped picking her up for school. Still, I'd see Arlene in psych class three times a week. We'd sit apart from one another even though Arlene would often come up and playfully peck me on the cheek or give me a hug. She seemed oblivious to the real pain that I felt and her open flirtatiousness only pissed me off. A lot of guys flunk out of school when their love life goes south. I did just the opposite.

Determined to show Arlene a stiff upper lip, and to succeed in my studies, I actually did very well that semester. I got a B in that psychology class. Maybe that professor took pity. At any rate, I received better grades that semester than I had ever gotten at Temple before.

The winter of my discontent finally gave way to spring 1960. On a sunny afternoon in May that I will never forget I waited for Arlene outside of a class she was taking on the second floor of Curtis Hall. She came out, as beautiful as ever, with her girlfriends. They all looked at me like I was a poor puppy who had just been run over by a car. I swept all vestiges of pride aside. I had never begged a girl for anything. I begged Arlene. I may have even cried. It was the most humiliating moment of my twenty-plus years on this earth. Worse even than getting my face pushed into a pile of horseshit by the Danowitz boys!

I told Arlene that I loved her. I needed her, I said. I missed her, I said. It would have made a great Sinatra song or a Woody Allen comedy. Take your pick! I knew then exactly how Frank felt when Ava dumped him. Arlene looked at me with pity in her eyes. "I'm sorry," she said. "But I need time. I need to think. But I'm very flattered!"

Goldman's rule number two: when a woman looks at you with nothing but pity in her eyes it is all over. The fat lady has sung. Women see emotional weakness in the male of the species as a major flaw. Forget about what the feminists have been saying since the Sixties. Men who cry or beg are seen by a majority of American women as major wussies! You want to elicit utter contempt from a woman? Just show her any sign of emotional weakness. American women do not like as Arnold has observed "girly men."

By that time Maury had long flown Arlene's coop. Maury was a great looking little guy and dozens of Mitten Hall lovelies were always flitting about him. Unlike me, he always had his pick. To Maury, Arlene was just another piece of ass. Over the next few years Maury and I remained good friends. We had even planned to team up after graduation. I never blamed him for what happened with Arlene. It would have happened anyway. Years later Maury came to visit when I was married and living on a farm in western Massachusetts. But, like many old friends from college days, we eventually lost touch as our lives took different direction. My old friend Maury Wolcoff died of cancer in August of 2001 at age 63.

On that fateful day in Curtis Hall, Arlene just turned uncomfortably away after telling me how flattered she was as she headed for the nearest stairwell. A guy I knew, "Jolly" Charlie Klein, grabbed my arm ushering me into an empty classroom. "Look out the window," Jolly Chollie said. I did. There beneath the window, not more than 100 feet from where we were perched, was a young man. He was tall, tanned and Hollywood handsome. He was surrounded by hundreds of cheering Temple students. Some campus ass-lick by the name of Oaky Miller introduced the young man: "Friends," the Oakster shouted above the din, "the United States Senator from Massachusetts, the next president of the United States, Senator John F. Kennedy." I never liked Oaky Miller. And he never liked me.

I had never heard of John F. Kennedy. I turned twenty-one on Election Day that year and I voted for him against Richard Nixon who looked like a sinister bastard who would sell his grandmother for green stamps. Both went on to become president. And finally, Nixon did sell his grandmother; although not literally. Oaky Miller headed for Hollywood, just the perfect place for a personality of his caliber, after he graduated. I once saw him on a Marlo Thomas TV show, *That Girl*. He was still obviously an ass-lick.

I was, at that point in time, totally apolitical. Kennedy was in Philly sweeping through the city's major college campuses where his handlers obviously saw an important Democratic voting block for JFK in Pennsylvania. He was closing out that long 1960 primary season as he campaigned for his sorry date with history and dreadful destiny. I remember him being very tan, almost glowing golden, and that his lustrous hair was a reddish burnt auburn. Of course, no one at that time knew he was a very ill man with Addison's disease. Kennedy made a short speech and the students applauded wildly. Even though I would teach the Kennedy presidency for years at Boston University and write *John F. Kennedy: Portrait of a President,* I cannot for the life of me recall a single thing the future president said that day. My heart was shattered and broken.

CHAPTER 24

I had to get out of the city. The summer was coming and I was seriously depressed. The Gansk had SallyAnn, Benny Stein had Myrna, Paul Rabinowitz had Sheila...and I?—what did I have?

I faced a hot Philly summer of acute angst and loneliness. William Styron has written that "...serious depressions do not disappear overnight." Over the years I have fought off serious depression by changing my environment. Instead of hitting a shrink, I hit the road. Usually, it has worked well. In the summer of 1960 it worked magnificently.

To make matters worse, for the first time since Nan left, there were troubles at home. My mother found a house she had always wanted about a mile from Diamond Street on Bryn Mawr Avenue a few yards from City Line. If you crossed City Line, you were out of Philly. Bryn Mawr Avenue was one of the nicest streets, lined with single family mansions, in the neighborhood. The house was, my father argued, priced beyond his means at $16,500—quite laughable as I write from my modest home valued at over $500,000! But my mother prevailed and Pop did something he always warned me against: buying a house without selling the one you own.

My father lived in mortal fear of debt throughout his life. My bills and my brother's are always current. As far as I know neither of us has ever paid a cent of interest on our credit cards and we have never even financed a new car (I finally broke this Goldman covenant when I purchased a new Mercedes in 2009 but I did get a 2% rate!). Thanks Pop!

Pop had gotten promoted at the Post Office. I never quite knew what it was he did exactly until that year when he was elevated to the Regional Office. He could have gone to Washington but, instead, chose to remain in Philadelphia working out of 30th Street. Pop was an expert budget man. He was soon traveling all over the country crunching numbers for the Post Office. A Sergeant in my reserve unit who worked at the Post Office told me, when he learned Louis Goldman was my Dad, that when Pop appeared on the main floor it was the same as a General officer appearing to revue the troops. I had seen this first-hand when I worked the main floor over a number of Christmas holidays: In the Philly Post Office Pop had clout.

Pop's promotion meant a substantial increase in salary and to Mom that welcome news translated into moving from our modest Diamond Street home. Mom and Pop passed papers on the house, a semi-detached brick row (one of six set apart from the old colonial mansions on upper Bryn Mawr Avenue) that spring and then the Arkay guys, under strict marching orders from Aunt Nan, came to renovate. They put in a new kitchen and remodeled the recreation room with a working wet bar that would become our first family room as well.

The renovations would take all spring and summer. The big move was planned for late summer or early fall. But Pop now had two houses and although he was only asking around $10,000 for the Diamond Street property, there were no initial takers. That winter Pop got deathly ill with whooping cough. He was in bed for the better part of three or four months and we were all pretty worried. He lost a lot of weight and looked terrible. It was the first time I had ever seen my seemingly indestructible father vulnerable. Pop claimed that the stress of carrying two homes had helped to make him sick. But I think Pop was just trying to make Mom feel guilty. It was she, after all, who had pushed so hard for the move.

By summer Pop was on the mend and Mom busied herself picking out color schemes for the rooms, getting the wall-to-wall carpeting in shape and shopping for drapes and new furniture. I didn't want to face the hassle of the move, going in the Army or being around the neighborhood where I might bump into Arlene. So I petitioned my reserve outfit to allow me to train without the unit in the fall at some other military post and then applied for a job at an overnight children's camp in the Poconos that would take me out of Philly for the entire summer.

Initially, my petition was denied, but Pop called a state senator he knew and I was allowed to appeal. The appeal was granted by a board of officers and I was cut orders to show up for two weeks of training that September before school started at Indiantown Gap, an ancient World War II military reservation in central Pennsylvania.

I was hired as a senior counselor in the boy's camp of Pocono Highlands, a coed camp in Marshall's Creek, Pennsylvania. When I was growing up in West Philly, overnight camp was a class delineator. If your parents could afford to send you to overnight camp, it meant you came from money. Needless to say, I never went to camp. Somehow my brother Kenny always managed to get them to send him to overnight camps as he grew up. Kenny says it was because Mom liked him better. I had spent all my summers in the steamy city until those few magic weeks down the shore in Atlantic City. The closest I had ever come to summer camp was the YMCA at 52nd and Sansom where an entire summer cost four bucks.

Summer camp was just what I needed to take my mind off the pain of parting from the first love of my young life. I lost myself in baseball, basketball, archery, tennis, and swimming in beautiful Reflection Lake. I ate well, put on some weight and made a horde of new friends.

Wonder of wonders, my skin finally cleared up! The ironic thing is that when Arlene broke up with me, I actually began to look pretty good for the first time in my life. My thin and gawky teenage body filled out with some muscle to the point that I no longer felt the need to wear a sweat shirt to the beach. I knew how a girl must feel when she grows nice tits. I had finally developed real muscles! At camp I enjoyed the fact that girls noticed me. That had never happened before.

Except for an occasional stomach-churning letter from one of my Harry's boys who mentioned seeing Arlene around the neighborhood, it turned out to be a wonderful summer. I liked the owners of the camp, Earl and Marian Weinberg. The Weinbergs left me to my own devices and, with assistance from an associate counselor and a CIT (Counselor in Training), I had an easy time of it. I liked the eight kids under our charge even though a few of them still wet their beds and I actually managed to find summer romance with a nice Jewish girl from Oradell, New Jersey.

Lillian Hacker was a first cousin of the rotund comedian Buddy Hackett. She lived in the heart of Soprano-land where her father owned a string of prosperous camera shops in Hackensack and Teaneck. Lillian was a freshman at Kent State University. She was a bit intense for my tastes, but I was always a sucker for girls with freckles—especially tall and slim girls with long legs and firm little tits. We spent every night together strolling by the archery ranges to the forested darkness behind the stables where we kissed and touched one another in magic places. Lil was a virgin and in my post-Arlene dementia I felt that you had to really love a girl to take her precious virginity. And thus Lillian Hacker emerged from our brief summer romance with her virtue intact even though there was one point where it was actually offered. My virgin policy would change drastically after that frustrating summer.

Mom and Pop visited on parent's day and I could see that my fourteen year-old-brother wanted very much to go to camp. That summer Ken, who was going through that teenage awkward stage, had opted to stay at home with our parents. It was to be his last such summer. Kenny went to summer camp until he was in college. Obviously, for the Goldman family, the year 1960 elevated them into the burgeoning American upper middle class.

The eight weeks of camp flew by quickly. I have always wondered what became of my weird Pocono Highlands friends Arnie Markowitz, Dave "Bingo" Banks," Steve "Swaps" Edelstein and Yale Gutnik. Camp friends, unlike the guys from the neighborhood, were always fleeting.

In early September I returned to our new house at 2435 Bryn Mawr Avenue and was promptly on the road again. Pop gave me the Olds to drive up to Indiantown Gap for two weeks of compulsory military service. I spent my time doing mostly nothing in a near-empty World War II vintage barracks. Besides a few other soldiers, the post was virtually deserted.

When I returned to Philly in mid-September I enrolled at Temple for the last part of my junior year and the first half of my senior year. The time in the Army proved to be fortuitous. Since I had left the family with no transportation for two weeks, Pop reached the conclusion that it was finally time for me to have my own car. That November I would turn twenty-one. I was the last one of all my friends to get my own car. Mostly the grandkids of eastern European immigrants, we had all arrived smack dab in the middle of the prototype postwar American dream—a single home with two cars parked in the driveway. It was 1960, life was good and the future beckoned our generation like a vast golden ribbon unfurling splendidly before us where everything and anything was possible. We could hardly envision the fact that in the coming decade America would undergo revolutionary change that would alter the nation's landscape for the rest of the century and the rest of our lives. Sometimes radical change is invisible; especially when you are in the midst of living it.

Pop went with me to a Chrysler dealership in Upper Darby where he negotiated the purchase of a brand new, four-door, cherry-red Valiant priced at, get this, $1,800. To the end of his life my father loved to negotiate the purchase of new cars with aggressive salesmen. Just a few weeks before he died, in his 92nd year, Pop accompanied my brother where he negotiated a pretty good deal on a new Toyota! Our father always got a kick out of that practice and we indulged him over the years in his firm belief that his two sons were incompetent when it came to major high ticket item purchases like cars or homes.

My new car was delivered by the end of that week. Of course, if I ever drove into town to work at Arkay, I was always obligated to give Aunt Nan a ride home unless I wanted to end up like some wayward contractors on her shit list! My aunt loved to save the twenty cents it cost for a subway or trolley ride.

I was so proud of my new Valiant. One of the first things I did was drive to Arlene's house. It was a warm Saturday morning. And it so happened that her parents were not home. I parked in front and rapped on the door. Arlene, her long hair down, answered the door in her blue bathrobe. We had not seen or spoken to one another since that painful day in May.

I showed her my new car out the window. She didn't appear overly impressed. She wanted to talk about the summer. She had heard that I had a new girlfriend. Was it true? Sort of, I lied. I was actually planning a weekend trip to Oradell, New Jersey that Thanksgiving weekend.

Arlene pulled me to her. We kissed and embraced as if nothing had happened and as if all those painful months didn't exist. When we finished Arlene told me that nothing had changed. She still didn't want to get back together. So, why did she do what she had just done? I had no idea. Women! Freud was right. What the hell do women want?

Then Arlene dropped a bombshell: she was dating a guy from Lower Merion by the name of Jay B. Lewis. I knew a little about this guy. And, from what I knew, I didn't like him. Not one bit. Jay Lewis's older brother, Alan "Monk" Lewis, hung out at Harry's with the older guys. He always drove a flashy convertible and, it was said, he came from a Main Line family with money—a lot of money. The Monk was four or five years older than my crowd. But he had always treated me with respect and never looked down on the younger element at the Spoon. I actually always liked the Monk.

He once bet a guy named Bobby Coult that I couldn't run the pool table. Bobby, related by his older sister's marriage to my second cousin, bet on me big and cleaned up. The Monk's younger brother Jay…well Jay B. Lewis was something else as far as I was concerned.

Rumor had it that Jay had married a neighborhood girl when they were both teenagers. I knew her slightly—actually more than slightly. The word out about this girl was that she put out to whoever showed up at her door. When I was thirteen or fourteen she was visiting a relative on the next block from Diamond Street. One hot summer night, on her aunt's porch, although she hardly knew me, she allowed me to play with her titties. I was twelve or thirteen at the time. By the time she met Jay Lewis, this girl was giving out a lot more than a little bare titty to the boys on Morse Street where she now lived. Apparently, so overcome with his first piece of ass, the flaming love-struck idiot headed to Elkton, Maryland and married this girl! Such things were often the subject of great scandal and gossip in our neighborhood. It was whispered that Jay's parents had gotten the marriage annulled and that the girl had been paid off handsomely. I never liked Jay Lewis (and the feeling was absolutely mutual!) who struck me as an arrogant, narcissistic rich kid who was always combing his greased down hair at the bowling alley as if he was Ed "Kookie" Byrnes.

Arlene's announcement about Jay Lewis floored me. How could she choose, I wondered, an asshole like Jay over an asshole like me with my sterling qualifications? Well, he did live across City Line in Lower Merion. Maybe it was money! That's it; it had to be money.

All right! I had a new car. I was entering my senior year of college. The world beckoned like a ripe piece of fruit for the picking. Screw you Arlene! Pissed off after Arlene told me that Jay had a nicer car (a Chevy Impala convertible) I took my leave and said goodbye. Over the next 43 years I only spoke to Arlene Rachman once.

Although I was to see Arlene around the Temple campus over the next year and a half and around the neighborhood over the ensuing years, we were not to speak again until early in 1972 when I was teaching history at Rutgers University in New Jersey.

I was happily married (or so I thought) and commuting to Philly from New England every week in 1971-72. By then, recovering from a brief period of hospitalization because of her husband's wandering libido, Arlene had divorced her philandering husband who, she told me, had run off with a neighbor friend's wife leaving her with two little girls to rear with very little financial support. Jesus! Wynnefield was worse than Peyton Place!

She was still as pretty as ever but I remember thinking back in '72 that it was good that we broke up. I probably would have married her and who knows what my life would have become. I probably would have never left Philadelphia. Without Arlene, I was free to begin a journey that was to take me into a world so far removed from the parochial bubble we had known in that little neighborhood that it might as well have been a rocket ship to the moon.

Of course, I did not let go easily. On a warm August Saturday night a few years later, I sat in my car outside Har Zion Temple on 54th Street with tears in my eyes. I could hear the loud and festive music inside. I could hear the sounds of happy people. I was devastated.

Inside the very same synagogue where I had been a Bar Mitzvah, Arlene Rachman and Jay Lewis celebrated their wedding. It was still a few years before Dustin Hoffman played Benjamin Braddock in *The Graduate*. I wasn't about to stand in that synagogue window screaming at the top of my lungs to stop that goddamn ceremony. Although, I must admit, the thought did occur to me. In the early 1980s a woman with whom I was just beginning a romantic involvement wrote me a long letter breaking off the relationship. I was well over forty. "It sounds," she wrote, "as though your notion of love is rather adolescent." Guilty as charged! I had not seen or heard from Arlene Rachman since 1972. I was told she had gone through a few more husbands and left Philadelphia in the late 1970's for Florida. But I didn't really know where she was and, in those ensuing years with the passage of healing time, I don't think I really cared. I still carried a picture of the two of us in my wallet taken by my mother when Arlene was fifteen and I was seventeen. It never occurred to me that she was always a part of my subconscious. You know: the house with a white picket fence; two kids; all of that. In 1999 an old friend called me from Philly. Jay Lewis, he informed me, had been killed when he fell asleep at the wheel while driving somewhere near Las Vegas. My friend had no idea where Arlene lived or what had happened in her life.

CHAPTER 25

The next year or so flew by in a blur. My life with women had come to a grinding halt. I did not date. I went to school, to work, home and studied. I was still not pulling top grades but I had achieved a plateau I never expected to reach: I was actually in sight of graduating from college and, above all else, I did not want to allow that degree to fall between the cracks. I would be the first Goldman to ever graduate college…blah, blah, blah. So, I concentrated on my studies.

From time to time I would pass by Arlene in a stairwell, in Mitten Hall or out on Broad Street. Sometimes I would see her with Jay at a local restaurant or at another neighborhood hang-out. She would sometimes smile demurely. Sometimes she would not even acknowledge my presence. But we never spoke. Every time I saw her the bottom would drop out of my stomach. I couldn't understand. How could she have shared what we shared for all those years, and then let it go? It was as if I didn't exist. As if I never existed.

Obviously, that woman who over twenty years later suggested that I had an adolescent notion about love was on the money. I may have been twenty-one but I still had a great deal to learn about women. In my last years at Temple, unfortunately, I did not learn much.

I was comfortably ensconced in the back room of our new house. Pop had the Arkay carpenters construct a long marble-top desk that faced the length of my windows and so I had a nice view of a rodent-infested wooded lot while I studied and, if I looked to the far left of our home, of City Line and the heavy city traffic. In my despair, I virtually cut myself off from my family and stayed in my room. My mother and father could hardly understand my grief. After all, they had never been young and in love! I brought an old ten-inch Philco television home from camp. With a TV and phone in my room, after dinner hardly anyone ever saw me.

My brother Kenny was six years younger. That six-year gap in our young lives was too much of a gap for me to ever become involved with him. Aside from taking care of some troubles he had in junior high and high school, I left my little brother to his own devices and friends. I kept my own counsel and we lived somewhat separate lives. We would grow closer many years later as adults. But he had his own friends and his own life. Ken was beginning to show talent as a creative writer. He was a good student and a good kid. But most of us, me included, missed the signals. Ken knew little about what was going on in my life and I probably knew less about his. His teenage trials almost totally escaped me as I was selfishly wrapped up in my own life.

I finished the first half of my senior year in college in 1961 and once again hired on at Pocono Highlands. With the same cast of characters returning to the boy's camp, I looked forward to that summer since, with a car, I would be one of the mobile elite among the staff. Most counselors were not permitted to have a car. But I was almost twenty-two, a veteran and I made it clear to management that I would not be treated like a teenager. To be fair, the Weinberg family didn't want their staff to have cars in order to avoid the probable legal difficulty they would face if someone got into an accident while they were working for the camp. The previous summer two staff members were killed in very freak accidents: one guy, a kitchen worker, slipped on a watermelon seed, hitting his head on a table, and died as result. A handyman we affectionately called "Jeepo" because he drove around camp in a Jeep lost his life that past fall in a fire shortly after the campers had gone home. So, the Weinberg family was not being unreasonable. The surest way to close down an overnight camp is to let it get out that somebody has gotten killed at the place.

I drove up to Marshall's Creek in late June and was immediately relieved to find out that Lillian Hacker was not returning for the summer. That would have been awkward. I had taken her out on New Year's Eve and, realizing that she could never replace Arlene, stopped communicating with her altogether. It helped that she was far away at Kent State in Ohio.

It was to become a Marty Goldman pattern that, like TV's Seinfeld, I would repeat many times over the years. Women are better at the game than men. This may sound wrong in this era of political correctness, but the first thing I always wanted to know about a woman is how she felt in bed. For me, the opening gambit in the war of the sexes has always been…well, sex. Smell, taste, moves, moans and groans…I wanted to know about all that stuff quickly. I was quite willing to get to know a woman; but only after I had seen her behave in bed. After my divorce that became my modus operandi. Like the lady wrote to me, "adolescent." Lillian Hacker probably ate her peas one at a time anyway. And I am sure she didn't like apple pie!

Women always have to tell you why they don't want to be with you. Men are with you one minute and then, like the birds of summer, they disappear without a word. I have always despised ending it. And so, I rarely have. I have disappeared from the lives of scores of women without a word. Like that old soldier, General Douglas MacArthur, I sort of just faded away.

Camp in the summer of 1961 was once again memorable. I met a girl from New York named Judy Shachter. Judy was a sophomore math major at Bryn Mawr College just outside of Philly and although she was hardly in Arlene's class in terms of looks (few women I have met are), her rapier wit and sarcastic intellect immediately grabbed me. Judy was one of the smartest girls I had ever known and so I could easily overlook her squat body and thick, stumpy legs. Besides, she knew how to use her tongue like a sword swallower.

We made out every night in my spot near the stables and had long conversations about things which I rarely talked about with the guys at Harry's: books, writers, poetry and music. I was probably as much enamored with Bryn Mawr College as with the girl. I was struck by the fact that a girl as bright as Judy, a math major no less, could be remotely interested in a dummy like me. Clearly, positive self-image was not one of my major strong suits.

Judy's siblings, an asthmatic, whiny brother and twin sisters, were campers. And thus her mother and father, New Yorkers, planned a visit on parent's day. Golfers, they booked lodging at the famous golf lodge, Shawnee-on-the-Delaware, owned and operated by the well known celebrity big bandleader, Fred Waring (and his Pennsylvanians!).

That weekend Judy's parents invited us to have dinner with them at the inn. I drove Judy to see her parents feeling anxious. First, I did not have the proper clothes for a fine dinner at a hetchy-petchy golfing resort where you could count the Jews (who went by on the highway!) and wore a short-sleeved sport shirt and chinos. Second, her parents were, according to Judy, fairly high-brow. The Shachters were Jewish but it didn't seem to be a major force in their family life. Judy seemed far more secular and much less provincial than the world I knew in Philly. She was unlike any Jewish girl I had ever met. She knew literature, math, music, poetry. In 1961 I didn't know shit!

Her father played violin in the New York Symphony. Music was a big thing in their lives. I had still never gone further than the music of American Bandstand. And her mother, she told me, had once been a professional singer. What kind of singer and who she sang with, Judy didn't say. And I never asked.

We arrived at Shawnee on time, met her parents and were ushered into the dining room. The problem was that the host would not let me in. I did not, he brilliantly observed, have a dinner jacket. Male diners were not admitted to Shawnee without a proper coat. Judy's mother glared at me as if I had a dread disease and had just fallen from the turnip truck and asked for Fred Waring. I was mortified and stifled a strong urge to pull a Three Stooges exit by running out of the place yelling woo-woo-woo like Curly Howard. Who brings a dinner jacket to summer camp in the Pocono Mountains?

Judy's father hadn't said much and had this "Is this little asshole banging my daughter?" look on his face. It is a look I have come to know well over the years. By the way, I was not banging his daughter, although I can honestly admit that I did have exactly that objective on our future dance card.

In a few moments the silver-haired Waring arrived wearing one of the ugliest dinner jackets I had ever seen. It was a sort of checkered thing reminiscent of the Minkman invented on Saturday Night Live by Dan Ackroyd. And, it didn't even fit him. Waring hugged and kissed Judy's mother on the cheek as if he knew her well calling her "Joanie." Then he took off his jacket and gave it to me. I was to wear

Fred Waring's ugly, ill-fitting dinner jacket through the entire evening. I felt like a dork; because I was a dork!

Dinner did not go great. The food was expensive and mediocre. The Shachters did not appear overly impressed with their daughter's summer romance. "What does your father do? Where did you say you go to school, Martin? Oh yes, Temple; in the city? Marketing? Is that really a major these days? What are your plans after graduation Martin?" That kind of horseshit: Plastics!

After dinner the lights went down, Fred Waring came out and began to lead his famous band in a medley of their hits from the 1930's and 1940's. I don't think I knew one frigging piece of music! After the set, with absolutely no warning, the spotlight landed right on our table and right on Judy's mother. She was a tall, stately woman who must have been quite a looker in her day—a lot more of a looker than her dumpy daughter.

What the hell was going on? Everybody in the goddamn place was staring; right at us! Waring spoke softly into the microphone. The spotlight lay brightly on Judy's mother. She didn't appear at all uncomfortable. "Ladies and Gentlemen," Waring noted, "we have with us tonight an old friend. You all remember the Lucky Strike Hit Parade. Ladies and gentlemen, welcome the great Joan Edwards from the Hit Parade! Joanie! How about singing a song for the audience?"

Joan Edwards? The name meant nothing to me. The Hit Parade? Sure, I used to watch the Lucky Strike Hit Parade on Saturday night TV in the 1950's with Snooky Lanson, Dorothy Collins and Giselle MacKenzie. The room exploded in applause. I may not have known Joan Edwards. But this *goyish* crowd sure as hell did. Mrs. Shachter stood up, apparently comfortable in the spotlight, acknowledged the applause and Fred Waring's kind words. She demurred from singing. "I don't sing anymore," she told the crowd as they continued to applaud. "I leave all that to my daughter Judith here." The spotlight then landed on Judy and the skinny doofus in the ugly checkered jacket sitting by her side.

Who the hell was Joan Edwards? It was another Mickey Rourke as Boogie-*Diner* moment. Things were obviously going on that I didn't know about. Joan Edwards was a very well-known and popular chanteuse in the forties who sang with the big bands ultimately grabbing a top spot on the famous radio Hit Parade beloved by Middle America during the trying days of WWII.

Among the young singers to appear with her was a crooner who had become something of a teenage rage at the time, a skinny kid in a bow-tie from Hoboken, New Jersey—Frank Sinatra. There is hardly a biography of Sinatra written that omits his many duets with the young Joan Edwards on *The Hit Parade.* In a tape recorded reminiscence of her father's early career, Nancy Sinatra points to Frank Sinatra's work with Joan Edwards on *The Hit Parade.* As something of a Sinatra scholar and lifelong Sinatra-phile, I now know the impact that Joan Edwards had on Old Blue Eyes early career. Imagine that! Mrs. Shachter and The Man himself! And me, your obedient servant, sitting right next to her totally in the dark!

When *The Hit Parade* moved to the new medium of television in the late forties Joan Edwards opted to leave show business behind, married and raised a family. A few years ago, when she died, Joan Edwards got a quarter-page obit in *The New York Times.* Naturally, it highlighted her work on radio in the 1940s with the Chairman of the Board.

After Waring finished his brief show, he swept into the audience shaking hands and finally pulled up a chair sitting at our table. People were staring at us. And there I was wearing Fred Waring's checkered Minkman! He made a lot of small talk, ignoring me almost completely.

"So," Waring finally said, "Judith! Your mother tells me you are quite a talented pianist. And you sing as well." You could have knocked me ass-over teacups. Judy never sang for me or even played the piano. At first Judy was quite modest. But when Fred Waring invited her to audition for his band, she took her shot. We both had scheduled a day off in the middle of the next week. Maybe, Judy suggested, I could drive her over to Shawnee and Waring could preview her stuff. I had planned a magic day of picnicking and whatever else I might luck into by an isolated waterfall hideaway and lake not far from Marshall's Creek.

But hey! I was a nice guy; and ever so naive. Sure, I told Waring. I'd be happy to bring Judy back for an "audition." The following Wednesday, in white t-shirts and shorts Judy and I showed up at Shawnee on the Delaware shortly before noon. Waring ushered her into a room with a nice piano and asked me if I wanted some coffee. He called over to the kitchen, walked me to the door of the room and when I left, shut the door behind me. I went for the coffee. Waring went for the pussy!

On the drive to my hidden lakefront waterfall Judy seemed very quiet. "What's the matter? Did I say something wrong?" I asked. Judy just shook her head. And then, after a few more miles she burst into tears. Fred Waring was a dirty old man. While she was playing the piano and singing, the old lecherous pervert reached over her to apparently demonstrate some key-work and he kissed her on the cheek while grabbing one of her big boobs. I pulled over. I was about to turn around, drive back to Shawnee and kick Fred Waring's skinny ancient Pennsylvanian ass. The crotchety old bastard must have easily been over seventy-five at the time!

And, Judy said, he was married. Judy begged me not to go back to the hotel. In a few minutes she finally calmed down, stopped crying and we proceeded to my romantic spot.

I never saw Fred Waring again. Like the Shachters, the horny old coot is dead. Don't ask me what became of his Pennsylvanians.

In the sixth week of camp a little girl in Judy's bunk reported to the head counselor that she had had a nightmare. She said that in her bad dream she saw Uncle Marty in Aunt Judy's bed. On top of Aunt Judy! Men in the girl's camp were strictly verboten. That day Marian Weinberg called me into the office. "Do you want to tell me what you were doing in the girl's camp last night? On second thought, I don't want to know." I liked Marian a lot. She had a realistic view of what camp was all about. "Marty, we really like you. But we can't let it get around that you got away with going into a girl's bunk late at night. We have to let you go. You've got until this evening to pack up and get out."

I wasn't angry at Marian. She had a camp to run. I had raging hormones to cope with. We had been heading down across the camp lines for most of the summer. You pays your money, you takes your choice! At least they had not caught Arnold Markowitz. Arnie was one of my closest camp friends. He had been seeing a girl he called "Double Cheeks" all that summer. Arnie had accompanied me that fateful night into the girl's camp for a liaison with Double Cheeks (sorry, I don't recall her real name!) At least Arnie would get through color war and the last two exciting weeks of camp with Double Cheeks; but not my Arnie. When he found that I had been summarily fired, Arnie Markowitz marched into the office announcing to any who would listen that he too had been part of that little girl's nightmare. In a few minutes Arnie was packing his things with me back at the bunk. And off both of us drove into the cruel Pocono mountain air.

It never occurred to me to ask then what the penalty would be for the women. It was 1961. Women didn't pay penalties back in those days: Boys bad; girls good. Looking back I can't even say it was worth it. It wasn't as if we were getting laid or anything at all like that.

The problem was that I couldn't go home. Although Arnie said his parents couldn't have cared less, I would have been in deep shit. Getting fired at camp and losing most of that summer's wages (since most counselors made their big money in tips) would have pissed the Pop off to no end. So, I told Arnie we had to hang around camp for three or four days and sleep in my car. We would sneak into camp late at night and get some food from the other counselors in our bunk and maybe even sneak back into the girl's camp for a late-night session with Judy and old Double Cheeks. Judy Shachter would have none of it. She couldn't afford to get in any more trouble and so after a day or two of surviving in my car, Arnie and I headed back to Philly. I would stay at Arnie's house for the rest of that week and then tell the folks that I left camp a week early. Arnie was right. His parents, in the midst of an ugly split, never asked a thing. And I, uncomfortable with poor Arnie's domestic situation made it home by the fifth or sixth day after we were fired.

I never told my parents what happened. And my Pop never asked how much I made in tips that summer. When school started, as I entered the last semester of my senior year, I drove up to Bryn Mawr

College, about twenty minutes from Philly, to see Judy Shachter. It would have made a great scene in one of those coming of age Sixties films or Phillip Roth books—The Heartbreak Schmuck meets Brenda Patimkin or Goodbye Philadelphia!

I had to go to the desk of her dorm where they called Judy on the phone to tell her that she had a visitor. I never did see Judy Shachter again. She told the desk to tell me that she was too busy studying for a math exam to come down and that, if I got a chance, I should give her a phone call. Like a lot of women I have known, Judy Shachter ate her peas one at a time (with a knife!). Even if her old lady did sing with Sinatra!

CHAPTER 26

My final semester at Temple was uneventful. My old friend Larry Laster, in his senior year at Penn State, had fixed me up with a girl who provided me with what I needed in that down period of my social life. She came to Philly a couple times between Thanksgiving and Christmas and we were able to spend some quality time at Alan Stahler's apartment on the Temple campus. Stahler was always good with a key to his digs when a sexual emergency arose.

But I was not very adept at sex without love in those days. As I grew into young manhood, I improved mightily, eventually mastering the technique of sex without guilt entirely. The Penn State girl soon faded from my life and in February, 1962 I became the first male of my generation in the extended Goldman clan to receive a college degree.

My grandfather, Max Goldman, had come to America a penniless Russian immigrant shortly after the turn of the century. Max died in 1937 barely able to speak the language of his adopted country. He left his vast brood to argue over his legacy—$100 in cash. A quarter century later Max Goldman's first grandson graduated from a university. Don't ever tell me America ain't a great country.

Little did I know, as I proudly sat with my pal Stanley "Benny" Stein and our beaming parents in the old Baptist Temple on the Temple campus listening to the world renowned anthropologist Margaret Mead deliver our class's commencement address, that our life's myriad problems had hardly been resolved. They were, like Professor Mead's interminably dull speech, just commencing.

Pop wanted to know immediately: "What are your plans? What are you going to do with your life?" This time, I had an answer. One he did not like.

Maury Wolcoff and I had made plans to go to California. We had both majored in marketing and advertising. Jobs were said to be plentiful out on the West Coast. I had long since forgiven Maury for sticking his tongue down Arlene's throat and whatever else he did. Jay B. Lewis, I logically reasoned, must have been doing far worse. Besides, my philosophy then and my philosophy now about men and women is basically the same: It always takes two to tango!

Maury and I had talked about the possibility of California incessantly for months. We both agreed. We would use February to plan the trip. We would drive my car since it was almost new. We would take a week or ten days to make a leisurely drive cross country, stopping to see some of the famous sights. And then we would find a cheap apartment, get jobs and begin to scan the beaches for those long-legged, golden-haired California surfer girls made so famous by Jan and Dean and the Beach Boys.

Our target date for leaving Philly was March 1, 1962. Pop was not at all happy. Pop would worry when I drove down the shore. He was having a lot of difficulty with me heading out to La La Land. As usual, fate, in the larger than life guise of Aunt Nan Goldman, intervened!

About a week after graduation Aunt Nan called me on the phone. Could I come downtown to Arkay for an important meeting with Sy Rochestie, Jerry Krevolin and Charlie Lotman. I drove downtown the next day and was ushered into Mr. Krevolin's private offices which were usually locked tight. Jerry Krevolin was behind his Dad's desk. Sy Rochestie and Charlie Lotman sat on the green leather couch. Aunt Nan was in a chair and another chair had been put in place for me.

"What's up guys?" I asked pleasantly. The Krevolins looked serious.

"Nan tells us you are planning to go to California," Jerry Krevolin said. "How firm are your plans?"

"Pretty firm," I answered honestly. "I have a friend who is sharing the driving and we plan to room together and find jobs. I'm pretty excited." Then Charlie Lotman spoke.

"I,…uh…we…want you to come work for me," Charlie said without any small talk.

"Doing what?" I asked. I had no ambition to be in the home remodeling business in any way, shape or form. Sales were definitely not my forte. And, after almost four years of conflict as a bookkeeper under Nan's tough and demanding thumb, I certainly had no wish to see her every day of my working week. I loved my Aunt Nan. On Rosh Hashanah, Passover, and other major holidays.

"I'm going to open a nightclub in Philly," Charlie said. "I want you to be the manager."

"Whoa! What the hell do I know about managing a nightclub?" I responded.

"You're a quick learner; you know how to keep the books…and, most important Marty…we all trust you not to steal," Sy Rochestie laughed.

Aunt Nan was beaming. It was as if I was being Bar Mitzvahed all over again.

It was 1962, the height of a popular new dance craze called "The Twist." In New York, the Peppermint Lounge was raking in big bucks with Twist pioneers like Joey Dee and the Starlighters. Charlie had found a property that had once been a movie theater. It was on the border of a changing North Philly neighborhood. In one direction was the encroaching ghetto; in the other was the Philly neighborhood known as West Oak Lane. Charlie Lotman felt it would be a perfect spot to draw hip crowds from both the black and white community.

The place would be called the Candy Cane Cafe. Charlie would put up most of the money (and the other Arkay guys would all have a piece). First, the place needed to be renovated. Charlie would use all the Arkay contractors and everything would be remodeled at cost. He had already been in touch with some booking agents and had gotten assurances that South Philly singing sensation Chubby (Ernest Evans) Checker would be on hand for opening night. At that time Chubby Checker's "The Twist" topped all the pop charts. The Twist was the rage in 1962.

Even American Bandstand's kids were busy twisting. Chubby Checker would assure a large crowd that would open the place at full tilt boogie. In 1962 the Chubster was a major draw and would help to insure the profitable cover charges we planned to put into operation.

People always ask me about music when they find out I grew up in Philly. Although I can't claim any special expertise about the music business or even "the Philly sound" in particular, Philadelphia, like Motown in Detroit, was developing a distinctive musical persona. It wasn't just old pop singers like Eddie Fisher, Al Alberts and the Four Aces and Mario Lanza or the newer stars like Frankie Avalon, Fabian, Bobby Rydell or the throng of doo-wop groups like Danny and the Juniors or the Dovells that were emerging on Philly's hip urban music scene. There was a musical marriage going on though few were aware of it at the time. My mother had spent her teenage years in Atlantic City, New Jersey graduating from Atlantic City High School. I grew to know its back streets almost as well as I knew those in Philly. Atlantic City and parts of South Jersey became my second home.

By the early 1960's, in addition to the Twist, Philly music was merging into a tough anthem-like declaration of the streets that was being rocked out in South Jersey's Somers Point (a few miles outside Atlantic City) at nightclubs like Bay Shore's and Tony Mart's; a South Jersey sound that would eventually fuse with the Philly beat into the urban rock anthems later put together so brilliantly by Bruce Springsteen and his E Street Band. It was no accident that Springsteen would win an Oscar and a Grammy for the gritty *Philadelphia*. Or write a great song like *Atlantic City*. To hear the Jersey-Philly sound merge into historical reality see that much underrated film, *Eddie and the Cruisers.*

I didn't know squat about the Twist. But I had hung around Somers Point enough to realize that American music in South Jersey and Philly was changing big time. Charlie Lotman's offer was more than attractive. That emerging South Jersey-Philly beat would eventually go hand-in-hand with any new club in the urban Philly sprawl; a club that I would be running. The possibilities, I fantasized, would be endless. Especially the possibilities with women!

It was an offer I found difficult to refuse. Starting salaries for college graduates in 1962 were hardly what they are today. Most of my friends were lucky if they could find jobs in sales or accounting that started anywhere near $100 a week. Charlie Lotman offered me $150 a week to start—plus three per cent of profits. Profit sharing was unheard of in those days for newly minted college grads.

I didn't need a minute to think about it. I accepted on the spot. Nan was happy; Pop was ecstatic. He wouldn't have to worry about me being on the road with all those drunks between Philly and L.A. And Mom wouldn't have to eat her heart out about me running off to marry some blonde surfer *shicksa*. The only thing I had to worry about was telling Maury.

But that wouldn't be so difficult. After all he *did* touch Arlene's body when she was ostensibly my girlfriend! Actually, Maury was great. He understood the opportunity before me and graciously allowed me to beg out of our great California adventure. In early March Maury left Philly for L.A. I was not to see or hear from him again for almost six years.

Within a few days, painters, carpenters, plumbers, electricians and other contractors were busy getting the Candy Cane ready for opening day in early April. I was to help supervise some of the work while working fulltime in the office with Nan. Things were moving along well. The dance floor was put in and the walls were painted a candy stripe red and white; tables were painted red with candy apple red chairs. My small office had one of those one-way windows that allowed me to look out over the entire dance floor without being seen. Charlie was sparing, it appeared, no expense. It was all shaping up quite nicely.

In the midst of all this excitement two guys from the neighborhood, Rocky Mintz (the same Rocky Mintz who once questioned me about a neighborhood gang incident) and a guy who lived a block from Diamond Street on Gainor Road, Mitch Lieberman, opened a club with Peppermint in the name downtown on Sansom Street.

Charlie didn't seem overly concerned but he did ask me to check the place out. I went down the week it opened and was greeted by my old pal Rocky Mintz. I had known Rocky since about the fifth grade and we were close friends in Junior High School. Eventually Rocky, with a reputation as one of the toughest street fighters in Wynnefield, took a different path.

He ultimately dropped out of Overbrook, but over the years we had remained fond of one another. Whenever Rocky drove his '49 red

Ford convertible up to Harry's, a lot of guys shit in their pants since it wasn't one of his regular hangouts. He was usually dropping by to kick somebody's ass. But not me; I always greeted Rocky Mintz with great affection. He reminded me of that fable where a guy removed a thorn from the paw of a lion…and that fierce lion never forgot. Over the years, Rocky never forgot Junior High School and always treated me with real respect, warmth and friendship.

Rocky was exuberant about his new place. It was packed with chicks, every table was occupied and a live band pounded hard rock and twist music out loudly over the sound system. It looked to me as if Rocky and Mitch Lieberman (an older Harry's denizen) had a winner.

Rocky had just begun to tell me some of the details of his new venture when he excused himself, making a beeline to the front door as the famed Jerry Blavat walked in with his entourage. At that time the Geator with the Heater was the hottest dance-party DJ in Philly. The Italian-Jewish, ex-Bandstander, it was said by no less a musical expert than well-known DJ Sid Mark, was on the verge of breaking out nationally. Jerry Blavat would, Mark actually predicted, be even bigger than Dick Clark. Needless to say, you never heard of the Geator if you are not from Philly or Jersey. It just never happened. The Geator did get a nationally syndicated TV shot in the Sixties, but like so many Dick Clark imitators, Jerry Blavat could never break out of his South Philly mold. He has remained a big fish in the small Philly music pond.

Today he still hosts his dance parties and spins records on some local AM stations. But his old Heater must be on the fritz because now he is just an aging, white-haired Geator like the rest of us.

I reported what I had seen to Charlie Lotman. Charlie thought that if the place on Sansom Street was packed, that we couldn't miss since we had a built-in audience that spanned at least three urban neighborhoods and no parking problems. This was before all the vaunted redevelopment in downtown Philly. Very few of Rocky Mintz's customers actually lived in the Sansom Street neighborhood. He drew most of his patrons from South or West Philly.

We had brochures printed up and scattered all over the adjoining neighborhoods. The brochures had our logo, a candy cane and announced our weekend opening in early April with a special surprise guest. To keep the public mildly titillated we had a life-size cutout of Chubby Checker put in the window that looked out over Ogontz Avenue.

To make a long and painful story short, the Candy Cane Cafe never opened. As a result of petitions of complaint signed by a number of local religious and neighborhood groups and sent to City Hall, our license was denied. With some experiences now behind me in City Hall politics in Boston, I can well understand the power wielded by church leaders and community groups.

But back in 1962, public relations was still pretty much in its infancy and none of us could have imagined that a dance club would be remotely threatening to any urban community. In retrospect, we should have been cognizant that a rock 'n roll night club where Whites and Blacks from two urban settings would congregate was just a formula for big trouble. We would have been closed down after the first stabbing or gang-fight anyway.

In addition, Philadelphia was clearly one of the most corrupt big cities in the nation. I don't know much about the Philly of the 21st Century; but in 1962 everybody in City Hall had their hand out. Charlie spent some big bucks. He hired an attorney; the lawyer, I was told, paid off in Licenses and Inspections. But in the end, with all the palms that finally had to be greased in City Hall, all the way to the top, Charlie finally threw in the towel.

I don't know what he lost in terms of four months rent and the expensive renovations. But it must have been a big number. Charlie gave up on the Candy Cane Cafe and Chubby Checker, growing ever chubbier, twisted off into the winds of show business oblivion making a living for the rest of his life as a golden oldie twisting again and again over the years like he did that summer.

So much for new dance fads: when the Twist finally faded so did Rocky Mintz's new night club. Charlie Lotman, Sy Rochestie and Jerry Krevolin were out the money. But they still had their secure jobs at Arkay with a steady salary. Me? I wasn't angry at Charlie or anyone but I was shit out of luck. Not to mention a job.

CHAPTER 27

I know. The first question to be asked is simply, "Why not join Maury Wolcoff in L.A.?" The answer is also simple. That guiding force in my life: inertia.

Unlike clinical depression, inertia is not a result of being melancholy or emotionally despondent. Inertia is a physical law, a force that goes something like this: bodies in motion tend to stay in motion; bodies at rest tend to remain at rest. Call it Goldman's rule of inertia. A Marty Goldman at rest tends to remain…well…at rest.

At any rate, I did not leave Philly for LA. I began to look for a job. Every Sunday the classified pages in the *Inquirer* were packed with opportunities for guys with my impeccable credentials. There was one advertisement that ran every week that caught my eye. It was from N. W. Ayer, a nationally known advertising agency. The ad stated that the agency was looking for new college grads who graduated with a major in marketing and advertising to train in their burgeoning departments. All I had to do was put a resume together and send it in. I fit N. W. Ayer's ad profile perfectly. So, I sent in my resume.

And waited; and waited…and waited.

Finally, greatly frustrated that my very polished resume did not elicit an immediate offer of CEO in training, I called the company and was directed to the Office of Personnel. Yes, a woman finally responded; they had my resume. Could I make myself available for a personal interview? Is the Pope Catholic?

I put on my best new suit, purchased from my dear friend Alvin Kolchins "Suit Club," went to the big N.W. Ayer building downtown and went through the interview which was unremarkable and fairly pro forma. Then I waited again. N.W. Ayer never called. That June I finally got a job through Temple University's excellent placement service as Traffic Manager in a small advertising agency that was located in Center City.

The agency, the Henry Goodsett Agency, was run by two Jews, rare in the ad business in those days, Henry S. Goodsett and Sol Silverstein who did the hiring. When I mentioned to Sol Silverstein that I had also applied to N.W. Ayer he just laughed. Ayer, he said, never hired Jews. "Never hired Jews?" What the hell did that mean?

Why wouldn't a company hire a Jew? Jews were everywhere in Philly. Practically everyone I knew was Jewish. With the exception of that troglodyte I ran into at Fort Knox, I had never before come face to face with anti-Semitism. Certainly, not in Philadelphia; the City of Brotherly Love!

I wasn't naive. I knew a lot about the Holocaust. I knew about the Klan. I was aware of the word "Kike" and also hazily aware that certain elite schools and colleges had "quotas." But I had not yet come across the brilliant work of Penn Professor, the late E. Digby Baltzell who demonstrated where real power resided in this country in his two classic works, *Philadelphia Gentlemen* and *The Protestant Elite*.

Irish Catholics may have been running City Hall from the turn of the century. But the people who really ran the city of Philadelphia lived out on the Main Line. They were big bankers, customer's men, lawyers and insurance brokers. Oh yes, they were also advertising execs. And these power-elite Philadelphians most certainly did not like Jews.

They rarely hung out under William Penn's big hat at City Hall. You could find these ancient motherfuckers at the Union League on Broad Street where, since the Civil War, they kept Blacks and Jews as far as possible from their clubs and their posh neighborhoods. While they sent their entitled kids to private academies on the Main Line that were also *Judenrein*, they sat on the Board of Education for generations to make sure that the Philly public schools continued to suck. It was no accident that so many schools were named for powerful WASPs like Judge Dimner Beeber and William B. Mann. They had the power…not to mention a lot of money; Old money.

I had never been hit head on with overt discrimination based on who I was or how I practiced my faith. That was and has always been bullshit to me. I could never comprehend that, with all the other troubles cropping up along life's brief, difficult path, how a person could be stupid enough to waste energy discriminating against anyone based on their race, sex, sexual preference or religion. Life was just too damn short for such crap.

Advertising, I quickly found out, was not for me. I liked working in a tiny agency with a small client list. But I did not like the tedium and boredom that came from checking with magazines and newspapers about half-bleeds or full-bleeds on their ad pages or learning and then setting the myriad forms of typeface. I could have given less of a shit about Roman or Gothic in the typeset of Goodsett's clients boring print advertisements.

Also, I was not setting the world on fire with my pay scale. Goodsett started me off at $75 a week. With parking, gas and lunches, my net $60.24 did not go very far each week. I was falling further and further into debt each week that I worked. And, truth be told, I was not a very good Traffic Manager. I spent a great deal of time gossiping with a fat secretary from Wynnefield or talking on the phone with Benny and the Gansk who were working in nearby office complexes. The fat secretary, who reminded me of a young Aunt Nan, would ask me to drive her home since she lived coincidentally on Diamond Street about two blocks from where I used to live. If I begged off, she would then rat me out to management and tell them I was always on the phone goofing off with my pals. One day my close friend Alvin Kolchins came to the office. Alvin was selling the Encyclopedia Brittanica and "Suit Clubs" for a downtown haberdasher called Irving's. You'd give Alv a dollar each week and he would fill out a card, place it in a lottery-like drawing and each week you could win a free suit. At some point, when you had enough dollars on your card, you could apply it towards the purchase of a new suit at Irving's. I never won a suit and I never had enough dollars to get one of Irving's expensive suits. Alvin Kolchins was one of those guys who could put horseshit in a bottle, mix in a little water and sell it as perfume. I have always supported my friend Alvin, both emotionally and financially, in all his many endeavors over the years. I have still yet to win a free suit!

Anyway, the fat secretary told the bosses that my friends were visiting the agency. I was called in by Sol Silverstein and fired. I also got a dressing down for the way I used English. They did not appreciate my frequent use of words like "Man!" "Cool!" or "Cat" in almost every sentence I wrote or spoke. They were, of course, correct. My Rat Pack language skills were inappropriate for the cool, button-down 1962 world of American advertising. I argued that the copy turned out by the agency was old-fashioned, stilted and stodgy. But my argument held no water with Sol Silverstein. I was still fired; and facing the fall unemployed with few prospects.

In late August I threw my name and transcripts into the hopper of the Philadelphia Board of Education. The School District was paying $20 a day for substitutes. Imagine my surprise when, in the first week of September, I was offered a fulltime teaching position at—get this—Overbrook High School, my alma mater; teaching Math, my very worst subject.

I accepted the job offer and found myself soon embroiled in fulltime teaching in Overbrook's Math Department chaired by an affable little man, Jonas Witman. It was to be the historic autumn of the Missiles of October. But for me John F. Kennedy's nuclear confrontation with Soviet Russia over Cuba and Castro was small potatoes: Compared to the Murder.

CHAPTER 28

By late October of 1962 a great many kids at Overbrook High School knew who had murdered Mrs. Clare Kramer; and so did I. The problem was that the Philly cops were baffled. For a time it looked as if somebody (or somebodies) might get away with a brutal murder.

I'd better go back to the beginning. This can get complicated. So pay attention.

On a crisp, sunny Friday afternoon in early October in Philadelphia, a nine-year-old girl returned to her Wynnefield Heights home from grade school to find her mother lying on the living room couch in a pool of blood, bludgeoned to death. The shocking sight of her mother's head, beat into a pulpy mass of human jelly, would haunt that poor little girl well into a much-troubled adulthood.

It was the next day, Saturday morning. I was at Danny the Barber's shop in the Marriott Motel on City Line Avenue. I picked up the morning *Inquirer* as I waited my turn. I looked up to see Danny giving Jay Lewis a razor-cut when Arlene Rachman walked in to the shop. I felt my stomach drop, like a plunging elevator, the usual fourteen floors. Two damn years and I still could not let go of my first girl completely. Arlene and Jay were now married a few months.

Arlene did not acknowledge my presence. It was ironic. Arlene's new husband Jay was also teaching at Overbrook High; in the Math Department. We rarely spoke to one another. Jay made no effort to hide the fact that he did not like me. Of course, the feeling was more than mutual. Because we had similar rosters, not only would I see Jay every day in the department office, but we also hung out in the third floor teacher's lounge during our lunch-break and off-periods. We even had the same lunch duties at the same time. There was no place else to go. So we suffered one another almost every day. I, with the painful knowledge that he was doing to the love of my young life what

I still longed to do. Him, with the knowledge that, wherever he was going each day when he returned home, I had been there many times for years before him.

In these days of enlightened sexual attitudes, perhaps that stuff does not matter to young people anymore. Not me. Call me old fashioned. Somehow, I just cannot imagine being good buddies with any guy who had ever fucked my wife! Then or now.

I imagine that Jay could not stomach the fact that his wife's ex-boyfriend was in his face every day. Never one to disguise my feelings, it was clear I couldn't stand him. I tried to be cool that particular day and buried my face in the paper. But I didn't read. I just sat there behind the newspaper and suffered the torture of the damned, wishing that I had chosen a different day to get a frigging haircut.

Finally, after what seemed like a long time, Jay and Arlene left. As Arlene walked out of the shop she did not even glance in my direction. Apparently, Jay Lewis made my ex-girl-friend acutely aware that she was not to ever acknowledge my existence. I still had not focused on the newspaper or its screaming headline. As I breathed a sigh of relief that they were finally gone, I eased myself into the barber's chair just as Danny said, "So Marty, what do you think about the murder?"

"Murder? What murder?" I responded with my stomach still knotted up like a pirate's winch. "You read the paper!" Danny said. "That murder over there on Country Club Road!"

Murder? Country Club Road? I grabbed the paper again. There it was; a bold headline. I scanned the copy. "Kramer...murdered...2400 block Country Club Road...daughter found her...dead."

The blood rushed to my head. I felt queasy. I dropped the newspaper, jumped out of the barber's chair muttering something like, "Sorry Danny, I gotta go!" I headed for my Valiant in the parking lot. As I sped across City Line Avenue and down Monument Road, my stomach was still in knots but it no longer had anything to do with Arlene Rachman or her husband. They were small potatoes at that moment.

One of my closest friends was a Judy Cramer. She lived on the 2400 block of Country Club Road. Judy was twenty-nine, had two young children, a five-year old, Howard and a seven-year-old, Lois. Howie Cramer had been one of the youngsters under my charge at Pocono Highlands. His mother Judy was a recent widow. She had lost her young husband Martin to cancer the year before and was trying to put her life back together while raising two kids. Lois was a cute, curly-haired moppet with a wonderful disposition considering the fact that she had recently lost her Daddy and, unlike her younger brother, was acutely aware of that loss.

Howard Cramer was my favorite kid in camp that year. I called him Heschie and he delighted in the fact that he was the only kid in the group of eight with a nickname. Over the summer of 1961 I became very close to little Heschie and continued to see him after the summer. I took him to the Philadelphia Zoo, to the movies and other places. Judy Cramer wisely understood that her son Heschie and I were good for one another. He had lost his father and needed a male role model; I had lost my girl forever that year and needed a diversion and a friend. Judy Cramer became that friend.

As time passed, I often went uninvited to Judy's to see the kids. I can't count the number of times I had stayed for dinner. And once, my parents even had Judy and the kids to our house. On occasion, I would happily stay with the kids if Judy went out on a date. I babysat a lot once Judy began dating again. My own social life must have been in the crapper. That I don't recall.

I lavished affection on little Howie and Lois and they returned that affection. Howie was one of those kids whose childhood innocence made every new discovery a delight and, at the same time, a challenge. He craved affection and I had plenty to give in those years. We would spend hours reading or playing games. I grew to love Heschie Cramer as if he were my own kid. And Judy Cramer welcomed my comings and goings without invitation as if I were a member of the family.

It took me three minutes to speed to Country Club Road from the Marriott. The cop cars were still all over the place. I parked, took a deep breath and rang Judy's bell. I don't know exactly what the cops were doing. Canvassing the neighborhood maybe; whatever it is cops do when there is a terrible crime. They didn't pay any attention to me as I leaned on the doorbell of Judy's house clutched by the starkest terror of my young lifetime.

Within a few seconds an ashen-faced Judy Cramer answered the door. We just hugged.

"God, I thought it was you! I thought it was you!" I exclaimed.

"You and everybody else in the world," Judy said. "My phone has been ringing off the hook. My mother almost had a stroke. Everybody thinks I'm dead."

I followed Judy into the house and she put on some coffee. We sat in her small kitchen with the two kids as she filled me in.

Another family, the Kramers, spelled with a K, lived halfway up the street, maybe ten doors up in the newly constructed row houses. Unless you grew up in cities like Newark, Baltimore or Philly, the concept of a row house may be foreign. A row house is a series of maybe fifty or sixty houses on one street built all in a row. Your walls border on two neighbor's walls. If they are thin, like they were on Diamond Street where I grew up, you can virtually put your ear to the wall and listen in on the conflicts, conversations, and whatever else takes place in an average family's life.

The newer homes on Country Club Road, built in the late fifties, had better soundproofing. So, apparently no one heard Clare Kramer's screams; if there were any screams. All Judy Cramer knew at that point was what was in the newspaper. The little Kramer girl had come home from school sometime on late Friday afternoon. She found her mother dead. The fall weather was still warm but apparently nobody on the street had seen or heard a thing. The rumor on the street was that someone had broken in to rob the house, found Mrs. Kramer home and killed her.

Nobody was saying anything about sexual assault. The Kramers, who had both escaped the Nazis during the Holocaust, were good neighbors but nobody knew much about them. They both usually were away at work at their small grocery store that the family ran in South Philadelphia. The Kramers worked long, hard hours and were not at home very much during the week. They were a quiet family who kept pretty much to themselves. There were two daughters: the nine-year old and a teenager who was in the eleventh grade at Overbrook High School. I did not know her although I had, of course, seen her in the halls on a number of occasions. Although I had two eleventh grade classes, she was not one of my students. Mrs. Kramer was in her early forties. It was an age that seemed old to me. Back then.

I stayed with Judy and the kids for a couple hours and, when I could see that she had things under control, I left. The neighborhood was crawling with cops and there was little to fear about leaving Judy and the kids alone. Whoever had killed Clare Kramer wouldn't be coming back soon. It was not really going to be a problem in my life. Right? Wrong!

As the weeks passed, I read the stories on the Kramer murder in the Philly press. *The Daily News*, the local tabloid, grabbed onto it like a bulldog. *The Bulletin* and *Inquirer* covered the story responsibly and it eventually fell into the middle pages of the papers as the trail grew colder and colder. Other Philly murders combined with the dangerous Cuban Missile Crisis drove the Kramer murder onto the local media's backburner.

To tell the truth, I didn't think much about it. It was sad, but I was a new teacher, with five classes a day to teach, lunch duty, study hall and forty students in each class. Math was always my very worst subject. I'd keep a step or two in front of the kids each day as we went through the Math problems in the text: "If a train leaves the station at 50 miles an hour and has to go to a city 100 miles away, how many hours does it take for the train to get to its destination?" Remember?

Overbrook High School was rampant with rumor. One rumor about who murdered Clare Kramer was that some local kids from the school were involved. I heard the kids in one of my classes whispering about it but I dismissed what I had heard as so much ill-informed gossip. In late October the Philadelphia Police finally made some arrests; but not for the murder of Mrs. Kramer.

A couple of young men from the neighborhood were arrested for being part of a major burglary ring. One of the houses they reportedly had burglarized on many occasions was the Kramer household. Like many European immigrants who had escaped the Nazis and lost everything they owned in the world in the process, the Kramers did not trust banks. Instead of putting the cash from their grocery business into a bank, they had apparently kept it at home squirreled away in a second-floor closet. Since their business was largely a cash business, there was allegedly a great deal of cash always hidden in that closet. Even Mr. Kramer, who was closely questioned by the police, did not seem aware of exactly how much money had been stolen over the weeks or months that his home was being repeatedly burglarized. The thing was that these kids never had to actually break in. They had a key. The Kramer teenager constantly threw parties and apparently a few kids from the neighborhood had stolen a key to the house after they had stumbled onto the family's stash in the closet. According to the newspapers, there was so much cash that the Kramers never even missed it when it was stolen. If they did miss the money, they never reported the thefts to the local cops.

However, the teenagers who were fingered for the robberies adamantly claimed that they had nothing to do with any murder. They would only cop to robbing the place. In terms of the homicide, the cops were back at square one. It seemed inconceivable that any of these guys could have committed so horrible a crime. After all, they were "nice" Jewish kids from the neighborhood! Actually, they were street punks—not cold-blooded killers. Philly bad-mouses maybe—but not rats!

One of the young men arrested was a guy I knew well...too well. He was the younger brother of Gloria Langnas, old Charlotte Cutler's best friend and neighbor. The Langnas family lived at 5633 Diamond Street right down the block from where I grew up. Mrs. Langnas (Norma) had grown up with my mother in the neighborhood. They had been childhood friends. Her son, Rodney, was nineteen when he was arrested for allegedly robbing the Kramer household on numerous occasions.

Rodney Langnas was not one of my Harry's buddies. Three or four years younger, Rodney was always a Harry's wannabe. We nicknamed him "the Rodent" and we'd often kick his skinny ass out of the back room of Harry's where we shot pool or played pinball. Three years was a giant age gap back then. To us the Rodent was just a punk little kid trying to grow up fast.

I hadn't paid much attention to Rodney while I was in school. Sometimes I'd see him around Overbrook when I came to pick up Arlene and ask after his sister Gloria and his mother. And once when I was a teacher I saw him in the front office and said hello. But that was about all. While I went to college Rodney Langnas had grown up. And the Philly streets which had beckoned so many of us had finally gotten him.

By nineteen, Rodney came of age. He had dropped out of high school and was on his way, it was rumored in Harry's circles, to becoming a major neighborhood gangster. I had no idea what he was actually into. And, truth be told, I didn't want to know. To me, he was just a punk kid with little direction in his lackluster life.

Rodney drove a shiny black Thunderbird convertible and had developed into a pretty good-looking young hunk as a result of working out and with so much time on his hands I heard he was scoring with a lot of girls in the high school. Somebody had hooked him up with a male modeling agency and there were Coca Cola billboards all over Philly and Jersey with Rodney dressed in a checkered clown suit sipping a Coke with a very cute girl. Some of the guys said that he was even going off to Hollywood as a result of the Coke signs.

I once ran into Rodney at the City Line bowling alley on 54th Street as he drove up in his T-Bird.

"Where'd you get the new wheels?" I asked. "I won big at the track in Jersey," he smiled furtively. I shrugged. I knew he was full of shit. But I wasn't part of that life anymore. If Rodney wanted to be a criminal, that was none of my business.

So, I wasn't at all surprised when he was arrested. Still, I couldn't imagine that he had anything at all to do with the Kramer murder. I knew the Rodent was a thief; I also knew he was not a killer.

A few days after the Rodent's arrest, I was approached in the hallway at school by another teacher, a guy from 56th and Diamond Street who had hung out at Harry's for years. Hy Mayerson was three years older. He had just graduated Temple University Law School and, like me, was teaching at the Brook before he got on with his professional life. He had an offbeat, fun-loving personality and had been a Harry's denizen with a crazy gang of guys that I really liked. Even nuttier than our gang of guys, if you can believe it, they were fixtures at Harry's for years.

Hy grew up on 56th and Diamond, down the street from me and across the street from the Langnas family. He was not a close friend because of that three-year age gap, but I had known Hy since I was seven or eight and always liked him. We had played touch football, box-ball, punch-ball and pickup in the streets for years. Hy was teaching in the Commercial Department at the time while he prepared for the Pennsylvania bar and a career as a Philadelphia lawyer. To my surprise, Hy informed me that he was representing Rodney Langnas and that Rodney told him to talk to me—that I could be of great help to support his case.

How could I help? Hy told me that the cops were trying to tie Rodney into the Kramer killing. Robbing the Kramer place was one thing, Hy said. But first degree murder was quite another. Pennsylvania still had the death penalty. The Rodent could get the chair!

Hy said that on that particular Friday, the very day of the murder, Rodney remembered seeing me during the lunch hour at Larry's Steaks on Lancaster Avenue, about a block from the high school. Hy said that if I somehow remembered seeing Rodney that I could fill in about an hour or so of his time on that day—a very crucial hour it turned out. If Hy could establish a full day's alibi for his client, there was no way the cops could link Rodney to the Kramer homicide. It was important. Did I remember seeing Rodney Langnas at Larry's Steaks around the noon hour on that October Friday of the Kramer murder?

Indeed, I did…indeed, I did. Of course, Hy could not have been aware of the fact that I had an almost photographic memory—that I could and would remember *everything* about that particular lunch hour on that particular day in October 1962.

What was I doing at Larry's Steaks?

When I was in high school, I was suspended on many occasions for skipping out of the building during lunch. Leaving school was prohibited but I abhorred the cafeteria food. In the ensuing years, not much had changed. The vice-principal, John Burke, who had suspended me on many occasions of skipping out of the cafeteria, was still vice-principal when I came back to teach at Overbrook. He often reminisced with me about my long record of school suspensions. The school's cafeteria food was still swill—even for the teachers. So, whenever I could I escaped to Harry's if I had two periods off back to back, a five minute drive across the Lancaster Avenue Bridge or Larry's Steaks a three-minute walk just up the street. You have never had a real Philly Cheese Steak smothered in ketchup and fried onions if you are not from Philly. Trust me. There is nothing in the world like a genuine Philadelphia Cheese Steak. Aside from Larry's there was Jim's at 63rd and Callowhill in West Philly or Pat's in South Philly. Jim's and Pat's were too far to hit in a forty-five minute lunch-break but Larry's was close to the school just up Lancaster Avenue. And since I could not be suspended anymore, I often walked up to Larry's to grab a Cheese Steak instead of suffering the terrible institutional food still served in the Overbrook High School cafeteria.

On that particular Friday I walked up to Larry's with another teacher, Phil Indictor. As we wolfed down our Cheese Steaks, Rodney Langnas walked in. He was wearing a beige crewneck sweater and black pants. I remembered that crewneck because with the weather still unseasonably warm, Rodney took off his sweater, forgetting to take it with him when he left. The counter waitress, a young black woman, had seen Rodney talking to me. So, when he left his sweater behind, she asked me to take it. I told her to just put the sweater behind the counter; that he would probably be back when he realized he had forgotten it.

When Rodney entered Larry's that day he saw me and Phil Indictor sitting across the room from his table. He got up, came over and said hello. Phil Indictor had been teaching for a couple of years and knew Rodney as a troublemaker in the school who had been expelled many times. But I had known Rodney since he was a little kid. And so I was very friendly. Besides, as I later told Phil Indictor, I had probably been expelled as many or more times as Rodney.

I remembered he made small talk. Rodney knew I was teaching at the Brook and asked how I liked it. I asked after his sisters and his family. We made some more small talk.

"What are you up to these days?" I asked.

"I'm starting Temple soon," the Rodent answered. I knew that had to be a load of heavy duty horse manure since before you could get into Temple University you had to first graduate high school. I was pretty damn sure that the Rodent hadn't yet accomplished that little detail at nineteen. The conversation lasted another minute or so. Rodney said so long and headed back to his table where he finished eating and left before we did. I can't say that he appeared uncomfortable or even out of sorts that day. To me, the exchange was not out of the ordinary. And, I soon forgot about it; until that day a few weeks later when Hy Mayerson stopped me in the hallway at Overbrook High School.

"Sure," I told Hy. I would be happy to tell anyone who wanted to know where Rodney Langnas was on that October Friday during the lunch hour. I could pinpoint it exactly in time because I had a written roster with my lunch hour plainly noted for that day. I remembered seeing him; as it turned out, too well.

"What about Lenny?" I asked.

"Lenny?" Hy asked quizzically; "Lenny who?"

"Lenny Engler," I answered. "Rodney wasn't alone. Lenny Engler was sitting with Rodney at lunch that day in Larry's. I saw them. They were definitely together."

Hy Mayerson went white. "Are you sure? On that day?" he stammered.

"Absolutely; one hundred percent!" I answered.

Then he looked me right in the eye. Hy knew what I knew. He knew that I knew he knew what I knew. We both knew who had probably killed Mrs. Kramer on that terrible day. Rodney Langnas, probably not hip to attorney-client privilege, had obviously not informed his attorney of everything. Maybe he had banked on the fact that I didn't know who he had been with at the restaurant. But I did! If Rodney had told his lawyer the whole truth about that day there is no doubt in my mind that Hy Mayerson would have ever approached me to fill in his client's lunch hour.

"What are you going to do?" Hy asked.

"Right now, not a goddamn thing," I said truthfully. "I have to think about things."

"Promise me one thing," Hy asked.

"Which is…?" I asked.

"That if you go to the cops or even to another lawyer…that you'll let me know," Hy said.

"You got it!" I promised. Then I turned and walked slowly to my next class. I was in a deep sweat. I thought I knew who had killed Clare Kramer. Or at least I was pretty sure that I knew. The question was: What was I going to do with that knowledge?

I didn't know Lenny Engler well. But I knew enough. Lenny Engler was a dangerous human being. He was a little older then me but his reputation in West Philly, Wynnefield and Overbrook Park was a long-established fact. In Junior High and High School you never wanted to get on the wrong side of Lenny Engler. He was one of those guys who would hurt you and take great delight in hurting you. He would walk into Harry's, put a sawbuck on the pool-table, lose a game of eight-ball and then dare the guy who had just bested him to take the money. Lenny Engler didn't just play at being a gangster. He was one; also a gangster with a very short fuse.

Physically, Lenny was not very imposing. He was about average height and a bit on the thin side. His face, even as a young adult approaching his mid-twenties, was blotchy and sometimes still troubled by teenage acne. If Lenny Engler's face reddened, with the veins popping out of his neck, you wanted to get out of his way; quickly.

Some guys said he carried a blade. Others said he always had a piece. I don't know. I do know that by any set of standards, then or now, Lenny Engler was one bad dude.

Fortunately, he didn't wander into Harry's often. People who knew him said he came from a large family with a lot of kids. I knew two of his siblings at the high school. The girl was tougher than the boy. And many teachers breathed a sigh of relief when she was not assigned to their classes. From Junior High on I had been warned to stay out of Lenny's way. And although I knew him, I am quite certain that he did not know me. I was very adept at staying out of his way.

Harry's would usually be open until 1 A.M. on weekends. Lenny once came into Harry's after midnight. I was shooting a rack alone in the back room. When Lenny walked in I put up my cue stick and made it an early night.

By 1962 Lenny Engler had done time. The rumor at Harry's was that it was hard time—federal time. I didn't know for sure. But I certainly did not want to be the one to finger him as the killer of Clare Kramer. My favorite superhero has always been Superman. But Superman was hardly heroic. Nobody could ever hurt him. If Lenny Engler came after me, he could hurt me; real bad.

Apparently, Rodney Langnas had banked on the fact that I would remember seeing him which is maybe why he stopped to say hello. I guess he also hoped that I would not recall that he was with anyone else that day at Larry's Steaks. He probably thought that I didn't even know Engler and, if I did, that I would hardly recall the two of them together.

He would have been half right. I did not *know* Lenny; but I certainly knew what he was and some of the things he had done. I knew that Lenny Engler could kill someone. Sometimes, the kind of memory I have can be a curse. In the David Lean classic film *Doctor Zhivago*, the secret policeman Yevgreb asks Zhivago's and Lara's young daughter how she learned to play the balalaika. Finally, he concludes, "Ah, it's a gift." Like my frigging memory. A gift, my ass!

CHAPTER 29

"Concealment, even of a crime in which one is oneself not a participant, is itself a crime—misprision of a felony—punishable by a statute enacted by the very first Congress and still on the books."
Gabriel Schoenfeld
Commentary, February 2007

That night I sat down with my Dad after dinner. With my mother and brother out of earshot, I related what had taken place with Hy Mayerson that day at school. Pop remembered Hy from Diamond Street but he did not know Rodney. He listened carefully as I told him my conclusion: that Rodney Langnas and Lenny Engler had killed Mrs. Kramer.

Pop was a very logical thinker. "First of all," Pop said, "just because you saw two guys having lunch, it doesn't mean that they committed a murder. Second of all, if they didn't do it and you cause them all kinds of trouble, they could sue. Third of all, mind your own business. If they did it, the cops will find out. They already have Langnas. If the other guy was involved, they'll break the Langnas kid. Stay out of it!"

The problem, I argued, was that the cops did not know about the other guy. "They'll find out. They have their ways," Pop said. "Stay out of it," he repeated.

My father was basically a very conservative person even though I think he voted for Democrats most of the time. I know he liked Bill Clinton as much as I despised him. Our arguments over the Clinton impeachment in 1998 were endless. As I grew older, it became clear that we both viewed the world differently. Pop would never consider writing a letter to the editor. He apparently didn't want anyone to know where he lived.

Still, Pop knew a lot more about cops than I did. We had a relative who was a detective on the force; the son of one of Pop's many uncles or cousins. Once in a while Pop would call this guy for a favor. I don't think I ever met him but over the years he was often mentioned around our dinner table. So, I decided to listen to my father. I did nothing. I told a few of the guys from Harry's that I knew who had killed Mrs. Kramer. But they only laughed. The Rodent? A killer? No way! An asshole? Maybe. But never a killer.

As the weeks passed, with the country mired in JFK's atomic eyeballing of the Russians over Missiles in Cuba, I'd run into Hy Mayerson in the hallway or in the teacher's lounge. He never brought up the Kramer murder again. He never mentioned a thing about his client or what was going on. The Cuban Missile Crisis came and went and the country breathed a well-earned sigh of relief that our big cities had not ended up being incinerated. At the time the Cuban Missile Crisis had little impact on my life. Although I would later write and teach many college classes about John F. Kennedy taking the nation to the very brink of nuclear conflagration, when it was going on, the Missile Crisis didn't bother me very much. I didn't lose a moment's sleep while JFK played nuclear chicken with Nikita Khrushchev. I taught my classes at the Brook and kept the knowledge of who I had seen at Larry's Steaks on the day of Clare Kramer's murder to myself.

It was a late Friday afternoon; a week before Thanksgiving. The Kramer case had been largely relegated to the back pages of the Philly papers and it didn't appear as if the cops were any closer to a resolution than they were back in October.

I had thought of little else. It bothered the hell out of me that a hardworking woman in a middle class neighborhood could not be safe in her own home. That a little girl had to come home from school to find her mother's mangled body. That not a single story linking Rodney Langnas to the various burglaries had ever mentioned Lenny Engler by name.

I left school around three o'clock that afternoon. As I pulled up in front of my house on Bryn Mawr Avenue the car radio blasted out the news that Rodney Langnas's lawyer(s) had filed a writ of *habeas corpus* which probably assured his imminent release from jail. I couldn't believe my ears. How could the goddamn cops be so inept? They had the right guy.

All they had to do was grill his ass. What had happened to the days of the old rubber hose? I guess I wasn't thinking clearly. I didn't call my Pop. I didn't call Hy Mayerson. I put the car in gear and headed for the police station at 63rd and Thompson, off Girard Avenue in West Philly. I was still wearing a dark tie and a blue herring-bone jacket as I walked up to the desk. I probably looked all of sixteen or seventeen. I was still being carded in bars well into my early thirties. The desk Sergeant asked gruffly if he could help me.

"Yes," I answered. "I'm a teacher at Overbrook High School. I would like to talk to Detective so and so." I had gleaned the name out of the newspaper stories. I do not recall that name today (Hey, I have a good memory but it ain't perfect!).

"Is this related to the Kramer murder?" the desk Sergeant asked perceptively.

"Yes…it is," I replied calmly. Inside, I was in absolute turmoil.

The desk Sergeant asked me to wait and I sat down. A few moments later he called me back to the desk. "They're sending a car from City Hall. They'll be here for you in about fifteen or twenty minutes. Two homicide detectives will pick you up."

"A car? A Red Car?" I thought. I didn't want to be riding around Philly in a Red Car. In those days you could see the Philly cops coming for miles. They all drove blood Red Cars. If a neighbor wanted you to stop playing ball in the alley behind their house, they would always threaten, "You'd better get your ass out of here or I'll call the Red Car!"

What the hell did I do? I felt a strong urge to run out of the cop station, drive home and get under the covers. I always felt safest in my room, in my bed, under the covers.

I want to say a few words about courage here. I do not want to give the impression that what I did took any courage. It was just something I did on the spur of the moment without any real serious or thoughtful introspection. I just did it without thinking about it. It wasn't heroic in any sense of the word. Heroic is what those firemen and cops were at the World Trade Center on September 11. I have friends where I live half the year in Florida; veterans of dozens of firefights in Vietnam. What they saw and did took real courage. They are true American heroes. I have often thought a great deal about courage. Would I have gone to Vietnam with my infantry outfit? At seventeen, the answer was probably. I was a kid and didn't know any better. By the time I was twenty-six, there is no way they could have ever gotten me to Vietnam. By then I knew it was a stupid and useless war. Although I had no special knowledge that Vietnam was a lost cause in the early years of the war, by the time I entered grad school I knew I would never allow some Asian guys I didn't know, some guys from a country I had never heard of and could not find on the map, to shoot my ass off for no discernible reason.

So, I am no hero. Not in the sense of my Vietnam veteran friends. But I am not a coward either. I recall being angry about the Kramer killing. I was angry that a woman couldn't be safe in her own house in my neighborhood. Something was very wrong with that.

I always believed that people had a basic right to be secure in their own homes. It could have been my mother (as eventually, it would be!). And what about the young Kramer children? They had lost a mother. Nobody deserved to lose a parent that way. I was also very angry about the cold-blooded killing of Mrs.Kramer. I didn't want whoever did it to get away with the crime.

At the same time, I was aware of violating a strict code of the Philly streets: never Rat.

And especially, never Rat to the cops! I had made up my mind. Pop was wrong. It was my business. I was going to Rat.

As it turned out they didn't send a Red Car. They sent a white, unmarked sedan with two plainclothes cops in the front seat. I got into the back seat for the short drive to City Hall. The two cops didn't say much. The one not driving asked, "So, you teach at the high school? What do you teach?"

"Math," I answered. "Math!" he exclaimed, "my worst subject!"

"Mine too," I said.

We arrived at City Hall a little before five o'clock. I was ushered in through a side door and escorted to Homicide. I passed a stocky guy in uniform with gold braid all over his cap. I immediately recognized Frank Rizzo, the toughest cop in the city of Philadelphia. I had once seen Rizzo step in front of an angry crowd who were protesting a neo-Nazi demonstration at the downtown theater showing the film *Exodus*. Rizzo challenged anybody in the crowd to cross a police line and take a punch at the Nazis. They would, he said, have to get by him first. Nobody in the angry crowd took Rizzo up on his offer and the Nazis left unscathed.

Within a few minutes a portly, bald detective came out and introduced himself. "Hi," he said, "I'm Larry Magen." Looking me over curiously, he said, "Do I know you?"

Sometimes life has strange and funny twists. Sometimes truth, as they say, is much stranger than fiction. Larry Magen knew me. He knew me well. When he was a young, beat patrolman, Larry Magen was at the Mann School crossing for the entire seven years I was in grade school. All the kids in the neighborhood knew and liked him. He watched me cross the street for seven years. As a teenager, because he remembered me from Mann School, Larry would often grab me and a lot of the guys off the street after some complaint, drive us around and then let us go with a warning. At the bowling alley on 54th Street he would drive up with a partner and corner me over the years. I can't count how many times Larry Magen had warned me to keep out of trouble. He was one of those law enforcement rarities in Philly: a Jewish cop and a friend to the teenagers who always caused him so much grief. When Larry used to see me on City Line with Arlene, he would flash me the high sign as he rode by in his patrol car. I was one of his success stories: a kid from the old neighborhood beat who never ended up in jail. I hadn't seen him in many years.

I reminded Larry how we knew one another. He immediately remembered me. I was not aware that Larry had risen to a homicide detective. Or that he had been assigned to the Kramer murder case.

"They tell me you're a teacher at Overbrook," Larry said cutting to the chase. "Whatcha got for us on the Kramer case?"

"First things first," I answered. "Where are you on this thing? I heard you are going to release Rodney Langnas."

"Looks that way," Magen said. "We can't hold on to him much longer. Whatcha got?"

"I don't want my name in the papers," I said. "You've got to promise that if I'm right, that you'll keep me out of the papers. I still have to live in Wynnefield. And teach at the Brook."

"We can do that," Magen promised.

"I don't want to testify," I said. "You've got to get it on your own. No trial where I testify."

"We'll try. I can't promise that. But we'll try," Magen said.

"Also, I am not signing anything," I said.

"Are you involved in this shit? Do you need a fucking lawyer," Magen asked pointedly.

"No lawyer. I just don't want to be hassled. I don't want my life turned upside down," I said.

"We'll do our best. I can't make any promises beyond that," Magen said impatiently. "Whatcha got?"

"Did you know that on the day of Mrs. Kramer's murder Rodney Langnas had lunch at Larry's Steaks on 59th and Lancaster Avenue?" I said.

"Yes. We are aware of that fact," Magen said.

"Did you know he wasn't alone?" I asked.

"No we did not! Who was he with?" Magen asked.

"He was with a guy from the neighborhood—Lenny Engler," I said.

"You saw them together?" Magen asked.

"I saw them. I spoke to Rodney. I can even tell you what he was wearing that day," I answered. Magen walked up to me, grabbed me and hugged me. I was taken completely aback. A tough Philly street cop does not usually give you warm bear hugs.

Magen knew Lenny. "We've spoken to Engler," he said. "He gave us *bupkas*." Magen did not say why they would have spoken to Lenny Engler and I didn't ask.

"Did he mention lunch with Rodney that day," I asked.

"No. He did not mention lunch with Rodney that day. We have nothing to tie him to Langnas at all during that day. I'm gonna have him picked up. I'm sorry but you're going to have to wait around. I need you to ID him positively. It's gonna take a while. Maybe you want to call home and tell them you'll be late for dinner? You want a coke or some coffee?"

I called home and told my mother I would not be coming home for supper. I didn't say why or where I was. No point in ruining my Pop's *Shabbat* dinner. Then I sat waiting alone in a small room at a long rectangular table sipping hot coffee. Another detective came in after about ten minutes to ask if I needed anything. I said no and he left. It was almost seven o'clock when Larry Magen returned.

"I'm going to take you to a room with a one-way window," he said. "We've got Lenny Engler in the next room. You'll be able to see him. He won't be able to see you. There's nothing to be afraid of. He will not see you. We need you to positively identify him as the person you saw eating lunch with Rodney Langnas on the day of Mrs. Kramer's murder. Can you do that?" Magen asked.

I could and I did. If I could keep from heaving up that acidic coffee since my stomach was churning by that point in full tilt boogie.

I was led into a room with a large glass window. I could see Lenny Engler sitting alone in a room at a table. His blotchy face was red. He appeared more angry than afraid. Magen remained with me. Another detective walked in and sat at the table facing Engler. Engler spoke first. I noticed his voice cracking a bit; perhaps an imperceptible octave higher than normal, if you had ever heard his act on the streets.

"Why are you hasseling me? You bastards have talked to me! I told you where I was.You got nothing on me!" Lenny exclaimed.

"Suppose we told you we can put you at Larry's Steaks that Friday with Rodney Langnas?" the detective sitting with him said.

In the room with me, Larry Magen asked me pointedly, "Is that the person you saw with Rodney Langnas at Larry's Steaks?"

"Yes," I answered in a low voice, swallowing hard. "Yes, it is. Lenny Engler."

Then the detective in the room with Engler opened the door. Standing off in the hallway, so that Engler could see him was Rodney Langnas. He was handcuffed. I could see Rodney being led away as the detective closed the door. Engler stared in stunned disbelief. It was obvious that the cops wanted Lenny to think that his buddy had finally given him up.

"Do you want to change your statement about that Friday?" the detective said sharply.

Engler looked like a trapped animal. His eyes scanned the room as if trying to find an exit, a way out. He looked straight at me even though I knew he could not see me. Then he put his head down on the table and began to sob. He made loud sounds but I couldn't make out a thing he was saying in between the sobbing since I could no longer see his face.

"That's it!" Larry Magen shouted. "We got 'em both!"

Magen then led me out of the room to another room where he asked me to sign a formal statement noting that I had seen Langnas and Engler at Larry's Steaks on the day of the Kramer murder. At first I refused. I didn't want to sign any statement but Magen informed me that without the document there would be no case, nothing to link the two men on that day. I had neglected to inform the cops that another teacher had been with me at Larry's. I didn't want to involve Phil Indictor in a murder investigation without his permission and, as it turned out, Indictor later told me he could not remember who I had talked to that day anyway. I signed the statement with great trepidation. Pop was going to really be upset.

Meanwhile, I could hear commotion. What was going on? Magen told me that some reporters had gotten wind that they had cracked the Kramer murder and that the place was beginning to fill with reporters. He would, he promised, get me out of a side door and have a car ready to whisk me back to 63rd and Thompson. He'd keep the reporters away.

He first told me what had happened at the Kramer house on the day of the murder. Engler had spilled his guts crying like a baby every step of the way. Some tough guy!

Rodney Langnas had been robbing the Kramer house for months with a key he glommed from the Kramer teenager's pocketbook at one of her parties. Langnas had hooked up with Lenny Engler at a pool room at 60th and Spruce in West Philly. I was glad to hear that the robbery had not been planned in Harry's backroom. Rodney had apparently bragged to Engler how he had been draining cash from the Kramer household as if it were his private Federal Reserve. Rodney had apparently involved other local teens in his weekly draining of cash from the Kramer household. However, he had never searched the entire house. That would take time and some extra manpower. There had, he told Engler, to be a lot more cash hidden around in that house. All Rodney needed was some help; some professional help. Lenny Engler was a professional.

So they made a plan. They would rob the house on a Friday morning when the family was away at school and at work. Engler enlisted a Negro friend who also hung out at the West Philly billiard parlor—one Lonnie Johnson. Johnson, in his twenties, was a petty thief who, according to Larry Magen, was no stranger to the Philly authorities.

On that particular Friday, Rodney drove up to the Kramer house in his black T-Bird with Johnson and Engler. He was the wheel man and would remain in the car if they needed to make a rapid getaway. Johnson and Engler entered the house. Johnson carried a crowbar to, he told his confederates, open any door or box that needed opening. The best laid plans...

Something went immediately wrong. Clare Kramer was home, upstairs on the second floor putting away laundry. She had heard the two men enter her home and then made a fatal mistake—the last mistake of her brief life. Instead, of picking up a phone and calling the cops, Mrs. Kramer came tearing down the stairs screaming at the top of her lungs.

Lonnie Johnson hit her with the crowbar; again, and again, and again. Engler told the police that he lost count of how many times Lonnie Johnson whacked Mrs. Kramer with that crowbar. He said that he had stood paralyzed, in fear of his own life as Johnson, apparently unnerved by the woman's screaming, just lost it. Engler also said something about Johnson picking up a table lamp but it wasn't clear, Magen told me, if he had whacked her with that lamp as well.

Before he knew it, Engler said, Mrs. Kramer was stone cold dead. They put her on the sofa; a nice touch. And then they got the hell out of there.

Rodney dropped Lonnie Johnson off after they tossed the crowbar down a sewer in West Philly. Then, less then an hour after Clare

Kramer was savagely beaten to death, Rodney Langnas and Lenny Engler decided to grab some lunch...at Larry's Steaks on Lancaster Avenue.

Magen hustled me out a side door. He said he intended to pick up Lonnie Johnson that very night. "I hope the black bastard resists because I wanna tune his black ass up if I get the chance," Magen said. I don't know if he ever got that chance but he did pick Johnson up the next day.

As I made my way out of City Hall I could see a horde of reporters waiting to find out how the cops had finally solved the Kramer murder. I don't recall much about the ride back to the station. I had a splitting headache. Or the drive to my house from the police station in West Philly. I felt shitty. I thought I had done the right thing. And I would do it again. But I took no joy in what I had done. Besides, now I had a task I hardly relished. I had to tell Pop!

CHAPTER 30

The next day, Saturday morning, the Kramer murder once again dominated the front pages of all three Philadelphia papers. Photos of Lonnie Johnson, Lenny Engler and Rodney Langnas, hustled past reporters in handcuffs by triumphant Philly cops, were in every paper too. The two broadsheets, *The Bulletin* and *The Inquirer*, reported the story straight down the line. Weeks of solid police work, connecting the dots, and a little luck, the papers noted, had enabled the crack Philadelphia Police Department to break the case.

Only *The Daily News*, the city's tabloid, came anywhere close to getting the story right. *The Daily News* hinted at a last-minute "secret witness" who came forward with vital information that the detectives used to link the three killers. After almost a decade as a reporter, columnist and editor for a number of Boston newspapers I learned a couple things about the press.

I learned that the tabloids usually developed better police sources than the larger dailies because their reporters often worked closer to the street where they became friends with the cops they covered in their various crime stories. Obviously, a *Daily News* reporter had a solid source deep in Philly's Homicide Bureau. Fortunately, that source kept Larry Magen's promise. My name never appeared in any Philly newspaper reporting on the resolution of the Kramer case.

That morning, as my father and I scanned the papers, I could see that he was unhappy.

"What's the matter, Pop?" I asked. "You don't think I did the right thing? I told you all along I knew who did it."

"That's not the point," my father said sharply. "You think this is over. I can tell you. It's not over. If I were you, I wouldn't go around bragging about this. Keep your mouth shut!"

On Monday morning the Kramer case was topic number one at school. In the teacher's lounge it was all anyone talked about. Most of the veteran teachers knew both Langnas and Engler from their infamous days at the Brook.

I listened intently to the conversations. Nobody seemed to have a clue as to how the case was finally solved. If Hy Mayerson knew what I had done, he never mentioned it. Facing a capital murder charge, Rodney Langnas had retained new and more experienced counsel. I didn't join in the conversations. Pop would have been proud. I kept my mouth shut.

Thanksgiving came and went; then Christmas and New Years. It was 1963—what was to be a fateful year in American history and, as it would turn out, a critical year in my life. I soon put the Kramer murder behind my thoughts and got on with my teaching. In January I was informed that my services would no longer be required in the Overbrook High math department. It wasn't that I had done a poor job. It had something to do with class numbers. So, in the spring semester I began to travel from school to school, filling in for absent teachers on a daily basis. It was actually easier since I had no classes to prepare. I was really a well-paid baby sitter.

Sometimes I'd be back at Overbrook; sometimes at Gratz or the three worst Junior High Schools in the city: Gillespie, Shoemaker or, the most horrid hellhole I have ever seen pass for a school, Fitzsimmons. I dreaded being sent to the Junior High Schools and, if I could get a full day of work at Arkay, would often pass if they called from those particular schools where organized chaos generally ruled the day and the dilapidated classrooms. To this day I still smile to myself when I hear a mayor, congressman, senator, governor or even the president pay lip service to improving American education. In the 1960s the best way to improve education in Philadelphia was to fire all the administrators, blow up these ancient schools and start over.

That spring I was surprised to receive a subpoena in the mail. I was ordered to make myself available for at least two weeks and maybe more for the trial of Rodney Langnas and Leonard Engler for the murder of Clare Kramer. As usual, my Pop was right.

I called Larry Magen and went off the charts. "What the fuck!" I yelled at Magen. "I thought we had a deal! What is this shit? A trial? No way. No fucking way! I am not testifying at any trial! I'll leave town first."

Detective Magen tried, with little success, to calm me down.

"Listen Marty, it isn't our fault. The D.A. needs you to make his case. It wasn't in our hands. It's his call. You gotta appear. If not, I'm gonna have to lock you up," Magen said.

"Lock me up?" I shouted. "After what I did for you guys! You're gonna lock me up?"

"That's the law Marty," Magen said. "You better be there. We can send a car but you gotta be there. Sorry."

"If I testify, the entire world will know that I ratted," I whined.

"We don't see it that way. You did the right thing. But we need you to be at the trial if the D.A. has to call you as a witness. You're on his list. Nothing I can do," Magen said.

I should have known. But, in those days there was no *Law and Order*. Joe Friday caught the bad guys every week on *Dragnet* and then a little crawl appeared on the screen to tell you that they were doing twenty-five to life in Alcatraz or Vacaville. You never saw a frigging trial. It was before Perry Mason. I had to appear at the goddamn trial. And then everybody in the world would find out what I had done. I began making plans in my head to enlist in the Merchant Marine on a freighter steaming to the Fiji Islands. As usual, inertia set in and took the day.

The week of the trial came. I put on a sharp suit and headed downtown to the courthouse. I took a bus and the subway. I didn't want to be driven by any cops. Magen and another detective met me out front and escorted me into the courthouse. Outside the courtroom, Norma Langnas, Rodney's mother, walked up to me. She didn't appear hostile. "Marty Goldman! What are you doing here?" she asked pleasantly. I tried to think of a good lie quickly but Mrs. Langnas answered her own question.

"I know," she said. "You know my Rodney. He's a good boy. You're a character witness."

I didn't bother to correct her. What the hell? She was a nice lady and had raised two terrific daughters. She didn't deserve this. I sat next to the two detectives in the courtroom not far from the table where the two defendants would sit with their attorneys. Within a few moments Engler and Langnas were led into the courtroom with their attorneys.

As he walked by me, Rodney acknowledged my presence with a half smile and a wink. Jesus! He didn't even look frightened. He knew! The cocky little bastard had to know! Engler, unlike Rodney, looked scared to death. It seemed that he had lost a lot of weight in jail. His clothes hung loosely on his thinner than usual frame. He actually appeared frail. Maybe he wasn't as tough as he always thought.

The judge, Vincent Caroll, an ancient Philly Irishman who enjoyed a well-earned reputation for being very tough on violent criminals, entered the courtroom. There was some preliminary bullshit between the judge and the attorneys. I could not hear what they were saying.

Finally, Judge Carroll addressed the two defendants. He asked them how they were going to plead. Both Langnas and Engler were standing as they spoke softly.

"Innocent," they murmured, one after the other. Judge Carroll glared at them.

"Fine," he said. "We are going to have a trial. But I want to tell you something before we get underway. This is a capital case. If the state of Pennsylvania enpanels a jury and goes to the expense of a long trial, and if that jury finds you guilty, I want you both to understand that it will be a First Degree verdict and that I will have the option of sending you to the electric chair. I want you both to understand that I intend to exercise that option."

From where I sat I could not see Lenny's or Rodney's face. They whispered to their lawyers. The lawyers then requested a recess. Judge Carroll gave them twenty minutes.

"What the hell is going on?" I asked a smiling Larry Magen.

"Kiddo, unless I miss my guess there ain't going to be a trial. I think you're off the hook," Magen said.

It turned out that Larry Magen was right. When the court reconvened, after consulting with their attorneys, Rodney Langnas and Leonard Engler changed their plea to "Guilty." I did not have to testify and no one ever found out that I was the guy who dimed them out.

Judge Carroll eventually sentenced them to life in prison for second degree murder. There was a bottom term like fifteen to life or ten to life. I have forgotten. It meant that they would serve the short boat after which the two would-be Philly hoods would be entitled to apply for parole. Rodney Langnas became something of a jailhouse lawyer and was constantly petitioning the Commonwealth of Pennsylvania to review his case. I don't know whether he ever got that review. I ran into his sister Gloria in Atlantic City in 1996. I asked Gloria how her brother was doing. She told me that he was fine. So I assume that Rodney served his time and eventually received his parole. Which was fine by me. Rodney was a wiseass, punk nineteen-year-old kid. He was not really a killer. He had never even entered the Kramer house that day. Still, if it wasn't for Rodney playing hoodlum, Mrs. Kramer would be playing with her grandkids today. You pays your money, you takes your choice!

Lonnie Johnson, tried separately, was given life without parole. I don't know what happened to him in prison or if he is back on the street today.

This Wynnefield, like Brigadoon, the mythical Scottish village, has largely disappeared into the hazy mists of time. But in the fall of 1962, it did exist. As the nation was perilously perched that autumn over the nuclear abyss, Wynnefield, the western-most neighborhood in Philadelphia, was still mired in the 1950's. With the Kennedy assassination, a year later, the Fifties would finally come to an end. Meanwhile, DeeDee Sharp, who had dropped out of Overbrook High, was hitting the charts with "Mashed Potato Time," Little Eva was doing "The Loco-Motion" and from Somerville, Massachusetts Bobby "Boris" Pickett and the Crypt Kickers were hitting the Halloween charts with "The Monster Mash;" just as Wynnefield was producing its own home-grown monsters. In a sense, those monsters signaled the end of my old neighborhood.

The Wynnefield I knew would never be the same. In a decade or so it would be gone.

There are, however, three postscripts to the Kramer murder in Philadelphia:

PS 1—sometime in the early 1970's the people who operated the Marriott Hotel on City Line noticed that a car had been parked in their lot for a number of days. They eventually called the cops when a foul smell began to emanate from the car. When the cops jimmied the trunk, they found Lenny Engler curled up inside with two slugs in his head. Lenny, who had been paroled shortly before he was found dead, had gotten as they say in South Boston, "two in the hat." As far as I know, Leonard Engler's killer(s?) has not yet been brought to justice. I should refrain from editorializing here or speaking ill of the dead, but the world was hardly the poorer without Lenny Engler in it. In the end, I suppose, he reaped exactly what he had sown.

PS 2—in the late 1970's I was dating a shrink in Philly. It wasn't a serious deal but I flew down a couple of times from Boston where I was living at the time. One night my psychologist friend and I were having drinks after dinner at a downtown restaurant. After a few drinks, she relaxed and began to speak about a few of her cases. She specialized in sexually dysfunctional women. There was one woman in particular she told me that broke her heart. The woman, attractive and in her mid-twenties, had a great deal of difficulty with men. Her patient wasn't gay, the shrink said, but she had great difficulty bringing any sexual relationship with the opposite sex to satisfactory consummation. What, I asked my shrink friend, did she think was at the root of this young woman's dilemma?

The shrink wasn't sure, but she felt certain that the problem was tied to her client's troubled childhood. When the woman was a little girl she had returned home from school one day to find her mother brutally murdered. It was, the shrink said, a highly publicized murder in the city at the time. Then I told the shrink her troubled client's name. She stared at me with wide eyes. "Impossible!" she cried out in stunned disbelief. "You've been living in New England. This happened almost two decades ago. How could you know? It's impossible! How could you know?"

Obviously, my shrink friend had no idea that I was from Bohemia! And, of course, I never told her.

PS 3—sometime in 2006 Philadelphia's *Jewish Exponent* had an obituary: Rodney B. Langnas, age 62, had died. There was no mention of the Kramer murder in the obit.

CHAPTER 31

The awful Kramer murder was behind me. The big question: what was I going to do with the rest of my life? I knew I couldn't stay in the broken Philly school system. I enjoyed teaching very much; I really liked the kids; but my fellow teachers were mostly, with few exceptions, dullards, dopes and dolts. Many teachers at the Brook went back to my days as a student. They were definitely not part of the solution. By 1962-63 Overbrook High School was about 75 per cent Negro. Those kids were getting the same educational screwing we got in the 1950's. I was just one teacher. One committed teacher does not a revolution make. Not in Philly. And race was beginning to rear its ugly head in Philly politics and education.

One day, while wondering aimlessly around Temple's campus that spring, I ran into John D. Stark, a young history professor who specialized in the American South and the Constitution.

Stark had been my American history survey teacher as a newly minted Duke University Ph.D. and he remembered me with some fondness. That anyone would remember me in a classroom was, back then, nothing short of a minor miracle. I rarely spoke up in any class I ever took.

Over coffee that day Stark laid out the academic possibilities for a potential career as a college professor after I poured my heart out about the frustration I felt teaching at a place like Overbrook High School. Stark recalled me from his classes. He knew that I had never been a top-notch student. But he offered a solution. I could worm my way into the M.A. program in history at Temple by studying Southern and Constitutional history with him. I would be admitted into the history program based on my grades in his courses. However, he would cut me no slack. I would have to earn good grades. Stark would also, he promised, oversee my Master's thesis.

I could take my classes at night and in the summers while continuing to teach high school. But first things first: I had always despised school. Studying had never been my forte. John Stark made it painfully clear that since I had never been accustomed to hard studying, that I would initially find the going tough. But he would be there to guide me; if I worked at it.

That summer I registered for Stark's course in The History of the American South and two other courses. One was an advanced political sociology course the department required.

I worked very hard and received the first grades of A in my entire academic career. In the meantime, my social life had picked up. I had begun seeing a young woman whom my friends and I had met the previous winter at a singles weekend at the Concord Hotel in the Catskills. She lived in Penn Valley on the Main Line in a beautiful home with a swimming pool. Her name was Trudy Shtatman; she had a cute nine-year-old sister, Andi, and a wild teenage brother, Kevy. Her father was a businessman with a couple of factories and some interests in a downtown Philly nightclub. His name was Ben Shtatman, he drove a big, new gold Caddie and looked like a gangster. The thing of it is that he probably was a gangster—in a Tony Soprano-like-mold, semi-legit. Physically, Bennie was a dead ringer for the late actor Sheldon Leonard who was a co-star with Sinatra in *Guys and Dolls* and always played gangsters. Like Sheldon Leonard, Mr. Shtatman talked out of the side of his mouth as if he didn't want too many people to hear him. He didn't seem to like me very much. But then Ben Shtatman didn't like too many people.

In June of 1963 Trudy and I became engaged. Ben and Vivien Shtatman, a stylish, attractive blonde woman in her forties, threw us a wonderful engagement party with a four-piece band, two bars, and catered food served by attentive waiters by their shimmering aquamarine pool. My nutty friend Denny Acker got smashed and threw all the cocktail glasses into the pool much to the chagrin of Louie Goldman who did not abide drunks of any type.

Denny met Trudy's best friend Marian Olderman at the party; they eventually married, had two kids and divorced. Both of them were dead by their mid-thirties. But that is another sad story. I always felt that Denny Acker's brief life would make a great movie.

All my aunts, uncles and cousins were invited. The Goldmans, basically a large family of lower middle class *schleppers,* couldn't believe my good fortune. One uncle or cousin after another whispered into my ear, "You got it made kiddo! Good work!" It was like a scene from *The Graduate.* Except it was real life and I was playing Dustin Hoffman's part.

Trudy was a wonderful girl. She had just graduated from Harcum Junior College and had a steady job as a claims adjuster in the local Waber-Odell Insurance Agency. She had long brunette hair with a killer body. And very big boobs! Trudy is probably one of the nicest women I have known. But she wasn't Arlene. I couldn't get Arlene out of my head. By fall 1963 I was back teaching fulltime at Overbrook, Arlene, I believed, was happily married and I still had to live with her husband Jay at school almost every day which reminded me of that painful fact. The rational side of me knew that a life with Arlene would forever be impossible.

But the romantic side of me just couldn't put those happy years between 1956 and 1960 to rest: Wordsworth's *Splendor in the Grass.* If the truth be known, I never would put them aside.

Still, Trudy loved me; the sex was…whatever it was…and Alvin Kolchins, my life's longtime doppelganger, convinced me in an extended conversation over cheeseburgers at Leof's Drugstore that it really didn't matter who you married; that after a while nobody was happy in most marriages anyway. As Alvin, the great philosopher often said, "M (he has always called me M!), cum is cum! It doesn't really matter where you put it!"

For the longest time I thought Alvin was right. The engagement party went swimmingly—until everyone went home and Trudy and I began un-wrapping our gifts. It was a little after six that evening when her father appeared in the living room where we were surrounded with dozens of unopened gifts. Mrs. Shtatman was on the couch and Trudy and I sat on the floor.

Ben Shtatman was carrying a suitcase. "Where are you going honey?" Trudy's mother Vivien cheerfully asked. "I'm leaving," Ben just as cheerfully answered. "I can't stay here anymore." And without another word, Ben hopped in his big gold Caddie and was gone.

Now you see that shit in the movies. It doesn't happen in real life, Right? Wrong! On the very happy day of his eldest and adoring daughter's engagement party, Ben Shtatman took a header off the high dive—with a broad he was screwing, only two years older than his twenty-one year-old daughter. Bennie ran off with a cocktail waitress from his nightclub on Locust Street. There was some point at which he did return but he soon left again…and that time it was finally for good. He left poor Vivien with a nine-year-old, a fourteen-year-old and a newly engaged, broken-hearted daughter who had worshipped her father. And not a hell of a lot of money!

I didn't see Ben Shtatman for many months. My philosopher friend Alvin told me it wasn't all so bad. Now Mr. Shtatman would have to invite me into the family business; out of sheer guilt. The thing is that I was conflicted. I wanted to be invited into the business. I was making about $5,000 a year as a teacher. My married friends were already making three and four times as much. I didn't want to run a factory or do whatever it is that one does to keep a dynamic business thriving. Making money was not a major motivating force as I was growing increasingly bookish and reading myself into oblivion. I had to play catch-up on a lifetime of second-tier education. Still, there was that comfortable Main Line lifestyle beckoning as opposed to the near poverty imposed by public service or academia. Also, I hardly minded those amazing Sunday dinners at the exclusive Radnor Country Club.

About three months after he left home and devastated his entire family, Ben Shtatman called to invite me to meet him for breakfast. Well, I thought, at least Alvin was right about one thing: here comes the job offer. Guilt is such a wonderfully powerful emotion.

We met for breakfast. After some preliminary small talk, Mr. Shtatman got down to it.

"You don't like me very much, do you?" he stated with a half-smile.

"No," I answered honestly. "I can't say that I do."

"I guess you pretty much think I'm a schmuck," he said.

"I wouldn't go that far," I answered, knowing full well the literal translation of that particular Yiddish word. I didn't want to insult the asshole.

"Let's just say that I am not one of your biggest fans," I added.

Now remember, I was about twenty-three and he was around forty-five.

"Well," he said, "all I'm going to say is that there are things you don't know about; could never know about."

"I know about your three kids," I responded brazenly. "I know they love you. That's all I have to know." It is so great to be twenty-three and to know all there is to know about life.

Ben changed the subject.

"I guess you think I'm going offer you a job…bring you into the business," he said. Shades of Phillip Roth's *Goodbye Columbus!* I was Neil sitting with Brenda Patimkin's loudmouthed father.

"To tell you the truth, I haven't thought about it," I lied.

"Well, I'm not offering you a job. I've got partners. And I'm selling the club and moving a lot of my operation south…to Tennessee. The move is going take some doing and I can't promise that there'll be a spot for you," he said.

Who was this guy, Vito Corleone?

"I didn't ask for a spot as I recall. I'm happy teaching. I'm at Temple in grad school. If everything goes all right I might go all the way to my doctorate," I said somewhat relieved that the decision about my non-career in business was easily already made for me.

"Yeah," Ben snickered. "But you don't make shit! You won't be able to support my daughter or a family on a teacher's salary. You don't know about that stuff. It ain't in those books you're always reading."

"Well, as I see it, that's my problem, not yours," I snapped back. No sense taking any shit from a guy I didn't like. Ben Shtatman was never going to be my boss. Or my father-in-law as it turned out. I never saw Ben Shtatman again. Good at his word, he moved to Mila, Tennessee after divorcing Trudy's mother. He sold his interest in the nightclub where he had made friends with the notorious local gangster moll-chanteuse Lillian Reis and the well-known comedienne Martha Raye. He moved his businesses and his young mistress whom he eventually married and subsequently divorced. I think he had a couple of kids with her. He was on wife number three, another cocktail waitress-type, sometime in the 1980s, when the cops found Ben Shtatman shot to death—murdered right in his Tennessee home. If Bennie Shtatman wasn't a gangster, maybe he should have been because this guy was definitely "hit." Ben always played life fast and very loose. His murder, as far as I know, has never been solved. Calling Robert Stack and *Unsolved Mysteries*!

CHAPTER 32

When I was a youngster, perhaps seven or eight, my father's former boss at the Post Office gave me a book for a Christmas present. The title of the book was *Lives of Poor Boys Who Became Famous*. It was a thick blue book with dense chapters on the lives of young men who had made very notable contributions after growing up in poverty. I recall reading passages on Benjamin Franklin, Samuel Johnson, and Calvin Coolidge among the many chapters in the book. It was not easy reading for a kid whose mainstay literature through high school was *Action, Detective, Batman, Superman* and *Whiz* comic books.

My father's former boss, Andy Young, was one reason behind my Dad's successful rise through the labyrinthine political-oriented maze that was the Philadelphia Post Office bureaucracy during the war. Andy Young had retired sometime in the 1940s to a small farm in Oxford, Pennsylvania where he lived with an unmarried daughter. But not before he assured an important promotion for my father that began what was to become an upwardly mobile career in the government for Lou Goldman; which was, in a way, very curious.

Andy Young was a Presbyterian. I didn't know then what a Protestant was but I had a definite instinct from the things my father said about most Christians whom he invariably saw as our enemies. Combined with his experiences of growing up an impoverished Jew in South Philadelphia was the fact that Pop had come of age in the 1920s when anti-Semitism was, on the heels of the Great Depression, at a fever pitch in the United States. It was then paralleled by the rise of Hitlerism, World War II and the Holocaust which only buttressed Pop's strong convictions about most *goyim*. I recall that every year when Easter rolled around Pop would caution me about playing in the schoolyard of St. Barbara's. Although no one ever beat me up in Wynnefield because I was Jewish, Pop never forgot the days he had to run for his life during Easter week in South Philly with the chilling taunts of "Sheeny," "Kike" and "Christ killer" ringing in his ears. Those nasty experiences pretty much shaped my father's world view over his lifetime. Years later when we were shopping for a decent assisted living facility shortly after Pop celebrated his ninetieth birthday, Louis Goldman caustically dismissed any facility that did not have a preponderance of, as he put it, *"Hebes."* And you must remember, unlike my mother who always loved going to services at Har Zion Temple where she worked in the library well into her mid-eighties, Pop had a measure of contempt for most rabbis who he saw as money grubbing charlatans, the organized Jewish religion and the over-organized Jewish community.

But Andy Young was different. He kind of adopted Pop as a young man and became his mentor. Pop would borrow a car and we would drive out for a visit to Andy Young on his farm at least once a year almost until the year old Andy passed away.

I remember walking out into the fields with Andy. He called each cow by name as the cow would slowly amble up to nuzzle him. Then Andy would treat me to a glass of fresh warm milk that he had milked by hand that very morning. For a city kid seeing cows, pigs, chickens, horses and Andy's truck garden was a real treat every year. From that time I often daydreamed of life on a farm myself. And when the chance presented itself many years later, I jumped at it with great anticipation. Some of my happiest years were spent on a large farm that I actually worked with a large truck garden for eight summers in central Massachusetts.

Usually Andy would sit a spell on his shaded porch with Pop over a glass of lemonade to discuss Post Office politics. It was all Greek to me but I had the run of the place and was able to entertain myself quite nicely on those yearly jaunts to Oxford. I remember passing a school on the way to Andy's. It was Lincoln University. "That's a college just for Negroes," Pop would say as we drove by the large front gate of the college. "Why do they need their own schools?" I asked once. "It's too complicated," Pop answered. "They just do."

I don't know what Pop's salary was in those days. It could not have been much because we could not afford our own car. I suppose Andy Young saw me as another of those poor boys in the book he gave me.

He would often tell me to pay attention in school because, he would say, I was a very bright youngster and could go as far as I wanted in the America that was coming. Andy Young gave the lie to my father's basic belief that all *goyim* were bigots.

Clearly, Pop's Jewish faith meant absolutely nothing to Andy Young who liked my Dad as well as his precocious kid. The message in his Christmas gift of that book was clear: I could be anything I wanted in this country; which was not exactly true after the Sixties. But we will get to that.

Anyway, I had made up my mind by the time I was around 23. I was not going to go into business and although I had a shit-load of catching up to do in terms of my rather limited educational achievements, I would work my ass off and eventually become that history professor much beloved by his adoring students for his abilities to bring the past to some measure of comprehensive life; like John Stark did for me.

I did very well at Temple University as a grad student, if not brilliantly. At least half of my grades were A's and the rest were commendable B's. The B-plus had not yet come into academic vogue in those days. The papers I wrote were well received and I chose to write my thesis on Huey Long, the Louisiana demagogue who turned on FDR and the New Deal before falling victim to an assassin's bullet in the mid-1930s. I felt equal to the other students in the program and by the summer of 1964 I was one course shy of completing the requirements for my M.A. degree. I was teaching History and English at Dobbins High School, a vocational and technical school for many impoverished kids of declining North Philly neighborhoods and the Kensington section of Philadelphia known derogatively as Fishtown (because it was Catholic and, yeah, Catholics still ate fish every Friday in those days).

The Dobbins kids were very nice and they enjoyed me as much as I enjoyed them. They may not have been the brightest kids that Philly has ever seen, but they were polite, funny and, to an extent, hungry for some good teaching. I have very fond memories of the Dobbins Tech kids. They were studying to be electricians, carpenters, hair dressers, restaurant workers and nurse's aides. Probably a jump up from what their parents had become. What I really liked was the fact that the school was integrated and racially balanced in 1964 and that both Blacks and Whites seemed to get along fine. I don't recall a single time I had to break up a fight.

The kids loved *The Count of Monte Cristo* and *Les Miserables* which we read word by tortured word in the English classes. The discussions about the travails of poor Edmund Dante and Jean Valjean opened a world they had never seen and would probably never know.

Still, they marveled at the vengeful Count and the heroic decency of the tortured Valjean.

In American history we fought the Civil War, abolished slavery, covered the marked racial progress of Reconstruction and got as far as the Second World War. The department chair was a wonderful woman who looked like a cleaning lady but she took me under her wing and eventually even tutored me for the Social Studies exam that I had to take to receive a permanent appointment in the Philly schools in the unlikely eventuality that I chose to call it a career.

I actually liked Dobbins better than Overbrook. It didn't seem as racially self-conscious and, as a result of one of the baseball coaches having a heart attack that spring, I also got to do some assistant coaching which held me in good stead with the tough White kids from Fishtown and the Blacks from North Philly who went out for baseball and also saw my bookish side in class. I was only 24 and could throw and hit as well as any kid on the Junior Varsity. Probably better since I had finally begun to put on some weight and fill out a little. A teacher who coaches always commands respect.

That spring I applied to about half a dozen graduate schools. Harvard wrote a perfunctory and discouraging letter. The Ivy League pipe puffers did not cotton to high school teachers with a Temple University pedigree at America's most elite institution; even one who had mended his wayward educational past. But Harvard was not alone. I was rejected by Rutgers (which is ironic, since years later I taught there!), Penn and a number of other first choice grad schools.

I was, however, accepted by the University of Delaware and the University of Maryland. Delaware offered nothing but admission. But

Maryland made an interesting offer: free tuition, room and board if I entered the university as a Faculty Resident in their housing program. I would be able to pursue my doctoral studies and, with a stipend that was almost as good as my yearly teacher's salary in Philly, I would also be able to live rent and food free. The only kicker was that I was engaged. And Trudy was pushing for us to set a date for the marriage.

My pal Alvin was wrong. By the early spring of 1964 Trudy Shtatman and I were history. I forget who broke up with whom. Maybe it was mutual. My mother seemed more devastated than Trudy and begged me to reconsider. I wavered but never folded.

I needed one more course to complete my Master's degree at Temple which I would take that summer. And then I would be off to the University of Maryland and the good life of the academy. But, as usual, fate stepped into my life. I was still slouching from Bohemia!

CHAPTER 33

With my thesis written and accepted I needed only three credits to complete my M.A. degree before moving down to College Park, Maryland. That was one course in those days. Sometimes the most trivial decision you make in this life alters not only your own life but the course of dozens of other people's lives as well. There were two courses to select from in the Temple catalogue in the last session that summer of 1964: The Protestant Reformation and Latin American history. I had little interest in either but religious history was never my thing. If I had taken on the Protestant Reformation there are a whole lot of marriages that would never have taken place in this life—not to mention my own. And that would mean that a great many of my closest friend's kids (Larry Lowenthal's and Alvin Kolchins's kids to name a few) would never have been born since, because of my own romantic connection, I would go on to introduce them to their future wives. Sound complicated? Hang on.

I chose the course on Latin America offered by a visiting professor from nearby Rutgers. Like most Temple history courses it was a packed classroom and consisted of an hour and a half of lectures each day for six weeks. On the first day of class I took my place, as I usually did, as far away from the professor as one could possibly get: on the last seat by the window on the back row. The class was held on the second floor of Temple's newest building. I had always had an aversion to Curtis Hall because it was the scene of my last debacle with Arlene Rachman who by 1964 was still "happily" married to a guy who everyone knew cheated on her from the beginning of their marriage. I also had heard through the grapevine that Arlene, who graduated Temple earlier that year, was the mother of a lovely little girl, Robin Ellen Lewis. But I was well over Arlene Rachman by mid-1964 and, no longer engaged to be married, on the alert for new romantic adventures. I was not looking to get involved and marriage was the furthest thing from my mind. But true love waits for no man's schedule in this life. Not to mention the fact that women want what they want when they want it!

On the first row in my summer school class in the summer of 1964 sat one of the cutest girls I had ever seen at Temple: she wore denim cutoffs and a colored t-shirt to class each day and when the professor called the role she answered "Here" to the name Andrea Leerman.

The class was pretty full and Andrea Leerman would never have noticed me if I didn't somehow stand out from the mob. So when the professor called my name, I invariably answered, "Present!" in a loud voice. Some of the women in the class twittered but Andrea never even turned around. Years later she admitted that she thought the guy who shouted out "Present!" was a bit of an "asshole." She asked questions once in a while in class but as the weeks passed it seemed clear that she never even noticed me. Or at least that is what I thought.

I don't recall much about the class. As I said, Latin American history has never been my thing. But I do recall telling a fellow history teacher from Dobbins who sat next to me in the class that I wanted to marry the girl in the cutoffs and T-shirt on the front row.

John Fitzpatrick merely laughed. But I wasn't kidding. From afar, I had fallen in love with that cute girl on the front row. Andrea Leerman was cute, brunette and not much more than five petite feet; but she had a great figure with perfect proportions, nice legs and looked ever so scrumptious in those T-shirts and tight shorts.

By mid-August on the last day of class I had still never spoken to the lovely Andrea Leerman. I had one day to make my move. Or I would probably never see her again and Josh Kolchins, Andrew Kolchins and Jessica Lowenthal would not have been born. These young people should bless the fact that I finally made that move. Well…at least somebody made it.

As I arrived on that last day of class about ten minutes early I noticed to my great joy that T-shirt girl, Andrea Leerman, was standing in the hall. "Say something…anything…," I said to myself. But I froze. Cool was never in my repertoire. As I walked by I said nothing. I went into the class, placed my books on the desk and walked back into the hallway. I had no idea what I was going to say. To my everlasting joy the girl in the T-shirt broke the ice. On the last day of the last hour of the last class I would ever take at Temple University I was to finally meet that girl who would forever change the course of my life; not to mention the lives of so many of my dearest friends.

"Do you have a match?" T-shirt girl asked.

"Shit!" I thought to myself, "Why in the hell did I ever stop smoking in the Army?"

"No, I'm sorry. I don't smoke," I said. Very cool!

"What good are you?" T-shirt girl quipped.

I was speechless. Nothing came to mind. I had nothing. I froze again. Here it was: the girl on the front row; the girl I had lusted after the entire summer asks me for a match and all I can come back with is the sorry-ass fact that I don't smoke. Smoking wasn't the big nasty that it has become back in those innocent days. When you are 24 you don't think much about cancer.

Actually, you don't think much about anything except sex and rock 'n roll.

I walked back into class totally dejected as I struggled to pay attention to the professor's last hour and a half on Simon Bolivar or some such bullshit. But lady luck was with me. As we exited the class, T-shirt girl was standing in the hall apparently awaiting her next class.

I put on my best Louie Goldman smile. "Hi," I said. "What are you waiting for?"

Brilliant! Not very, I know. But it was 1964!

"I have another class," T-shirt girl answered pleasantly smiling back. I had passed GO!

Now I just had to miss getting the Go to Jail card and collect my $200.

"Cut it," I said.

"Why should I do that?" T-shirt girl asked still smiling.

"To have a cup of coffee with me," I answered—the epitome of 1950's cool.

Andrea Leerman cut that class and we had that cup of coffee. About a year later, on August 21, 1965, we were married.

CHAPTER 34

Andi Leerman grew up in the working class neighborhood of Logan, off Roosevelt Boulevard on the way to northeast Philadelphia and the somewhat newer neighborhood of Oxford Circle. If you drive up the Boulevard today you will see a great many of those row houses boarded up. Apparently the neighborhood is sinking and many properties have been condemned. The city of Philadelphia, run by a long succession of grossly incompetent pinheads, allowed them to sink lower and lower, rotting like brown stained teeth in a malformed mouth.

The product of a difficult childhood, Andi lost her mother to Alzheimer's before she was ten. Her father Irv Leerman, the proprietor of a hardware and dry goods store in Kensington, had remarried and Andi didn't like the new arrangement even though Mr. Leerman's second wife, Rose, seemed nice enough to me. So, as a teenager, Andi chose to live with her older sister and brother-in-law Yerma and Lou Vizak and their growing family on Eighth Street in Logan. An excellent student, she graduated Olney High School and was awarded a full scholarship to Temple University whizzing through the nearby commuter college in just a little over three years majoring in Sociology.

When I met her, Andi was a graduating senior and had already been accepted to a Ph.D. program in Temple's Sociology department as a teaching assistant for the following year. I had just three weeks before I left Philadelphia for Maryland. After a two week trip to New England with my mother, father and our little terrier Rusty, I had about ten days left to win Andi's heart. She wasn't going to make it very easy.

First, Andi was involved with another guy. Ironically, he came from my neighborhood but since he was younger I didn't know him. Second, that relationship had become sexual.

Back then, in the Stone Age, young men didn't take kindly to a woman's sexuality unless it was exclusively with them. I had rarely encountered a young woman who was sexually experienced. I had briefly dated a beautiful girl named Sue Sager from Overbrook Park whose virtue remained intact. And the fault was hardly mine. She married an old Atlantic City pal, Brent Toll, shortly after we stopped going out and they are still married today.

I recall being more than a little upset when Andi leveled with me about her relationship and how far it had progressed. What was even worse, Andi informed me, she would not sleep with more than one person at a time. And I was, she pulled no punches, not on her current bunk-mate list. Even as a pinch hitter.

Andi had made this painfully clear on our initial date to the 1964 World's Fair in Flushing Meadow, New York. After a wonderful day of sampling exotic foods from all over the world and attending the endless exhibitions at the Fair, we were caught in an unscheduled summer downpour and soaked to our skin. I cannily suggested a quick drive into Manhattan where I would graciously spring for a hotel room as we awaited the drying of our wet garments. Pretty slick, huh? I would get Andi's clothes off without even trying!

The hotel cost about twenty-six bucks—not a small sum in 1964. We lay in the bed, naked as the day we were both born while our clothes dried. We hugged and kissed. But Andi just would not budge.

"I'm not going to make love with you," she said. "It wouldn't be fair to Fred" (the name of her erstwhile Philly beau).

And so, with my wallet lighter some twenty-six extra bucks but our clothes dry, Andi and I headed down the Jersey Turnpike back to Philly. Her, with her morality intact; me, a sadder and wiser, but poorer little horn dog.

The next week Andi was to leave for a week's vacation in Atlantic City. She had booked a room at a very nice hotel about a block down from the Steel Pier on Pennsylvania Avenue. With nothing else to do that third week in August I graciously offered to save Andi a trip on the bus and drove her to the shore. My brother Ken was working in his beloved Atlantic City that summer and I figured, if worse came to worse, I could always bunk in with him. He had a small apartment up near the old President Hotel on Providence Avenue.

Worse did not come to worse and Andi finally allowed me to share her bed; not to mention the free hotel room. Bye, bye, Freddy pie!

I sprung for meals and we ended up having a very romantic week. As it turned out Andrea Leerman and I shared a very similar view of the world—we loved those old Miss Marple/Agatha Christie mystery films with Margaret Rutherford; we loved Italian food; and we were both what would have then been considered radical left in terms of our political orientation and worldview. In 1964 the word *radical* had a very different meaning than it did by the end of that tumultuous decade.

Radical in 1964 was looking at "Race" as the most important problem facing the United States. Viet Nam had not yet heated up and the American public had hardly stirred with the 15,000 American "military advisors" who were placed in-country by John F. Kennedy; the ongoing Cold War seemed under some semblance of control with the fall of Nikita Khrushchev after the Soviet leader was bested by JFK in the October Missile Crisis of 1962; and, aside from the discomfiting Kennedy assassination reverberations, the only thing of consequence in the initial months of 1964 was the American arrival of the Beatles— no big deal then to Andi or me—and the coincidental fact that the Democratic Party was holding its quadrennial nominating convention in, of all places, Atlantic City, New Jersey during that magical week we were there.

I was busy falling in love with Andrea Leerman. By 1964 I had finally completed my eight-year military obligation to Uncle and that November I looked forward to an Honorable Discharge along with full and final separation from the American military. I briefly flirted with the idea of re-upping—it was said I would make Sergeant if I signed up for another reserve tour—but Southeast Asia seemed to be heating up and even though Lyndon Johnson had promised that no American boy would ever have to die for a war that Asian boys should be fighting, I didn't believe him. LBJ turned out to be a major league bullshit artist. It was to begin a lifetime of cynical skepticism for me when it came to most politicians and authority figures.

The Democratic convention in 1964 was not exactly a nominating convention. It was much more of a coronation. The purpose in 1964 for Democrats of all stripes was to crown Lyndon B. Johnson, the murdered King Arthur's lackluster successor vice-president who most probably would have been dumped from the ticket altogether had the Prince of Camelot lived. Now the wealthy and crafty Texan was running the country and his party...and the Atlantic City convention...and, unbeknownst to the American people to whom he lied incessantly, was about to drop the country waist-deep in the big muddy of Southeast Asia.

The only suspense of 1964 was the question over who was going to be LBJ's running mate since he had served since November 22, 1963 without a vice-president. There were rumors (probably put out by ex-New Frontiersmen now in pained exile) that Bobby Kennedy would be President Johnson's pick. But Johnson despised the Kennedys and "the Harvards" that Camelot had enticed to Washington. And word soon leaked out that Johnson was going to choose the very liberal and popular Minnesota Senator Hubert H. Humphery as his running mate.

With Arizona Senator Barry Goldwater as the opposition, it would be a cakewalk for the Johnson-Humphery team and everyone but the politically obtuse knew it.

I can't say that I was politically sophisticated in 1964. I had voted for JFK against Nixon in 1960—a no-brainer as far as I was concerned. Truth be told, I knew practically nothing about JFK. I knew even less about Lyndon B. Johnson. Andi and I would spend our days of that magic week at the beach, getting up early and, after a hearty breakfast, head for the rays. But by the third day, we were getting bored and since Convention Hall was just a mile or so walk up the Boardwalk we headed up to the Democratic Convention to witness the historical action first-hand just as things were heating up and getting interesting.

The convention, micro-managed by LBJ's numerous lickspittles, had very little to excite the American people beyond that question of who the President would pick to run with him. Bobby Kennedy had given a very powerful speech after standing for what observers said was a twenty minute ovation from the floor. According to those inside the hall, there wasn't a dry eye among the delegates or in the cynical press corps. In effect, RFK stole the President's thunder that day. Thus LBJ hated him even more. But there was one problem and, as it turned out, it became the single most important historical event of the 1964 Democratic convention.

In 1964 there were very few Negro delegates at the Democratic convention—especially from the South. Southern delegations still with powerful segregationist platforms were largely lily-white and one of the top reasons the Democratic Party was so rankly hypocritical as the party of the people. Race was a problem that the Democrats had straddled since the Civil War and certainly since the New Deal and FDR when they couldn't even pass anti-lynching legislation.

Earlier that summer three civil rights workers had disappeared in Mississippi. That state had been targeted by student-based civil rights groups as one of the most racially oppressed states in the Union. Volunteers, largely made up of southern Black and northeast Jewish students on summer break, streamed into various southern states to register Black voters and establish freedom schools in Black churches where segregated school districts had shut down rather than allow the great-grandchildren of slaves to cross the racial border of what was even then sub-standard White schools. One of the welcome offshoots of all that civil rights activity in Mississippi was the establishment of the Mississippi Freedom Party, a black branch of the state's Democrats.

Led by local activists like Mrs. Fannie Lou Hamer, the Mississippi Freedom Party made it's way to Atlantic City to challenge the state's racist white Democratic establishment.

As far as Lyndon B. Johnson was concerned it was like being invited to barbecue at his sprawling Texas ranch on the Pedernales and shitting on his lawn right in front of First Lady Bird. The Mississippi Black delegates were throwing a monkey wrench into Johnson's big Atlantic City barbecue. And the Big Bopper didn't like it. Not even a little bit.

In an era before TV became as powerful in the political process as it is today, it still made for very bad TV—the Black delegates were refused seating and were then ejected from the floor of Convention

Hall. Many of them marched out onto the Boardwalk where a sit-in had begun with all the ensuing chaos such a widely publicized act might attract. Since the early 1960's sit-ins had become standard operating procedure in the civil rights movement.

The Mississippi Freedom delegates were led by a tough movement activist, Robert Moses, who, initially, would not compromise. The last I heard, Bob Moses was still alive and living a quietly anonymous life in Cambridge, Massachusetts teaching mathematics. He does not give interviews and apparently has no nostalgic affection for those halcyon days.

Bob Moses, a giant among the many pygmies who began to swell the Negro leadership ranks in the Sixties, insisted on the moral right of Black representation on the convention floor. Many Black leaders like Martin Luther King. Jr., and Roy Wilkins, pressed by White liberal allies like Joseph Rauh, Hubert Humphrey and Walter Mondale, were divided and sought to compromise over the sticky and potentially embarrassing Mississippi Freedom delegation problem.

Andi and I came upon the convention site just as the Black delegates were walking out of the overflowing Hall. "Join us, sit in with us," many of the young Black civil rights activists shouted to the gathering and curious throngs on the Boardwalk.

We didn't hesitate for a second. The issue was crystal clear: the bigoted Democrats were excluding Black delegates from the convention. As if both parties hadn't done that for the better part of a century! Of course, we were totally ignorant of the fact that three other southern Democratic delegations (Tennessee, North Carolina and Georgia) actually had Negro delegates officially *included* in their respective delegations. What the hell! We were young. And so Andi and I, falling in love and politically naive, joined the Blacks from Mississippi with other sympathetic Whites from the crowd to sit in and protest the exclusion of the Mississippi Freedom Party.

We were going to become part of American history and our own history at the same time.

A number of things happened during the two days we sat in with the Mississippi Freedom Democrats. I am not sure of the order of events but here is what Andi and I saw and heard: The news slowly filtered through the sit-in crowd that the bodies of the missing civil rights workers had been found buried in shallow graves in Philadelphia, Mississippi. Andrew Goodman, Michael Schwerner and James Chaney had been murdered in cold blood. By who? No one knew for certain then. As it turned out, Schwerner, Goodman and Chaney had been arrested by local authorities late at night on a country road for God knows what and then turned over to their murderers by the very men who had been sworn to uphold the law down there. No one ever went to jail for the killings. There may have been trials but the local redneck juries found everyone innocent. A book *Three Lives for Mississippi* resulted. And then, sometime in the 90s a film, *Mississippi Burning,* came out that fictionally depicted the event. The movie, starring Gene Hackman and Willem Defoe, was a typical by-product of liberal Hollywood. Recently there was news that they are reopening the case because of some Illinois high school kids. I am sure that Chaney, Goodman and Schwerner would be so very pleased almost a half century later! My solution back then has remained the same as it is today: find out for sure who did it and place a 9 mm Glock behind their ear, smile and give them what they deserve—two in the hat.

After the shock of the killings spread through the delegation, a number of the Blacks began singing "We Shall Overcome" and "Ain't Nobody Gonna Turn Me 'Round." Soon we all joined in. At the time, few of us had ever heard of Philadelphia, Mississippi. For some odd reason we all believed that singing would bring civil rights to the country after more than a century of discrimination when it would really only come after some old-fashioned Philly ass kicking.

Another memorable moment was when the American Nazi Party arrived on the scene from Arlington, Virginia to grab up their share of the free publicity on the Boardwalk. These jackbooted cretins were soon picketing and demonstrating against the Black Mississippians hurling the typical racial invective of their mentor and leader George Lincoln Rockwell. The Atlantic City police initially set up a skirmish line to protect the morons who had arrived in full swastika-ed regalia.

But the Blacks and Whites in the crowd surged forward and, if the cops had not protected the Nazi pinheads, the angry mob would most certainly have ripped those large Nazi pieces of shit into smaller pieces of shit. A few years later Rockewell was assassinated by one of his own swastika-ed bean brains.

That night was apparently Lyndon B. Johnson's birthday. We were still sitting in when President Johnson and Senator Humphrey appeared above the crowd on a Convention Hall balcony. I had never been so close to a president before. There he was, the Big Bopper himself, in all his gawky glory, waving to the boardwalk crowds as a boat about a half-mile offshore lit up with fireworks with a flag as the backdrop and the likeness of LBJ in the foreground of the flaming display. Happy birthday Mr. President! And by the way, thanks so much for Viet Nam!

The President of the United States was all smiles. He couldn't hear the shouts from our section of the sit-in that he should put his convention where the moon don't shine. I remember being struck about how thin and sickly Johnson appeared. With his gleaming hair slicked straight back he was a dead ringer for Lurch from the Addams family.

That summer of 1964 was to be my entry into a fascinating world where politics, history and my graduate studies converged. I had found my life's work as well as my calling. Of course, I didn't know it at the moment.

I was in love.

CHAPTER 35

In 1964 the University of Maryland was a school more tied to the politics and mores of Virginia than to that of neighboring Pennsylvania or Delaware. For all intents and purposes Maryland was a southern school with a southern outlook. As the Faculty Resident of a newly built dorm, Easton Hall, the university provided a comfortable, new tastefully furnished suite on the 8th floor. The students under my charge numbered around fifty and, with only a few exceptions, were a rowdy bunch of beer-swilling good old boys. The female dorm within a few yards, Denton Hall, in those pre-parietal days was totally off limits to men.

On Friday nights most of my young charges would drink themselves all the way through to Sunday. Sometimes they came back to the dorm so shit-faced that they would crap or vomit in the elevators and smear their vomit and feces all over the elevator buttons. Dorm fires were a weekly constant whenever these numbskulls threw lit cigarettes down the trash chutes. We were constantly interrupted in our evening studies with fire alarms that often forced evacuation into the cold fall nights. But the job paid well (about $4,000 including room, board and tuition). I did my best to ride herd on the worst miscreants on the 8th floor and made friends with a number of the other Faculty Residents. I have fond memories of Joe Danek, Mike Holden and Tom Ingram and our nightly pizza-beer runs into College Park.

The Maryland history program was another problem altogether. I made friends with a few other grad students. John Haller, who went on to become an excellent historian, became a lifelong friend although we have been out of touch for some years now. Last I heard he was out of teaching history and a dean at the University of Colorado in Greeley. He had a fine temperament and would have made a great college president because college presidents have to put up with so much bullshit from the spoiled tenured faculty who think they crap cream cheese.

I was woefully unprepared for the rigors of full-time graduate study in what was then a tough program. The other Ph.D. students were mostly young men (and a few women) who had come from decent schools where they had majored in history with graduate study as their ultimate goal. Even though I was armed with an M.A., I was hardly prepared for the rigorous program at Maryland. Unlike Temple University where many of the professors were mediocre, the history faculty at Maryland were published scholars and largely well known in their fields.

I decided to concentrate on Russian history and took almost every course I could in that area of concentration. The problem was that the professor who taught Russian history was a taciturn ex-marine with a Ph.D. from Princeton who seemed to view his students as an impediment to his own time for research. If his ultimate goal was to torment students, he did a good job.

Professor George Yaney made life as miserable as he could for his Russian history students. The first impediment he put in front of his students was a geography test that had to be passed before continuing on in the course of study. You literally had to memorize the entire map of the Soviet Union. I failed the map exam twice before finally narrowly passing Yaney's silly rite of initiation. Memorizing the map of Russia was like Algebra—useless. After all, if you wanted to find a city, a river or a mountain all you had to do was look on the goddamn map!

By that time I was two to three weeks behind in my reading and preparation. As a result, I only received a C in the first blue book exam. I went to see Yaney as often as time allowed but he always seemed annoyed when I came by during his office hours. I also had a seminar in American history with a kindly old duffer by the name of Sam Merrill. Merrill, who had been at Maryland since the Great Flood, held the seminar in the evening at his comfortable suburban home not far from campus. One night he thrilled our small class by bringing the well-known scholar John Hope Franklin for a visit and a lecture. Franklin, a pioneer in American Negro history and, even back in '64, was a superstar to all of the students and he had already achieved legendary status in the profession through his teaching and scholarship. Over the ensuing years I saw Professor Franklin on a number of occasions and would remind him of that wonderful night in 1964 when he led our seminar. One of the seminar students was so taken with the gentle professor that he went on to become Franklin's teaching assistant at the University of Chicago.

My third course that semester was a German language reading course to prepare for my first required language exam on the path to my doctorate degree. It was a difficult transition to make from Temple University where I at least had one champion in the department. I never did find my John Stark at Maryland and although I completed the first semester with a B in Russian history, a B plus in the seminar and a pass in German I was not at all comfortable going into my second semester—especially since all of my course work would be with the dour Yaney in the Russian field.

In addition life in Easton Hall was deteriorating as the students in my charge began to sink lower in their studies and grades and deeper into their weekend beer swilling. I did my best to tutor and mentor some of the students but some were beyond redemption and dropped out of college altogether returning to the many small towns surrounding Baltimore from whence they had originally come for stopgap jobs in gas stations, fast food joints and future lives of quiet desperation until those Friday nights when endless beer kegs could be guzzled to cushion their lackluster lives.

Four things occurred at Maryland in the spring of 1965 that changed the course of my life. Andrea Leerman had been visiting me regularly and by New Year's we had decided to get married in the summer of 1965. She would give up her Temple fellowship and move down to Maryland where we would live in graduate student housing.

The second thing was the heating up of the war in Viet Nam. Protests began to break out all over campus that spring. My job, as a Faculty Resident, was to see that they did not spill over into the dorms or cafeterias. At that time I didn't know enough about Viet Nam to have an informed opinion so I did what it is wise to do when you don't know very much about a given subject: I shut up.

Another event which was to have a profound influence on my future studies and career was a one-day symposium with three intellectuals whose names were unfamiliar to me at the time: Hannah Arendt, a chain smoking political scientist, had recently published a controversial work entitled *Eichmann in Jerusalem*. The Holocaust had not yet become the academic discipline that it is today. In fact, the word Holocaust was hardly in common usage in 1965. Arendt, whose earlier book *The Origins of Totalitarianism* had become required reading for any serious student of Communism and Nazism, had covered the Eichmann trial in Israel. In her latest book she had posited a number of controversial theories about Eichmann and the Nazis. Eichmann, Arendt maintained, was only a small cog in the Nazi killing machine and maybe even not a very important one. Eichmann, in her view, a small-minded man and a petty bureaucrat, represented the banality of evil. And although he might have well deserved the death penalty, executing this rather irrelevant little man had little meaning beyond the propaganda coup Prime Minister David Ben Gurion planned it to be for the government and nation of Israel. What was worse, as far as the Jewish community was concerned, Arendt had some very critical things to say about the victims of the Nazis who she believed went to their deaths like lambs to the slaughter.

Arendt created a major controversy when she argued that if the Jews of Europe had only fought back or resisted the Nazis in any fashion, even when at death's door in the killing camps, many more Jews would have survived.

Of course, when I attended this symposium, the only two books I had recently read about the Nazis were William Shirer's *The Rise and Fall of the Third Reich* and Alan Bullock's one volume biography *Hitler: A Study in Tyranny*. Not so her protagonists on the symposium panel: Dwight MacDonald, a well known New York magazine writer and the intellectually pugnacious Norman Podhoretz, the young editor of a magazine I had never heard of: *Commentary*. *Commentary*, one of the foremost intellectual periodicals in the nation, would inform my geopolitical, ideological and social philosophy for the rest of the century. I was mesmerized by Podhoretz as he dissected and deconstructed Arendt's flimsy thesis and then, strand by strand, took it and, to her chagrin, the great German scholar herself, apart.

I had never seen the likes of Podhoretz: a tough minded Jewish intellectual who took no prisoners and, over the many years I read and observed him, no shit from anyone. He even took on the pugnacious Norman Mailer! Better informed about critical issues than any academic I have ever known, Podhoretz became a must read for me. If Podhoretz wrote it over the years, I had to read it. And although I wasn't always in lock-step with his thinking, I wasn't far off his mark whether it was the Middle East, Iraq, Iran, Southeast Asia, terrorism or the ongoing American briar patch of race and race politics. It was this symposium, more than anything else that stoked my lifelong interest, study and ultimately teaching of the Holocaust and Jewish Studies. But that was much later in my career.

The last event—the event that ended my career as a University of Maryland student was a result of my own carelessness and a trait I quickly discarded after my time at College Park.

Up until my time at Maryland I was a fairly trusting soul. If you were friendly toward me then I was generally friendly to you. There were two graduate students, let's call them Dick and Perry, (like the two killers of the Clutter family in Truman Capote's classic *In Cold Blood*) who I knew from the Russian classes. But I did not know them well. I usually sat with them and maybe even had coffee with them a few times. I had decided not to return to the dorm program and was therefore vying for a teaching assistantship to replace my lost income.

Andi and I had already staked a claim to married student housing which was more than reasonable. But still, we needed some income until Andi could line up a possible teaching job in the nearby Montgomery County schools. What I did not know is that Dick and Perry, who were both pursuing Master's degrees, had also applied for teaching spots in the large Maryland history department.

One day, near the end of the spring term Professor Yaney called me to his office. Two students, he informed me, had come to him to claim that I had cheated in a recent exam. "How did I cheat?" I asked Yaney incredulous. And who were the students? Yaney would not say.

"I'd rather not say," Yaney icily said, "but it was the second time these students came to me."

I looked Yaney in the eye, hardly intimidated. "That's pure bullshit!" I spit out. "Did you speak to either of these students during an exam?" Yaney asked. I thought hard. I vaguely recalled sitting near these two assholes but I tried to answer as honestly as I could. "Well, I might have exclaimed after reading one of your exam questions to nobody in particular 'What the hell is this?' But I certainly did not ask for help in an essay exam where you were sitting or standing no more than fifteen feet from where I sat. It was an essay exam. How does one cheat in an essay exam with the professor right there? It's bullshit, pure and simple!" Yaney was notorious for asking the most obscure possible questions in his bluebooks. It had always seemed to me that the prick took some perverted pleasure in seeing his students squirm or even fail.

"Nevertheless," Yaney exploded, "this is a very serious charge. You are to stop coming to all my classes." The professor, in effect, kicked me out of all my classes at the university.

"In other words you are finding me guilty without a trial," I said.

"That's my prerogative and that's the end of it," Yaney coldly responded.

To make a long and somewhat painful story short, through a professor at Temple who had attended the University of Maryland for her Ph.D. I was put in touch with the chair of the University of Maryland's graduate board. He too was a history professor who specialized in European intellectual history and when we met he seemed like a decent guy.

He appeared horrified that Yaney had kicked me out of his classes. He informed me that he believed my rights had been violated and that, at the very least, I had a right to a faculty hearing before the University's graduate board. The board was made up of professors from the department but other professors were on the board as well or free to attend.

A close friend and beer drinking buddy of mine who was a professor in the Botany Department told me he would sit in on the hearing if I wanted. He also told me something I did not know but was rapidly concluding: that George Yaney, the ex-marine, thought he was still at Parris Island and that many faculty members saw him as a bit of an asshole.

The graduate board met. I stated my case. Yaney stated his. The two students who had charged me with cheating did not appear. The graduate board quickly concluded that Yaney had acted precipitously and unfairly. They clearly understood that although I might well have spoken during an exam that my words had little application insofar as the charges of cheating were concerned. They reinstated me in the program and that was the end of it; and the end of my time at the University of Maryland.

Dick, the guy who allegedly went to Yaney and charged me with cheating, got that teaching assistantship. I got a thank you but no thanks. I don't know what Perry ever got. My hope is that it was something catching. The history professor who had helped me called me to his office and told me that I was welcome to stay in the department. However, as he duly noted, everyone in the department was well aware of the matter and Yaney had some friends. I had embarrassed him in front of the entire department.

I would be wiser, he said, to move on. Andrea and I discussed the matter and we both agreed it would be far wiser to return to Philly. She had a neighbor who worked on the Parkway for the Board of Education. Since I had placed highly in the Social Studies exams the previous year, Andrea's neighbor saw little difficulty in my reappointment, this time as a permanent history teacher, to the Philadelphia school system.

I got myself a summer job at a suburban day camp. By mid-July I took an appointment in the history department at West Philadelphia High School not far from the Penn campus on Walnut Street. And on August 21, 1965 Andrea Leerman and I were married. We had a traditional Jewish wedding at a synagogue in the Mt. Airy section of the city with all our friends and family. We honeymooned in Puerto Rico and St. Thomas—my first time on an airplane. We found a reasonable one bedroom apartment in a high rise in Germantown, one of the only integrated neighborhoods in Philly. Andi had a teaching fellowship in the doctoral program in Sociology at Temple University where she would teach freshman Sociology and study fulltime for her Ph.D. And although Temple did not yet have a doctoral program in history, I enrolled in two evening courses with the idea of applying the credits toward the eventuality of a Ph.D. in history at Temple which was in the works.

Andi and I would meet in Mitten Hall on those nights, grab a bite to eat and then I would head for class while she went to the library or her office. Since we had only one car, a new '65 maroon Mustang, Andi generally used public transportation since Temple was not that far from Germantown. Except on the nights she would wait until my class was over and then, both exhausted after a day that started at 6 A.M. and ended at around 10 P.M., we'd head happily home together.

It was not to be an easy year. I would drive to West Philly down the winding Wissahickon Drive and through Fairmount Park every day where I taught four courses in American history and one section in Current Events at West Philadelphia High School. This was to be my goodbye year to the City of Brotherly Love, the city of my birth, the beloved city of my childhood where I had come of age and the only place I had ever really known.

CHAPTER 36

I don't remember much about my wedding. I suppose it was typical of many I attended countless times. I have never been much for weddings since—especially because at least half of the marriages in the United States since the 1960s usually ended up in divorce anyway.

One thing I do recall clearly was the rabbi. We shared the same last name. About a week before our wedding Rabbi Goldman called me and asked to see me and my prospective bride in his study. We made the appointment. Andrea asked me what Rabbi Goldman could possibly want since he did not know us. I knew rabbis, I told her. They were sensitive and spiritual.

The rabbi, I believed, probably wanted to get to know us before the ceremony and to offer us some kindly chosen words of rabbinical wisdom as we pledged our future lives to one another.

Now the truth is that I did not know rabbis. Rabbi David Goldstein at Har Zion had never spoken to me once in seven years except on the day of my bar mitzvah. After that he never spoke to me again. My father believed that many rabbis were bullshit artists. It was an ongoing argument between us over the years—especially when a number of prominent rabbis in the greater Boston area numbered among my close friends. But, I am forced to report that my Dad was closer to being right than I ever was. Most rabbis, as Louie Goldman always believed I am sad to conclude, are full of shit. They cater largely to their wealthiest congregants, kissing their fat cat asses and view the rank and file synagogue members as so many *schleppers*, an unwelcome burden that, at the least, must be tolerated. Jewish America ain't *Anitevkah*.

Back to our wise and prescient sage, Rabbi Goldman, who was certainly not a *Fiddler on the Roof*. About a week before our wedding Andrea and I appeared at the synagogue where we sat nervously in the rabbi's study awaiting his words of wisdom for two young adults who were about to embark on one of life's more hazardous journeys—the troublesome and vexing state of holy matrimony.

The rabbi smiled benignly and made some small talk. Then he issued his much anticipated words of wisdom: "I get two hundred dollars; the cantor gets a hundred. The sexton gets seventy-five. Please, if you will, cash, no checks! In three separate envelopes. Preferably, new tens and twenties," Rabbi Goldman intoned in a mellifluous voice.

"What the fuck," I thought to myself, "is a sexton? And more important, what the fuck does he do that is going to cost us seventy-five bucks?

On August 21, 1965 Andrea Leerman became Mrs. Martin S. Goldman as we entered the strange and difficult world of marriage—a brand new experience for both of us.

I don't recall a thing about the ceremony or very much about the large party held in the synagogue afterwards. All our friends and family were there. And there was a band. I do remember asking Rabbi "Capone" about the length of the service when we met in his well-appointed study. His response was interesting: "If I think a couple is deeply in love," the Rabbi responded, "they get the long service. If I think neither is deeply committed, they get a quickie. It all depends."

"How can you tell?" I queried Rabbi Numbnuts. Truthfully, I can't recall his answer. All I can tell you is that the ceremony seemed to go by very quickly and I don't recall a word that the Rabbi said.

We settled into the state of matrimony comfortably. We furnished our spacious one bedroom on Johnson and Greene Streets with bargain furniture my mother found for us at Van Sciver's on City Line. The Duval Manor was not a palace but it was comfortable and affordable at $100 a month including heat. We looked out over the parking lot in the back of the building from the eighth floor but beyond we could see the still leafy streets of Germantown where the stately old Victorian mansions built in the late 18th century were still mostly inhabited by older Whites who had refused to flee the changing racial demography of the neighborhood.

My teaching at West Philadelphia High School went well. I had four eleventh grade sections of American history. All my students were Black. I don't recall seeing a single White student in the entire school. One of the sections was an advanced class made up of some pretty bright kids. I recall always looking forward to that class. The students were bright, inquisitive, and polite. Most were headed for college. I had very few discipline problems.

We went through the Colonial period, the American Revolution, the Federal era and by Christmas headed toward the years before the Civil War. The department was chaired by a very nice woman, Helen Ainsley. She saw to it that her teachers had a minimum of bullshit to put up with—an era in the Philadelphia school system when bullshit became standard operating procedure for most beginning teachers. There were things like study hall, hall duty, lunch duty etc. It was enough to drive a young and ambitious teacher out of the system and Helen seemed to understand that in order to keep her younger charges happily on the payroll, she would have to run some interference for them.

Like the time when one of the Vice-Principals chewed me out in front of my homeroom class for wrongly filling out some endless form that we were forced to turn in every day. This asshole had embarrassed me in front of the kids—always a no-no in my book.

I told Helen and she went right to the principal himself. I don't recall his name but he forced that asshole Vice-Principal to apologize to me. And right in front of my class!

The other classes I had consisted of average kids who were probably not very much interested in American history. But they were for the most part respectful and, as the year progressed, I grew very fond of some of them.

However, it was my colleagues that got to me. Some of the older teachers were just going through the paces. Many of them had second and even third jobs. And too many of the younger teachers were dullards or, worse, dopes. Like the genius who taught American history and told me he had skipped slavery because he didn't want to make his Black students uncomfortable.

It wasn't a big deal then and it doesn't seem a big deal now. Race in 1965 was hardly the awesome barrier it became in urban school settings a few years later. Remember, this was right before the Black Power movement and schmucks like Stokely Carmichael. Excuse me: the late lamented Kwame Toure!

I did have some friends at West Philly. Some Wynnefield guys were on the faculty. An old pal and Overbrook classmate, Bernie Ivens from Hazelhurst Street was in the Math Department. Bernie had been a major basketball star at Temple. And one of the coaches was Steve Kane whose father owned Kane's Pharmacy on Lebanon Avenue.

I think Kane was an assistant coach to Joey Goldenberg, a legendary Temple University basketball player who starred with Guy Rodgers who had made it to the pros.

In the History Department I was close friends with Herb Showell, a Black guy who had also gone to Overbrook High and now lived in West Philly. Herb and I would hang out together and commiserate about the old days at the Brook (Overbrook) and how fucked the kids were in terms of the education they were receiving in the Philly schools. If you think they were screwed then, can you imagine what the kids in West Philly get today! Overbrook High and West Philadelphia High, at this writing, are still open! And little has changed in either of these educational dungeons.

The year went by quickly and before I knew it spring was in the air. In Philly, as opposed to New England where spring arrives on chilled and padded feet, spring comes early. It usually warms up by April.

I was deeply troubled. The idea of returning to West Philadelphia High for another year was not something I looked forward to with great anticipation. Andrea suggested that I get my resume together and file it with the office of placement at Temple University.

The university's placement office had gotten me a job in advertising. There was no reason to believe that they couldn't do the same in the field of teaching. So, as Andrea had suggested, I set the wheels in motion that would change both our lives forever. It was to be the end of inertia!

By April I got my first bite. Temple University had a campus in Ambler, Pennsylvania not far from Philadelphia. The history department had an opening for the following September. I knocked the interview out of the ballpark and within days was offered a job to teach history and government at a substantial raise from my Philadelphia salary.

With the reduced teaching load (from 25 classroom hours a week to 12) I could again concentrate on a doctorate. I happily accepted the written offer from Temple's president and that, I thought, would be that.

But a few days later I received a call from a man who identified himself as the chairman of the History Department at a school I'd never even heard of—Worcester Polytechnic Institute in a place I had never heard of—Worcester, Massachusetts. His name was Claude Scheiffley and he told me he had an opening for a history teacher in his department. He asked if I would meet him for an interview in New York City.

I had nothing to lose except the time it took to take the train to the Big Apple and readily agreed to the meeting at Grand Central Station. The interview, over drinks, went fine and the old man took to me (as I did to him). He had been teaching at Tech (the nickname of Worcester Polytechnic Institute) since the 1930s and had only recently been named to the chairmanship of the Department of History and Modern Languages—an academic merger I thought somewhat strange but who was I to look a gift horse in the mouth?

Professor Scheiffley was a graduate of the University of Pennsylvania and he remarked that when he was a student at Penn in the 1930's, West Philadelphia High School was known as one of the finest schools in the city. I was not about to bust his bubble. West Philly High School should have been torn down in the 1940's. It had no athletic fields (I believe they shared some facilities with a local Catholic school) and by the 1960's was just another ugly gang-ridden ghetto school where most of its graduates were doomed to lives of quiet desperation ignored by the city fathers under William Penn's statue and the federal fathers sucking at the trough in the District of Columbia. Sure, some West Philly kids went to college. I had five classes with forty students in each class. Out of 200 students only one of my classes could possibly be ticketed for higher learning and of those forty kids about half would never make it. Figure it out—a school with about 4,000 students with a very high dropout rate and less than ten per cent would ever have a bite at the ever shrinking apple of the American dream.

Sure, I told the New England professor, West Philadelphia High School was still among the best educational institutions in the city of Philadelphia.

I returned to Philly and told Andrea that we had a real dilemma. Now they wanted me to come to Worcester, Massachusetts for an interview with the college's dean and the President. I went. The interviews went very well. The college's president, Harry Storke, had been commanding general of NATO forces in Europe before taking over the presidency. He liked the fact that I was a veteran since even back in the 1960's few academics ever served in the armed services. Temple University graciously allowed me to bow out of our deal.

I received a substantial bump up from my proffered Temple salary, moving expenses and best of all, although I was to teach four history classes at twelve hours a week, a three-day schedule for my first year. Worcester Poly had Saturday classes in those days but I was spared that agony during my first year. This would enable me to find a niche in the doctoral program in history at Clark University, a quality small liberal arts college only a five-minute drive from Tech. In addition, the perks were amazing for someone coming out of a ghetto school in downtown Philly. There was a fully equipped gym with a pool; tennis courts; indoor basketball courts where I played at least an hour every day; a first-rate faculty dining room where the food was amazing and cheap. And wonder of all wonders, my very own office with my name stenciled on the door where I could study, daydream, prepare my lectures or just read. And, oh yes, meet with students. You have no idea what an office with a desk, phone and bookcases could mean to a young teacher emerging from the dregs of an ancient Philadelphia ghetto high school.

Andrea and I drove to New England that June to look for an apartment. We found a three bedroom about a block from the leafy campus near a beautiful park where we could take our little Lab Whiskey. The apartment, the first floor of a two family, had a garage and a fireplace and at $125 plus utilities a month was reasonable considering that Andrea would soon be teaching English lit at Doherty, the best and newest high school in the city. One of my colleagues in the history department who became a lifelong friend, Richard Greene, was on the Worcester School Committee and he helped open some doors for Andrea, who had given up her doctoral fellowship in Sociology at Temple, to go in another direction. Now some feminists would moan and cringe, wet their knickers and be appalled at that. But that is what most women did back in those prehistoric days when dinosaurs walked the earth; not, perhaps, the way the world should have been or one would have hoped it to have been. This was simply the world as it was. Ask Hillary Clinton!

CHAPTER 37

The best thing that happened in the next seven years was an amazing stroke of good luck: life on a large working dairy farm. Andrea had been appointed to the English department at a new high school in Worcester, Doherty Memorial, I was comfortably ensconced at Tech and was accepted into the doctoral program in history at Clark University by mid-1967. But our real stroke of luck came in December of 1966. We were not too happy with our new landlords who lived directly above us and each week after Thanksgiving we began to scour the Worcester *Telegram and Gazette* for a new place to live. Our rent of $125 a month was not the problem. Two spinster sisters owned the home at 44 Sagamore Road and they constantly bothered us about our dog, parking and a number of other minor annoyances.

For some reason I had violated my father's lifelong dictum of never writing a letter to the editor. By this time I was deeply opposed to the Viet Nam fiasco. I had read Bernard Fall's excellent book about the French debacle in Nam and realized that American kids dying in Southeast Asia was by far beyond stupid. Communism was a coat of many evils but a monolith it was not and the United States had very little to fear about South Viet Nam falling to Ho Chi Minh who was as much a nationalist as he was a communist; and he had little affection for the Chinese communists. At any rate one weekend in December my letter to the editor about the war was published and it so happened that I saw an advertisement for a small single home located on a large dairy farm in the rolling hills just beyond the city limits of Worcester in the small rural town (back then) of Auburn, Massachusetts.

I called the number given in the ad and a man who answered the phone was initially quite circumspect; until he found out that I was a history professor at Tech, that my wife was also a teacher and that I was the author of the anti-war letter he had read that very day in the local paper. His name was Adna Cutting (how's that for a John O'Hara novel!) and he was the owner of Hillcrest Dairy, probably the largest dairy business in Central Massachusetts. Mr. Cutting (he was always Mr. Cutting to us) invited us to his home on a hillside on the west side of a farm that seemed to go on for miles and miles in every direction. His home was a colonial and comfortably appointed but far from ostentatious.

He introduced Andrea and me to his wife and then took us for a ride around his farm. Mr. Cutting was grandfatherly warm and he questioned us about our lives intensely. I was worried about Jewish being a problem and although it came up at one point, it did not appear to be an issue with the old man. Why was that always an issue with me?

He pointed to a nearby hillside some miles from the farm. "That is where Robert Goddard fired off his first rocket," he said. I knew of Goddard, the father of America's space program. He was a professor at both Tech and Clark at one point and we discussed Goddard as well as the relative merits of the space program. Then he took us to the home he had for rent which lay on a large tract of land not far from a number of other Hillcrest properties occupied by his herdsman and the farm handyman. Mr. Cutting's daughter lived with her husband Donald Post and three kids in a large home not far from the small house for rent overlooking the lush green rolling hills of central Massachusetts just beyond Hillcrest Farms. His son Charles had a house next to his.

The house itself was something I could only have imagined in a dream. It was a stone and wood rancher. It had two bedrooms, a large living room and a small but cozy kitchen. Light streamed through the large windows in the living room and picture window that framed the rolling hills of central Massachusetts for miles in the back. Mr. Cutting proudly showed us the home which had once been a bowling alley that had been converted to a far more livable and comfortable space.

Mr. Cutting was willing, he said, to paint it for his new tenants, put down new carpeting in all the rooms and new linoleum in the kitchen and bath. In addition, he would put in a new washer and dryer. The only thing we would have to buy was a refrigerator.

In effect, we were moving into a completely refurbished home with virtually everything brand spanking new. For two city kids out of West Philly and Logan it was a dream come true.

To cap off our little honeymoon cottage the second bedroom had a large open hearth stone fireplace that worked and made for years of cozy winter evenings when our cottage was buried by many feet of snow for weeks at a time. There was a hidden trap door cut in the carpeting to a basement where we were able to store many cords of firewood to keep the cottage warm and cozy through the next seven and a half years of long, hard New England winters.

In addition Mr. Cutting gave us a garage space near the barn so that we would never have to dig out our car in the winter. I soon purchased a medium sized Honda motorcycle so that Andrea could take the car on days when I didn't have to be in Worcester. That came in handy two years later when I left Tech to finish my Ph.D. at Clark which was about fifteen minutes away from our farm using back country roads. And, he told us, he expected that I would take advantage of the vast acreage of Hillcrest Dairy. His farm workers, Henry Dunn and Bill Seamons would see to it that a tract of land would be cleared every spring so that I could plant a large garden of vegetables. Bill Seamons and his extended family were our closest neighbors. And, as the years passed, our families became friends. If something in our small home needed fixing, one of the Seamons or Henry Dunn would be on the scene in a matter of minutes. It gave me a new take on the idea of city versus country life. The Seamons were the kind of neighbors you got used to seeing in Mayberry on the old Andy Griffith show.

But Hillcrest Farm wasn't a TV show. For the next seven and a half years it became the centrifugal force in our daily lives.

Bill's son Dick worked for a heating company and was married to a terrific young woman named Mary. Mary and Dick who lived on the first floor of Bill's two-family home also owned by the Cuttings had twin boys, Kevin and Kurt. The friendly twins, both blonde haired, were like members of our family and we grew close.

One horrible night when the twins were about three, Kurt came down with some kind of a fever. Rushed to the hospital he soon fell into a coma. Kevin and Kurt were constantly knocking on our door to come in and play with our black Lab Whiskey. Within the week little Kurt Seamons died. It was a tragic blow felt by everyone on the farm. Can there be anything in life worse than losing a child? Andi and I shared in the Seamons family's deep grief and went to the funeral. For a time I visited little Kurt's gravesite not far from the farm on my way to school trying to make some sense out of it all. I never had an epiphany of any sort. The death of a child, any child, has no rhyme, no reason.

A few years later Mary Seamons gave birth to a little girl. Mary, who was a practicing Catholic, seemed to take little Kurt's death in some measure of stride never losing her ever-present faith and sense of humor but I am certain to this day she has never gotten over it. Who would?

Over the years when we would throw house parties and even barbecues with softball games on the open fields in front of our home I could tell that some of the grad students at Clark were somewhat envious of our rural lifestyle. After all, the code of most graduate students is to suffer in gentle poverty. Hillcrest Farm was a far cry from the privation imposed upon most graduate student life in the 1960's.

So between January 1967 (when we moved to the farm) and May of 1973 when we were asked to leave life was good. Actually, it was better than good.

Andrea settled into her teaching at the high school where she was soon recognized as a masterful instructor and well-liked by her students and colleagues. She also entered a M.Ed. program at Worcester State College. At the same time I grew comfortable over at Clark and by 1968 moved over there full time to complete my doctoral studies. In 1968 I took a year of leave from Tech where I was able to keep most of our benefits and secretly hoped that things would go so well at Clark that I would not have to return. I liked the school well enough but scientists and engineers did not take the history courses as seriously as my liberal arts students at Clark. As it turned out, after a falling out with the new department chair at Worcester Tech, I was invited back for a final year of teaching but since I was able to cobble together an income at Clark that actually surpassed the $7500 a year I had reached at Tech, I ultimately declined to return for that final year. I was offered full tuition in the doctoral program, a teaching assistantship in Political Science and a university fellowship that put my income from the department at well over $5,000. In addition Clark University allowed me to teach a number of courses in my specialty, "Negro History," in their evening and summer programs. I actually offered the very first Black Studies courses ever given at Clark: "American Negro History," "Race as an Idea in American History," "Black Political Thought" and "The History of the South." As word spread that Clark had a guy who could teach Black history, I was invited to teach for a couple years over at Holy Cross and to top it all off by 1970 I added a grad course in Black history to my dance card at nearby Fitchburg State College.

The graduate program in history at Clark University was concentrated and vigorous. Being a small department, History only took about a half dozen new students a year. Contrast that with a Ph.D. factory like say Rutgers in New Jersey that easily accepted 75 to 100 new students a year and you can begin to appreciate the intimacy of such a small department with a close-knit faculty and graduate student body. Our professors became friends as well as mentors and the graduate students, although competitive like all ambitious grad students who constantly jockey for position and recognition, were more like a family. We held daily get-togethers, pot luck dinner parties and even grad student picnics.

My good fortune continued as I was appointed to be the teaching assistant of Professor Knud Rasmussen who taught the large freshman class in Political Science of between 150-200 students each year. Knud, who had grown up in Copenhagen, Denmark, was in his forties and he quickly became my closest friend at Clark. He had sparkling blue eyes, blonde hair and a quick but subtle wit. Knud also had an eye for a well-turned skirt and in the late sixties the co-eds wore mostly minis or cutoffs!

Andrea and I shared many a happy dinner with him and his wife Ginny in their comfortable Holden, Massachusetts home. Knud and I bonded so well that he allowed me to design part of the curriculum and although I was responsible for the three weekly discussion sections, I also gave a series of lectures over the course of each semester on Communism and Totalitarianism. Our friendship grew quickly so that when the long mid-winter study session came in January and February, Knud invited me to accompany him on a trip to his native Denmark where we would both lecture on American politics and study Danish Political Culture to a small group of about a dozen students from Clark at the impressive University of Copenhagen. Knud even asked the History Department to help underwrite my participation and the chairman, Gerry Grob, generously not only approved my assisting Knud but kicked in with a travel stipend from the department as well. And so, after only one semester at Clark I was off to Denmark for the mid-winter semester of 1969.

Denmark was an eye-opening experience for a 29-year-old who had barely been beyond West Philadelphia. The Danes are a remarkable and friendly people, comfortable in their own skins and, at that time, far advanced from other western democracies in their attitude toward sex and morality. The Clark students were typical of the times in that they were mostly upper middle class Jewish kids from very affluent homes. One of the student's fathers was a law partner in New York City with the famous and well-known attorney Louis Nizer. We spent our time meeting Danish professors, students, journalists and high school teachers.

For me the two high spots of the mid-term we spent in Denmark was an overnight train trip for a weekend in Berlin where, for the first time, I could still see a city that had not quite recovered from the ravages of World War II. I can't say that I was comfortable in Berlin in 1969 as I passed many amputees walking with canes because of war injuries. How many Nazis, I wondered, did I pass on the German streets, in the restaurants and plazas? One of the fun parts of the weekend was going to a German movie house to watch *Gone with the Wind* and *Dr. Zhivago* in German.

The other memorable part of the trip was a weekend drive up the Danish coast to Knud's parent's home in Jutland where he grew up.

The Rasmussen family still lived in the quaint fishing village where my friend had lived as a boy under the Nazi occupation. Knud's mother and father welcomed us to their comfortable home with a wonderful Danish luncheon with all kinds of delicacies I had never tasted before, and one day Mr. Rasmussen took me to the beaches by the North Sea where the German bunkers still stood waiting for an invasion by the Allies that never came. I still have a photo of me dancing on top of one of the German bunkers standing silent watch over the tumultuous North Sea—a bit of sticking it to the Nazis with an American Jew dancing on the skeleton remnant of what was to be their thousand year Reich!

I made up the Denmark trip to Andrea the following summer when the two of us flew off to Europe where we backpacked through Luxembourg, France, Italy, Germany, Denmark and Holland. We spent the better part of that remarkable summer visiting the major capitols of Europe and hit the museums, restaurants and high spots of Paris, Rome, Munich (after a day trip to Dachau concentration camp outside of Munich we both agreed to skip Berlin!), Copenhagen and Amsterdam. We stayed in pensions, youth hostels and cheap hotels. Imagine a room in Paris for four bucks a night! The only downside of the trip was that we had to board our black Labrador Retriever Ripper over much of that summer.

The years I spent at Clark University were magic. There were endless discussions over gallons of coffee in the student union about every conceivable topic under the sun. My close friend David Goodman, a year ahead of me in his studies, and I spent hours discussing history and life. David was from Hicksville, Long Island and was, for my money, the brightest grad student in the department. He and his wife Marilyn, an artist who also taught in the Worcester schools art programs, spent a great deal of time with us on the farm, going to the movies and trying to find decent, reasonable restaurants in provincial Worcester, Massachusetts which was no easy task. As I recall we found Renee and Leo's for great Italian food and Putnam's downtown for the greatest baked stuffed twin lobster I have ever tasted. The locals called the place Put's…but coming from Philly we didn't much like that nickname!

Every spring the fields in front of our house on the farm would be tilled by tractor by Bill or Henry and I was permitted to work a large tract to plant and grow whatever I wanted. Because the herder had died during our first winter, the number of cattle on the farm had dwindled to about a dozen. The herd was gradually built up again so that when we left there were almost 150 prize cows. The fierce New England winters were mostly spent in front of our large stone fireplace in our back room that overlooked the rolling hills of Central Massachusetts. I passed my written and oral exams in 1970 and 1971 concentrating in the broad field of American history with an emphasis on American Negro history; my other two fields were German history with an emphasis on the Nazi period and the Holocaust and Political Theory where I studied the great political thinkers from Plato and Aristotle to Hegel, Kant and Marx. Shortly after I passed my oral exams, in the spring of 1971, Andrea and I flew out to the University of Michigan where I presented a paper on Black History before a combined audience of students and faculty. I was offered an appointment at the university's satellite campus in Dearborn. I didn't relish living in Ann Arbor, a college town or in Dearborn which was ugly and flat. So I procrastinated. A few weeks later my American history professor at Clark, Gerry Grob, who had moved to Rutgers University called to offer me a one-year appointment in Afro-American history replacing another former mentor of mine from Temple, Seth Scheiner, who was going off on a sabbatical. Since my dissertation research topic had to do with Philadelphia I made a quick decision to take the Rutgers offer. I would drive down to Philly on a Sunday or Monday, live with my family, research my dissertation all week, teach my courses on a one-day schedule on a Friday and head back to New England every weekend from New Brunswick, New Jersey.

It was both a wise and foolish decision. First, I had put the University of Michigan on hold taking the real chance that the offer of a tenure-track spot might not be held for an entire year. The good part of the choice was that it gave me a chance to spend a wonderful year with my mother and father who were not at all happy about my decision to leave Philadelphia in 1966. The really foolish part of my decision that year was the weekly commuting between Philadelphia and New England. Even though I was still relatively young, the weekly round-trip commute took a toll on me physically and, worst of all, on our marriage.

And so I started commuting to Philly in September 1971. My friend Murray Freedman, the scholarly director of the American Jewish Committee in Philadelphia, introduced me to a real character by the name of Maxwell Whiteman who was the historian and curmudgeon in residence at the Union League of Philadelphia. The Union League, founded during the Civil War by a group of wealthy anti-slavery (not abolitionists!) men who basically ran Philadelphia was to be the topic of my Ph.D. thesis. Although he was not remotely an academic (Max, in fact, had nothing but disdain for academic historians!) or a trained scholar, Whiteman, as the archivist of the Union League, had done pioneering work in Black and Jewish history. Ironically, by the turn of the century the Union League which had long since abandoned its quest for equal rights for Black Americans had restricted the club from admitting Jewish members. And Maxwell Whiteman was Jewish. He gave me unrestricted access to the Union League's 19th century records for the better part of that year as I worked to prove a pet theory that had long been percolating in my mind—that the real enemies of Black Americans were their friends: the Liberals. You must remember that during the Civil War and Reconstruction, the Republicans, the elite of American political and social circles, were the Liberals of that era. Was I guilty of "historical present-ism" (looking at the past from the perspective of the present)? You bet!

I was also able to catch up with many old friends. The Gansk, (Paul Gansky) now comfortably ensconced in his father's lucrative insurance agency, American Integrity (how is that for a misleading name!) was a block or so away from the Union League. And the Gansk made the Xerox facilities of his agency available to me so that instead of taking notes all I had to do was pile up the documents every day and, with Max's kind permission, take the materials over to the Gansk's office after 5 P.M. every evening, duplicate them and bring them back the next day.

The Gansk was going through some terrible times in his marriage to Sallyann (it soon ended in divorce) so we spent most weeknights eating out together and commiserating mostly about the troubles in the Gansk's married life. That sadness soon ended when he met another woman and within a year or so they were living together. They married a year or two later and Paul and Ester Gansky remain happily married to this day. The Gansks live the manor life of an English squire on a huge farm outside of Philly where they have many horses, dogs, an amazing art collection and quite a nice existence with a 110-foot boat that is bigger than most houses, Fox Hunting at the Radnor Hunt and traveling the world in great style. I also caught up with Stanley (Benny) and Myrna Stein and Alvin and Diane Kolchins (Diane Meltzer was one of Andrea's closest friends and we had fixed them up shortly after we were married). Larry Laster, my hand grenade carrying buddy from the 1950's, had gone from blowing up houses and robbing gas stations to a Ph.D. and a full professorship in bio-statistics at the University of Pennsylvania. I often joined him, his wife Linda and their three kids at their home in Valley Forge. Of all the guys, over the years, I stayed in close touch with Larry and his burgeoning tribe. We often vacationed together every summer on Martha's Vineyard which for a good part of the 1970's became our special summer retreat. Still, it was a difficult forty weeks although my parents were very happy to have their eldest son back home on a weekly basis in 1971 and 1972.

The year flew by quickly, the research went well and teaching at Rutgers was no problem. I had many Black students in my classes and never once did any student throughout that entire year question the fact that a White guy was teaching Black History. One day, my Dad came up to listen to me lecture a class on the Harlem Renaissance. Of course, my Dad had never heard of the Harlem Renaissance. It was the first and only time my Dad heard me lecture. After the class which lasted about 90 minutes his only comment driving back to Philly was, "Where did you learn about all that stuff? And how come nobody ever heard of it?" I think it was his way of saying he approved. But I'm certain he still wondered what I was going to do with my life.

Before I knew it I was facing the lazy summer of 1972 whiling away my days on Hillcrest Farm, teaching summer school at Clark and working my large tract of land growing all the veggies one could possibly imagine. We shared a house on the Vineyard for part of the summer with my friends from Philly Larry and Linda Laster and Dick and Sharon Donahue. Dick taught history at Andrea's high school. It was to be our last carefree summer living an idyllic peaceful and rural life in Central Massachusetts.

CHAPTER 38

That fall I accepted a teaching appointment at Worcester State College, one of the half dozen or so teacher's colleges in the Massachusetts state system. I signed on full time to teach The History of Education and to supervise the college's Social Studies student teachers who were spread around the region's many high schools. I can't say that Worcester State College was the academic setting of my dreams. The students were, for the most part, lackluster and mediocre. One student that I supervised at a high school in Holden, Massachusetts actually made incredible misstatements of historical fact in one of the classes I monitored. I was on campus one day a week and spent the rest of the week going to the various schools in the region to watch my charges teach and to evaluate them. I shuddered at the thought of some of them going into the profession. But it was a job. And a job was a job.

One of those days was spent at Doherty Memorial where I had a chance to watch Andrea teach in her English classes. Andrea was a master teacher and very well liked by her students who were among the most advanced in the school. She spent hours at home preparing classes and grading essay papers. As the year progressed Andrea had done so well that she was offered the directorship of an alternative program that the city of Worcester was putting into operation for exceptionally gifted students.

My work at Worcester State concluded in January of 1973. From January through June, with the exception of a single course I was teaching at Clark University, The History of the South, I was unemployed. It began to produce some tension between Andrea and me which I chose to avoid thinking about. With my credentials, I didn't think that I had a worry in the world. I should have listened closer. I might have heard God laughing.

By early spring I had not heard from the University of Michigan and so I wrote to ask about the previous year's offer and whether we should be packing our bags for Ann Arbor. The chairman wrote back somewhat apologetically for as he put it "keeping you on tenterhooks": the department had been instructed by the Grand Viziers of that academic kingdom to hire "a person of color" for the position. No matter, I thought. I didn't really want to live in Michigan anyway; so far from the Atlantic Ocean. And I was still very marketable. Or so I thought. I had already published two scholarly articles while in grad school. I had introduced the subject in question, Afro-American History, at some very fine institutions of higher learning. I was halfway through my dissertation. So, I put my resume together and, after attending a number of academic history organization meetings where it was encouraging to see so many jobs in Black Studies available, I sent out over fifty responses to openings at some of the best universities in the country. I heard back from Tufts University, Vanderbilt, Penn State, Wellesley College and a score of other nationally ranked academic institutions: the answers, if not on a cheesy form letter, were basically the same. The history departments were committed to the principles of "equality" by enforcing the federally mandated program of "Affirmative Action" and therefore they were looking for a man or woman "of color" (preferably a woman—a twofer) to join their faculties. It was the first time I would tilt, like Don Quixote, against the storm tossed windmill of Affirmative Action as it began to sweep the country and especially the nation's college campuses. It would certainly not be the last.

To put it mildly, I was devastated. All I had worked toward and for since 1963 was in dire jeopardy. After all, I had banked on the fact that trained academics knew more about overt discrimination in the history of the United States than most government bureaucrats? Could they be so stupid as to "discriminate to end discrimination?" It was a phrase I was to employ on many occasions for years to come as the battle lines were drawn. And it was an eye opener for me in many ways: academics and scholars, whom I had held in such high esteem for so many years, were just like ostriches with their heads in the sand.

Except for the fact that most academics I was to come across over the years didn't have their heads stuck in the sand; their heads were firmly entrenched up their own asses!

But that was hardly our only problem that spring. One disaster seemed to follow another. In early April we received a letter evicting us from the farm, our home and our way of life. Mr. Cutting Sr. had died a few years before 1973 and his only son and principle heir, Charles Cutting, was running the dairy farm and the business. Charlie, like his Dad, liked us and told us we had nothing to fear from him; that nothing would change. But Charlie Cutting, only in his early forties, died suddenly. And his sister, who then inherited the dairy business and the farm, had little affection over the years for Andrea or me. Whenever our Labradors, first Whiskey and then both Rippers, would run the hundred or so yards to her house which was on a hill directly behind our house, we would receive an angry phone call. We never bitched when her big Collie, Breezy, ran over to our place and pooped on the lawn. But then we didn't own the lawn!

I knew she didn't care a whit for us when our black Labrador followed the paperboy down the road to the highway one early evening on a snowy Friday in December of 1970. The Ripper, only a year old at the time, was hit by a car out on the highway and when I got there he looked up at me sadly and died right in my arms. Andrea and I were both so grief-stricken that we attempted to replace the Ripper immediately. A fellow grad student at Clark who raised Labradors told of us of a professor at Dartmouth College who bred Labradors. We called and within 24 hours we had a three month old adorable black Lab puppy. We named him Ripper II and he lived a long and happy life dying in 1983. But our neighbor of many years, Mr. Cutting's snarky daughter, never even called to tell us how sorry she was that we had lost our original Ripper. We rarely spoke to her and her wimp of a husband after that.

So Andrea and I had a major dilemma. We had to decide whether to fight the unfair eviction notice or move. That May, unwilling to stay where we were not wanted, we moved.

CHAPTER 39

When the moving van emptied the last of our possessions from our little house on the farm I walked in for one long last look while Andrea waited in the car. I felt an overwhelming sense of loss and although we had found a very comfortable two story home on a beautiful crystal clear lake about a half-hour away, something deep within me told me that things would never be the same. And they were not.

The seven years at Hillcrest Farm with the Baker family (Charlie Baker, who lived in a large white house right next door, was a French professor at Holy Cross and he, his wife Joan and their five great kids had become like family to Andrea and me) and the other farm families had been among the happiest years in my adult life. Somehow, as I stood in that old stone house to say a final goodbye, I realized that an important segment of my life was really over. I would never be fortunate enough to live on such a vast tract of land again; nor would I have the acres and acres of land for such a large garden every year (although I have rarely been without a vegetable garden wherever I lived). And what about us: Andrea and me? It was imperceptible at the time. But change was coming in our relationship.

In May of 1973 we moved to the small central Massachusetts town of Spencer. Spencer, Massachusetts is, perhaps, famous for one thing: the Trappist monastery where the cloistered monks chant Vespers a couple times a day and where, in their medieval surroundings, they have enough land to grow fruit trees that make that great jam and jelly that you see in so many supermarkets. We had found a newly built modern home on Cranberry Lake and although the rent was more than double what we were paying on the farm it was a beautiful home right on the beach of a four-mile long crystal clear lake that was wonderful for boating, fishing and swimming. Our new landlords, a young couple with two kids, lived in the newly constructed home next door and seemed like very nice people.

I had sold my motorcycle shortly before we moved from the farm and took that money to purchase a used 17-foot speed boat that we moored directly in front of our house off our small sandy beach. May was unusually warm that year. From our spacious deck we could survey most of the lake and Ripper and I were soon taking cruises all around the lake or swimming the half-mile across on almost a daily basis. I have always been a strong swimmer and made the mile-long swim up and back with little difficulty. As I approached our shore the Ripper would often dive into the lake like he was shot out of a canon and he'd often accompany me for the last couple hundred yards or so.

Summer was coming soon and even though I was unemployed, with the promise of only a single summer school course to teach at Clark University, I was somewhat sanguine about my situation. Not so Andrea. She would come home every day to find me either sitting in my boat in the middle of the lake or sunning myself on the deck reading mystery novels. We began to argue and it didn't help much that I wasn't working at all on alleviating my employment dilemma. I should have understood that Andrea was working hard and, having accepted the new position in the Worcester schools, was experiencing pressures of her own at work. But, far too centered on my own dilemma, I didn't attempt to understand her problems. I had worked hard over four years at Clark University and it seemed as if the academic world was shitting on me.

I would scan *The New York Times* educational section every Sunday, send out my resume and wait for responses that rarely came. Each day I would ritualistically head to our mailbox and then scan the few letters that would arrive proclaiming the usual formulated rejections to my inquiries about an advertised job opening in this or that particular history department around the country.

What finally tore it for me was when Clark University itself announced an opening for an assistant professor of African-American History. Richard Ford, a White historian, was already tenured in African History so I thought that, even though the long-standing position of the department was never to hire one of their own grad students, I had a shot. I went to see the chairman, Professor Theodore

Von Laue. Von Laue, the son of a very prominent and brave German physicist who had been a leading anti-Nazi, graciously agreed to see me. We sparred for a bit and then Professor Von Laue got right to the point. He was charged, he informed me, by the Clark administration to bring a Black person to the campus. My counter argument about ghettoizing the discipline, that Black History wasn't the only position that ought to be considered for an able Black scholar—why not Math, Physics, Psychology or Geography I argued—was not effective with Von Laue. Even though, as a specialist in Russian history (his book *Why Lenin?—Why Stalin?* was a standard monograph used in many college courses across the country), Von Laue knew better than most that what the university was proposing was not far removed from the Soviet attempt at thought control—in other words, that only a Black could teach about Blacks; that only a woman could teach about women; which ultimately leads to the stupid but somewhat insane position that to study Roman history you better find yourself an ancient Roman! But in the 1970's that was, unbelievably enough, the direction in which too many American colleges and universities were heading. Black Studies were on the road to becoming Black bullshit.

Professor Von Laue held his ground. He would search the country, he said, to hire the most talented and qualified Black scholar he could find for the university. "But what if you can't find a qualified Black scholar?" I asked. Would I then be considered? Von Laue didn't offer me a straight answer. And that was the end of it. Von Laue never did find the qualified Black scholar that he was looking for and the job opening was left unfilled in 1973 and 1974 and 1975. Finally, the position was withdrawn. The students, Black and White, who had taken over an administration building in 1972 to demand the hiring of Black faculty and Black Studies had graduated or left the university and so, like so many academic decisions, in the end nothing was done.

I lost track of what was happening in Clark's history department after that. I did note that at some point Clark brought to its campus a very famous and well-qualified Black scholar who had made his academic bones with an in-depth sociological study of the Black Muslim movement in America. This fellow was brought to Clark with a great deal of publicity and fanfare. Within a year of his appointment two women came forward and charged him with sexual harassment. Apparently, this old duffer would invite good looking chicks up to his office and then grope them. It was a scandal of major proportion reaching from Worcester to Boston and all around the state. It rocked the tight-knit Clark community. I always wondered what Professor Von Laue thought about it all. But I never got a chance to ask him. He retired and died a few years later. Too bad, I thought, when I heard that he had died, that the son never had the guts and courage of the father. Von Laue, who had seen firsthand what Nazism and racial politics could do to a country, was tenured and he knew that hiring a teacher based on his or her race was wrong. He should have told the Clark administration to go to hell.

CHAPTER 40

Sometime in June my close friend from Clark University, David Goodman, called to offer me information about a job opening. Dave had separated from his wife Marilyn shortly after completing his Ph.D. (they would eventually divorce) and he was soon faced with a dilemma similar to mine: the academic world was closed to White Ph.D.s of almost any caliber. Dave Goodman, in my mind the best history student in that crop that was at Clark between 1968 and 1972, had settled for a job in Washington, D.C. with ARBA—The American Revolution Bicentennial Administration, a White House commission begun under President Lyndon Johnson who had assumed that he might still be president in 1976 since, having become president in 1963 with the assassination of JFK, Johnson was constitutionally permitted to run again in 1968 and 1972. My guess is that the commission was originally set in motion to aggrandize Johnson in the last year of his presidency as it coincided with the 200th birthday of the United States.

David had been hired as a historian in the Heritage section of the Bicentennial Administration and the Commission, which was funded to the astounding tune of around $20 million a year—a small sum I was told when it came to government spending in D.C.—and there was a job opening for someone who had some expertise in ethnic and minority studies. Dave had given the head of the section an article I had published about Black History and the boss, a Ph.D. himself, quickly decided to bring me down to D.C. for an interview. The interview was *pro forma* even though I was told they would have preferred a Black Ph.D. for the position, and an offer of a job was made at twice the salary I could ever have expected in any academic setting.

You might think I was happy about all this. I was not. First of all, I had no idea what my job responsibilities would be and even after an entire year in D.C. it still wasn't made clear. Second, it made me sad to think that the government would spend so much money on a job title as Program Officer and Director of Ethnic and Minority Heritage (whatever the hell that was!) while no reputable college or university could find a space for me at half the salary the government was willing to shell out—a salary I would have gratefully accepted.

My first inclination was to tell the good folks in D.C., "Thanks, but no thanks." I didn't want to go. I didn't want to leave New England. I didn't want to live in the Washington area. I didn't want to move again. I hated the idea of a July and August in Washington—the two most stifling months of the year in our nation's capital.

Andrea wouldn't hear of it. She was, she argued, willing to give up the directorship of the Worcester school system's Alternative Education Program, once more diverting her life and professional career, in order to redirect my own career. Remember, Andrea had given up a great spot in Temple University's Ph.D. program in Sociology for me when we moved to Massachusetts. Now she was willing to give up everything she had worked for in Worcester for almost eight years. She would find a job in the government once we got settled in D.C. and the Bicentennial, which we both thought might actually be a good stepping stone to other more important government service options.

I had long wanted to take a look at the CIA where I knew competent scholars were often hired as national security specialists and analysts. Although I was hardly interested in becoming an American James Bond type, one of our guys in the history program at Clark University, James Pavitt, had actually wormed his way into the CIA after being drafted with two years in Army intelligence in Germany and serving on the staff of a hack Massachusetts congressman who just happened to be on the House Intelligence Committee.

When Pavitt and his wife Ramsey left Clark Andrea and I threw them a going away party at the farm. We had both been close with the Pavitts during their year at Clark. All the grad students were there and we presented Jim with a watch to remember his time with us. Well liked by everyone at Clark, Jim Pavitt apparently did so brilliantly at the cloak and dagger games played by the CIA, or he had made his way around the back-stabbing, ass-kissing bureaucratic government maze very well—take your pick—that by September 11, 2001 he had risen to CIA Director George Tenet's number two man as head of the Directorate of Operations (DO)—the entire clandestine spy service that had so obviously dropped that big terrorist ball in the fight against Al Qaeda costing 3,000 innocent Americans their lives and shattering the nation to its core like Pearl Harbor in 1941 and the Assassination of John F. Kennedy in 1963.

Pavitt had served the CIA in the White House during Bush 41 and was one of the few CIA guys trusted to brief Bush 43 on whatever it is presidents get briefed about shortly after George W. Bush was elected. As it turned out I was to see the CIA close-up; only in a much different capacity than my old grad school buddy Jim Pavitt.

And so, with Andrea's strong urging, I finally accepted the Bicentennial job and we made preparations for the move to the Washington area. Our new landlords graciously let us out of our two-year lease and I, with no small trepidation, drove down to D.C. Andrea would close out our affairs in Massachusetts and I, for most of the summer, would stay with Andrea's cousins Michael and Ellensue Gross and their young kids Mindy and Peter. Michael and Ellensue were from Philly but Michael, who had a Ph.D. in science, worked at the NIH (National Institute of Health). They had a lovely, spacious home in Rockville, Maryland and they made my summer stay welcoming and comfortable. Michael's brother, Winnie Gross had also moved to the D.C. area and had opened a jewelry emporium called "Creative Goldsmith's" in, of all places, the Watergate complex. From time to time we all worked in that jewelry store—Michael Gross had a piece of the place—to help out on busy weekends.

I started work at the Bicentennial in mid-July of 1973. Our offices which housed about 150 professional and support staff were located in the antique town houses along Jackson Place and rented space on K Street NW—all part of the New Executive office complex where thousands toiled as part of the White House staff to bolster the failing presidency of Richard M. Nixon while The Trickster scrambled to avoid the ever entangling web he himself had spun of Watergate deceit. I was given a spacious office right next to my friend Dave Goodman.

Although it did not have a window—which in the government is a measure of how important you are—it did have a couch and a small credenza that could also serve as a mini-bar. I was also given a full-time secretary. The only problem is that I didn't know what to tell her to do. Because, simply enough, I had absolutely no idea what I was supposed to do. And nobody, to Dave Goodman's and my own eternal amusement, ever came around to tell us.

Andrea flew down in August and we found a comfortable town house in Reston, Virginia where we paid three times the rent we had paid on the farm. What the hell! I was making twice what I would have made in most colleges. We moved to Reston that September and things soon settled into a livable routine. Andrea quickly found a good job at the NIE (National Institute of Education) and we were both making the long commute to the city either by bus or in a car pool that we had set up in Reston. Wasn't it great that there were so many alphabet soup government agencies that had so much money to spread around that they could hire unemployed academics at the drop of a hat? Another Clark grad student, Sid Hart, also made his way into government service as a historian at the National Portrait Gallery. There was little room in the academic world for White guys in the early 1970's. But our government was always there, thankfully, to pick up the slack! Sort of like welfare for Ph.d.s.

CHAPTER 41

There were some major events over the next eighteen months that were to have a marked effect on the rest of my life. The first was the appointment of Secretary of the Navy John Warner to serve as head Administrator of the Bicentennial. Before Warner married Elizabeth Taylor he was married to a Mellon (of the very wealthy Pittsburgh, Pennsylvania Mellons). The family had been major contributors to the Nixon political coffers and as a reward the corrupt President appointed Warner as Secretary of the Navy. Even though Warner was in the process of a messy divorce he was hardly abandoned by the politically powerful Mellon family. But President Nixon, as the rumor mill went in the small-town gossip of the District, had little respect for Warner's intellectual abilities and quickly moved him out of the Pentagon. Of course, they had to find a spot for Warner. What better place to bury him than deep in the moribund Bicentennial Administration where, Nixon must have imagined, Warner might never have been heard from again. As was his ongoing problem with so many people as president, Nixon underestimated Warner just as he underestimated Senator Sam Irvin, Judge John Sirica and John Dean not to mention the American people.

So my problem, as only one hustling staffer of about 150 hustling staffers, not a simple one, was how to reach Mr. Warner and to make him take notice of my varied talents and put them to the most effective use. Warner had taken a handful of Navy people with him from the Pentagon into the Bicentennial Administration. That thick layer of protective Navy blue was not at all easy to penetrate; at first. At the time I had no idea that Warner, that sly boots, was sleeping with Barbara Walters. I guess there is no accounting for taste. His, not hers!

The second event had nothing to do with my job but affected my performance, my psyche and the stability of my family for many months and years afterward. It was an incident that has never been far removed from my consciousness. My brother Ken and I still can't let it go almost 40 years later.

The phone call came to me in Virginia on the last Sunday of September, 1973 around 10:30 P.M. The caller was my brother Ken. I knew from the moment he spoke from his tone what had happened. I just couldn't know how bad it was. When I answered the phone Ken's first sentence said it all:

"Are you sitting down?" he asked. I answered with a question: "Are they alive?"

"Yes," Kenny said, "but it's bad."

For years, even when I stayed with my parents during my year at Rutgers, I had been begging them to sell the house and move. But my mother loved that house, enjoyed tending to her rose bushes and had lived in our cozy Philly neighborhood almost all of her life. Wynnefield, like many American neighborhoods in the 1960's and 1970's, was in the process of great urban flux. Blacks were moving into the neighborhood in increasing numbers and Jews, as was their wont, were fleeing in droves across City Line out of the city. When the largest synagogue, Har Zion Temple, where my brother and I had been a bar mitzvah, moved the handwriting was on the proverbial wall. I had actually published a couple of pieces on the problem of the changes that were taking place in my old neighborhood and had predicted in no uncertain terms that Wynnefield, as an integrated polity, was a fanciful dream that was doomed. Although many misguided liberal pundits were writing articles in periodicals like *Philadelphia Magazine* and *The Jewish Exponent* that Wynnefield could be a model for the new integration—a city neighborhood where, if the Whites (make that Jews!) only stayed put during the influx of Blacks, a great lesson could be taught the world: that Blacks and Whites could share the same neighborhood and that the world would be a much better place. *Cumbaya!* Of course, in a perfect world they would have been correct. But the world of race, running, riot and robbing in West Philly by 1970 was far from perfect.

By the time I received my brother's phone call that Sunday night two of my childhood friend's mothers had been brutally murdered in their own homes in Wynnefield. And those were the ones I knew about. I always had it in the back of my mind that...well...no...I would just shut it out of my mind because it was too horrible to contemplate; which is why I wanted my aging parents to move.

This is what had happened that day: on Sunday morning around noon my father went out to walk Rusty, our little terrier. When he got back to the house he found that two men had broken into the house through the basement off the back alley which was fairly hidden from the street and from the heavy traffic that passed by about half a block away on City Line Avenue. The two men who had a gun demanded that my father give them a large sum of money. They knew they said that he had at least $10,000 in cash in the house. Whoever had given them that information certainly did not know Louie Goldman. My father never kept large denominations of money in the house. My father told them, truthfully, that he did not have anything like that kind of money in the house. He gave them what he had. They took his wallet, watch, signet ring, keys and then they pistol-whipped him and tied him up and gagged him. Then they took my mother upstairs where one of them raped her. They also beat her around the face and head.

They then proceeded to ransack the entire house taking anything of value they could find where they casually carried it out to my Dad's car, a late model brown Chevy. After a few hours in the house they had a debate. One of them wanted to shoot my mother and father. One of them didn't want to shoot them. They held that debate in front of my father. My Dad later told me that while they were debating his life and death that the only thought that went through his mind was, "I wish they still had the death penalty in Pennsylvania!" Of course, *they* did not. After all, the death penalty as so many well-meaning idiots teach and preach in our colleges and universities is barbaric. The death penalty for law abiding citizens...well, that's just fine.

Meanwhile, Rusty was barking at them. One of them was going to shoot the dog when my father pleaded that they put him in a large closet downstairs. They put the dog in the closet where he apparently settled down. After tying my poor hysterical mother up and smacking her around some more they looted the rest of the house. They had held my parents captive for almost six hours before they finally left taking our family car filled to the brim with our stuff.

My parents might never have been found in time if it hadn't been for the dog. Rusty, cooped up in that closet, began to bark his head off. My father said that the dog might have barked for almost two hours. Our neighbor and close friend, Dr. Arthur Mashbit, heard Rusty barking. He knew that Rusty hardly ever barked except when a bicycle went by the house. But the dog wasn't on the porch outside. Somehow, Dr. Mashbit either forced the front door or got into the house through the broken window in the basement. I never asked. He found my parents, untied them and called the cops. Then my parents called my brother who lived about an hour away.

After my brother's phone call I awakened Andrea, told her what I knew had transpired and we began to throw some things haphazardly into a bag for the three hour trip to Philadelphia. It was easily after 11 P.M. when we finally left Virginia. I have no idea why and thus I can't tell you why I did it, but I owned a. 22 caliber Ruger which I had purchased while we lived on the farm. I threw that loaded gun in the back seat of our new Mustang as we left for Philly. People were always breaking down on the highway near our farm and we had been awakened on more than one occasion in the middle of the night by someone seeking help. Because we lived a somewhat isolated existence I thought it was wise to have a weapon in the house. I would not have had the weapon with any kids around but you never knew when Dick and Perry might show up.

On the long drive to Philly we said very little to one another as I held my foot to the floor. I was lost in the grotesque thoughts of what had happened to my parents when somewhere late at night on that sparsely traveled Route 95 highway between Wilmington, Delaware and Philly my father's Chevy roared past us; it was between 12:30 and 1 A.M.

As Dad's car flew by I could see two Black guys in the front seat. There was nothing in the back seat. They had apparently driven my family's stuff down to Baltimore and gotten rid of it.

They were easily hitting between 80 and 90 miles an hour when they passed. I decided to chase them. At first I tried to follow them at a safe distance and hoped that they would pull into one of the rest stations. What, you may ask, was I going to do if the two men had pulled into a rest stop? My answer, whether you choose to believe me or not, is easy: I was going to kill them.

As I pushed the Mustang to speeds approaching 85 and then 90 miles an hour, the guys in my Dad's Chevy must have realized that they had someone on their tail. They had to be going over 100 miles an hour. They were pulling out of range. Andrea started screaming at me, begging me to slow down and give up the chase; which, after some minutes, I reluctantly did.

When we got to Philly I immediately called the cops to alert them to the fact that I had seen my father's car on Route 95 outside of Philly. The car, like the two criminals, was never found.

My parents had both been to the hospital and were at home when we arrived sometime after 1 A.M. My mother's cheek was swollen and black and blue. One of her eyes was swollen shut. Her lip was spread and split. It even hurt her to cry which, of course, she did. My father wouldn't talk about it. I did my best that night to honor his silence. I could not even imagine how they felt.

Don't get me wrong here. I am not bellyaching. Everybody in this life suffers loss and pain. Nobody escapes life's myriad difficulties. And nobody gets out alive. It is what life is partly all about; Yin and Yang. There is the good and the bad. There is health and disease; triumph and tragedy. But this was different. This was something that shouldn't have been part of our life—of anyone's life. Nobody should have seen what Ken and I saw on that late Sunday night in September. And no children should ever come home to what we did—the utter and undeserved devastation of a family and their home. Tornadoes, tsunamis and hurricanes are terrible events and families are devastated and lives are lost, homes are destroyed with peace of mind forever ruined. But those catastrophes are far beyond human control. Not this. This was man made. Two men had made a decision to do great evil. This had struck at our very soul. And that is all I want to write about our arrival on that loathsome night.

The next day, Monday, our house was filled with cops. Smudge marks were all over the place from the finger printing crews. If they got any usable prints they never told us. Philly detectives attempted to question my parents but with little luck. There was no question that my mother would ever be able to identify either of the two men. My father's description of the men was a bit better but helped little.

A Black detective came and sat with me in my old room. He was afraid, he said, that even if they caught these guys that they could never be taken to trial. Forget about the stuff that was taken, he said. That would be long gone. However, he told me, he knew that I had seen them and that I had chased them. What did I think I was going to do if I somehow had caught up to the two men? I told him. He smiled understandingly and said that I would have been foolish to even have attempted to capture them. Of course, that had never been part of my plan. And then he said something that I will never forget:

"Listen man, I've seen your Mom. I promise you if I catch up to these two son-of-a-bitches I will save the state of Pennsylvania a trial," the detective said.

"That would," I responded coldly, "be fine with me."

Of course, they never did catch the guys who brutalized my parents. And while the next days flashed by in a blur here, as close as I can recall, is what happened.

The Philadelphia newspapers played up the home invasion big. *The Daily News* put the incident on their front page that Monday and both the *Inquirer* and *Bulletin* also gave my parents long day of trauma extensive coverage. Phone calls flowed in from local reporters. Relatives we had not seen in years came out of the woodwork. It was strange since the papers never used my mother or father's names. Everybody had advice for us; some good; some bad; some stupid.

Most of the time, we didn't want to talk about it with the press. That Monday night we went to the local Horn and Hardart's for dinner and somebody near our table was reading *The Daily News.* When my mother saw the bold screaming headline about the housebreak she became hysterical and we had to leave.

The next day we moved my parents out of their house. They never came back except to pick up a few belongings. They went to live with their close friends Joe and Lillian Stein. Joe Stein had been my Dad's pal since childhood and he and his wife, Aunt Lil, did their best to make my mother and father as comfortable as possible in their spacious home in nearby Wynnewood.

I wanted my parents to move to Margate, two towns removed from Atlantic City. My mother loved the Jersey shore and I thought that it would be best for her to return to a place that had some happy memories—a comfort zone from her childhood. My Dad, who had only retired in 1972, detested the shore and wouldn't hear of it. We had one of the first real heated arguments in my adult life. But my father was adamant. He would not consider New Jersey.

After a few days of trying to find a livable and affordable home we found a newly developed complex of garden style apartments and town homes in Penn Valley—not really more than ten minutes from the home that my parents had left, but in effect a world away.

We put the house up for sale and within a matter of weeks my parents were safely ensconced in their new home—a second floor town house with an impregnable front door in what was called Oak Hill Estates. That, however, was only part of the problem we solved. The other part was far more difficult to resolve.

My mother had always been somewhat of a carefree personality. When I was a teenager we would jitterbug in front of the TV in the early days of Bandstand. Mom loved to dance. No more. She was a woman who could sleep anywhere at the drop of a hat. Her mind, unlike so many of my generation, was uncluttered with worry and always seemed clear. From the time we were little kids my mother had been a most resourceful and athletic person. In 1957 she was head girls counselor at a camp in the Pocono Mountains. She had taught in the Philadelphia night school programs for many years traveling weekly as far north as Frankford High School and had even once been named teacher of the year in the Philadelphia Evening Program. That, after owning her own business—a yarn shop which she had named Ken-Mar (after her two boys). She taught knitting and all kinds of crafts and was, way ahead of the coming hippy generation, a creative artist and craftsperson in her own right. My brother and I still have pieces she lovingly and meticulously crafted hanging proudly in our homes.

With the brutal invasion of her sanctuary and body it seemed that Mom's spirit was broken; her joy of living crushed beyond any repair. This was a woman who had really enjoyed life. That joy was gone never to fully return. I called a rape crisis hotline that I recall was run out of the University of Pennsylvania. They were quite willing to see my mother. But she would have none of it. Her loving sons could not help. Every time we brought the matter up she became hysterical. One time she completely lost it and screamed at me to just leave her alone. For years after that day, I would visit on holidays and whenever I could get to Philadelphia. Sometimes I would be awakened in the middle of the night from the guest bedroom where I slept by a light in the nearby dining room only to find my mother sitting at the dining room table in the middle of the night playing solitaire. At first, I would try to talk to her but I couldn't really help. The truth is I didn't really know what to say. She wouldn't seek any professional help and she refused to ever discuss the demons that now haunted her waking hours and refused her so many nights of rest.

For years, even in her seventies and then into her late eighties she could never enjoy a complete night's sleep. Only when the dark clouds of dementia finally overtook her in the last few years of her life was the memory of that terrible night erased for the benefit of a full and decent night's sleep.

After most of that week in Philly we returned to Virginia. It was more than difficult getting back to the routine of working at the Bicentennial and what I accurately perceived as a bullshit job doing mostly nothing for no one and getting a handsome salary to do it. My colleagues and friends at the Commission who knew what had happened did their best to give me a few weeks respite to catch my breath. I needed those few weeks and more. I was on the phone every day for hours with my brother and my parents. I had a boulder in the pit of my stomach and it took many months for it to go away.

But there was one more shoe to drop that week. A *Bulletin* columnist by the name of Adrian Lee had somehow gotten wind that I had been a teacher of Black History at Clark University and Rutgers. Like any good reporter Lee tracked me down in Virginia. His first question was a stunner: "How does it feel," he asked, "to have taught about Black people's history in a college and then to have your mother attacked by two Blacks?" My answer must not have pleased him. "I really would be so much happier," I snapped, "if the two men in question had been White!"

Lee was not about to print that little rejoinder. But he did go out to the house, looked around outside and went on to write an insipid column about the unpredictable savagery that drove my parents from their beloved home and neighborhood. He used my mother's dying rose garden as a metaphor for the loss of the tranquility and sanctity of their home.

In retrospect I should never have spoken with a reporter. It was my first lesson about what reporters really do. Whenever I see those pseudo reporter assholes on TV waving a microphone in some poor suffering bastard's puss and asking, "How does it feel...?" I go back to that conversation with Lee where I experience an overwhelming and unquenchable desire to find the reporter and shove that microphone up his or her ass. Years later, when I became editor of a Boston newspaper, I made it a point never to play that stupid game and I often instructed my reporters to be as solicitous as possible with the victims of violent crime in the Boston area. Once when an elderly woman with the last name, ironically enough, of Goldman was robbed and brutally assaulted in her home in a Boston neighborhood, I spiked the photos of the woman taken by our staff photographer. Her face had been badly beaten by an intruder and I recalled how much it would have pained me to see my mother's picture plastered in any Philly newspaper.

However, like anything else in life even tragedy and trauma must eventually be put aside for the realities of everyday living. Andrea, like any decent wife, could not have been more supportive during that horrid week. But Andrea and I had a life in Washington, D.C.; and so both of us returned to our hectic life of daily commuting, work and trying to find our little piece of the American dream. I didn't know it but our dream was on its way to becoming a nightmare.

CHAPTER 42

Over the next year and a half a lot was going on in our lives. As the trauma of September faded into the winter months of 1974 I found that, even with the appointment of John Warner, the Bicentennial was frozen like almost every other government agency in the icy blast that was known as "Watergate." I had been invited that spring to speak about the 200th anniversary of America at a small state college in Paterson, New Jersey. I accepted the engagement with little inkling that it would bring some unwanted attention to me in Washington. The friendly and appreciative college students shepherded me about the campus and it was, I believed, just another wasted and routine trip where little was actually accomplished. But I was wrong.

At the student assembly after I spoke briefly I answered what I thought was a rather unimportant question relating to the Nixon administration's well publicized travails. My answer to whatever the question was came out as I intended—bland and politically obtuse. What I did not know was that a *New York Times* stringer was in the audience and that Sunday, even though the article was buried, I was quoted in the paper. The Nixon White House was furious. I was told by one of John Warner's aides that if Nixon wasn't on his way out— he resigned the presidency just 6 or 7 weeks later—that I would have been fired. Nobody gets quoted in the *New York Times* I was informed, without official permission from the Ayatollahs who sat on that white Mount Olympus on Pennsylvania Avenue across Lafayette Park from Jackson Place NW.

I had also attempted to set something in motion at the Bicentennial that I thought would be constructive. In the final analysis it was not. But I was able to throw away a shit-load of money.

I called it BERC—the Bicentennial Ethnic-Racial Coalition. I identified leaders of ethnic and racial groups all over the country and, after contacting them and identifying myself, invited them to a two-day, all expense paid conference in D.C. about the future of racial-ethnic relations in the United States and how these leaders and their groups might relate to the 200th birthday of their nation. While anything of real substance I would propose was shot down by a team of gray-suited lawyers attached to the Bicentennial Administration, it appeared that the Bicentennial always had plenty of money to spend on bullshit.

We held the meetings at a major Washington hotel where we put the members of BERC up and the two days of food, lodging and travel must have cost the government a pretty penny. Of course, when conference day came it was John Warner who was front and center. I did all of the organizing, all of the contacting and cajoling, all of the heavy lifting with endless meetings and in-house in-fighting. But it was Warner and a Catholic priest by the name of Monsignor Geno Baroni who basked in the limelight and glory of that two-day meeting. It was to be my first lesson in the Washington bureaucratic maze: you do all the work and other people get all the credit. That was to be validated years later when I became friendly with some of Senator Edward Kennedy's top staff people.

I had met Father Baroni early on during the summer of 1973 and we had become good friends over the months meeting often for breakfast or lunch. On one such occasion Geno brought along his good friend from Chicago, the best-selling writer-priest, Father Andrew Greeley.

Monsignor Geno Baroni was head of the National Center for Urban Ethnic Affairs and a very decent human being. He viewed the rising ethnic movement so well described by his friend Michael Novak in his book *The Rise of the Unmeltable Ethnics,* as an answer to the Black consciousness movement symbolized in the Sixties by the slogan "Black Power." Geno had a great deal of cache in the growing ethnic consciousness which was sweeping the country in the 1970's. When Jimmy Carter was elected president he appointed Geno as an undersecretary at HUD (Housing and Urban Development)—to my understanding the first such appointment of a Catholic priest to a sub-cabinet level in American history.

I made sure to balance the various Jewish, Italian, Irish, Polish, German and other ethnic groups with Black leaders as well. We actually invited Jesse Jackson to represent Operation PUSH. Of course, with an invitation from a Republican White House, he didn't show up; even for a freebee. But his wife, Jacqueline Jackson, did—not that she added any great substance to the festivities. Two Black brothers, the DeForrests, represented the Afro-American Bicentennial which was also based in D.C. All told we hosted about a hundred people. The program itself was innocuous. Many of the invited academics like Professor Seth Scheiner of Rutgers University couldn't understand what the point of the whole affair was all about; which was fine because I didn't have a clue myself. But, in the end, Mr. Warner was happy and almost everyone who attended felt that what had taken place, although benign, was mostly positive because at least a network of sorts had been established. In fact, the attendees were so pleased that we brought them all back for a second round later in the year. Once again, little was accomplished.

One person who was not at all pleased was the Director of the Republican National Committee in Washington—a guy I had heard about; but only vaguely. He had once been a congressman from Texas and Nixon, who the grapevine said had little respect for the guy because of his blueblood and Ivy League credentials (Andover and Yale) thought that the RNC was a good place to stash this boob (Nixon thought he was a boob; not me!).

As head of the RNC he wrote John Warner an official letter that was delivered and circulated all around the White House. He charged Warner with being at best uninformed or at worst naive and noted that Geno Baroni represented a radical and left-leaning faction within the enemy ranks of the Democratic Party. He also argued that Warner had been misled by his staff that had left out the authentic ethnic leaders from various Eastern European groups—groups that were, of course, in the hip pocket of the Republican party.

After getting a copy of the letter I looked into some of the individuals and groups that the head of the RNC was touting and complaining about. Most of them were little better than anti-Communist proto-fascists even though, on the far right, they seemingly allied themselves with the Republicans. Although the letter did not mention my name specifically, it was clear: this guy who headed the RNC was putting my ass between the crosshairs.

My only sin was one of omission. It was true that the groups which were mostly obscure Eastern European organizations like Latvians, Ukrainians and Estonian named in the RNC letter had not been invited; but not because I had decided to leave them out. I simply did not know that they existed. But, thankfully, I had not gone to the Democratic National Committee even though I had chosen many of the attendees with the help of Geno Baroni without checking out their political affiliations. Of course, I should have realized that most of the people he invited swung from the left or Democratic side of the plate. So I was the naive one; not John Warner who had never questioned the list of attendees at any juncture of the operation. At bottom John Warner, a Virginia patrician who I mistakenly saw as clueless about the struggles of working class Americans, was a very decent man. Warner would spend his weekends in Virginia horse country at his farm-like estate Atoka, which had once belonged to another patrician and somewhat clueless American family, John and Jackie Kennedy. But I was from Bohemia and this is not the way I had intended to impress the head of the Bicentennial who was golden ticketed. Shortly thereafter John Warner would astonish the astonish-proof political world of D.C. by becoming Number Eight to the First Lady of Hollywood, (picture a bejeweled Elizabeth Taylor dressed in checkered gingham down home at Atoka baking brownies waiting for her man to wipe the cow flop from his boots!), divorce Liz and become boy-toy of the First Lady of American TV Barbara Wa-Wa and through the luck (?) of a plane crash serve as the longtime United States senator from the state of Virginia.

By now you must have a clue that the man who signed the RNC letter had some real clout in the world of Washington's internecine politics where everyone eventually eats their children. He did: his name was George Herbert Walker Bush. Like Warner, Bush was a patrician; unlike Warner, Bush had a long political pedigree. His father, Senator Prescott Bush was the estimable senator from Connecticut which led a long line of little Bushes to Andover and Yale. The Bush family has long tried to relinquish their cooler Puritan New England aura for the hotter Texas climes where real men are…well, real men? However, there has always been much more Kennebunkport Striper to the Bushes genetic makeup than Panhandle Armadillo. Of course George Bush would go on from heading the RNC to head the CIA (was Gerald Ford nuts or did Bush have naked pictures of President Ford cavorting with his cat?), American ambassador to China, the Vice-Presidency as a reward for not trashing the Great Communicator too badly in 1980, and…well…the rest is the stuff of Hollywood legend. Like Jimmy Stewart, Mr. Bush went to Washington and eventually beat a fairly decent Massachusetts Greek stiff who tried to ride a tank to the White House all the while looking like Mickey Mouse at a Disneyland party in Orlando, Florida.

Warner could easily have called me into the woodshed and reamed me good. In fact, he never even mentioned the letter and as far as I knew, unless he called George Bush personally, I never saw any official response to the RNC that came out of Warner's shop.

To be absolutely truthful, I did have an ulterior motive that I shared with no one in the creation of BERC. Noting how important ethnic consciousness was becoming across the country I thought that maybe I could join the next presidential campaign with my lists of ethnic leaders from around the country who I now knew on a first-name basis. There were a great many Polish and Italian votes in Chicago and I had brought two of the key ethnic leaders of those two voting blocs to D.C. Having worked very hard in Massachusetts to elect George McGovern in 1972, I was still a nominally committed Democrat in 1974. Of course, I had no idea who the Democratic nominee would be and whatever was in the back of my devious mind never did come to any consequence or fruition.

By the time the Democrats nominated Jimmy Carter in 1976 I was long gone from the D.C. scene in Washington and the silly leftwing politics that I had embraced since voting for John F. Kennedy in 1960. I suppose Geno Baroni had the same idea that I did and hence his appointment as one of the High Pajanjdrums over at HUD during the tiresome and malaise-filled Carter years.

CHAPTER 43

I did finally crack the inner sanctum of that invisible Navy Blue wall that surrounded the Warner regime at the Bicentennial. My wife Andrea had become very friendly as a result of her work at the NIE (National Institute of Education) with a professor of Soviet Studies at George Washington University. This guy was, according to Andrea, very tight with the Nixon man who had been Secretary of the Navy and who was now, as the fates would have it, my boss.

I asked Andrea to request that this guy tell Warner that he had a gem in the rough on his staff who wasn't being utilized in a creative or useful way. I had just returned from a long trip to New Orleans and a well-known Black school in Louisiana, Grambling College. At Grambling I had met with the all the academic deans and the President of the college. Like college types everywhere I went, they were only interested in how much money the Feds were going to cough up for this or that program. When I got back to Washington I was pleased to see a note on my desk thanking me for my Grambling memo and requesting me to call the boss's secretary. Obviously, Andrea's pal had worked fast. Mr. Warner wanted to see me.

I made an appointment with John Warner's secretary and within a week I was standing in front of the boss himself. Warner made some small talk about his recent party in his palatial Georgetown mansion where he had invited all the staff to meet the man who was on the threshold of becoming President of the United States, Gerald Ford. Then he got to the point.

He was invited, he said, to give the commencement address at Indiana State University in Terre Haute that year. He wanted me to go to the campus, scout out the territory, meet with the university's leadership and then carefully craft his commencement speech using the information I gathered about what students and faculty were thinking in the week I would spend in Indiana, the American heartland.

Needless to say, I was thrilled. Here was a real job. I was to advance John Warner's trip to a major American university. This was not a bullshit job; it was real and, in my mind, the first real work I had been assigned since arriving in Washington. And not only was I to advance Mr. Warner's appearance at Indiana State but I was chosen to write his speech. The Gods were good. Who could know where John Warner might be heading in Washington? (This was shortly before he became Mr. Elizabeth Taylor and Senator John Warner!). If I performed brilliantly I might even head there with him.

I spent an interesting week in Indiana. I attended classes; I met with professors, deans and the school's president. I even hitched up with some dimwit who headed the college's fledgling Black Studies program. It didn't take me more than a few minutes to realize that this Black bozo had been hired to cajole the restless Black students at the college into an uneasy silence. His knowledge of the discipline was not even superficial and no deeper than your average Junior High School teacher's intellectual approaches to an 8th grade history class. I remember thinking how sad it was that there must have been tens of thousands of guys like me—completely shut out from academic life and American education because of historical forces far beyond our control. And then I would think of the Civil War where 600,000 Americans died for a lost cause, of lynching where over the better part of a century over 5,000 innocent Black men and women lost their lives, and of the Holocaust where 6 million…well, I hope you get my point. Who the hell was I to bitch about where life had taken me? At least I was getting a nice fat paycheck every week.

When I returned to Washington the first thing I did was to write a long report on what was on the mind of the people I had met at Indiana State. From the president of the college to the professors and students I reported to Mr. Warner on their interests and concerns. Of course, as we faced the summer of 1974 the major concern on everyone's mind was Watergate; that and the economy, which, to my way of thinking compared to today (2011), wasn't all that bad. As I recall gasoline was selling for a bit above forty cents a gallon in 1973-74—sort of funny when gas is approaching $4.00 a gallon as I write this. My rent of a brand new two-floor townhouse in Reston, Virginia was $275 a month and a few months later when Andrea and I bought our first home, a newly constructed single home for $59,000, my mortgage payment was $335 a month.

At any rate I sat down to write the best damn commencement address ever given by anyone in D.C. since JFK hit the academic bricks at American University in 1963. I wrote and rewrote. And then I rewrote again. The effort took me the better part of a week and I will never forget how proud I was when I took the pages of my long-labored efforts over to Warner's office in Jackson Place. My secretary had worked on nothing else that week.

Then I waited; and waited. Finally, a note arrived from Warner thanking me for my fine memo about academic life and concerns at Indiana State University. A few weeks later I received my official copy of John Warner's commencement address. It ran on for many pages. But the writing was totally unfamiliar. Where were my brilliant lines and observations? Where were the points I had made about American history and the Founding Fathers like Madison, Adams and Jefferson? What about the concerns of the students and faculty I had so meticulously crafted into my major league address? They were nowhere to be found in the address as delivered by John Warner.

I couldn't believe my eyes! I had flown to Terre Haute, booked an expensive room at a fine hotel, ate well on the government dole, rented a car and spent that harried week running around that fucking campus talking to anyone and everyone and all I could find were two damn lines of the entire commencement address I had turned in to Warner's office.

I called a good buddy, the Bicentennial's congressional liaison, a crafty Democratic operative who had survived the Johnson Vice-Presidency and then the Big Bopper's lame administration and, after Johnson jumped ship leaving so many decent staffers stranded in the D.C. jungle, been hired by the Nixon boys because they needed a Democrat to run interference with those pain-in-the-ass Democrats on the Hill. He had been a protégé of President Johnson. He laughed when I informed him of my frustration and chagrin.

"Don't you know Marty? Warner has an entire stable of speech writers over here. They probably vetted your work, hacked it to pieces and what you got, what Warner got, was their finished product, not yours. No matter how good your work was; do you think for a minute they were going to allow it to sneak through? You were treading on their turf. Every speech everybody gives in this town is usually the work of a committee," he said sympathetically. Then he said, "That's the way Washington works Marty; get used to it! You had a nice time in Indiana? No? Enjoy yourself; roll with the punches."

Well, to make a long story short, I didn't roll with the punches. I put my resume together and began shipping it all over the nation's capitol and the country. I started to apply to universities again; to the Congress and to, of all places, Jewish organizations. What did I know about organized Jewish life in America? To tell the truth: not a hell of a lot.

CHAPTER 44

There were a number of events that dovetailed late in 1974 during my last months of sucking on the government teat.

The first, and most important, was that I became a national news story. How did that happen?

In the last months of my time in Massachusetts I must have applied to between 50 and 100 colleges and universities for a job. As I wrote earlier, most of the responses I received were bleakly negative. But on one occasion I received a phone call from the chairman of the Black Studies Department at my alma mater Temple University in Philadelphia. His name was Odeyo Ayaga, obviously an African— as it turned out he was from Nigeria. Professor Ayaga called, he said, because he had my resume in his hand and he was impressed. Professor Ayaga informed me that he had an opening for an assistant professor who would offer courses in American Black History. Would I be interested in coming to Temple University? Is the Pope Catholic?

Ayaga went on to outline the position, the salary and all the perks that would come with the appointment. Temple had recently become a state university in the Pennsylvania system and their salaries in 1973 were a lot more competitive than most private colleges. We chatted for a few minutes and Ayaga made it seemingly clear that coming down for an interview to Philly would only be a formality—that the job was in the bag. Just before I hung up it occurred to me that the good professor thought he was talking to a Black person. I informed Ayaga that I was White and after a few seconds of stammering incoherence Ayaga withdrew the invitation for me to come to Philadelphia. The Nigerian, who barely spoke understandable English, hardly knew what anyone else would instantly have known from my last name; not only that I was White but that I was also Jewish. The Afro-Centric Black Studies program, an academic sandbox, at Temple University hardly had room for anyone of my religious persuasion or race. I allowed the professor of African bigotry to get off the hook gracefully and promptly forgot about it. After all, Temple University was no worse than Tufts, Penn State, Vanderbilt, Wellesley or a host of other universities to which I had applied. It never even occurred to me to make something out of it. And I would not have if...

If a few months later I had not received a phone call from a young woman saying she was calling on behalf of the Black Studies program at Temple University. Would I still be, she asked, interested in being considered for the position at Temple to which I had applied some months before? Of course, I replied, I would be interested. However, I asked, did she know that I was White? No, she answered. She did not. The position, she made clear, was not available to anyone who was White.

"Suppose," I asked her, "I told you I would not hire you for a position because you are Black?"

"That would be racist!" she snapped at me.

"If the shoe fits," I retorted, "perhaps you had best try it on!"

The woman hung up on me.

For the first time I was really pissed off. And as my Daddy once told me it is much better to get pissed off than pissed on. I decided to write a letter to Marvin Wachman, the new President of Temple University. After all I had worked hard over six years to obtain two degrees from that institution; I was an alumnus for whatever that was worth. I had long known of Dr. Marvin Wachman. First, Wachman came to Temple from Lincoln University—that Black college in Oxford, Pennsylvania that Pop and I passed all those times on our way to Andy Young's farm when I was a boy. And irony of all ironies, Dr. Wachman was a historian who had taught and specialized in, of all subjects, Black American History. From his name I also assumed that he was Jewish.

Within a few weeks I received a reply from President Wachman. In a page-long letter Wachman assured me that he had looked into the matter and that I had been treated abominably, that there had been some "poor communication" on the part of the Department chairman human relations-wise and that what I had experienced was not part of any normal hiring practice within his large institution. President Wachman apologized on behalf of the University and then wished me well in my future job search. He didn't say that he was going to ream Professor Ayaga's Afro-Centric ass (which I later heard he did!) or discipline what was clearly an out of control Department on his campus that was discriminating in its hiring policies and teaching students for all intents and purposes that the world was flat; nor did he say anything about the possibility of a job with the school. All of which pissed me off even further.

"Screw this!" I said to myself after receiving Wachman's incriminating letter. It was proof positive that I had been the victim of overt hiring discrimination. I shared the letter with my friend Dr. Murray Freedman, Executive Director of the American Jewish Committee in Philadelphia and he agreed that what Temple had done not only violated the spirit of the law but was also an unconscionable violation of my civil rights. To make a long story short, Murray got me a pro bono attorney from the legal arm of the local American Jewish Committee; the attorney, after meeting with me once, filed an official claim with the appropriate state government department (The Equal Opportunity Commission of Pennsylvania or some such bureaucracy) and we waited. Sometime in 1974 when I was in D.C. the Commission came back with a clear-cut finding against Temple University. Murray called me at home to give me the good news and asked what I wanted to do.

What were my options? First, Murray wanted me to know that President Wachman was bullshit. He had inadvertently provided me with the legal ammunition that I then utilized for the finding in my favor. Murray informed me that the President of Temple was actually a friend of his and that he didn't want to alienate the folks at Temple since he was attempting to set up some kind of institute of Jewish Studies there himself. He would appreciate it, he said, if I would accept some form of remuneration from the university and go quietly into the night.

In retrospect, I should have nailed Wachman, Ayaga and Temple's Black Studies charade to the barn door. But, although I didn't give a fig for anyone at Temple, I certainly didn't want to hurt Murray Freedman or a Jewish human relations organization that had provided pro bono legal advice and work on my behalf. I might even have bargained my way to a job and gone home to live in the town of my birth where my parents would have been thrilled. But instead I settled for the difference in salary between what I would have made at Temple that year and what I actually did make—not an unsubstantial figure in 1974 numbers.

When the American Jewish Committee in Philadelphia issued a press release touting our mutual triumph over the forces of Temple University discrimination the media hounds of hell were unleashed. *The Philadelphia Inquirer,* usually leaning toward predictable political correctness, not only reported the story fairly; they placed a lead editorial on their opinion page saying that what Temple had done was wrong and that the university deserved to pay for it. *The Wall Street Journal* reported the story touting my victory as the first reverse discrimination case in academia. The local papers in Worcester, *The Worcester Telegram* and *The Worcester Gazette* called me in Virginia and eventually reported the case accurately with editorials and columns about a Clark University professor who had been the victim of reverse discrimination. The Associated Press picked up the story which ran in many newspapers around the country. And then, to top off the media storm, *The Philadelphia Inquirer* sent a reporter to my home in Virginia for a long in-depth piece about me and Ayaga that was to run in the Inky's Sunday magazine, *Today.* The article which came out in early 1974 depicted Ayaga in a very negative light—it actually made him look like an idiot—and made me look like a local hero; which I clearly was not. They even sent a photographer down to our house in Reston where you can see a page-wide photo in the article of Andrea and me looking off forlornly into space. *The Jewish Exponent*, Philadelphia's Jewish Federation newspaper which has always been widely read in Philly's activist Jewish community also had a number of articles on the Temple case.

Believe it or not, when the media hullabaloo finally died down I was relieved. Although I always wanted to write the stories, I really didn't enjoy being the story. And Andrea, who was always somewhat shy, wasn't too sad to see the phone finally stop ringing and the newspaper stories stop coming.

However, that was not the end of it. I was soon contacted by a Professor by the name of Miro Todorovich. Professor Todorovich informed me that he was the head of a growing university group that called itself UNCRA—the University National Center for Rational Alternatives. UNCRA was organized, Professor Todorovich said, to combat the destructive policies of Affirmative Action and political correctness that were sweeping American campuses in the late Sixties and early Seventies. UNCRA, he maintained, wanted to publicize my particular case. Would I be opposed to allowing his group to use me as an example of what was happening on American college campuses? I told the professor that he could use my case any way he wanted and that I would make myself available to him and his colleagues any time they wanted.

After being written up by the UNCRA in-house newsletter, I was soon receiving letters of support from professors and students from around the country. Some of the tales that were related in these letters to me were even worse than my own. The famed New York philosophy professor Sidney Hook even wrote me a kind note of support. Networking with these sympathetic academics was, if nothing else, encouraging. Although it never did lead to a tenure track job, it was reassuring to know that I was not alone in my dilemma and that there were still a few rational minds at work in our institutions of higher learning. Not everyone in academia had succumbed to the madness that was sweeping American campuses during this sad period of American history. However, my opinion of most academics has never been very high.

CHAPTER 45

The last piece of my D.C. life fell into place in late 1974 when I was invited to testify before the House Subcommittee on Education. I had carefully preserved all the many letters of rejection I had received—especially those claiming that they were looking to fill an academic spot with a Black person. I couldn't imagine how anyone would have reacted if any job at that point in American history would have been listed, "For Whites only!" Those letters, in my eyes, had now become important historical documents. I had letters proving my point from Penn State, Temple, Tufts, Vanderbilt and quite a few other places where idiocy had clearly been substituted for the usually solid academic thinking of the day. For two weeks before my testimony I wrote up and prepared what I was going to say. If nothing else I was going to put every pipe-puffing asshole in every college and university history department that was playing Affirmative Action games on the spot and on the record—the Congressional Record that is. I carefully prepared my testimony as if it were a lecture in Intro Political Science to the Clark University freshmen class.

The day came and I made my way to the hearing room on Capitol Hill where I spoke for well over an hour and a half. Everything I said was fully documented. I made nothing up. I never cited a college or university that did not go on the record with a written letter; even though there were many institutions that were a great deal smarter than the ones I had the goods on. For example, in 1973 and 1974 I had attended the meetings of the two most prominent professional organizations in my discipline—the American Historical Society in New York and the Organization of American Historians in Denver. I went through an endless series of personal interviews in sweaty hotel rooms in which it was clear to me that no White candidate would ever be considered for a position. But if the interviewer did not go on the record in the course of the interview I felt obligated to always give that institution the benefit of the doubt. Thus, the colleges and universities I ratted out to the congressional subcommittee were clearly guilty of the stupidity of reverse discrimination. I was the judge and jury. And there was to be no appeal even though there was plenty of bitching about my testimony in the months that followed.

The congressmen, both Republicans and Democrats, could not have been more attentive or responsive to my testimony. I recall being queried, after my testimony, by Rep. John Dingell of Michigan. On February 11, 2009 Congressman Dingell made the history books by becoming the longest serving Member in the history of the U.S. House of Representatives. What, Dingell asked me, would be my remedy? My answer was succinct and to the point: either stop what was going on or watch American universities become places where people would be hired for their sex or their race and not their expertise; which is exactly what happened over the last forty years or so in American higher education. Quantitatively you can find more ideological morons teaching on American college campuses today than in a discount moron shop. My testimony before the subcommittee is reprinted in the Congressional Record of 1974 so that future writers and historians of this period will at least have a small clue as to how it got to be this way.

Shortly, after my testimony I received a phone call at my home from Michigan Congressman John Conyers. My friend in the Bicentennial had spread my resume around Capitol Hill and apparently Congressman Conyers got a copy and read one of my published articles dealing with the Black History experience that was sweeping the country. Conyers it seemed did not have a clue about my recent testimony but told me that he was extremely impressed with the article I had published in the academic journal, *Social Studies*. I was flattered that a congressman of his stature would read anything I had written much less an essay on the Black experience.

I knew a little about Congressman Conyers—an outspoken, attractive Black legislator with an eye for good looking women and natty suits. He had been a major vote on the House Judiciary Committee in the 1974 decision to impeach President Nixon—a decision that did not lead to Nixon's impeachment but rather to his resignation.

My good friend Joe Bruno, who worked the Congress for the Bicentennial, had spread my resume around on the Hill. I would have preferred a congressman like the liberal Democrat from the North Shore of Boston, Rep. Michael Harrington. I had always admired Mike Harrington's politics and his ability to look the system in the eye and stand his ground. But there was a long line of people who wanted to work on Harrington's staff and although I met Harrington where we eventually spoke about the possibilities of me becoming a staffer, I never got an invite for a return session. Unlike my Clark University friend Jim Pavitt who had turned a few years of toil in one of the lamest Massachusetts congressional offices into a covert operative's life at the CIA, I wanted to work for someone who really had a future in American politics and was not asleep at the switch. As it turned out Congressman Harrington became frustrated with the endless D.C. political game and walked away from politics for good shortly thereafter.

John Conyers was different. Representing Black Detroit, he was smart and ambitious. Conyers had not yet enshrouded himself in his Al Sharpton persona playing on nothing but the politics of race. He had an opening on his staff and he wanted to hire someone with my background and experience. Could I, he asked, take three or four days off and come over to his office and work there? If I fit in, the job would be mine for the asking. I had a great deal of comp time coming to me and one Monday just about a month before Christmas 1974 I showed up bright-eyed and bushy tailed at the congressman's spacious suite of offices.

I sat down with Conyers in his spacious office for a chat and he told me he wanted to see how well I might adjust to his staff. Then he gave me a number of puzzling assignments having to do with Black jazz and Black folk music—subjects which were far removed from my historical area of expertise. Then Conyers left for a trip, ostensibly to Detroit, but it was clear to me as I overheard people talking that few in the office really knew where he was. I took my assigned desk and utilizing the availability and resources of the Library of Congress went to work on Black music. I remember cobbling together some type of report. But it wasn't very good.

The Conyers congressional staff was integrated with just as many White staffers as Black. I liked that. What I didn't like, listening to the office banter for three days, was that most of the people who worked for Conyers were to the left of Chairman Mao. I said little to anyone, kept to myself, turned my work in after three days and went home. I never heard from John Conyers or anyone connected to him. I chalked the experience up to my winning taciturn personality which had the uncanny ability to accomplish the opposite effect of Dale Carnegie—never to win friends or influence people. The John Conyers congressional shop must not have liked people from Bohemia.

CHAPTER 46

"(S)he slept a summer by my side,
(S)he filled my days with endless wonder...
but (s)he was gone when Autumn came."
Broadway's *Les Miserables*

By now you must have some clue that all was not well on the domestic scene in Reston, Virginia. By the summer of 1974 Andrea and I had purchased a newly constructed home not far from the house we rented. It was a well-appointed and comfortable three-bedroom single home which we had fun furnishing. We spent $700 on our first color TV and bought the best furniture we could find in posh Georgetown boutiques. I suppose we both thought that a real home of our own filled with nice stuff would solve the problems we were shoving hard under our new shag carpets.

I cared deeply for Andrea but I take the blame for rarely being able to show it. Too wrapped up in the personal frustrations and sadness of my sinking professional life, I did not pay attention to a marriage that had been rapidly deteriorating for some time. Andrea had sacrificed a great deal on my behalf and we both had little to show for it.

Read any marriage manual or book on divorce and you will find the author usually telling you that when a marriage fails it is on both partners. My marriage had been failing for a long time...and sorry Dr. Ruth and Dr. Laura...but it was largely my fault. I saw the handwriting on the wall early on shortly before we vacated Hillcrest Farm. I chose to ignore it. We were growing distant. But I did nothing, or damn little, to put a brake on the snowball of marital indifference rolling down a hill that became a landslide. Andrea and I tried counseling in Washington but the shrink was either wrong or I was too damn angry—maybe both. By the time we recognized the elephant in the room it was too late. We went to see a psychiatrist who specialized in failing marriages. The shrink asked us if we wanted to save our marriage. I said yes. Andrea said she didn't know. That should have answered the question for me right then; but when it came to personal relationships—especially relationships with women—I had always been a slow learner.

In the fall of 1973 when the Yom Kippur War broke out in the Middle East I began paying attention to Jewish politics for the first time in my life. You might recall that Israel was in a precarious position for a few days that fall and that if Nixon/Kissinger had not come to the rescue with some needed crucial military aid a real disaster might have ensued. Golda Meir, Israel's Prime Minister would never forget what Nixon had done for her country during those dangerous days. Anyway, the situation, unlike the '67 War, had raised my Jewish consciousness sufficiently for me to place a call over to the national headquarters of the B'nai B'rith in D.C. which was within walking distance of my office. I went over to offer assistance or moral support or whatever I could do and in the ensuing months made some good friends over there. I was actually responsible for a small grant the Bicentennial awarded the agency for one of their projects. When I began to circulate my resume I naturally sent some copies over to my friends at B'nai B'rith.

One of my friends sent my resume to the New York headquarters of the Anti-Defamation League where it ended up on the desk of the Director of National Programs for ADL, a guy by the name of Ted Freedman. In the fall of 1974, shortly after my congressional testimony, I took the train to New York City to meet with Freedman. The Anti-Defamation League in those days went by the name of the Anti-Defamation League of B'nai B'rith. But, in reality, the Anti-Defamation League was a completely independent organization and, while they accepted some financial support from B'nai B'rith, sometime by the late 1970's the tenuous affiliation with the B'nai B'rith who could never control the tough-minded Jews who ran the ADL came to an abrupt end. Eventually the ADL broke completely with B'nai B'rith over Affirmative Action which they condemned both morally and legally placing *amicus* briefs before the Supreme Court.

I didn't understand Jewish inter and intra-agency politics at the time but Freedman was attempting to become a major power within the boughs of the Anti-Defamation League. The two co-national directors were well up in age and they would soon retire. If Freedman had his people firmly placed in each section of the country in important regional ADL offices and if those people could make some creative waves that were felt agency-wide, maybe he would have a shot at becoming national director. Freedman's creative idea was to hire a half a dozen new positions he would control from New York. These so-called "Education Directors" would be placed in Boston, New York City, Atlanta, Chicago and Los Angeles. All Freedman needed was a green light from the budget people in the agency to green light the hires.

My interview went well. Freedman made it clear that he wanted to hire me for the Boston office where I could possibly introduce the many ADL human relations programs into the powerful institutions of higher learning that dotted the city of Boston and the vast New England countryside. Given my work at the Bicentennial, the ADL seemed a natural transition for me especially with a nice raise from my government salary and a great many other perks which included moving expenses from Virginia with a weekly expense and travel account. I liked Freedman immediately and told him that I wanted to come to work for the ADL. Although I needed a great deal of study to catch up on Middle East History, Israel, Jewish politics and the American Jewish community—topics about which I knew almost nothing—I had mastered Black History and American History. The Jewish stuff would be a cakewalk.

There were, however, political problems. The New England regional office had a director in Boston who had been running the ADL ship since the end of World War II. He would have to approve Freedman putting another staffer into his office and although that staffer would be answerable to New York through Freedman, he would also have to work closely with the Boston office staff as well. I took that political bull by the horns. I had a good friend at the American Jewish Committee who had been one of my invitees to the

Bicentennial ethnic conferences. I called him. Since his offices were on the 4th Floor of the so-called "Jewish Pentagon" that housed almost every Jewish organization in Boston on Franklin Street across the way from Filene's Basement in the area called "Downtown Crossing" my friend could easily go up to the 5th Floor where the ADL's suite was located and put in a good word for me. My friend, Phil Perlmutter, not only did that but he told the ADL director that I would be a good hire and that I would be a real asset to the work of the ADL throughout New England. Although they were fierce rivals and would remain so throughout my eight years at the ADL, the director took Perlmutter's word without making me come to Boston for an interview.

However, months passed and I heard no more from the ADL. Then one early Saturday morning in January 1975 the phone rang. It was Ted Freedman. The position in Boston had been budgeted. When could I wrap things up in D.C. and leave for New England? I wrote John Warner a letter of resignation where I thanked him for allowing me to do some creative work at the Bicentennial and made arrangements to arrive in Boston by mid-February. When I hung up with Freedman Andrea and I should have been elated. Andrea began to cry. She was happy, she said, that I had finally gotten a job that I really wanted. But I was going to Boston alone. She was going to stay in Washington at her job and maybe after a time we could put things back together.

She would see. Another thing I learned: you don't put broken marriages back together long distance. The distance has the problem of getting in the way.

CHAPTER 47

In early February, 1974 I packed up my new Ford Granada (Andrea kept our '72 Mustang) with all my worldly belongings, kissed my wife goodbye, said a sad so long to our large Labrador, Ripper, and drove to Philadelphia where I stayed with my parents and brother Ken for a few days. I recall being vague about the state of my marriage but you couldn't get much past Louie Goldman who knew that something was amiss. However, my Pop, a private person in his own right, never pressed me for details. My brother, hipper and more attuned to my moods, finally got it out of me. I was going to Boston alone. Andrea and I had separated.

I soon arrived in snowy Boston and after a week at a friend's apartment I found a squalid little Myrtle Street apartment in a basement on Beacon Hill within a five-minute walk of my office. I signed a six-month lease at $165 a month (for which the ADL had agreed to pay) and set out to understand the complex internecine world of Jewish politics in Boston and New England. It wasn't easy. But I had a wonderful colleague by the name of Isadore Zack who took me under his wing and did his best to quickly show me the ropes.

Iz Zack or "Z" as we all called him had been with the ADL since the mid 1940's after he had served in the Army. He had been, in his day, quite a baseball player and had even gained the eye and friendship of Tom Yawkey the longtime owner of the fabulous Boston Red Sox. Mr. Yawkey saw to it that every year "Z" had a press pass for all the home games which "Z" often shared with me. I was still a Phillies fan but it didn't take me long to fall in love with the Sox and let them break my heart year after year until 2004. My favorite ballplayer became Carl Yazstremski. I finally met my hero Yaz on the very last day he played for the Sox in 1983 when I sat in the reserved private box between Yaz's father and Massachusetts Governor Ed King. Not bad for a kid from West Philly, huh?

The Anti-Defamation League had a division which it called "Civil Rights." Although it was largely made up of lawyers in every office, in Boston Isadore Zack was the Civil Rights Director. The name "Civil Rights" was actually a misnomer. Zack had been in Military Intelligence during his service in World War II and had actually operated a clandestine operation with offices in Brookline, Massachusetts with a few other intelligence officers looking for escaped Nazi war prisoners and any other subversive activity that might have been used against the American war effort. My pal Zack was actually a Jewish James Bond. He knew more about covert anti-Israel Arab operations, neo-Nazis and Klansmen and any other anti-Semitic activity in the five New England states than any one in the FBI, the Boston Civil Disorders Unit in the Boston Police Department or any other law enforcement agency. In fact, law enforcement people often came to the office where they started with "Z" and his incredible files whenever they wanted some information on a radical or subversive group that had come to make trouble in Boston. And remember, it was 1975—forced busing had come to Boston and the Klan and Neo-Nazi types were coming out of the woodwork in South Boston.

The Anti-Defamation League's public relations are that it is a human relations agency that fights for civil rights and against discrimination for all religions and ethnic groups. That much is absolutely true. But the ADL is much more than that. In many respects the ADL is the canary in the coal mine. The ADL is an early warning system for the American Jewish community. As such, besides research and public opinion surveys, it often conducts covert operations against the enemies of the Jewish people. Once in awhile the ADL gets some bad press, as in San Francisco where an ADL director put the agency on the spot and ended up in hot water after being accused of "spying" on certain groups and people.

The object Zack told me was to keep my mouth shut and never discuss what went on in the office with anyone but fellow ADL staffers. Iz Zack did a great deal that he could not or would not share with me. I knew that he had a budget to spend on the penetration of various anti-Israel or Neo-Nazi individuals and groups that worked against the interests of American and world Jewry. He had people on his payroll whose job it was to penetrate these groups, report back to him and he, in turn, would share the information he gleaned with New York and, if given the go signal, with law enforcement people in the New England region. It was not long before I came to know the Police Commissioner of Boston, the head of the Civil Disorders Unit of the Boston Police Department, a contact agent in the FBI and other assorted law enforcement personnel whose job it was to monitor groups that might do unlawful or dangerous things in Boston. For example, by the time I left the ADL I knew a great deal more about international terrorism than when I started. I eventually even lectured on International Terrorism before a number of groups in Boston and ultimately even taught a course on "The History of Terrorism" at a New England college.

Zack taught me a lot and he worked under the difficult situation of having an immediate superior who did not think his work all that important. However, because Zack, like me, really answered to the directors in New York, there was little the New England Director could do to deter his work. The Regional Director made it clear to me on a number of occasions that he considered the cloak and dagger aspect of the Civil Rights division's work to be so much bullshit. I suspended judgment until I had seen for myself what was going on in Boston—especially on the college campuses where anti-Israel activity, like so much else on the leftist fringes of American life, was reaching a virulent stage in the late 1970's and early 1980's.

Although I never adopted the knee-jerk reaction that disagreement with Israeli policy was tantamount to being anti-Semitic, I came across many critics of Israel who had no great love for the Jewish people. Some of them, even on college campuses, were Jew haters; or self-hating Jews.

Trying my best to ignore my still shattering marriage, I threw myself fully into my work. The first six months were basically a learning curve. The Director would often send me out to the hinterlands to speak before any group that required a speaker on Jewish topics. That work was mostly on weekends. I recall once driving to Hanover, New Hampshire, the home of Dartmouth College, about three and a half hours from Boston to deliver a twenty minute address on current developments in the Middle East. I sat through an abominably boring two-hour meeting of some local Jewish group before these clods finally had me do my twenty minutes on whatever it was that was going on that week between Israel and the Palestinians. On another occasion I drove all the way up to Augusta, Maine where there was a small Jewish community. A local family agreed to put me up on a Friday night after the local Shabbat services. Since they did not have a synagogue, the service was held in a local church. Imagine my surprise when the President of the congregation announced that I was there to conduct the service since they did not have a Rabbi either. Now I can read Hebrew fluently (I can't translate very well but when it comes to conducting a Shabbat service I am about as lost as Moses was in the Sinai). The congregation couldn't believe that somebody who was the Education Director of the Anti-Defamation League wasn't at least a graduate of the Hebrew Union Seminary. I did my best to explain that ADL was a largely secular organization and got through the night by speaking on what else—current developments in the Middle East.

Eventually Andrea brought Ripper up to stay with me and the two of us enjoyed a wonderful weekend of reconciliation in Gloucester that spring. It was like I was dating my wife. In the beginning it worked and we actually looked for a place to live in downtown Boston together. Andrea came to Boston for the July 4th celebration that summer. I had fallen down in the Public Garden next to the Boston Common one Sunday and fractured my ankle. I was still on crutches when I picked Andi up at Logan Airport. Again we spent a nice weekend going to that fabulous July 4th concert at the Half Shell on the Charles River where we heard Arthur Fiedler and the Boston Pops bring in America's 199th birthday. It was obvious that we still cared for one another...very obvious if you get my drift. But by the end of that weekend it was apparent to me that Andrea remained adamant about not coming to Boston. Our relationship or whatever it had become seemed to be in limbo.

Ripper's presence took some of the loneliness out of the equation. If I had nothing to do on a weekend, since I did not really know a soul in Boston, I would often not speak to anyone but the dog after leaving the office at five o'clock on Friday until coming to work on the following Monday morning. Ripper usually didn't say much but he was great company.

That August I found a very nice modern one-bedroom apartment at Tremont-on-the-Common, a high-rise that towered over the Boston Common. Andrea sent most of our furniture and all my books to Boston courtesy of the ADL and I moved into far more comfortable surroundings than the basement walk-down on Beacon Hill flat I had suffered in since February. Andrea had moved out of our house in Reston which we put up for sale. She was living in Georgetown with two women I did not know. So, in effect I had a mortgage and rent to worry about until our Virginia house was sold. That took the better part of a year.

On one weekend late in September I had been invited to dinner at Mikki and Mike Ritvo's home in Newton. Mikki was the Dean of Women at Lesley College in Cambridge and I had asked that she chair my Education Committee at ADL. Her husband Mike was a radiologist. I left Mikki and Mike's house a little after ten that night and as usual drove to my parking spot under the Boston Common. The parking spot cost me about $30 a month as opposed to the more expensive spot that would have been far more convenient and, as it turned out, much safer in my protected building. As I emerged from the lower level of the Common lot into a completely dark and deserted Boston Common somewhere around 11 P.M., I began to hastily make my way toward my apartment building about 200 yards from the lot's exit onto the Common. I just wasn't fast enough.

Two Black guys came out of the shadows and blocked my way out of the park onto Tremont Street. One of them demanded, "Just give us your stuff man!" The other pulled a knife. I punched the guy without the knife in the mouth. Then they knocked me down and proceeded to beat the shit out of me. They took my wallet, my new watch which my parents had given me, my glasses and my shoes. The wallet had about a hundred bucks in it. They took the cash and left the credit cards and threw the wallet down at me. Then the one I hit said to the guy with the knife, "Stick 'im! Stick 'im!" I was hurting down on the ground but still conscious of the debate that ensued. The guy with the knife didn't want to stab me and demurred. His buddy pressed him. I interjected a thought into the debate: "Listen guys, if you stick me and I live, they'll find you. It's not really a good idea." They apparently agreed and walked off casually into the night down Tremont Street and towards the famous Combat Zone. For a moment I thought that if I followed them and saw a cop—where is a goddamn cop when you need one?—that maybe I could get my stuff back. But without shoes, hurting mightily from the beating and ever mindful of getting knifed I watched the two muggers disappear into the Zone, dragged my ass across the street and into my building where the ever-present concierge obligingly called the Boston constabulary.

The Boston cops were very sympathetic. What the hell was I doing in the Boston Common after dark? Didn't I have any brains? Was I an idiot? Didn't I know what went on in the Common at night? What was the chance, I asked, they would find these guys and get my stuff back? About one in a million, they said truthfully. Did I want to go to the hospital? No. Then sign this form and we'll get back to you. Did you ever hear from them?

The first person I called when finally getting into my apartment was Andrea. Big mistake; it was like talking to a stranger. A month or so before we were looking for apartments and making plans to be together; now she might as well have been on Mars. It wasn't that she didn't care about what had happened to me. To me it was that she didn't seem to care. I decided that weekend that I didn't want to date my wife any longer. I don't know when she decided.

A few days after the mugging I went to see a lawyer—a very bright and decent Boston lawyer who rarely took divorce cases, a guy I had met through the ADL work. Andrea Goldman got her own lawyer and to make a long, story short we eventually sold our house in Virginia and in about a year or so we were both single again. The divorce was painful for both of us. I think our divorce was ultimately as amicable as "amicable" divorces go. You'll have to ask Andrea Leerman for her opinion. And as Forrest Gump would say, "That's all I have to say about that!"

CHAPTER 48

Over the next two years I threw myself into the work of the Anti-Defamation League. I had become a true believer. I liked the agency; I totally agreed with ADL policy, I liked the people in New York and most of my Boston colleagues. In short order I was able to get a $25,000 grant from the Massachusetts Foundation for the Humanities for work with various ethnic groups in the four corners of the state; I quarterbacked a major teacher's conference on "Teaching the Holocaust," cooperating with other Jewish organizations in Boston (which is rarely done!), the creative superintendent of the Brookline Public Schools, Dr. Robert Sperber and other local educators. We anticipated that we would get fifty or so teachers to attend our conference. On the day of the meeting we had about 300 Junior and Senior High School teachers from every corner of the state. I was able to present a paper on "Teaching the Holocaust" which I later published in an academic journal. I was also able to reconnect with an old friend, Professor Paul Bookbinder, a panelist at the conference who taught German history at the University of Massachusetts in Boston.

That conference was so successful that we held a second one at Holy Cross in Worcester where I became friendly with Governor Michael Dukakis's wife Kitty Dukakis who took a major interest in Holocaust education. As keynote speaker I invited an old friend, Dr. Franklin Littell, who had founded the graduate program in Holocaust studies at Temple University. Because I had taken a Ph.D. field in German History at Clark University with major emphasis on the Nazi period, Holocaust Education was right down my alley. One of the major accomplishments of these two conferences was the creation of a Holocaust education program by two Brookline teachers that was called "Facing History." Today that program is a multi-million dollar nation-wide program still run by one of those teachers, Margot

Strom, with offices in cities around the country. Their curriculum has changed the nature of the concept of Moral Education in the Social Studies in virtually every major school system in the country. The credit belongs to Margot Strom and Bill Parsons, the two dynamic Junior High teachers with a dream and vision.

Aside from my personal life going into the crapper it was a wonderful and creative two years. As Education Director of the ADL I was free to go in almost any direction I wanted. I had more freedom to do what I wanted in the first three years at ADL than in any job I have ever had. I set up a series of Human Relations workshops for Boston teachers, most of whom were Black, who were on the firing line in 1975 with forced busing coming to virtually every neighborhood in the city. I brought in ADL's National Education Director, Walter Plotch, from New York to work with me and the teachers. Plotch, a creative guy in his own right, was a specialist in human relations, race relations, ethnic education and defusing tense educational situations. And no neighborhoods or urban school system could have been more tense between 1975 and 1977 then those in the city of Boston.

I loved the city of Boston and enjoyed the freedom of exploring the streets and neighborhoods or bicycling along the Charles River, going to the theater district only a block from my apartment building, shopping at Filene's Basement, and eating at the new restaurants in what was to become Quincy Market on the waterfront. I also made friends with an up and coming ambitious city councilor by the name of Raymond Flynn, a leader of the anti-Busing movement in South Boston. Flynn, who had a brief career with the Boston Celtics, was an enigma to many liberals—especially at *The Boston Globe,* Boston's newspaper of record.

Flynn, a longtime neighborhood advocate, certainly was no racist. I had met him as one of the leaders of a major Southie demonstration against the Klan and Neo-Nazis who were attempting to infiltrate the chaotic situation to take advantage of the tumultuous conditions caused by the problems of Forced Busing. Succeeding Mayor Kevin White, he became mayor of Boston in 1983. I also met and befriended a portly young State Representative who spoke out of the side of his mouth with a tough New Jersey accent. His name was Barney Frank.

Within a matter of months I was helping to put ADL on the educational map of Boston and New England. I made it my business to acquaint myself with some major journalists in the city. I met one of the greatest urban journalists in the country, Alan Lupo who wrote for the *Globe* and *Boston Phoenix* during my early years in Boston. (My first hire as a columnist when I became editor of *The Boston Ledger* was Al Lupo who by that time had become a longtime friend). I invited Joan Vennochi, a very capable city reporter who was covering education and busing to lunch. I also managed to become acquainted with the editor of the *Globe's* Op-ed pages, Helen Donovan. Helen's Dad was Hedley Donovan, the well-respected editor of *Time Magazine*. My connection with Helen enabled me to place some highly controversial columns on the subject of Affirmative Action onto the op-ed pages of the *Globe*. One the eve of the famous Bakke Decision by the Supreme Court the *Globe* placed one of my columns opposite the well-known civil rights leader who headed the Urban League—Vernon Jordan who would become a household name in the Clinton/Lewinsky scandal. A week or so after my column was published in the *Globe*, *Time Magazine* devoted an entire section to its cover story—the Bakke Case. And guess who they quoted as a major opponent of Affirmative Action? "Martin S. Goldman of B'nai B'rith said, 'One does not end discrimination by discriminating.'" Well, they almost got it right!

By the end of 1978 I had published more than a half-dozen Op-ed pieces in the *Globe*. So I decided to branch out. I contacted editors from other sections of the paper and began to take on assignments for major features. Then I contacted editors at other Boston newspapers. Bob Sales, the genial editor of the *Boston Phoenix*, became a good friend and I was able to do some very creative in-depth pieces for that weekly paper in the ensuing years with a writing partner who was to become one of my dearest friends, Michael Kort.

Since my writing did not interfere with my ADL work, or in some cases actually enhanced that work since I was taking editorial positions that were the stated national policies of the agency, nobody objected. The Director often wanted to know what I was writing about and I always felt he was jealous of my growing public visibility and political connections. But I was getting the ADL into the newspapers on almost a bi-weekly basis and so for a time he held his fire and left me to my own devices answerable only to New York. Our lay leadership liked the idea of seeing a byline by someone they knew on a professional basis and, for the most part, agreed with my stated positions.

I wrote about Nazi war criminals, Jimmy Carter and the Jews (among other long features for Bernie Hyatt, publisher of *The Jewish Advocate*), Ronald Reagan, violence on the transit system of Boston, crime, Soviet Jewry, and just about anything that popped into my head. In late 1978 I began to write for the *Globe's* major competitor, the tabloid *Boston Herald* where the editorial page editor, Shelley Cohen, a fellow Philadelphian published almost anything I sent over. *The Globe* and *The Herald* didn't seem to care that I was writing for both papers; or maybe they didn't know it.

At the same time I was able to make some strong and lasting personal friendships. Larry Lowenthal, a Ph.D. in English Literature from New York University called me one day and invited me to lunch. Larry was the Director of the Zionist House on Commonwealth Avenue. When we met Larry was in the middle of a painful divorce. He had two young children; a tenuous hold on an organization that was not considered an A-list player in Boston's elite Jewish world and well…Larry Lowenthal is one of the smartest people I have ever known. A born teacher and speaker, Larry would give a lecture on just about anything: American literature, Jewish comedy, film, Israel or whatever. Larry would lecture when the refrigerator light went on. He still does.

Larry and I became the closest of friends from the first day we met over lunch at a downtown Boston restaurant, Purcell's. We would throw well-attended parties on weekends to meet women; we would meet for years almost every Sunday for brunch at a Brookline deli, Jack and Marion's. We loved The English Tearoom and ate there at least once a week for dinner until the place disappeared. Larry had lived in Tel Aviv, Israel and taught for many years at Hebrew University. He had even been in the Israeli Defense Force during the Yom Kippur War. Like me, Larry was committed to the health and survival of the

Jewish state. He came back to America around the time I had come to Boston but we didn't actually meet until 1977. When we were single we spoke at least once a day—sometimes for hours. I can't report how many times I awakened poor Larry, an incurable insomniac, from a deep sleep when I returned from a well-known Cambridge bar where I hung out to report that "I finally met the woman of my dreams!" Unfortunately, I seemed to dream a lot.

Larry owned a comfortable home on the Cape in the woods of Truro a few minutes from the beach. I spent many happy weekends with Larry at his Cape Cod house and once Ripper and I even joined his Dad, Louie Lowenthal, for a week or so of late summer vacation. Eventually I introduced Larry to his second wife, Pauline Gerson, ironically the younger sister of my ex-wife's best friend. They married in 1983 and in 1986 had a beautiful little girl, Jessica, who has already graduated from college and is a grad student at the Heller School at Brandeis.

Then there was Father Robert Bullock. He became my friend, confidante and in a very important sense, my moral compass and teacher. We met on the Catholic-Jewish Committee and our friendship remained solid until his untimely death in 2004. At the time we met Bob headed up the Campus Ministry of the Archdiocese in Boston. But, I believe, because of his strong attachment to the Jewish community and their issues, Father Bullock, who was called derisively "the Jew priest" by a few jealous competitors, fell out of favor with the powers that be in the Archdiocese—namely the new Cardinal Madeiros who unlike Cardinal Cushing didn't have a strong affinity for Catholic-Jewish relations.

But Bob landed on his feet by becoming the Catholic Chaplain at Brandeis University where he worked closely for a number of years with the popular and well-liked campus Hillel Rabbi Al Axelrad. Bob became active with the ADL and often spoke at our board meetings and many academic conferences. He ultimately found a loving home at Facing History where he was Chairman of the Board for a while and where he remained active until his death.

Eventually Bob took a parish at Our Lady of Sorrows, a church in Sharon, Massachusetts where he quickly became one of the most beloved priests in the Archdiocese. But he remained a powerful moral voice in New England's large Catholic community. When Cardinal Bernard Law, who had become a great friend to Boston Jewry, found himself caught up in the ugly sexual abuse scandal of pederast priests in his Archdiocese, it was Bob Bullock who not only got on the Cardinal's case but eventually called for Law, who was clearly guilty of sweeping so much criminal perversion under the rug, to step down; which he eventually did.

I would get together with Bob often for lunch until I left Massachusetts. Sometimes, Bob did not wear the collar. He had an old gray tweed jacket that he favored with blue jeans. One time we were having lunch in Quincy Market and two young women at the next table were smiling at us—or I should say they were smiling at Bob. When I found out that they were indeed interested in meeting Bob who was tall, red-haired, Hollywood handsome and had the most killer smile I have ever known, I simply said, "You girls are barking up the wrong parish." They didn't know what the hell I was talking about but Bob just cracked up.

I was honored to be one of the two or three Jews invited to celebrate Bob's fiftieth birthday. Bob was a man who was always interested in what his friends were doing. He would always start lunch with a question: "So Martin, what are you reading these days?" We would often share our latest treasured finds in books and authors. When I was at the end of my career at Merrimack College, an Augustinian Catholic school, Bob would come up to the North Andover campus for lunch at least once a month and he also served on my education committee there.

Bob was an intellectual who knew more about the Holocaust and Israel than most Jews. I am glad that my mother and father lived long enough to meet Father Bullock. They had heard his name for many years and Bob, because of our many discussions over the years, always felt he knew them. They finally met in 1996 at one of my Merrimack College dinners and spent an enjoyable evening together. My aging mother lived up to Bob's expectations colored by many years of my stories and descriptions of the perfect "Jewish mother."

On another occasion Bob and I met for dinner. I was writing a novel and was having trouble with the ending where the protagonist had to commit a murder. Bob and I played out the scene and I took notes of our conversation exactly as we said the words. The character in my book goes to his best friend, a priest, in an attempt to acquire justification for an act he knows he must commit for what he truly believes is the greater good. Bob played his part with perfection. The book, the first in a trilogy, will be published after Book two. Book number one came out in 2006.

Father Robert Bullock died in 2004 after a brief battle with cancer. I have never known a man as decent, moral and honorable as Bob Bullock. And I am quite certain I never will. God must have had important work for Bob to do because He took him from us much too soon. I am not ashamed to say that I loved him. My Boston experience was illuminated and made golden by having Father Robert Bullock in my life.

One summer weekend in 1976 I was taking the ferry from Woods Hole to Martha's Vineyard. The Vineyard had been Andrea's and my favorite spot on earth to vacation and relax. I didn't often go there after our divorce—bad vibes; painful memories!

But that year a friend convinced me to go with her for a couple of days. On the ferry she introduced me to a guy staring over the boat's rail at the dark swirling sea between Woods Hole and the island. He was about my age and was also on his way to the Vineyard. "Marty," she said, "say hello to Alan." We talked for a few minutes, found out we were both recently divorced, that we had a great deal in common (we were both academics and came from a Jewish urban background) and then the ferry arrived at Vineyard Haven and we parted. I had no idea that he was, even then in his late thirties, a nationally known academic personality.

To make another long story short the Alan I was introduced to on the Vineyard ferry was Alan Dershowitz, Felix Frankfurter Professor of Law at Harvard University. During the 1970's and 1980's Alan became a close friend, a source of legal support and partner in some fun adventures. We vacationed at the Vineyard often; we hung out nightly for many years over dinner and drinks at the Harvest in Cambridge; we worked together on any number of Jewish issues; and best of all, during the cold winter of 1982 we shared a suite and stories we may or may not relate to our grandchildren at Club Med on the Caribbean island of Guadalupe. We told the women we met that week that we were Air Traffic Controllers!

I was around Alan's house often during the months of his defense of accused attempted murderer, Claus Von Bulow. His final argument that I watched before the Rhode Island Supreme Court should remain a classic in American legal history and taught in every Law school in America. You want to see a great movie? See *Reversal of Fortune* where the late Ron Silver absolutely nails Dersh. Alan, whose public persona is far different than the *mensche* he actually is, often gets hammered in the press unfairly, and although he is very capable of defending himself as a tough Jew out of Boro Park in Brooklyn, nobody better badmouth the Dersh in front of me.

Once, Alan even traveled with me all the way to Philly to speak for no fee (he usually commands between $10,000 and $15,000 a speech) at my parent's synagogue, Har Zion. My mother and father loved him and he was always more than gracious to my parents on the many occasions when he met them. Alan was also to act as my attorney in some later troubles that I got myself into. He saved me thousands of dollars in lawyer's fees. Once when he appeared as my counsel when I was being deposed by the actress Vanessa Redgrave's hotshot New York attorneys, one of the opposing attorneys just put his head down and sighed when Alan walked into the room, unpacked his briefcase and sat down to represent me over many difficult hours.

But the real story of the next two years began in the fall of 1977. I was planning a well-earned vacation to the Caribbean. I had hardly taken a day off since I arrived in Boston. That was when my friend Michael Kort who by then was working on the 4th Floor of 72 Franklin Street for the American Jewish Committee changed my vacation plans. Mike came up to my office and said simply, "Let's go to Russia."

CHAPTER 49

I met Michael and Carol Kort early in 1977 at the Newton home of Mikki Ritvo, the chairman of ADL's education committee. Michael, a Ph.D. in Russian History from New York University, was looking for a fulltime job and I guess he thought I could help him. In fact, when my friend Iz Zack retired in 1978 I pitched Mike to the ADL as the new Civil Rights director and he would have been hired except for the fact that New York was dead set on a lawyer for the spot.

Like many academics of that era who were forced to piece their incomes together with non-tenure teaching or other campus jobs, Mike had bounced around quite a bit and he was discouraged to say the least. Carol, one of the world's amazing women, was doing public relations at Lesley College in Cambridge and they lived in a very comfortable apartment on Garden Street right off Harvard Square. Disappointed that he could not connect with the ADL Mike didn't give up and when there was an opening at the American Jewish Committee for an assistant director I prevailed on my then girl-friend, Karen Osborne, the other assistant director, to put in a good word for Mike with the director. And Mike got the job.

The American Jewish Committee and the American Jewish Congress, both housed in the same building (called "The Jewish Pentagon") as the ADL, were actually fierce competitors. They rarely worked together, rarely shared information and to make matters even more complicated a fourth competitor was the local Jewish Community Relations Council (funded by the local Jewish Federation, the CJP— The Combined Jewish Philanthropies), by 1977 headed by my friend and mentor Phil Perlmutter who the ADL director in Boston detested. Sometime in 1978 or 1979 to further complicate matters Phil's older brother, Nathan Perlmutter, became National Director of the ADL. That made it difficult for everybody involved because these defense agencies were so competitive. But the Boston ADL director had to walk on eggshells because he couldn't very well take on the brother of his New York boss in a full frontal attack; though he did his best behind the scenes to undermine the Council.

My life became more difficult because of my strong relationship with Iz Zack and friendship with Phil Perlmutter but there was little the Director could do since I still basically answered to New York. As one might surmise, one of the major problems of the American Jewish community is that it is over-organized and wastes a hell of a lot of money on agencies that basically do the same damn thing! I would often joke that sometimes we fought with one another more than we did with the Arabs; which was actually no joke. For many Jews the agency or organization of their choice becomes sort of like their synagogue—a place where they could live out their Jewish commitment without the ambiguous spiritual conflict of religion and ritual intruding.

By the time Mike went to work for the American Jewish Committee we had become very close friends because of the many things we had in common: our neo-conservative politics, our strong affinity as Jews (Mike and Carol had lived in Israel early in their marriage), our educational backgrounds, our failure to land tenure track university jobs—all of this very similar even though Mike had grown up in New York and I had grown up in Philly. And we both loved Carol albeit in different ways.

When Mike came up to my office and suggested a trip to Russia I thought he was off kilter. Why Russia? Why on God's green earth would I want to go to Russia? Well, Mike explained, there was the very real problem of *the Refuseniks*, those Soviet Jews who were refused the right to emigrate and were being oppressed by the government of Leonid Brezhnev. To tell the truth, I hardly knew a thing about the Soviet Jewish situation other than what I would sometimes read in the Jewish press or *The New York Times*.

The first thing I did was get hold of a number of books and articles about Soviet Jewry. The local head of Amnesty International, Josh Rubenstein, was a scholar on the plight of Soviet Jews. I read his articles. And they led me to other articles and books. It was an eye-opener. Although many Jews had emigrated to the United States and Israel since World War II, there were still between two and four million Jews in the Soviet Union. Russian Anti-Semitism was as deeply embedded in the Soviet soul over the centuries as Christianity or even Communism. The Soviet system had done its best to eliminate the Jewish religion, Jewish tradition and the Hebrew language from their large Jewish minority. But in 1967, with the overwhelming Israeli victory in the Six Day War, Russian Jewry's image of itself had been transformed. Soviet Jewry could be said to have had a great awakening as Zionism took deep root. Those Russian Jews who sought freedom of religion or emigration to Israel were in desperate straits as the government did its best to erase all vestiges of Jewish nationalism and culture. Jew hatred in Russia was such that the possibility of another debacle similar to the Holocaust was not out of the question according to the wisest and most competent scholars.

Mike Kort had become acquainted with two local women, Bailey Barron and Judy Patkin, who worked for an organization—yes, another Jewish organization!—called Action for Soviet Jewry. Action, like other groups in cities all over the United States, would send American tourists into the Soviet Union to meet with the leading *Refuseniks* armed with both moral and some measure of financial support. There were two agencies in the Jewish community designed to service the problems of Soviet Jewry: the Union of Councils and the National Conference for Soviet Jewry. Action for Soviet Jewry, a Boston-based outfit, was affiliated with the Union of Councils one of whose leading supporters was Bob Gordon, the philanthropic owner and founder of the Store 24 chain in New England. It was Bob Gordon who financed the trips into the Soviet Union.

To further complicate matters a leading Moscow *Refusenik*, Anatoly Scharansky, had recently been arrested by the KGB and charged with being a spy for the CIA and sent off to the notorious Lefotorvo Prison where he was awaiting trial. His new wife Avital had made a number of trips to the States to connect with various organizations on her husband's behalf. She had stopped in Boston where Judy Patkin and Bailey Barron hosted her for Action for Soviet Jewry and where the group dedicated itself to actively taking up Scharansky's difficult cause. At best Scharansky faced many years under harsh conditions in a Soviet prison or even a Gulag. At worst, he faced the death penalty.

If Mike and I could meet up with some of his fellow *Refuseniks,* we were told, they could supply us with vital materials for Scharansky's defense at his upcoming trial. *Time Magazine* thought the Scharansky case was important enough to make it a cover story. Anatoly Scharansky might have been a giant pain-in-the-ass to the Soviets and the KGB as one of the most outspoken *Refuseniks* who had a definite knack for getting together with western travelers and journalists. A CIA operative, he was not. CIA operatives, especially in-country, are close-mouthed. Scharansky talked to anyone who would listen. Ironically, unbeknownst to us at the time, Professor Alan Dershowitz had signed on to defend the accused Russian Jew who could have been sentenced to death. The Soviets used to have a real passion for executing spies they deemed as traitors to their beloved Motherland (Read David Wise, *Spy: The Inside Story of How the FBI's Robert Hanssen Betrayed America,* (New York, 2002).

Mike and I met with Bailey Barron over coffee at Hebrew College in Brookline. Bailey was in charge of sending people into Russia. An attractive, bright woman in her forties who lived in Sudbury, Massachusetts, Bailey Barron was deeply committed to alleviating the plight of Jews in the Soviet Union and she carefully questioned me to see how much I knew about the problem and whether Action should approve sending us into the heart of darkness. Mike, as a Ph.D. in Russian History was definitely qualified to go. But Bailey, who eventually became a lifelong friend, had apparently heard some negative things about me and wanted to check me out for herself. I apparently passed muster in the interview and it was agreed that we would be off to the Soviet Union over Thanksgiving week, 1977.

I want to note here that there was nothing overly heroic or brave about going into the Soviet Union in these years. Hundreds of American Jews preceded us; and hundreds, if not thousands would follow. My retrospective take on the Soviet Jewry problem is that our generation was painfully aware of the failure of American Jewry to act during the years of the Holocaust 1933-1945. I had been lecturing on the Holocaust for years by that time and had read scores of studies related to what America, the Roosevelt administration and the Jewish community did and did not do for European Jewry. The scholars and teachers had done their consciousness raising work well. Our generation could never be accused of standing idly by while our Russian brethren were being oppressed by Soviet anti-Semitism. In cities like New York, Philadelphia, Chicago, Boston, Atlanta and Miami, to name a few, tourists were being organized, trained and sent into the belly of the beast to let the *Refuseniks* know that they did not stand alone.

I spent the weeks before the trip training for the long, cold Russian nights and what would be a great deal of walking. I would get up early every day and, with the Ripper, jog the Boston Common twice—about two miles of running every day. I would also bike the paths along the Charles River to Brookline and back once or twice a week. By the time we left for Russia, for a sedentary guy in his late thirties I was in terrific shape.

Getting into the Soviet Union at the height of the Cold War was not as easy as it is today. You had to apply for a visa through the Soviet embassy in D.C. That meant that you had to give a reason for your travel and, if the Soviet bureaucrats didn't like the reason, your visa might be rejected. The Soviets were always on the lookout for "cutouts"— spies who were not officially connected to America's vast intelligence apparatus but who might be sent into the country to disappear into Soviet society while reporting back about whatever it is they were sent in to report about. A "cutout" was different than a "legend"—that was a spy sent in whose identity was totally fabricated and who had really never existed as the person they were supposedly being. "Legends," if they actually existed, had prolonged stays in the countries where they were operating. We hoped to get in and out as quickly as possible.

Mike and I filled out the necessary forms for our visas saying that we were high school teachers who were interested in learning about Soviet art and culture. Our passports were legitimate and the only thing that wasn't accurate on our visa applications was our profession and our reason for going to Russia. There is no doubt that our applications would have been rejected if we listed our professional Jewish agency affiliations. The two visas were approved.

The second problem related to going into the Soviet Union was the fact that you just couldn't fly into Russia, get off the plane, tip your hat and go on your way. You had to enter the country with a group of other American tourists who would always be met at the airport by a Russian representative of the Soviet Intourist Agency that was responsible for overseeing all incoming travelers. That Intourist person usually stayed with the group throughout the entire trip and, while ostensibly accommodating the American tourist's silly questions and needs, would also immediately report any untoward or suspicious conduct. Mike and I were forewarned that most Intourist representatives, usually attractive young women, were in reality KGB agents working for the notorious Soviet Secret police—a combination of our FBI and CIA. Their job was to look for any suspicious activity on the part of tourists and report it.

We were also warned never to speak to one another about what we were doing in our hotel rooms which Bailey warned us were usually bugged. Mike and I solved that little problem by picking up one of those children's thingamajigs which you could write on, then lift up and watch it automatically erase. We used those toys to great advantage during the many days we spent in Russia. When we visited with Soviet Jews we always brought our little toys along just in case.

Our day of departure arrived in late November. Mike and I drove down to his in-laws in Orange, New Jersey, stayed the night and the next day went to JFK Airport for the long flight into what I would eventually call "The Land of Frozen Hearts."

Mike's father-in-law, Jack Chvat, was in the clothing business and he generously supplied us with two expensive leather jackets, two ski jackets and other assorted clothing which we could use to aid the *Refuseniks* we would meet financially. The Soviet Union was bereft in those days of most consumer goods. Mike and I carried backpacks loaded with Levi jeans, leather jackets, Beatles and Rolling Stones albums and assorted BIC pens as well as other technical devices like small calculators and pocket tape recorders. We both wore parka-type ski jackets. When we went through Soviet customs I remember the agent smiling knowingly at me. All that gear in my backpack along with half a dozen *Time* magazines, he well knew, meant that I wasn't in Russia to see the fabled art museums. Leather jackets could bring between $150-$200 American on any Russian street. Levis were selling for $100-$150. A twenty-cent BIC pen could command as much as $10; a Beatles album went for over $50. One thing I learned quickly on our Soviet sojourn was that Communism wasn't working very well. Aside from the Communists, who could purchase consumer goods at special government-run stores called the GUM, the average Soviet citizen couldn't even get toilet paper or a pair of shoes that fit without a hassle. The Russian middle classes were suffering along with the poor for the impossible dream of a totally leveled society. One day we were walking in downtown Moscow when dozens of Russian men and women began running by us toward…well, we didn't know where. Mike asked a passerby in Russian what all the commotion was about: "Toilet paper!" he answered as he ran off. A bunch of guys were selling toilet paper from the back of a truck! You didn't have to sit in an oak-paneled D.C. think tank or in the hallowed halls of the State Department to understand that the old fools in the Politburo were sitting in the Titanic on top of a melting iceberg.

It didn't take long for our fellow Americans to realize that Mike and I were not in the country to tour the sites and museums. For the most part, we disappeared every morning after breakfast and did not show up again until well after dinner and sometimes not until the wee hours of the next morning. The Intourist guide immediately knew that we were often missing. But how could she have known where we were each day? Mike spoke enough passable Russian to get us to our targeted destinations by taxi. We always knew something about the person or persons we were going to see. We had even viewed photos of the individuals we were visiting so we would know if the person who answered the door of those vast sterile apartment complexes was the person we were supposed to visit. Often we would call ahead to let the people know we were coming to see them. Mike did the calling and mostly spoke in Russian if the individual didn't have passable English. Mike knew enough to say very little over the phone beyond the fact that we wanted to visit. In many cases we were expected.

Our trip started out in Leningrad (St. Petersburg since 1990), probably the most beautiful and most European of all Russian big cities. I will not go into the names of everyone we visited; by the time we left Leningrad we had seen over a dozen *Refuseniks* and listened to similar tales of Soviet Jewish woe. Our full trip report was written and filed with Action for Soviet Jewry when we returned to the States. (I still have a copy). As we traveled around Leningrad we unloaded our Levi jeans, jackets, pens, tape recorders and record albums to the Jewish families in need. In Leningrad we did nothing out of the ordinary that other American Jews behind and ahead of us did not do for many years.

The other Americans on our tour were mostly from Texas. Many soon suspected wrongly that we were some kind of spies. A few people actually asked us where we went each day and what it was we were doing. I would respond that Mike and I didn't like to be regimented and that we wanted to go off on our own to see the country. I don't know if they believed me but the questions went no further.

On each floor of the hotel as you got off the elevator there was an elderly Russian woman sitting taking note of who was in and out of the hotel floor. Undoubtedly, these women were reporting on us too. But nobody could possibly know, once we hit the Russian street, where we went and what we were doing. Often, we didn't know where we were going until we got there. And we never spoke of our plans openly in our hotel room.

We were sometimes stopped on the streets by young men asking if we had dollars to trade or jeans to sell. Fortunately, Bailey Barron had warned us about these types. Some were just young Russian guys hustling to make a few rubles by exchanging valuable American dollars for Russian money—a crime in the Soviet Union. Others may have been agents. You just never knew; but we were stopped by a lot of people asking about money or blue jeans. I once asked some old guy who stopped to chat with us about America on the street how he knew we were Americans. His answer was interesting: "By your glasses and by the way you walk. You look into people's eyes!" I began to notice that most Russians making their way through the cold streets of Leningrad and Moscow walked with their heads down and rarely looked anyone directly in the eye. Maybe it was the weather; maybe it was the country; maybe it was the system.

After we left Leningrad about mid-week, we traveled by rail to the small town of Kalinin. We walked the streets of the town but there were no synagogues or Jews to be found. The Nazis had apparently done their work during the war and the town appeared *Judenrein.*

Our next stop was Moscow, a colder, grayer and more cheerless city than Leningrad. It was in Moscow that our real work was done. Again we visited with over a dozen families and one defrocked Jewish scientist from the Academy of Science, Victor Brailovski, who was doing menial work for a scientist of his stature in order to survive. He presented us both with scientific medals (I still have my medal). Brailovski lives in Israel today and is a renowned mathematician.

There were, however, two very important meetings that were to make our trip somewhat more unique than the average Jewish American traveler's. On Thanksgiving night, a Thursday which had absolutely no meaning to Muscovites, we stopped at the threadbare apartment of a diminutive *Refusenik* by the name of Boris Katz. Boris, a computer specialist, and his wife Natalya had been refused emigration to the United States because the Soviet authorities accused them of harboring "State Secrets." Fired from his job by applying for a visa, Boris was forced to travel many miles from Moscow each day to work at a menial job to make ends meet for his family which also included a new-born baby girl named Jessica.

The Katz family's situation was hardly different from most Jewish families we had met in Leningrad and Moscow but for some reason there was chemistry between Boris and myself. Over a few short hours on an icy Russian night in 1977 we bonded powerfully and there was an affinity between the two of us as we spoke of life in Russia and the United States. Perhaps it was because his mother and two brothers had already emigrated and were living in Cambridge, Massachusetts. Perhaps it was that the Katz family seemed so typical to me—they were the Russian Jewish Everyman whose plight, over steaming Russian tea and cookies, seemed so poignant on my favorite holiday, Thanksgiving. When we left Boris and Natalya's home it was snowing hard. Maybe it was snow melting on our faces; maybe it was tears. Who knows? Boris walked us to a taxi and we hugged like brothers, both of us painfully aware that we would probably never see one another again. I resolved that when I returned to Boston that I would write about the Katz family because, in my eyes, they were the representative *Refusenik* family.

However, the most important meeting took place a day after Thanksgiving at the modest Gorky Street apartment of the leading *Refuseniks* in the Soviet Union, Vladimir and Mascha Slepak. If Andrei Sakharov was the leader of the Russian dissidents, Vladimir Slepak was the old lion of the Soviet Jewish movement. Everyone knew him— especially, as it turned out, the KGB. His Moscow apartment was the place everyone came for counsel, strategy and emotional support. There is no question that it was always watched by the KGB.

Slepak's father, a leading Bolshevik, had even named him after Vladimir Lenin. When Slepak was a boy his father sent his son to Comsomol, the Communist Youth League where it was expected that he would follow in his father's footsteps as an active Communist. Long story short: Vladimir Slepak broke with his father and the Party, became a Zionist and sought emigration to Israel. His father never spoke to him again. The late Jewish writer Chaim Potok chronicled the Slepak family's painful history and struggles in his excellent book, *The Gates of November*.

Mike and I came to the Slepaks through another courageous *Refusenik* who we had met in the beginning of that week, Dina Beilina. She promised us that Slepak would produce the materials we would need to get back to the West for Anatoly Scharansky's defense. Also present that night was Ida Nudel, another well-known leader in the movement. She was also what the Russian Jews called "A Prisoner of Zion" who had been dismissed from her job in 1972 and had to get by on menial work to survive. I believe she tutored Jewish children in

Hebrew. After years of difficulty with the Soviet authorities, she was eventually permitted to immigrate to Israel in 1987.

Over strong cups of Russian tea and some kind of soup the Slepaks produced the materials we were looking for: about 200 manuscript pages written in tiny Russian script. How, Mike asked Slepak who did not speak English as well as Mike spoke Russian, did they expect us to get this manuscript out of Russia and past a close inspection at the airport where they would obviously be looking for something like a large packet of papers? "Do you have a good camera?" Slepak asked Mike in Russian. As it happened, I did. I had a new, hi-powered Olympus that I had purchased especially for the trip. It was in my backpack. It was shortly after 10 P.M. when I started to take one picture, one page at a time of the extensive manuscript while Slepak, Ida Nudel and Dina Beilina took turns holding a powerful light on the materials. I had used 5 rolls of film that had 36 shots on each roll by the time I finished taking the photos. It took about three to four hours before the picture taking was completed because, unlike a photo of a person or a building, my hand had to be perfectly steady before snapping each photograph.

We left the Slepak's apartment emotionally and physically drained around 2 A.M. But not before someone mentioned that we had come to visit on Vladimir's birthday. By the time we got to the Slepak's we had given away all our jeans, jackets, records and other valuable items. It was our last stop. Our backpacks were virtually empty. I felt embarrassed that we were leaving the most important group we would visit with nothing but a thank you for their gracious hospitality. I was wearing a brand new olive-green ski parka that I had picked up in Filene's Basement just prior to our trip. I took off my parka and insisted that Volodya, as Slepak insisted on being called, take it. At first he refused. But he didn't take much prodding. The $50 parka would easily bring over $200 on the Moscow streets. Slepak, a bear of a man with a thick beard who was a much huskier man than me, tried on my parka which was a large. It fit like a glove because, like my Dad had taught me, I always bought things about a size larger than I needed. Years later I met up with Slepak who was standing with

Elie Wiesel and Anatoly (now Natan) Scharansky to head up a march on the Ellipse in Washington, D.C. for Soviet Jewry in January, 1987. I asked Scharansky to tell Slepak that I was the guy who had given him my ski jacket so many years before in Moscow. Slepak looked at me blankly and told Scharansky in Russian, "I have no idea what this fellow is talking about." So much for no good deed going unpunished; or remembered!

A few months after our visit the Slepaks were arrested and, under trumped up charges, sent into exile in Siberia where they suffered for years until, under relentless pressure from American senators like Henry "Scoop" Jackson, human rights and Jewish advocacy groups, the Soviet government finally permitted them to immigrate to Israel in 1987. I guess the Russians thought they were well rid of a family of "troublemakers" who somehow, even in exile, kept their names in the Western press.

I felt good about giving my parka to Slepak for his birthday; that is until I hit the icy cold Russian streets with just a flimsy shirt to protect me from the elements. Snow was swirling around us stinging our eyes and sticking to my Boston-watch cap as we made our way back to our hotel, about a thirty-minute walk, because we could not find a taxi that early in the morning. Endless walking around the snowy Russian streets with little rest, terrible food or sometimes no food had taken its toll. Within two days I had a fever that broke out into the flu by the time I was back in the States. But that was the least of our problems. How were we going to make sure that the five rolls of film for the Scharansky defense would make it safely out of the Soviet Union?

Mike and I had agreed on one thing at the beginning of our trip: we both had to agree on whatever decisions were made. And each of had a veto over any major decision. We were leaving Russia in two days after the meeting at the Slepaks. We decided to take a chance and approach one of the Texans who were on the tour. We would explain nothing but would ask an American tourist to take the five rolls of film in his or her bags until we were on the plane and out of Soviet airspace. All we would promise was that if the American got in trouble during the inspection by Soviet customs officers that we would step forward and admit that the film belonged to us. Pretty damn flimsy!

We approached an attractive young woman in the hotel lobby who we had spoken with a couple of times. She had appeared very friendly and quite curious about us during the time we traveled in Russia. We made our pitch. She looked at us skeptically. "I knew you two were up to something! No way!" she exclaimed walking quickly away and never spoke to either of us again. Our next "victim" was an attractive woman from Texas in her early forties with the unusual name of Kleita Peacock. We made the pitch about our film and she smiled. "Do you both promise that if I get in trouble you two will make it right?" she asked. We promised; and we meant it. We gave her the film and in a few hours we were all off to the airport for the long flight back to the States.

The lines were long at the airport outside of Moscow. So Mike and I decided to separate just to be careful. Mike was at the head of the line and I was about twenty-five people behind him. He was about to check in with his baggage when a non-descript man in a brown suit walked up to him, took him by the arm and led him away. Holy shit! What was I going to tell Carol? She was going into her eighth month of pregnancy. I was going home without Mike! How would I tell Carol that some guy had grabbed Mike and then disappeared?

I didn't have to worry. In about seven minutes as I reached the head of the check-in line a man with closely cropped hair in a gray suit walked up to me, grabbed my arm and led me away without a word. He took me into a room off to the side of the airport's lobby. He pointed to a chair and barked at me in Russian. I guess he meant for me to sit down. I sat down.

The man continued to speak to me in a loud voice. Since he spoke Russian I had no idea what he was saying. I told him to speak English. He only barked louder. Then he pointed to my luggage. I figured that he meant I should open my bags. They were practically empty. We had given everything away. I opened them and handed him my backpack. He rifled through my stuff: underwear went flying; a few shirts; two pair of pants (khakis and jeans); a sweater; nothing else. The man seemed agitated and yelled at me some more in Russian. Then he opened up my backpack. It too was practically empty. He grabbed a can of spray deodorant and shook it; nothing but deodorant. He took a tube of toothpaste and cut it open with a pocketknife. Nothing but Colgate! He seemed more disappointed than pissed and began to speak a little more softly; but still in Russian. I said in English again that I did not understand what he was saying and that if there was a problem that I would like to speak to an official at the American embassy. I think he understood the words "American embassy" because he threw his hands up and motioned for me to put my stuff back in the backpack and valise. I did. Then he led me back into the airport and to the head of the line where I checked in.

Gray-suit smiled at me, shook his head and walked away. I checked in with my luggage and walked to the area where the rest of the tour group was waiting to board the plane.

Mike was already there smiling. That is when we began calling each other "Frick" and "Frack"—the two most bumbling undercover guys ever to enter and get out of the Soviet Union. Michael had obviously gone through the very same process with Mr. Brown-suit. The two guys, Mike said, were KGB and they were looking for something. Of course, they didn't find it.

On the plane back to the States we retrieved our five rolls of film from Ms. Peacock. She asked if we would tell her what we were doing. I took her address and promised to write her the full story once we were back in the States and had delivered our film. Back in the States, after recovering from the flu, I turned our film in and was told that it was being sent to England for processing. I eventually wrote Ms. Peacock and told her what it was "Frick" and "Frack" were doing in the Soviet Union.

But that was not to be the end of the story. In some ways it was just the beginning.

Postscript: Anatoly Scharansky was in prison under intense interrogation from March of 1977 until July 1978. Scharansky apparently did not break under interrogation and was finally tried without being defended by Alan Dershowitz. Acting as his own attorney, according to reports he did a fairly credible job considering that his principal accuser was also another Soviet Jew, Sanya Lipavsky. Scharansky escaped the death penalty but was found guilty and received a thirteen-year sentence. The prosecution had asked for fifteen years so maybe he got off light! At any rate under pressure for years by stalwart figurers like French President Francois Mitterand and President Ronald Reagan, Scharansky was eventually released in a spy swap where, like in a bad Hollywood movie, the so-called spies from two countries were driven to a bridge and exchanged. The only thing missing was Orson Welles as Harry Lime!

Scharansky immigrated to Israel where he changed his first name to Natan and became an elected official as a conservative member of the Likud Party and one of George W. Bush's favorite authors.

However, in 1998 Scharansky published his long-awaited memoir, *Fear No Evil*, of his travails as a Jewish dissident in the Soviet Union. And that is where things got very curious.

In his book Scharansky tells the story of a KGB interrogator coming into his cell at Lefortovo Prison and throwing down a manuscript that the KGB man tells Scharansky was intercepted at the Moscow Airport. It was, according to Scharansky, a copy of the materials that Mike Kort and I smuggled out of Russia. The KGB man sneered at Scharansky and even told him that the materials were taken from an American "tourist" named "Gold." Gold!

This took place shortly after Mike and I returned from the Soviet Union. If I was indeed the "Gold" (could there have been two "Golds?") that the KGB man was referring to then he was lying or this could never have happened. Because Mike and I got the film of the manuscript out of the Soviet Union and it was, according to our sources, sent on to England for processing and translation. So there are some questions here:

1. How could the KGB man have known my name unless he was the KGB guy who interrogated me at the airport? Maybe I had been reported by the Intourist aide for going off the tourist reservation.

2. Was there a report filed by the KGB with my name on it saying I gave up the manuscript we had on film? If so, the report was a lie.

I did not give it up because I did not have it. It was in the luggage of a woman from Texas.

3. If Scharansky was in touch with other dissidents that we met up with, did they give him my name and tell him what we had been doing in Moscow on his behalf?

4. Where did the KGB agent get our manuscript? Was it sent from England? Or the U.S.? Or was there a KGB infiltrator in Moscow who was trusted by the *Refuseniks?*

Clearly, I do not know the answers to any of these questions. But since I do know that Michael Kort and I got the five rolls of film out of Russia to the United States here are some possibilities:

1. The Jewish pipeline was penetrated by a Soviet double agent who worked in the U.S. or England and he or she sent our materials back into Russia to the KGB.

2. We are lying; none of this happened; and we never got the film out of Russia because we made the whole thing up and there was no film.

3. Natan Scharansky was not telling the truth in his memoir.

4. There were two Americans with the last name of "Gold." If so, how did the second Gold get hold of that manuscript and how could he have been so stupid as to have it on his person at the airport? Was I the smart "Gold?"

Take your pick!

CHAPTER 50

By early January 1978 I was back in my comfortable Sam Spade-like Boston office on Franklin Street to my mundane world as Education Director of the Anti-Defamation League when the phone call came. It was from a Jewish FBI agent I had gotten to know from working at the ADL. The agent, with whom I had met for lunch and coffee a couple of times over the last two years, wanted to know if I was willing to come in to be debriefed about my recent trip to the Soviet Union.

I was surprised. How did he know that I had been in Russia? He wouldn't or couldn't say. Then, no I responded, I was not interested in coming in to the FBI field office to be debriefed since I knew that the FBI had no abiding interest in the emigration of oppressed Soviet Jews.

Then he hit me with a real whammy. There were, he claimed, Soviet agents infiltrating the United States through the good offices of the American Soviet Jewish movement. The people in the movement, the FBI agent claimed, were not even aware that the KGB had penetrated their operations. He then asked if I was willing to go to work as an FBI informant although he did not use that word. My job, he said, would be to attend all meetings, rallies and related get-togethers and report back to the FBI on what was taking place and who was doing what. They obviously wanted me to name names! Names were the name of his game.

Now I am as patriotic as the next guy. And I, unlike too many academic types, have no major beef with the FBI or the CIA or any government agency that is designed to make American lives more secure. Actually, I support the FBI and the CIA (as you will see). In addition, I was acutely aware of the role of the *Judenrat* (the European Jewish Councils) that cooperated with the Nazis during the Holocaust. Not that the FBI were anything like Nazis, but I would not have been comfortable reporting on the activities of many good people I admired. No, I was not at all interested in attending meetings or rallies and reporting back to the FBI. I was happy with my job and although I would have relished at one time working for the FBI, by 1978 it was much too late in my career to become a G-Man. Besides, I don't do bleeding very well. The FBI agent thanked me and that should have been that when it came to Soviet Jewry. Except for the fact that it was not!

On January 18, 1978 I published a piece in *The Boston Globe* op-ed page called "Trapped in the Land of Frozen Hearts." It was my homage to the Katz family and their plight in Moscow. I told of our Thanksgiving night spent bonding and I meticulously outlined the family's precarious situation that I found to be so typical of the plight of Soviet Jewry. I was proud of the piece but must admit that few in the Boston media were moved by my article. The only response I really remember getting came from Boris Katz's mother, Khaika Landsman who lived in Cambridge. She, of course, was deeply appreciative but aside from some other Katz family members and the Action for Soviet Jewry people, it was an early morning winter's yawn over "pass me the coffee." The op-ed editor noted that she would be glad to publish anything else I had to say about Soviet Jewry. But my interests lay elsewhere and I told her that I would continue to submit my op-ed thoughts on a variety of other subjects.

The phone call came to my home in Boston late one icy winter's night at the end of January. It was Boris Katz in Moscow. I was so amazed that I could be talking to someone in Moscow that I did not even think to ask how he had gotten my phone number. At first, I couldn't understand what the problem was because Boris, with his thick Russian accent, wasn't explaining it coherently. I got him to calm down and speak slowly. And this is what he told me.

His baby daughter, Jessica, was gravely ill. He had taken her to the hospital in Moscow but was told there was nothing the Russian pediatricians could do for the baby. "What is the problem?" I asked. The baby had stopped eating and was slowly starving to death. She wouldn't take mother's milk and she was losing weight. Boris made it clear that if something wasn't done that he felt the baby would die in a matter of days.

"Hey Boris," I said. "I'm in Boston, Massachusetts. You're in Moscow. There are a few thousand miles between us; and an ocean or two. What the hell can I do here in Boston?"

"Mar-teen," he said in that thick accent. "You must help us. The baby will die. Please!"

I took Boris's phone number and told him to give me until the next day to figure out what, if anything at all, could be done.

Before ringing off I asked Boris if he thought his treatment by the Soviet medical people at the hospital had anything to do with his being a *Refusenik*. No, he answered. He did not think so. "Great!" I thought to myself. I couldn't even make a case for Soviet anti-Semitism.

I immediately called Mike Kort. Mike said he would think on it and meet me the next day in my office on the fifth floor. Mike's office was on the fourth floor. There had to be something we could do; but what?

The next months passed by in a blur of feverish activity. I am hard pressed to exactly recall who did what. But this is the closest I can come to what actually happened. The four activists in the forefront of the situation were Mike Kort from the American Jewish Committee, Bailey Barron and Judy Patkin from Action for Soviet Jewry and me from the ADL. Much of the financial support came from the ever-charitable Bob Gordon, CEO of Store 24 and the guy who had financed our original sojourn to the Soviet Union. Somebody, probably Bailey Barron or Judy Patkin, got to a Boston pediatrician, Dr. Richard Feinbloom. As it turned out Dr. Feinbloom had been to the Soviet Union along with his wife as part of a group called Physicians for Social Responsibility. He was keenly aware of the situation for Jews in Russia who wanted to emigrate. Feinbloom called me the next night at home. I told him as much as I knew, gave him Boris Katz's Moscow phone number and after a conversation with Boris, the doctor called me with his diagnosis which turned out to be right on the money.

Jessica Katz, according to Dr. Feinbloom, was suffering a somewhat common infant malady called "Mal-absorption Syndrome."

Basically the problem was that the infant could not absorb nutrients from mother's milk or from most infant formulas. It had something to do with the inability of the infant's digestive system to take in nutrition at an early stage of development. Soviet pediatrics, the doctor told me, were light years behind American medicine in dealing with this problem. However, there was an easy solution. American pharmaceutical research had developed an infant formula called Pregestimal (predigested formula) to deal with this very serious but resolvable medical situation. Our problem had nothing to do with Soviet anti-Semitism. It had everything to do with the fact that the Russian doctors had no treatment for Mal-absorption Syndrome; and the fact that the Soviet medical officials were possibly embarrassed by the fact that they could not treat the common childhood malady and so did little or nothing.

Over the next days we all sprang into action. We got cases and cases of Pregestimal and every week for the next ten months or so tourists who entered the Soviet Union carried in their luggage as many cans of the stuff as they could pack. Within two weeks or so Pregestimal was flowing without any problem into Moscow and right to the Katz household. Long story short: the Pregestimal worked, as Dr. Feinbloom had predicted, and aside from a few scares over the next months when supplies trickled down or Jessica developed a fever, Jessica Katz slowly recovered.

But, after meeting with Mrs. Landsman, the grandmother, and the Katz brothers in Cambridge, it was apparent to all of us—Mike, Bailey, Judy and myself—that we couldn't keep up the traffic indefinitely and that our goal should be to publicize the Katz family's problem in the local media with the hope that *The Boston Globe, The Boston Herald* or even some of the TV stations would become interested. Over the next two or three months I published a number of anti-Soviet pieces in both papers focusing on the emigration and health plight of the Katzes, their Boston relatives and the failure of the Soviets to treat the baby. Action for Soviet Jewry, led by Judy and Bailey, put media kits together with the full story of the Katz family's dire situation and we sent them off to the western world: Congressman, senators, reporters (print, radio and TV), wealthy Jews, leading Catholic clergy—just about anyone who might listen or help. By March I received a call from a local reporter at Channel 7, the CBS affiliate at the time in Boston. Could she come to the ADL office to do an on-camera interview? Do I love the Phillies?

The reporter's name was Charlene Mitchell, a gorgeous black woman who seemed to be a real comer at the station and in Boston's competitive but small TV market. Although we didn't know one another, we hit it off and the interview about the plight of a sick baby stuck in the Soviet Union because of her parent's *Refusenik* status (according to the Soviets, it was Natalya Katz who was in possession of state secrets which precluded their leaving Russia), struck a real chord with Mitchell. After the interview Mitchell asked me to make a deal with her. If I promised to call her with whatever new developments broke with the family over time, she would get first dibs at the story, and she in turn would put our efforts on camera before the New England TV audience whenever we wanted as things progressed.

I don't recall how many times we went on TV over the next ten months or so with the plight of Jessica Katz. But it was a lot. Mitchell lived up to her part of the deal and would show up with a camera crew at 72 Franklin Street, across the street from Filene's, whenever I called.

Mike Kort, a bit shyer than I (actually a lot shyer), never once complained that I was getting all the TV exposure. And neither did the women from Action for Soviet Jewry. Our goal was to keep the story going because as far as we all knew Jessica Katz's illness, while arrested for the time being, was hardly cured. I spoke to Boris many times over the next months and he continued to report that Jessica's progress was painfully slow if barely visible. The main problem was that the baby was not gaining weight, she seemed sluggish he said and if the Pregestimal didn't come in for a given week, "the Littlest *Refusenik*" as the media called her, would slip back into feverish illness. So, it seemed as if we were all playing a holding game at best.

That is until we got in touch with Senator Edward Kennedy. I can't recall for sure which of us first made contact with Kennedy's senate office. Or maybe, after seeing so many stories in the papers or on TV, they got in touch with us. I know I spoke with the Senator's staff on so many occasions that I came to see some of his staffers as friends and spoke to them on a first-name basis. And they always took my calls. Now one thing you can still say about the Kennedys: when it came to picking staffers for their senate offices or the White House, those staffs were always first rate. You couldn't be a slacker or a dope or an apparatchik and work for a Kennedy on the policy side. Of course, the political side was far different. But I never had to deal with the ambitious slugs and hangers-on from the senator's political realm. Senator Ted Kennedy's policy people were brilliant and always got right to the heart of any situation as it cropped up. Their help in this situation was immense.

Although I spoke with a great many people in Kennedy's D.C. office over the next months, the staffer I remember best was Jan Kalicki (pronounced Kalitsky). Jan was a Ph.D. and an expert on foreign policy. I believe he staffed the Foreign Relations Committee on which Ted Kennedy sat. By 1978 I had met Senator Ted Kennedy a number of times and each time, although he professed recognition, my take was that he didn't have the foggiest notion who I was or what I did. One time I even met him, one on one, in the lobby of a downtown Boston hotel, where I cheerfully escorted him into a public meeting introducing him to each person on the dais. I have a number of photos proving this particular event in case you are skeptical. Whether or not Kennedy knew I was the guy partially quarterbacking the Katz family's cause is up for debate; my guess is probably not.

At any rate my contact guy in the senator's office was, besides his press secretary, Jan Kalicki.

Jan was always sympathetic and inordinately helpful over the months as they passed. He often offered up helpful ideas as well. By the way, I still had my job with the ADL and, although I spent about ninety percent of my time that entire year on the Katz's plight working the media or making speeches before Jewish groups, college students and temples, I did my best to keep up with the endless meetings and other mundane bureaucratic bullshit that an ADL staffer is forced to endure. For some reason I never quite understood, the Director never stopped me from whatever it was I was doing in the area of Soviet Jewry (which was hardly an ADL priority in 1978-79). He could be difficult in so many other ways…but when it came to a Soviet Jewish family in trouble, and all the TV time I was racking up on the nightly news with Charlene Mitchell, he stayed out of my way and always seemed supportive after the weekly updates I would give him on the Katz case.

When Jan Kalicki asked one day what our goals were I gave him the simplest answer possible: we want the entire Katz family out of Russia (by then Boris and Natalya were pregnant with another child on the way).

Once again: long story short. Late that summer or early in the fall Ted Kennedy traveled to the Soviet Union for a meeting with Premier Leonid Brezhnev. Tell me that the Kennedy name didn't carry cache in major foreign circles and I'll sell you the Bourne Bridge to the Cape. Senator Kennedy presented the Russian premier with a list of people he had probably gotten from Kalicki who had gotten the list from us. On it were Boris, Natalya and Jessica Katz and some other prominent *Refuseniks*. Remember, Brezhnev's best intelligence in late 1978 was that there was great disillusionment with Jimmy Carter—especially among American Jews (which is probably why Jimmy Carter has always practiced ugly payback to the Jews and Israel as our worst president and worst ex-president in American history). While the senator was far from ready to announce going against a sitting Democratic president, Premier Brezhnev must have been aware that Senator Edward M. Kennedy could possibly become "President Kennedy" in 1980.

Late that November, exactly a year after we met with the Katz family in Moscow, Senator Kennedy's office announced publicly that the Katz family was soon to be on a flight to Boston from Moscow. Kalicki called me to inform me that Brezhnev had folded his tent, and that Boris and his family were going to be free. Could we all come to Logan Airport that Friday with the Senator to greet the family as they got off the plane?

We all met Senator Kennedy in the VIP lounge at Logan Airport that last Friday in November. Bailey, Mike, Judy, Dr. Feinbloom, Boris's two brothers, Victor and Mischa, and his mother, Khaika (Clara) Landsman, and I waited with tremendous pride that our mutual efforts had gotten a sick baby and her entire family out of the Soviet Union. I spoke privately with the Senator who spent much of his time speaking into a nearby telephone on a table. We made some small talk, talked about the past year-long effort and, when I got close to the Senator, I could tell he was fairly well lit for so early in the afternoon. The smell of the alcohol he had obviously consumed at lunch was unmistakable.

I tried to give credit where credit was due—to the excellent work of Jan Kalicki who I believe was the one staffer who got the senator focused on our Soviet problem. Kennedy acknowledged that Jan was a valuable and trusted member of his staff and then went back to his phone after some photos were taken (I still have them!).

By four o'clock the plane from Russia had landed and off came Boris, Natalya, Jessica and their new-born baby girl, Gabriella. What I didn't anticipate was the mob scene at the airport. Of course, Charlene Mitchell was there with her TV crew; but so was NBC, ABC and every other TV news, radio and newspaper operation in the western world. There were literally hundreds of people I never saw before watching from behind a cordon when Boris, who recognized me instantly, rushed into my arms for a bear-hug with tears in both our eyes (I have a photo of that too!). Kennedy, looking uncomfortable, stood there sober and dry-eyed. But he also seemed somewhat amazed at the crush of media and humanity. He kept saying to me as I stood next to him, "Isn't this something!" I don't know who alerted all the media. I just know, aside from a piece on our triumph that Mike Kort and I had penned for *The Boston Globe* the next day and Charlene Mitchell from Channel 7, I never spoke to another soul.

That night, to my mother's everlasting amazement in Philadelphia as she watched her eldest son standing next to Senator Ted Kennedy at Logan Airport, Walter Cronkite reported on the happy and festive arrival of the Katz family in Boston, Massachusetts. It was an amazingly great feeling of accomplishment after so many meetings, brick walls and frustrations over the course of a long year. All of our long hours of work and plans had seemingly come to a successful fruition.

But for some reason the fates were not smiling. What is that old saying about snatching defeat from the jaws of victory?

CHAPTER 51

In the midst of all the euphoria at the airport none of us were paying very much attention to a number of little details.

First, Jessica Katz looked terrific. Her face was round, pink and cherubic and she hardly looked like an infant who had been at death's door for most of the year. The media, who had dubbed Jessica Katz "the Littlest *Refusenik*" over the course of that year, smelled blood in the water and like the good tiger sharks they were, some reporters began to circle in for the kill.

Second, none of us were aware that *The New York Times* had sent a Boston stringer to the airport to cover the arrival of the Katz family. I was busy trying to live up to my deal with Charlene Mitchell, who had certainly been good to me personally over the course of the year, and see that she got an exclusive with the family in the midst of all the tumult at Logan Airport. Charlene got her exclusive and seemed very appreciative that I didn't forget her and her crew.

An NBC national TV reporter, Robert Hager, had approached me at the airport. Where would we all be that evening? I told Hager that as far as I knew we were all going back to the grandmother's apartment for a quiet celebratory dinner in Cambridge. Hager wanted to come to the apartment with a news crew for an interview with the family.

I didn't know Hager personally but I had certainly seen his reporting over the years. A first-rate journalist who always seemed to get his stories right, Hager reported in a low key but matter of fact manner. So I arranged with the family for the NBC crew to come to Cambridge that evening for an interview. They did and the interview, of which no one but the immediate family took any part, went very well. As I recall, it aired that Saturday night on the NBC national news.

What none of us could have possibly known was that, at the airport, the *Times* stringer had turned to someone in the crowd to ask how it was that baby Jessica looked so well. After all, he said, we had been selling the media that the child was at death's door for almost a year! Well, not exactly. We all had actually stopped calling it a matter of life and death by the previous April when it had become apparent to the Bostonians involved that Jessica Katz was slowly improving as a result of the Pregestimal. But that little point escaped the *Times* reporter whose antenna went up when the person to whom he had addressed his question about Jessica's robust looks replied, "I guess we really all fooled you!"

Now I have no idea who it was who had spouted that nonsense to the *Times*. Bailey Barron later that week said that it was some scatter-brained volunteer from Action who had little professional expertise in dealing with reporters. But it hardly mattered. The next day, Saturday, *The New York Times* reported that the American public, Senator Kennedy, and Mr. Peanut had been hoodwinked by a group of aggressive Soviet Jewry activists: primarily Bailey Barron, Judy Patkin, Michael Kort and your obedient servant were the scam artists who had willfully misled the press, the public and the politicians.

The next day, Sunday, was even worse. The lead editorial in the *Times* was headlined "Jessica Kats (sic) Riding Hood." What none of us knew at the time was the fact that the editor of the editorial page, Max Frankel, had a bee in his bonnet for Jewish activists whom he was convinced were interfering with and doing serious damage to American foreign policy. Frankel, a German Jew who had escaped Hitler's Germany as a youngster, saw the issues with the Soviets in much larger terms than we did. Sometimes, though, the big picture is not the prism from which to peer into the human element in a particular page of Jewish history.

Frankel felt that, with the Cold War still raging, some American Jews were playing with nuclear fire whenever they did anything that went beyond the approval of the State Department to piss off the Russians. Well, he was right about one thing: we often did our best to piss off the Russians. But once again, as a student and teacher of the Holocaust for many decades, I never did anything just to piss off the Russians. Whatever any of us did when it came to Soviet Jewry, I always felt, was a direct result of what the American Jewish community did not do between 1933 and 1945 that ultimately resulted in the decimation of one-third of world Jewry. There were still between 2 and 3 million Jews in the Soviet Union. If Brezhnev and company were making life miserable for them…well, it was a problem that good people like Bailey Barron, Bob Gordon and Judy Patkin would not let go unresolved if they could possibly do something about it.

So Max Frankel was more than wrong. He was a German Jewish ostrich with his head in the sand—or more likely, like many at the *Times* over the years, up his ass!

The "Jessica Kats Riding Hood" piece was a killer. It argued that all our efforts were based on a fairy tale—a big lie which we had propagated to achieve our dubious ends.

It was one thing for *The Boston Globe* to hammer you. You could simply fail to send the piece on to the New York ADL office and they would never be the wiser; but *The New York Times?* In 1978 *The New York Times* was still the only paper of record in these United States. In my world it was the Bible. If the *Times* printed it, so it went, it had to be true!

However, we were not without resources in the media of our own. Bailey Barron's brother, who I came to know and respect very much over the years, is Sydney Schanberg—at that time the city columnist for the *Times*. You might remember Sydney Schanberg as the Pulitzer Prize winning reporter whose reportage from Cambodia when the country fell to the genocidal Khmer Rouge in 1975 was superb. Sydney went on to pen a small book, *The Death and Life of Dith Pran,* which became the Oscar nominated film *The Killing Fields* in 1984 starring Sam Waterston as Sydney Schanberg.

Of course, Sydney had to tread lightly at the *Times* whose policy, first and foremost in those heady days, was to never admit to making a journalistic mistake. As historian Arthur M. Schlesinger, Jr., noted in his journal of a fancy New York dinner party he attended in 1980 where one of his least favorite people, Max Frankel, was present, "The *Times* has a terrible effect on people who work for it. They cannot bear any criticism of anything the *Times* ever does; they act as if it were lese-majeste."

Sydney reached the stringer in Boston who had first reported the story and got the reporter to go back and at least get our side of the story; which he did. However, the part with our side of the Katz epic which was reported accurately was buried in the inner pages of the paper and didn't get the kind of exposure we had all hoped it would get.

As for Max Frankel, Sydney got nowhere. Frankel adamantly refused to issue a retraction of his vicious and fractious essay on our efforts to get the Katz family out of Russia. Frankel simply dug in his Germanic heels.

Meanwhile, I had some serious problems of my own. Bailey Barron and Judy Patkin were volunteers. I was the Director of Education for the New England regional office of the Anti-Defamation League. That Monday the Director of the Boston office received an angry phone call from Arnold Forster, the titular director of the Civil Rights division of the League but who was in reality the co-director of the ADL along with the national director, Ben Epstein. Forster initially asked my boss if he had ever met me. Forster didn't seem to know who I was. Of course, Forster and I had met on a number of occasions. I even picked him up once at Logan Airport and drove him around the city of Boston. But to Forster, one of the national ADL leaders with an ego almost as big as his mouth, I was just another lick-spittle hired to see that the Grand Pajandrums of the ADL found their way from Logan Airport to Harvard Yard and back again. Forster was, according to my Director, livid about the *Times* reporting. He never actually spoke to me. In Forster's mind I had knowingly embarrassed the ADL by lying to the Old Gray Lady for many months. Lying to the *Times,* in the inner sanctum of the ADL where the *Times* was akin to the Old Testament, could be an executable offense.

Arnold Forster told the Boston Director to fire me immediately. Once again, the New England Regional Director stepped up to the plate on my behalf. I suppose he was acutely aware that we had done a good and decent thing and, wherever the truth lay, we had truly aided in getting a Soviet Jewish family to the West and to freedom. He also knew that we were pressing the *Times* hard for a retraction or, at the very least, for coverage of our side of the story. As I said, we did get the Boston stringer to write our version of events. And when that appeared a few days later, it apparently ameliorated the order for my execution issued by the overly excitable Mr. Forster. So I wasn't fired.

But I wasn't quite done with the likes of Max Frankel. I desperately wanted him to know the truth of the matter and how much damage his editorial had done to so many decent and dedicated people. So I put a media kit together which proved along a timeline I carefully traced for him exactly what we had done, when we had done it and how we had done it. An inveterate saver of any paper trail I have ever left in this life, I had an entire large carton filled with copies of every newspaper story, every memo, every meeting, and every letter I had received or written on behalf of Boris Katz and his family over the course of the last eleven months. I sent the material to Frankel in a packet with a long letter that I hoped would explain exactly what had transpired from the time Mike and I returned from the Soviet Union and how no one had ever misled the media in any way. I made the mistake, in the last line of my letter to Frankel, of telling him that I was ashamed of him as a Jew. What do you want? I had just turned forty that November and was still filled with piss and vinegar. I guess I knew it would piss him off but I had to let Frankel know what an asshole I thought he was (and is!)

Frankel chose to ignore all the materials I sent that proved our case beyond a shadow of a doubt. None of it mattered to him when American Jews without portfolio took it upon themselves to screw with official American foreign policy. I didn't know then that Max Frankel was one of those New York types who partied hearty with the effete New York literati set and especially the two magnificent Normans (Podhoretz—one of my personal heroes—and Mailer). A few weeks later Frankel wrote me back a long, scathing letter explaining why he chose to nail us to the barn door with his editorial and, in his last line to me, made it quite clear that what I had written about our efforts and work in behalf of the Katz family had made him sad; but what I had written in that line about his lack of Jewish commitment really made him angry. As they say in West Philly, "Tough shit!" When it comes to Jews like Max Frankel, I'm firmly in the Schlesinger, Jr., corner.

The last time I saw Jessica Katz in person was at her *bat mitzvah* sometime around 1982. She seemed healthy, well brought up and very adjusted to her new life in the United States. Unlike her parents and grandmother she spoke flawless English.

And then on August 25, 2009, the day Senator Kennedy died, who should appear on the national news but a grown thirty-something Jessica Katz. Attractive, well spoken and living in New York, Jessica made sure to tell the interviewer that Senator Edward M. Kennedy had saved her life as well as that of her family. Well...duh...yeah. That would be true; but only partly. Ted Kennedy did travel to the Soviet Union to petition Leonid Brezhnev on behalf of the Katz family. But there were a whole cartload of decent people, who worked for the better part of a year to get the Pregestimal into the Soviet Union; who relentlessly worked the media every day; who's daily lives for that year started and ended with the Katz family; and who almost lost their very livelihood because of those efforts. Not to mention the tenacity of a grandmother and two uncles who never gave up on their family.

What about Senator Kennedy's amazing staff? They labored assiduously in behalf of the Katz family and the only mention they have ever gotten...is right here! Scanning the internet recently I came across some bozo from Ohio who worked in Congressman Tom Lukens's office on the Hill at the time of the Katz case claiming credit for saving Jessica Katz. Apparently our "hero" had written a letter to Senator Kennedy on the Congressman's stationary asking Kennedy to go to the Soviet Union on behalf of the Katz family. Obviously, this bozo had no idea that hundreds of letters were written, thousands of media packets sent out and endless calls were made to any senator or congressman on the Hill who would listen. It was nice that this guy wrote a letter to a U.S. Senator. But his letter was only one of hundreds!

"The Littlest *Refusenik*" and Lukens's ego-centric former staffer need a quick history lesson. A lot of hands went into the cake that baked its way to freedom in the West for the family of Jessica Katz.

CHAPTER 52

The Katz family saga had made me aware of a number of things. I knew that my days at the Anti-Defamation League in Boston were numbered. Kissing rich Jewish ass was not what I wanted to do with the rest of my life. While I supported the politics of the ADL (neo-conservative, pro-Israel, anti-bigotry, pro-civil rights), I despised the endless emphasis that New York forced on the professional staff to raise money, raise money, raise money! Not to mention the stifling bureaucracy within the agency.

It took another three years for me to figure exactly what it was that I wanted to do. At the end of 1983 the ADL and I parted amicably when I refused an assignment to direct a number of offices far removed from Boston which had become, for better or worse, my home town. I was not offered the Boston office when the Director retired. And I was not about to move to Seattle, Pittsburgh or West Palm Beach, Florida!

By that time my close friend Michael Kort, a Ph.D. in Russian history, had joined the faculty of Boston University as a history professor. But in 1979 things were not all that clear for either of us. Mike detested his job at the American Jewish Committee as assistant director. I barely tolerated my job at the ADL because administrative changes in New York had put me under the oppressive thumb of a virtual tyrant who delighted in harassing staffers who, in the reorganization, had found themselves in his department and under his malignant control.

Without the Katz family to worry about in 1979, I was mostly turning out quarterly News Letters about anti-Semitism and neo-Nazis in Providence, Rhode Island, Portland, Maine or Worcester, making Sunday morning speeches to the B'nai B'rith, a Jewish organization that had little reason to exist but at the time was affiliated tenuously with the ADL, forced into organizing fundraisers that celebrated people who hardly deserved to be honored as well as writing endless press releases for Arnie Forster's newest film on Israel. This ego-centric

Mandarin squandered thousands of ADL's precious dollars making these desultory movies about Israeli archeology digs and old burial sites in Jerusalem; and then he would pressure the regional offices to get his damn films shown in cities across America. We actually got somebody on the local PBS station to show one of his stupid films. But he constantly haunted my boss who in turn would constantly haunt me to get a Forster-produced film, starring Arnold Forster of course, on local TV.

Sharing our mutual discontent with our lot, Michael and I decided to write freelance as a team to see if Boston journalism might have a solution to our woes. We contacted Bob Sales, the editor at the *Boston Phoenix* and after a friendly lunch Sales agreed to credential us as reporters for the *Phoenix,* a very popular and hip Boston alternative weekly. Mike and I would work on stories mostly on weekends but sometimes, since we were only separated by one floor at the Boston Jewish Pentagon, as 72 Franklin Street was called, we were able to discuss stories we might work together.

Bob Sales was as good as his word. He published stories we wrote on Boston crime; shoplifting in the big Boston chains and department stores and a number of other topics that cropped up throughout the early part of 1979. Once in a while he even gave us the cover of the book. I recall rushing to the Out of Town News in Harvard Square on a number of occasions to get my early copy of *The Phoenix* with our by-lines splashed on the cover.

Meanwhile, I was still submitting columns to the *Boston Globe* and the *Boston Herald* where the op-ed editors published virtually everything I sent in. By mid-1979 Mike and I were establishing ourselves as a team who could do an in-depth investigative piece on just about anything. Bob Sales always seemed to like our ideas for stories. It looked as if we were on our way as journalists if only we could come up with that big Boston story—the story that every writer dreams will one day drop into their laps.

That summer of 1979 the big story dropped into our laps.

I was talking, as I frequently did in those months, with Tom Southwick, Senator Ted Kennedy's press secretary in D.C. As a result of the Katz family and my connection with *the Boston Phoenix* Southwick and I would speak from time to time. Early in July, in the course of a conversation, Southwick dropped me a bomb. He said something along the lines of, "Well, when we declare soon for the presidency…" I immediately stopped him. "Uh, Tom, we weren't off the record here. You just told me Teddy is running against Jimmy Carter." There was a brief moment of silence. And then Southwick, begged off the line. Clearly, Kennedy's usually adroit press guy had screwed up big time.

Now you have to know that in July of 1979 nobody had a clue that Senator Edward M. Kennedy was going to challenge Jimmy Carter, a fellow Democrat and a sitting president. Even Kennedy family insiders like the Kennedy's court historian Arthur M. Schlesinger, Jr., were in the dark about Ted Kennedy's political plans for 1980. In July of '79 Schlesinger hoped Kennedy would run. Bitten hard by the White House bug during the Thousand Days of JFK, Schlesinger, devastated by Robert Kennedy's assassination in 1968, salivated at the thought of the next Kennedy installed in the Oval Office. Besides, like many Democrats after three years of the inept Peanut Farmer, Schlesinger despised Carter. But even after many lunches and meetings with the Senator, the old history professor didn't have a clue. Schlesinger's *Journals* entry for July 11, 1979 reads;

> "Ted was up, and we saw him a couple of times. My feeling is confirmed that, so long as he is not out, he is in; but that he will not initiate a contest against Carter nor even declare a candidacy; instead he will submit himself to events and let events take their course."

Thus, even those closest to Kennedy had no idea that by mid-Summer 1979 the decision had been made. Kennedy was going to run. Tom Southwick, Kennedy's press guy, had unwittingly let the proverbial cat out of the bag. And I was now holding the bag.

Sure, there was a great deal of dissatisfaction with Jimmy Carter (I had written a scathing long think piece for *The Jewish Advocate* which I titled "President Carter and the Jews.") and a lot of people were urging Kennedy to run. But Kennedy, with the ghost of Chappaquiddick still hovering, was like a reluctant debutante at her first cotillion. Southwick, who was obviously deep inside the Kennedy closed tent had inadvertently dropped a vital story in my lap. The question was what was I going to do with it?

Mike Kort and I went over to see Bob Sales at *the Phoenix*. I told Bob of my discussion with Southwick and asked if he would finance a trip for Mike and me to travel to D.C. to nail down the Kennedy story. Each of us had about a month of vacation that summer so we had plenty of time to research the story and write it.

Bob Sales agreed. It was a hell of a story. But, Sales warned, what will you do if your story goes south? It was always wise, Sales told us, to have a backup plan—another story possibility so that the trip (and his newspaper's money) would not be wasted. Did we have a backup story?

As a matter of fact, we did.

CHAPTER 53

I have always had an abiding interest in the American intelligence community. Even though I have never offered a course on the History of American Intelligence, in 1998-99 I taught a course on The History of Terrorism and the Assassination of JFK where I naturally lectured on many occasions on the Central Intelligence Agency. I had read virtually every academic study ever written on the CIA and knew more about the place than the average layman who thought that Felix Leiter, James Bond's CIA counterpart, was what the Company was all about.

In my first year of grad school at Clark University in 1968-69 one of my fellow grad students also became a social friend. His name was James Pavitt. A graduate of the University of Missouri, Pavitt came to Worcester with his wife Ramsey as an NDEA (National Defense Education Act) Fellow in Clark's Ph.D. program in history.

Unfortunately or fortunately for Pavitt he was drafted at the end of his first year at Clark and ended up in the Army. My wife and I threw him a going-away party with the entire history department at our farm but after Pavitt left Worcester I never saw or heard from him again.

However, I followed his career with great interest. After attending the Army's foreign language school and a stint in Germany in Military Intelligence, Pavitt went to work for a sleepy Massachusetts congressman by the name of Harold Donahue. Donahue had the reputation of being a lightweight (like so many Massachusetts congressman of that era) and somewhat ineffective but he did sit on the influential Intelligence Committee. Within a short time James Pavitt found himself working for the CIA.

I'm not sure how but everyone in the history department at Clark knew what Jim was doing and some people often spoke derisively of Pavitt as a CIA Spook (undercover Spy) since it was a time when liberal academic distrust of the Agency was very high.

Interestingly, the last seminar Pavitt and I took together at Clark University focused for a number of weeks on the sneak attack by the Japanese on Pearl Harbor in 1941. We were assigned the classic 1962 study *Pearl Harbor: Warning and Decision* by Roberta Wohlstetter. Since there were only three or four students, including Pavitt and me, in the seminar I wish I could recall what his take was on Pearl Harbor. My memory is good. But it ain't that good!

I offer this seemingly trivial footnote about Pearl Harbor because on September 11, 2001 the very same James Pavitt had risen through the CIA's ranks to become DDO (Deputy Director of Operations) where he managed the CIA's worldwide clandestine operations that cost at least half of the CIA's multi-billion dollar yearly budget. Pavitt served in that position from 1999 to 2004 when he suddenly resigned (a day after George Tenet) in the wake of that massive intelligence failure dealing with "Weapons of Mass Destruction" that had been the Bush administration's main rationale for the second Iraq War that cost another 5,000 American lives and probably (a conservative estimate) the lives of at least 100,000 Iraqis (and at this writing is still going on).

Pavitt was second in the Agency only to George Tenet, the DCIA (Director of Central Intelligence) and Pavitt, in the course of his amazing bureaucratic ascent, had personally briefed presidents from Bush 41 through Bush 43 (as well as many congressional leaders) on the problems of terrorism, national security and American intelligence. More than any standout spook in the Company, including the ubiquitous and somewhat nutty Michael Scheuer (head of the Bin Laden Unit) and Tyler Drumheller (Chief of the CIA's covert European operations) and the mysterious Joseph Cofer Black, (Director of the CIA's Counter Terrorist Center 1999-2002), Jim Pavitt should have been on top of Osama Bin Laden and Al Qaeda's devious plans. Keeping a step or two ahead of Bin Laden and Al Qaeda was hardly above Jim Pavitt's pay grade.

Pavitt sat astride of that expensive and extensive network of CIA covert operations costing U.S. taxpayers billions (not millions!) that stretched across the length and breadth of the globe.

My purpose here is not to take Jim Pavitt, the CIA and 9-11 to task. I hardly know enough historical fact to explain, with its vast worldwide resources, how the CIA failed to prevent September 11, 2001. Scholars like James Bamford, Michael Scheur and many others have called Jim Pavitt to account for being too cautious, too conservative, too un-original and too bureaucratically entrenched as head of the Directorate of Operations. I don't know the historical truth about Pavitt's real responsibility for the dismal failure of American intelligence that led to 9-11. So I leave that verdict to a future Roberta Wohlstetter with access to files that will someday, hopefully, be de-classified.

My interest in James Pavitt goes back to that summer of 1979.

By the summer of 1979 a number of CIA operatives had been assassinated around the world. The head of station in Beirut, Lebanon and the head of station in Athens, Greece were kidnapped and murdered. And other CIA people were being identified and named by a far left-wing group headquartered in D.C. which put out a small periodical titled *Covert Action Information Bulletin*.

Eventually the group even published a much despised book that listed and named CIA agents all around the world. Thumbing through the book that summer I was surprised to see the name of my old grad school buddy James L. Pavitt.

It wasn't difficult to figure out how these creeps were identifying CIA operatives in foreign capitols around the world. As the people in the group who we interviewed were happy to confirm later for Mike and me, they simply worked off published State Department personnel lists which were printed by the Government Printing Office and could be easily purchased at the State Department. Once they figured out who the CIA operatives were, they would publish their names in local newspapers in the cities or country where the CIA officers were stationed. It didn't take long for the enemies of the United States to figure out who they were, where they lived and, if the Company did not get them out quick enough, they would be targeted and possibly murdered. It was, at the time, a priority problem within the ranks at Langley.

For example, if you looked up a name like John Smith and you saw that Smith had been in the military where he had served in foreign capitols or was listed as an Intelligence Officer during his hitch, it was a fairly good bet that if the State Department listed our Mr. Smith as a political officer or an economic attaché, he was an undercover CIA guy. The chance was very good that our fictional Mr. Smith had been stationed in the particular country covertly under aegis of the State Department but was, in reality, a spy.

Michael Kort and I discussed the problem at length. These D.C. lefties were legally (it is now against the law to disclose the identity of a CIA agent or any American intelligence officer) disclosing the identities of men and women who were putting their lives on the line during the still very hot Cold War. It made our blood boil as we examined the problem and we thought that the difficulty the CIA was having with these heinous exposures ought to be brought to light so that the American public would know what was being done against our country right in their nation's capitol. And, we wondered, how many lawmakers in D.C. were aware of the problem?

Our problem, of course, was getting into the CIA. In 1979, in the middle of the Iran hostage crisis, the CIA wasn't too sanguine about opening their doors to a pair of journalists from *the Boston Phoenix*. We placed a call to the *Covert Information* people, and thinking that we were sympathetic to what they were doing because we were writing for *the Phoenix*, they readily agreed to meet with us in their Washington offices and cooperate on an in-depth story. Getting into the CIA was a little tougher—especially since I wanted the top guy, Jimmy Carter's CIA director, Admiral Stansfield Turner.

My two years in D.C. now came into play. You will recall that I had worked for John Warner at the Bicentennial. Warner had come to the Bicentennial immediately after serving in the Nixon Administration as Secretary of the Navy. As a result he brought a number of career Navy personnel along with him. One of them was a pretty straight shooting guy by the name of Captain Herb Hetu. You should know that in the Navy a Captain's rank is not above Lieutenant but is right below Admiral—a Naval Captain is equal to a full-bird Colonel in the Army. As it turned out, by the summer of 1979, Herb Hetu and a number of other Navy guys I knew were working for the CIA. I quickly called some old friends in D.C. and found out that Hetu was serving Stansfield Turner as the chief Public Information officer in the CIA.

I placed a call to the CIA and asked for Captain Hetu. Within a moment or so I had him on the line. Captain Hetu remembered me from my time with Warner but we were never what I would call friends. Hetu was also painfully aware of the problem with the public naming of CIA personnel around the globe. In fact, as he told me, it was a problem of high priority and one that the CIA was at that very time in the process of trying to resolve.

I explained what Mike and I wanted to do. At first Herb was naturally reticent. *The Boston Phoenix* was not exactly required reading in the inner sanctum of the CIA because of its well-known alternative and predictable far-left slant. Captain Hetu only wanted to make sure that green-lighting us into the CIA would not make the situation worse than it already was.

I assured him that we had the best intentions and told him what we wanted to do if we could get to the right people. When I told him that we not only wanted Stansfield Turner but that we also needed to interview a "covert operative" currently working undercover as well as the legal people at the CIA, Herb laughingly responded that it was probably not going to happen. Once again he asked for my word that we were not out to do a number on the CIA. And once again I assured him that we were doing the story right down the middle of the road without political qualification. Mike and I just wanted to report the facts without editorializing. Hetu said he'd get back to me.

And he did. At the end of July Mike and I left for Washington, stopping off overnight at my parents in Philadelphia and then driving the final leg of our trip into that Wilderness of Mirrors in Langley, Virginia.

CHAPTER 54

Bob Sales turned out to be right. The Kennedy story went south.

Our first stop in D.C. was Senator Kennedy's office. Tom Southwick sheepishly ushered us into the Senator's inner offices. Over coffee he literally begged us not to do the story. It would be, he said, highly embarrassing and possibly cost him his job. Yes, he admitted, Senator Kennedy was running for the presidency. But the announcement was still many months away and what he had said to me over the phone was an inadvertent slip of the tongue.

Kennedy, as well as his people we were informed, would not cooperate with any story we had in mind. Thus, we simply had one line which, of course, was eminently deniable. However, if we agreed not to do the story, Southwick promised, we would have access to the Senator anytime we wanted in the course of what would be a dynamite campaign where Ted Kennedy was going to attempt to unseat a sitting president in his own party. Southwick was offering us an IOU for some future access to a candidate who would obviously be sought after by all the journalistic big-foots like Bob Woodward and David Broder in the Washington press corps.

Not wanting to ruffle Senator Kennedy's feathers or, at the same time, to cause his press secretary more grief than he normally experienced in such a pressure cooker of a job, Mike and I left with the naive hope that we would get to Kennedy sometime in the near future. But there was to be no near future for another Kennedy in the White House.

As it turned out Kennedy did announce for the presidency early the next year. He turned out to be a dismal candidate; his campaign was a political disaster from the very beginning what with Bob Shrum and many of the old Kennedy hands like brother-in-law Stephen Smith at odds with one another over crafting a sellable message and running things; and after the Roger Mudd interview on CBS everyone knew that Ted Kennedy was political toast and that, for better or worse, Jimmy Carter would once again be the Democratic candidate in 1980.

So, sadly we were never able to cash Southwick's Ted Kennedy IOU. And that is the closest I ever came to that really big story—until the 2004 presidential election and John Forbes Kerry. We will get to that.

However, we still had our CIA story. We headed for Langley, Virginia.

Admitted to the CIA parking lot, we walked past the statue of Nathan Hale, America's first spy, standing his silent vigil in front of CIA headquarters in Langley. The CIA, with its modern architecture, reminds one of a post-1960 college campus in states like Florida. As you walk around the "campus" that view is reinforced by the casual dress and professorial demeanor of many of the CIA's employees. Long hair, casual dress and beards were not in short supply at the CIA in 1979.

Mike and I were ushered into that large reception area of the main building by an armed guard where there is a wall adorned with dozens of stars—each star representing an agent killed in the line of duty. There we waited for Herb Hetu to meet us so that we could get the lapel passes that would allow us entry into the CIA's inner sanctum. After accomplishing our credentialing, Herb led us upstairs to the seventh floor office of CIA director Admiral Stansfield Turner. I recall Mike and I staring at one another in wide-eyed disbelief. We were actually getting a face to face with the head of U.S. intelligence.

Admiral Turner greeted us warmly in his spacious well-appointed long rectangular office and we sat down in the center of Turner's digs on a large comfortable beige couch with a coffee table. Stan Turner seemed right out of central casting for the job. With a warm and disarming smile Admiral Turner was Hollywood handsome and could easily have replaced Henry Fonda or Frederick March as the presidents in *Fail Safe* or *Seven Days in May*.

Captain Hetu made the intros and placed a tape recorder on the coffee table. And we, in turn, placed our tape recorder right next to his. Both recorders were voice activated.

"Well," Turner said, "let's get to it!"

We had already interviewed the people who were exposing CIA agents around the world and we knew almost all there was to know about their politics, motivation and methodology. They had been quite open and candid in our interview believing that they were talking to two left-wing alternative press reporters who couldn't have been more sympathetic to their activities. Although Mike and I did the interviewing straight down the middle without editorial comment or input, we had done nothing to disabuse them of their preconceived notion about us. If they wanted to think we liked to see CIA agents getting whacked in foreign capitols, well…that was their business.

Our first question for the CIA director went along the lines of, "How much damage were these anti-CIA activists actually causing to CIA and American intelligence operations around the globe?"

Turner was inordinately candid and straight forward. The Covert Action people, he told us, were hurting the CIA badly. In addition to the agents who had already lost their lives, operatives like my old grad school friend James Pavitt, named in their major publication, had to be pulled out of assigned stations and reassigned because exposing them put their work as well as their lives and the lives of all their contacts in grave jeopardy. And the CIA legal people, Turner said, were looking into ways to counter their devious efforts legislatively. In addition, measures had already been put into place to change CIA policy in regard to providing cover for covert agents in regard to their entree into the various capitols and trouble spots of the world.

Our interview, which went on for a little less than an hour, could not have gone better.

Whatever questions we asked were answered honestly by Admiral Turner. He did not attempt to minimize the damage that had been done or the importance of the story. Unlike too many politicians and government bureaucrats who, when asked a question by an interviewer rarely answer the question posed and dance around it, Turner responded to all our questioning with an answer that made sense and rounded out all the parts of the story that needed further clarification.

When we finally ended the interview and the tape recorders were no longer running, I turned to Admiral Turner with one final question. I don't think Herb Hetu appreciated this question but it was not going into our story anyway. Though it was not off the record, at the time I felt compelled to ask it. Over three decades later it is still, I think, a pertinent question because I firmly believe that right now (March, 2011) the greatest danger to the United States is Iran (not Iraq; certainly not Afghanistan; maybe Pakistan) and the possibility that fundamentalist Muslim madmen who have an apocalyptic vision of life on this planet will soon control nuclear devices.

"What happened in Iran? How did you miss the signals?" I asked the CIA director. By that time the Iranian hostage crisis was one of the major news stories of the year as the Shah had abdicated, the Iranian revolutionaries had seized the American embassy and the Ayatollah Khomeini had returned from France to run the Iranian revolution that was to ultimately cost the lives of first thousands and then, in the Iran-Iraq war, millions.

Without missing a beat Admiral Turner looked me in the eye and said, "We screwed up!" And that was the end of the interview. He did not go into any more detail than that.

As we left the seventh floor to meet with a CIA lawyer and an operative who was currently working undercover, Captain Hetu remarked in the elevator that he thought the interview went well considering the fact that few journalists ever got face time with the Admiral. He did not reproach me for going into the Iran screw-up. Our interview with the CIA legal counsel and the undercover operative did not reveal much more for our story. I remember asking the CIA undercover (who over the years I have seen interviewed on TV) what the real damage was as a result of the exposure of agents. The guy thought for a few seconds and then replied that the CIA relied on the power of mystique to accomplish many of their ends and if that mystique was ultimately threatened, CIA case officers would have greater difficulty recruiting locals in various countries where the CIA was conducting sensitive covert operations. And that could lead, he said, to a grave danger to the United States in countries where intelligence was paramount in the successful pursuit of the nation's Cold War objectives. Remember, it was 1979.

Mike and I returned to Boston content with the fact that we were bringing a major story to light for the New England alternative press's audience. We worked on the story diligently for the better part of the next two weeks. And we fought a lot. That was how Mike and I got to complete every story we did together. Arguing with one another over this paragraph or that phrase inevitably produced a cleaner, more concise and clearer manuscript. When we were finished we had a story of almost 5,000 words that we were proud to turn in. It was, we both were convinced, the best work we had ever done together. We didn't editorialize. We simply laid out both sides of the issue and, although our sympathies were with the intelligence community, I don't believe that bias ever entered into our manuscript. The reader had the option to choose sides for themselves.

But things at the *Boston Phoenix* had changed in our absence. Our editor, Bob Sales, had left to become managing editor of *the Boston Herald* and he had been replaced by a new editor, Richard Gaines. Long story short: Gaines spiked our CIA story without any explanation. Maybe he was nervous about a new editor producing a major story in liberal Boston that didn't say that the CIA sucked. I don't really know. He paid us for it and he paid our expenses. But the CIA story, as we wrote it, never saw the light of print.

A few weeks later I asked Mike if he would mind if I watered our story down for an opinion piece of about 500 words that I could publish in *the Boston Herald*. Mike, who was aware of the fact that I had been publishing columns in the *Herald* for some time, generously allowed me to publish the piece with my by-line. And so, in the end, the story was told. But not in the way we wanted to tell it or in the way it should have been told.

Eventually in 1982, the Congress passed the Intelligence Identities Protection Act that made it against the law to divulge the identity of an American intelligence agent. I don't know if our efforts had any effect on that legislation but I do know that when Valerie Plame Wilson was exposed as a covert agent in the imbroglio leading up to Bush 43's Iraq

War, that whoever had revealed her identity may not have broken the spirit or the substance of that law. But, aside from the late Robert D. Novak's column naming Plame (who by that time had been outed by others), the 1982 law should be enforced.

CHAPTER 55

After the frustration of losing what had been our best work together to the unsympathetic spike, Mike and I went back to work at our respective jobs and stopped writing together. In short order Mike, who had a Ph.D. in history from New York University, left the American Jewish Committee for a spot at Boston University's College of Basic Studies where he was eventually tenured. In the ensuing years Michael Kort has produced a prodigious amount of scholarly work. His book, *The Soviet Colossus* was a Book of the Month Club selection and, utilized in college courses around the country, is still in print. His other works on the Cold War and the decision to drop the atomic bombs on Japan (not to mention over a dozen biographies and regional studies) at the end of World War II rank Mike among the top historians in my book. Sometimes we still wax nostalgic about what "Frick" and "Frack" (our *nom de plumes*) might have achieved if our CIA story had not been killed. Who knows? Kortward and Goldstein maybe?

In the summer of 1980 the ADL sent me to Israel and Egypt on a staff tour. In the Middle East we traveled across the border into Lebanon with a contingent of Israeli soldiers escorted by the Christian *Falange* who were friendly to the Israelis; we visited a pro-Israeli Lebanese radio station that was blown up by Palestinian terrorists some years later; we met with virtually every major Israeli politician including Yitzhak Rabin (assassinated as Prime Minister by a Jewish fanatic in 1995) with whom we had lunch. We attended seminars at various think tanks, visited *moshaves and kibbutzes* and got to see many Israeli military installations including the amazing and heroic young Israeli pilots who were manning F-15s and F-16s at the secluded airbase Ramat David.

After a week or so in Cairo, Egypt I returned to Israel to spend the remaining weeks of that summer living with the ADL's Israel director, Harry Wall, an American who had immigrated to Israel, in his spacious ocean front apartment in the Arab town of Jaffa outside of Tel Aviv. I also spent a few days in an Arab village outside of the Old City. I left when I was warned by a friendly local that I was possibly a target if violence was to break out in the village. The guy told me that there were Arab villagers who would happily cut my throat.

Other than that I settled back into my job at the Anti-Defamation League without any idea of where my life might be headed. For the next three years I virtually treaded water. I suppose if I had had a family I might have been a bit more ambitious. As it was, unlike so many of my friends, I remained alone except for a brief move-in relationship that lasted about a year or so with a very nice woman named Karen Osborne. Karen, a small town girl from western Ohio was a convert to Judaism when she was in grad school at Harvard. She worked with Mike Kort at the American Jewish Committee and we began dating in 1978. We moved into a comfy town house in suburban Newton Highlands during that summer. Karen's major ambition in life was to live and work in the Big Apple. I liked New York; but only for a brief visit. Somewhere along the line life had taken the boy out of Philly and Philly out of the boy. By 1979 Karen Osborne was on her way to New York City as a freelancer via a small academic publication at Rutgers University. After welcoming the New Year of 1980 in with her at her new apartment, I never saw or heard from her again. I was still Bob Feller when it came to lasting relationships with women—the all-time strikeout king!

By 1981 I had left Newton after a disastrous series of housemates convinced me that the only answer to yearly rent increases as well as my endless and obvious bachelorhood was to buy my own home and live alone. I found a battered three-bedroom rancher in a small town, Sudbury, about twenty-five miles west of Boston. The property had a four-stall barn (where I eventually kept chickens) and over fifty trees right on the border of the dark and wooded Hapgood Marsh where one could easily get lost for days in the miles of wilderness surrounding what was still in some respects a rural Massachusetts village. I used to cross country ski for hours in the long winters of my Sudbury years. Once or twice I got lost skiing those woods with the new lady in my life—Ann Marchette, who conveniently lived just around the corner from Autumn Street on Barton Drive with her two young boys, Josh and Benjie.

With darkness approaching early in the winter afternoons, that can be scary. Luckily I would always find my way home—even in the winter darkness.

By 1983 the ADL and I parted ways. My colleague and friend Lenny Zakim had been elevated to director of the Boston office and, although New York offered me options of other offices, I didn't want to work under Lenny and so I opted out. On a visit to Boston the national director, the very capable Nathan Perlmutter, took me aside and asked why I hadn't come to him. He could, he told me, have helped keep me in the agency. I admired guys like Nate immensely (Nathan Perlmutter, only in his early sixties, succumbed to cancer just a few years later and was replaced by Abe Foxman as national director). And I liked the kind of things the Anti-Defamation League stood for and allowed me to do. But the bottom line of ADL, as for most Jewish organizations, was always money. And money was not something that was ever a major interest of mine. Somehow, I always seemed to get by.

I briefly went to work doing press for the burgeoning mayoral campaign of my old friend Ray Flynn. Flynn allowed me access to a desk right in his own City Council office in City Hall and for the next four months I went there every day to try and get Flynn the recognition he so sorely needed to give legitimacy to a campaign that was short on money and, aside from his traditional South Boston leeches and hangers-on, short on experienced political talent. None of the press wise guys gave Flynn a chance to win and although I liked him very much I honestly didn't think he had much of a shot either. When Flynn hired a campaign manager by the name of Ray Dooley, I took my leave. I didn't like Dooley or his leftist politics much and he clearly didn't like me. But I continued to support Ray for mayor and actually published a number of columns on his behalf. Needless to say Ray Flynn succeeded Kevin White as mayor of Boston in 1983!

Fortunately, after almost a decade with the ADL, I had a very generous severance package and what with a door opening for me to teach a couple of courses at Boston University, I wasn't in any danger of going under financially. Although my first mortgage rate was 17% (thanks Jimmy Carter!), somehow I didn't go under and lasted it out until I was able to negotiate a more reasonable interest rate by refinancing a new mortgage.

And then the fates stepped in. Pat Whitley, a well-known radio talk show host in Boston, called me. I had been a guest a number of times on all the Boston talk shows of that era. I had appeared with the most popular Boston talk show host, Jerry Williams, a number of times. I had also been a guest on Avi Nelson's show, on David Brudnoy's show and on Pat Whitley's show. It turned out that Pat had just purchased an AM station in Natick, Massachusetts (about fifteen minutes from my house in Sudbury). The next day I went to the station, WTTP—Touch 1060!—met with Pat and solidified a twice weekly four-hour format for myself dealing mostly with political topics of concern to the New England Jewish community. Of course, in my way of thinking that included the Boston race for mayor and the upcoming 1984 presidential campaign. Pat assured me that the station's signal would get to Rhode Island and New Hampshire in addition to the greater Boston area—and thus was born KOL New England, the Voice of New England.

For the next year or so I combined my teaching at Boston University with my talk show and was also able to fill in for anybody at the station who took a sick day or a personal day. It was a happy and productive year even though I was well aware that I, at the approaching age of 44, was treading financial and professional water. Over the next year my guest list included well-known writers like Bill Novak and Ron Radosh, academics like Alan Dershowitz, some show business people passing through Boston and well-known Massachusetts politicians like Barney Frank and John Kerry who was by 1984 running for the U.S. Senate. On two occasions I even hosted the most notorious rabbi in America or Israel, the head of the Jewish Defense League Meir Kahane, in studio. For years after that, whenever he visited Boston, Rabbi Kahane would call and chat. Although we vehemently disagreed with one another on almost every Jewish issue, we always seemed to get along well. I liked him and he liked me. The calls stopped when

Rabbi Kahane was assassinated in New York City by an Arab fanatic in the early 1990s.

But the real story that came out of that year was my budding relationship with Lieutenant Governor John Forbes Kerry. Kerry, in 1984, would be trading in his do-nothing office far removed both physically and politically from that of Governor Michael Dukakis for the much more important title of United States senator. And that is a story that I have never written about; until now.

CHAPTER 56

It began with a phone call from an old girlfriend. I was still at the ADL. It was around late 1980. Would I be interested in meeting and having a cup of coffee with a prominent Boston lawyer about my age who had some political ambitions? His name, she told me, was John Kerry.

In 1980 most people outside of Boston never heard of John Forbes Kerry. But I suffer that syndrome of indelible memory. I easily recalled a young former naval officer testifying before the Senate Foreign Relations Committee (also called the Fulbright Hearings) about the Vietnam War. I watched his April, 1971 testimony with my then-wife and was struck by it and the disheveled young man in green fatigues on national TV. The former Swift Boat commander asked the politicians a disarming question, "How do you ask a man to be the last man to die for a mistake?" Exactly! I had come to a similar conclusion by 1966: the war in Viet Nam was a huge mistake; a war that cost the lives of over 50,000 American servicemen; not to mention the over one million Vietnamese that were lost. And so much of America's national treasure! Lyndon Johnson's lame attempt at Guns and Butter!

I remember turning to my wife and saying something like, "Get that guy a haircut, take off the worn olive green field jacket and replace it with a nice pin-striped suit and he could be president someday." This was the same John Kerry who my old girlfriend wanted me to meet.

After his time as an activist with the Vietnam Veterans against the War, John Kerry had returned to New England, went to Boston College Law School, ran for Congress and lost, spent some time as an assistant district attorney for an aging DA by the name of John Droney in Middlesex County and then set up a law practice with an attractive female partner he had known since law school. In addition, Kerry appeared from time to time on one of those terminally boring local Sunday TV shows called "Five on 5" that nobody watches except political junkies, their families and nerds (like me). So, sure I knew who John Kerry was and sure, I told my ex-girlfriend, I would be happy to meet him.

A few days later I walked into John Kerry's unimpressive law offices at 60 State Street in downtown Boston and was immediately ushered into his small but comfortable inner office. A tattered but large American flag was framed on the wall near his desk. Probably from his Swift Boat, I assumed. How Kennedy-like I thought to myself. I seemed to recall a similarly framed tattered flag in Ted Kennedy's office which had ostensibly once belonged to his martyred brother JFK.

Kerry waved for me to sit down. He was on the phone. Kerry cupped his hand over the speaker part of the phone and mouthed the words, "Peter Yarrow." I thought to myself, "How many Bostonians would ever know who the hell Peter Yarrow was?" Was that a test? Because I certainly knew who Peter Yarrow was: one-third of my favorite folk music group who I had seen in concert at least three or four times, *Peter, Paul and Mary.*

Kerry finished his conversation with Yarrow and then turned to me with his full attention. We chatted amiably and made small talk: about his military service; about mine; about Boston; about politics. At no time did Kerry try to impress me with his war record or the fact that some people considered him "a hero"—(a fact widely disputed by the book *Unfit for Command* that undoubtedly helped sink Kerry's presidential aspirations in 2004).

We talked about what he had heard about me; about what I had heard (and knew) about him. Kerry flattered me that he had read some of my columns in the *Globe* and *Herald.* I flattered him back relaying the fact that I had watched him on Channel 5 on many a Sunday and had been impressed (not a lie by the way). And I couldn't help but recall his 1971 testimony before the Senate Foreign Relations Committee (a committee he now ironically chairs!) and the comment I had made to my then wife. Kerry didn't respond at all when I mentioned the possibility of the presidency. It was 1980—twenty-four years before his disastrous run for the gold.

Then Kerry turned to the ostensible reason that he had acceded to our meeting.

"If you were me and were thinking of running for office in this state," Kerry posited, "what office would you pick?" I only had to think about the question for a few seconds.

In 1982, the next election cycle, I knew through people close to Michael Dukakis that the former Massachusetts governor who had been defeated by the very conservative Ed King in a Democratic primary in 1978 had decided to make a comeback. The Duke already had a loyal Brookline liberal constituency that would serve as his base, an ambitious former staff salivating for their former boss's return from political exile, a nice stash of campaign cash and a clear shot at unseating the unpopular Governor King who had sent him packing ingnominiously from the State House in '78. The Duke and his forces, led by his fellow Greek Svengali John Sasso, had been plotting their return to Bulfinch's Golden Dome from political anonymity for almost four years. They too had ambitions far beyond the stifling confines of the tiny Bay State.

So Governor was out of the question. Paul Tsongas, the low-key but bright, honest and effective Massachusetts senator, had crushed Republican Ed Brooke in the 1978 U.S. Senate race. And nobody, unless bereft of their senses, would ever take on Teddy Kennedy. Not in Massachusetts where Kennedys were still kings. So, there was only one office that offered John Kerry any semblance of an ongoing political career. And it was undoubtedly the worst office anyone could ever want to inhabit in the Bay State—the do-nothing, coat-holding, and thankless job of Lieutenant Governor.

So I answered Kerry's question: "Lieutenant Governor," I said.

Kerry smiled knowingly. Obviously, I was not the first political wise guy to give him that answer. And I certainly did not flatter myself by thinking I was the first person he had asked that question.

"Well," Kerry said, "that is exactly my thought on the subject."

"Will you be running?" I asked.

"I'm not sure yet. But if I do run I wonder if I can count on your help," he said.

I had no idea what he meant. I certainly couldn't give him big money; I couldn't go to work in the campaign. I had already run into some trouble in the fall of 1980 helping out in Barney Frank's first congressional race. If you work for the ADL, a non-profit, you are not supposed to get involved in politics. Of course, just about everybody I knew in the agency in those days happily violated that stupid rule. I had done a fundraiser for Barney at the Brook House. I had known Barney for years; and also served behind the scenes in some political maneuvering during the campaign (which Barney eventually won). Over the years I have met Barney for breakfast on many occasions. Despite my differences with him politically, I have always liked him and consider him a committed and honest politician with the ultimate idea of doing good for his district and the country.

Anyway, our conversation ended amiably and Kerry asked me to keep in touch.

I was surprised a few weeks later in January 1981 to receive a phone call from somebody (it wasn't Kerry) inviting me to sit at the table Kerry's firm had taken at Boston College for the annual Martin Luther King, Jr., Memorial Breakfast. I had attended the King breakfast off and on over the years. For any ambitious Boston pol the King breakfast is a must show. Every weepy liberal within fifty miles of Boston comes out to sit with his Black brothers and sisters of Boston, to eat the soggy bacon and eggs, to listen to terminally boring and bullshit speechifying and then to join hands in the singing of "We Shall Overcome." You'll even find a few politically ambitious Republicans at the King breakfast each year. Republicans are allowed to overcome in Massachusetts too—only not too much.

Looking around the crowd over the years I always used to think, "Overcome what?"

Most of the blacks in the audience were "buppies" made up of either high-profile church leaders in New England, high-powered Black attorneys or Blacks who had cushy, high paying jobs in state or federal government. You can be sure you won't be finding too many brothers and sisters from the 'hood' of Roxbury at these yearly soirees.

Anyway, I went. I ate the bad eggs; I listened to the boring speeches; and yes, I joined hands and sang "We Shall Overcome." And I sat next to John Kerry and his law partner, one of the most gorgeous blonde-haired, deep blue-eyed women I had ever laid my tired and unmarried eyes on.

After the breakfast Kerry asked me if he could give me a lift to my office which was only a few blocks from his office at 60 State Street. We made small talk on the ride downtown. I recall Kerry telling me that he didn't know how I could cope, on a daily basis, with the tough job of dealing with the endless problem of anti-Semitic violence and discrimination that flooded our offices. By that time I had been in the agency for six years. I guess I was used to it. Kerry dropped me at 72 Franklin Street and he and his law partner continued on to their State Street offices.

As soon as I got back to my office I picked up the phone and called my ex-girlfriend.

"Could you possibly get me Roanne's home phone number?" I asked.

Roanne was John Kerry's law partner.

"Why?" she asked.

"I want to ask her out to dinner," I replied.

There was dead silence on the line for about ten seconds.

"Uh, that wouldn't be a good idea, Marty," my ex-girlfriend said.

"Why?" Stanny Dumm asked.

Ten seconds of silence again.

"Just not a good idea," she finally said.

Mr. and Mrs. Goldman didn't raise an idiot for a son. Nobody had to hit me over the head with a sledge hammer. I got it. It took a bit... but I got it.

"Uh...Kerry and Roanne..." I said.

"You didn't hear it from me," she answered.

And that was it for me, John Kerry and Roanne Sragow. Or so I thought.

CHAPTER 57

Over the next year or so I saw little of John Kerry or his attractive law partner. But then Kerry announced that he was running for Lieutenant Governor. Even though the field was crowded with some very talented young up and coming Massachusetts pols, the media was focused on the Dukakis comeback and Kerry and company got short shrift from the predictable Boston press corps. Nobody gave much of a damn who the next Lieutenant Governor of Massachusetts was going to be; except for John Kerry and Ms. Sragow.

And John Kerry was as aware of that little factoid as anyone.

At some point in 1982 the law firm of Kerry and Sragow had gotten a con named George Reissfelder out of prison. It was a pro bono case with the possibility of a lot of publicity. Reisssfelder had been, according to press reports, wrongly convicted of a 1967 murder and had been unjustly imprisoned at MCI Walpole for years. Their efforts on Reissfelder's behalf received a lot of press in the state and, since I had become friendly with Roanne over that past year or so, I thought maybe there was a good book in the story—or at the least an in-depth magazine piece. Shortly after Reissfelder's release Roanne and I got together for a friendly lunch. We discussed the Reissfelder case and Roanne told me that she had done most of the real legal legwork while John took the vast majority of the media glory. It was, she told me, part of their master plan for his upcoming political race. There was no bitterness. This was a woman who knew exactly what she wanted and where she wanted to go. Of course, I didn't mention the little fact that John Kerry was still married to the former Julia Thorne and that they had two young daughters, Alexandra and Vanessa, and as far as the public knew, everything in the Kerry household looked rosy.—kind of like the Schwarzeneggers. That was, as far as I was concerned, none of my business.

Clearly, though there might have been a great story behind the Reissfelder case, Roanne wasn't going to be the one to write it and, no she said, they didn't want a book or a movie or anything beyond the publicity which the law firm of Kerry-Sragow had already garnered. So I got no sale on the possibility of a Reissfelder book or article beyond what the Kerry-loving *Boston Phoenix* had already published. George Reissfelder apparently didn't much capitalize on his fifteen minutes of Bay State fame. In March of 1991 he was found dead in Quincy, Massachusetts of a cocaine overdose.

The next time I saw Roanne and Kerry was at Alan Dershowitz's Brattle Street home in Cambridge sometime in the early fall of 1982. Kerry had already declared for Lieutenant Governor (as I knew he would) and one Saturday night that autumn he was lined up for a TV debate with the other candidates in the field at a nearby TV studio. A group put together by the Harvard Law professor hosted a small fund raiser for Kerry after the debate. We watched the boring debate at Dershowitz's house (after all who really cares who is the Lieutenant Governor of Massachusetts?) and about fifteen minutes after it was over in walked Kerry and Roanne. It was still none of my business but I wondered where Kerry's wife Julia was that night. The skinny on Julia was that she was inordinately shy, hated the phoniness of politics and preferred to stay at home with her young daughters. Still, it occurred to me, that if Kerry continued to show up at campaign events with Roanne Sragow that people would...well, talk. And, of course in Boston, talk they did.

That previous summer I was Alan Dershowitz's guest for the better part of a week at a rented home in Chilmark on Martha's Vineyard. One night over dinner I recall telling Alan about Roanne and Kerry and my lame-ass attempt to take her out the previous year (before I knew about their legal "partnership"). Nonplussed, Dersh who apparently knew what Roanne looked like asked if I had her phone number. It so happened that I did. Dersh, never a shrinking violet like me, excused himself, found a phone in the restaurant and called her on the spot. He returned to the table smiling; "I have a date with her next week." I shrugged. Who was I to even attempt to understand the strange vagaries of women? "*Mazel tov*," I said. I have no idea whatever, if anything, transpired between Dersh and Roanne Sragow that summer. I never asked and Alan never mentioned her again—except when she was appointed as a district court judge by outgoing Governor Michael Dukakis in 1991 and, for some strange reason, the Dukakis people barred Alan from attending her swearing in at the State House; which pissed the good law professor off in no uncertain terms since he went ballistic and very public over the incident. After all, at the time in the early 1980s, no matter what the crazy circumstances were, they were both single, over twenty-one and consenting adults! At any rate I was in the dark—not a bad place to be considering.

The next memory I have of Kerry that year was of a mammoth fundraiser he held at the Hynes Convention Center in downtown Boston. There were hundreds, maybe even thousands, of people present to hear the future Lieutenant Governor of Massachusetts lauded by performers like Peter, Paul and Mary (Peter Travers once again!), Robin Williams and Chevy Chase. This time, when Kerry took the stage to be hero worshipped by these show biz elites, he was accompanied by his loving wife Julia. She looked really uncomfortable up there…but at least she was up there. The great folk singing trio and the comedians were on stage for hours. In fact, the manic and peripatetic Williams was at his zenith of possibly being the most hilarious comedian I have ever had the privilege to see from the vantage point of my seats right up front in the third or fourth row. The night was an unqualified success. Kerry put a lot of cash into his campaign coffers and the loving Boston media, impressed as we all were with Kerry's ability to pull Hollywood show biz types into the Hub, virtually anointed him as the Bay State's next second in command.

After John Kerry was elected Lieutenant Governor I rarely saw him. Like I said, that office is usually a death sentence for aspiring Bay State pols. Kerry was so far removed from Michael Dukakis's corner offices on the third floor of the State House that it was actually a hike from his office to the Governor's digs.

Once in a while I would bump into Roanne around Downtown Crossing or in Filene's Basement but the extent of our relationship was mostly relegated to small talk when we met. I was having my own problems at the ADL and it really wasn't until the early winter of 1984 that I reconnected with John Kerry. The circumstances were sad.

Senator Paul Tsongas, one of the most decent and capable pols I have ever known, had been elected in 1978 defeating Republican Senator Edward Brooke, the only Black at the time in the U.S. Senate. I knew a number of people connected to the Tsongas campaign and had even supplied the campaign with long lists of possible Jewish donors. While Paul Tsongas was an extremely dedicated senator, some in the Jewish community were not happy with his evenhanded approach to the Israeli-Palestinian issues of that time.

My office hosted a number of successful meetings over the years with the senator and we had maintained cordial relations in spite of our obvious disagreements over Middle East policy. What I liked and most respected about Tsongas was the fact that he never seemed reticent to vehemently disagree with his core constituency—and in Massachusetts the greater Boston Jewish community had always been a central part of that constituency.

In early 1984 Senator Tsongas went public with his diagnosis of a virulent lymphoma and he quickly announced that he was retiring from the Senate after only one term. That announcement set off a firestorm of speculation and media frenzy as candidates for Tsongas's seat came out of the woodwork before it even got a chance to get cold.

There was Congressman Ed Markey; Attorney General and former Congressman Jim Shannon; and, of course, Lieutenant Governor John Kerry among the front runners jockeying hard for position.

About a week after he announced for Tsongas's senate seat Kerry called me at home. I had already parted ways with the ADL. I was teaching history at Boston University's Metropolitan College and hosting a radio talk show for eight hours a week while also filling in at the station, WTTP-1060 AM, for some of the other talk jocks.

Could I, Kerry asked, come down to the State House and see him? The next morning I made my way into Kerry's desultory place of exile under Bulfinch's famed Golden Dome in the Massachusetts State House.

As I was escorted into the Lieutenant Governor's office, Kerry was on the phone. He put his hand over the receiver and mouthed the words, "Paul Simon." Since I didn't think that Kerry was having a tet a tet with the senator from Illinois, I had to assume that he was talking with the better half of Garfunkel. But I never asked. Apparently Kerry had forgotten that he had done the same thing in our initial meeting. I guess he thought celebrity would impress dummies like me.

Kerry and celebrities! It was something John Kerry apparently never learned. Many working class voters look askance at politicians who surround themselves with airheaded Hollywood types. I love Streisand and Springsteen. But I could care less who they think should live at 1600 Pennsylvania Avenue or what they say about the Iraq War or any war.

No small talk for Kerry this time. After finishing his conversation with "Paul Simon," Kerry got right down to business.

"I'm running for the Senate. I want you with me," he said.

"I'm with you!" I answered.

"No…I mean in the campaign," he said.

"Doing?" I asked.

"What do you think you can do? What would you want to do?" he asked.

"Well, I did some press for Ray Flynn in the early part of the Boston mayor's race in '83 and I handled the press for the ADL for years," I said. And then there was my talk radio show and my writing in the *Globe*, *Herald* and *Phoenix*. I knew the major players in the Boston media as well as anyone.

"No," Kerry said. "I already have somebody in that slot."

He sure did; a very attractive woman with about an inch deep of media experience.

"What about foreign policy?" I asked somewhat unhappy with Kerry's obvious politically correct approach to the one hot-button issue I despised—affirmative action.

"No," he answered. "I've hired Michal Regunberg to do my foreign policy stuff."

I knew Michal Regunberg well. We had once dated and had a longstanding off and on friendship. Michal wasn't an inch deep. A

Brandeis grad, she was very bright, had worked in both TV and radio and knew her way around Massachusetts liberal politics.

"So," I asked, "what do you think I could do?"

"I think you know the Jewish community in Massachusetts. I want you to be my liaison to the state's Jewish community," Kerry answered.

John Kerry had done his homework. I did know the major Jewish players in Boston, Worcester, New Bedford, Fall River and Springfield—the key cities in the Bay State.

But then so what! I knew them. But what did that mean. The Massachusetts Jewish community was liberal, but they had no more affinity for John Kerry than they did for say Ed Markey or James Shannon. I was pretty sure the political pie was somewhat evenly divided.

However, my radio show wasn't going that well. By 1984 Boston University was making noises that my course on the Presidency of John F. Kennedy wasn't "cost effective" and I still had, thanks to Jimmy Carter, a 17% interest rate on my mortgage.

I accepted Kerry's offer; with one caveat.

"John," I said, "I don't want to have to go through hoops in order to talk to you. I'll do my best to connect you with the Jewish community. But if I have to talk to you, I don't want to stand in line."

Kerry agreed and promised access throughout the campaign. We came to an easy agreement on salary and I headed for the door. As I reached the door I stopped, turned to the Lieutenant Governor of Massachusetts and said, "Oh yeah John, one other thing. If I do a good job and you win...don't fuck me!"

Kerry smiled, came out from behind his desk, walked over and put his arm around my shoulder and said, "Don't worry Marty! I never fuck my friends!"

On February 25, 1984 Norma Nathan, *the Boston Herald's* well-known gossip writer dropped an item in her popular "The Eye" column under the bold headline: "Goldman goes with John Kerry." It read in part:

> *John Kerry, candidate for the U.S. Senate, had* (sic) *prioritized the Jewish vote in his upcoming campaign. Kerry has named*

Marty Goldman of Sudbury, former public affairs director of the Anti-Defamation League, as liaison to the Jewish community and fundraiser.

Public Affairs Director of the ADL? Oh well. She spelled my name right.

CHAPTER 58

The following week I showed up at Kerry's campaign headquarters, was assigned a desk and got down to work. I connected with a few Boston liberal attorneys who agreed to host a fundraiser at one of their homes. I called a number of big givers from my ADL lists but at that particular moment many political players were hedging their bets. The race seemed too close to call and apparently a great many people didn't want to hook up with the losing team. Kerry, Markey and Shannon were political peas in a liberal pod. Their differences were so few that the Kerry campaign was having difficulty gaining a foothold in the bastion of American liberalism.

After all, what could you attack Markey or Shannon on when you invariably held the same lockstep liberal positions?

After a few days on the job Ron Rosenblith, the campaign manager, asked me to meet him for breakfast. I didn't know Rosenblith but had heard about him. He had been active in Brookline liberal politics; he was close to Kerry (how close I never really knew) and knew next to squat about the Jewish world outside of Brookline, Massachusetts.

At first Rosenblith, who didn't know me, tried to butter me up with "this is the opportunity of a lifetime" and that we were getting in on the ground floor of something really big. That if John Kerry won this senate seat, someday the White House would be in the cards. After the pep talk and encouragement came the deluge.

As campaign manager, Rosenblith informed me in no uncertain terms, all contacts with the candidate were to go through him. The law was laid down. I was not to contact our candidate unless I informed Rosenblith first and received approval. That was the initial of the proverbial straws that broke the camel's back.

I didn't like Rosenblith. And I came to know quickly that he didn't like me. Every morning there was a staff meeting behind closed doors.

On no occasion was I ever invited into the staff meetings. Although my desk was right next to Michal Regunberg's I was never asked into the inner sanctums of the Kerry campaign. Kerry's mother, a delightful little old lady, would often come in and we'd chat over coffee and donuts. And I also got to know his brother Cameron, a convert to Judaism who the campaign seemed to keep way in the closet. In effect, I had no idea what was going on, what the issues were or what the campaign strategy was about. Even Michal Regunberg, a genuine policy wonk who was rarely invited into the senior staff meetings herself, seemed to be in the dark. It was like working in a vacuum. After about three weeks I stopped coming into the headquarters and worked from home. I could just as easily make my calls from home and save on gas and parking. As it turned out nobody seemed to miss me.

From time to time somebody in the campaign would call and ask what I was working on. One day I was in the headquarters working on a fundraiser and the wife of the guy who had agreed to host the party called and for about forty-five minutes she drove me nutty over the flower arrangements. I felt like telling her to stick the flower arrangements up her pampered ass. But, in the best interest of the campaign, I held my deadly tongue. Not once did anyone ask me a policy question that was in any way related to the Jewish community or the Middle East. It became evident that my real job was to be a funnel—money from Jews into the Kerry campaign. It's sad but if you ask me, the one thing in his long political career that John Kerry has always been about…is money. Before anything, even love, John Kerry has always been about money.

It was around that time that I knew the Kerry Senate campaign and me were going to part our ways. I tried calling the candidate. He never returned my calls. And so I just stopped coming in. To this day I don't have any idea if the flower arrangements at that fundraiser were appropriate.

Long story short: Kerry beat his Democratic primary opposition and went on to crush his poor Republican opponent, businessman Ray Shamie in the general. And I never heard from the Kerry campaign again.

That summer I took a job teaching at MCI Norfolk and the adjacent Bay State prison in the Boston University prison education program and worked part time at the Framingham Jewish Federation doing office work to make ends meet. My radio show was on the road to cancellation when I received a call at home from Kerry's Republican opponent, Ray Shamie himself. Shamie had run for the senate against Ted Kennedy and in Kennedy country had been crushed. Now, a little better known, he was taking on John Kerry after defeating Richard Nixon's former Attorney General, the blue-blooded Elliot Richardson in the primary.

Could I, Shamie asked, stop at his house on my way to my classes at Norfolk Prison? Since Shamie lived in nearby Walpole, Massachusetts I could and did.

Ray Shamie seemed like an amiable, down-to-earth guy for a multi-millionaire. But after a few minutes of conversation it was clear to me that he had little understanding of Massachusetts politics. He had heard, he told me, that I had left the Kerry campaign and that I was somewhat disillusioned with the candidate. Could I tell him anything that he might use?

The first thing I said was, "Let's take a walk." Familiar with Richard Nixon's audio taping devices I had to assume that Shamie's well-appointed home office was wired for sound. Paranoid? Maybe. But sometimes even paranoids, as they say, have enemies. We walked around a small lake that was adjacent to Shamie's spacious and well-kept property.

First, I told Shamie in no uncertain terms that he didn't have a snowball in hell's chance to beat John Kerry in the election (Kerry beat him 55-45%). Nobody knew him and Massachusetts was at its liberal zenith. He vehemently disagreed. Then I said that while I did have some differences with the campaign and certainly with the campaign manager that I had never really had a falling out with the candidate himself. And third, I told Shamie that there was little I could do for him. I was a registered Democrat (albeit of a conservative bent) and had only voted for a Republican once in my life—Ronald Reagan (by 1984 of course).

Shamie disagreed with me again. He would win he said. He wanted to call a press conference with me at his side to ward off any hint that he was an anti-Semite. Why, I asked, would anyone think such a terrible thing?

For one thing Shamie told me, he was of Lebanese extraction. And even though he was a Christian, he said that the Kerry people were painting him as an Arab and an enemy of Israel. He also worried that the Kerry people had infiltrated his campaign and asked me if I knew anything about that. I did not; even though far worse things were typical in the Bay State political wars.

Shamie said that the Kerry campaign had been dropping hints to the media that he had anti-Jewish literature on his bookshelves and he wanted someone with credibility in the Jewish community to counter these charges. I laughed and told Shamie that if someone came into my house and looked on my bookshelves that they would find *Mein Kampf* along with biographies of Goebbels, Goering, Hitler, Hess, Bormann and Himmler to name only a few of the more notorious Nazis. Not to mention over a hundred other books on Nazi Germany (one of my Ph.D. fields).

We talked for a few more minutes but Shamie soon realized that he could not get me to sit with him at a press conference and I had to get to MCI Norfolk to teach my courses. I never saw or heard from Shamie who lost the election that fall. The only good thing that came out of Shamie's abortive senatorial campaign was a revived Massachusetts Republican party and the production of some top level campaign aides who went on to somewhat lead the Republican party in the Bay State into the twenty-first century in politics and journalism: Joe Malone, a Shamie acolyte, became State Treasurer and if he hadn't hired some inordinately corrupt bozos at the state lottery or allied himself with some of his neer do well Waltham pals he might have even made governor. But Malone, who had joined me for breakfast and lunch on a number of occasions, just couldn't separate himself from hangers-on who saw his political success as a golden opportunity to bilk the system. Todd Domke became a major Republican pundit and consultant and Jeff Jacoby went on to become a columnist at the

Boston Herald and at this writing is the lone conservative voice over at the *Boston Globe;* and Charlie Manning is one of the most sought after Republican spokesman in the state. As for Ray Shamie himself, after doing more than anyone to revive the moribund fortunes of the Massachusetts Republican party, he died of cancer in 1999.

By the spring of 1985 I was editing the weekly arts section of *the Boston Ledger, the Brookline Citizen* and *the Allston-Brighton Item* in addition to writing a weekly column (mostly about politics) that appeared in all of the Citizen Group publications And I had somehow managed to extend my stay at Boston University where my Kennedy and Black history courses still flourished along with a survey section of American history. I would often go to meet my friends for dinner at the Harvest on Brattle Street in Cambridge just a ten minute drive from the newspaper's offices on Harvard Street in Brookline. On Thursday nights the Harvest bar and restaurant became for me the place where everybody knew your name. A lot of writers like Robert B. Parker and Robin Cook hung out at the Harvest. By the early 1980s I was spending three to four nights a week at the Harvest. The place became my only conduit to meeting women for the better part of a decade and I was to eventually meet a woman there, Ann Marchette, with whom I had an on and off again (she might say mostly off; I would say mostly on) relationship for over twenty years. It lasted from 1982 to 2003. Ironically, although we first met at the Harvest, she lived right around the corner from me facing a tranquil pond in Sudbury.

One Thursday night I was having dinner alone (my Israeli buddy Eli Rappaport, a Harvard University biologist and Dersh were both apparently late) when who should walk into the restaurant but Senator John Kerry and Roanne Sragow. Seeing me eating alone Kerry walked right up to my table and asked if I minded if he and Roanne could join me for dinner.

Now remember, there was no bad blood between Kerry and me. I didn't know if he had any idea why I had left the campaign and to be honest, at the time, I didn't really care. My problem had always been with Ron Rosenblith who, I had heard through the grapevine, had moved to Washington to start some political internet newsletter called *The Hotline*. I had no idea what it was all about As far as Ron Rosenblith was concerned I never felt that Washington's gain was Brookline's loss.

Roanne was her ever pleasant and attractive self as John Kerry and I made small talk. "How do you like life in D.C.?" I asked. "It's a real blast," Kerry answered. "I'm having a ball." I didn't ask at what and I certainly didn't bring up his marriage. I had read in the papers that Kerry had finally separated from his long-suffering wife Julia. Was Kerry living with Roanne? I had no idea. We had our dinner, made our small talk, Alan Dershowitz arrived, sat with us and made some more small talk and the evening passed without anything of remarkable note to report.

And that was the last time I ever laid eyes on John F. Kerry in person. But it was hardly the end of our relationship.

CHAPTER 59

From 1985 to mid-1990 I had the good fortune to work for the publisher of Citizen Group Publications. Fred Phinney was the owner-publisher of five long standing weeklies in the greater Boston area. His father had begun *the Boston Ledger* and *the Brookline Citizen* almost fifty years before I came aboard. In the years that I worked as an editor/columnist for Phinney I was a virtual writing machine and Fred didn't mind that I continued to teach at Boston University. In addition to editing the arts section of all the papers, *This Week,* and writing a weekly column, by 1987 I had become editor of *the Boston Ledger* and authored an additional column called initially "B& L at the B & D" (Bagels and Lox at the B and D Deli in Brookline; get it?) where I held court over breakfast every Thursday while interviewing the major politicians in the Bay State. Years later we moved the breakfast to lunch at Matt Garrett's on Harvard Street and renamed the column MG2 (Marty Goldman at Matt Garrett's) where I eventually lunched with Mayor Kevin White, Lieutenant Governor Evelyn Murphy, Senate President William "Billy" Bulger (brother of the notorious Boston gangster James "Whitey" Bulger who is just below Osama Bin Ladin on the FBI's most wanted list) and a number of Boston sports stars including Boston Celtics greats like M.L. Carr and Dave "Big Red" Cowens.

According to Joe Kennedy, who ran for Congress in the 8th District in 1986, his political guru Michael Goldman (no relation!) told him that "before he sat down with the *Boston Globe,* he had best sit down with Marty Goldman who could put him in the *Boston Ledger* and *the Allston-Brighton Item.*" Now I don't know if Joe Kennedy was shining me...but I do know that Michael Goldman always had his major clients coming to the B& D deli for breakfast with me over many years.

As time passed almost everybody who was anybody in Massachusetts politics jockeyed for position from my Thursday morning perch at the B & D (Joe Kennedy returned for breakfast twice). After a few columns I didn't have to invite anyone. City councilors, state reps, state senators and others in power in the state would often call me at the paper to request a breakfast date.

In all the years I wrote I never once wrote a column about Senator John F. Kerry. I did, at one point, rip a good friend of his who was running against Joe Kennedy in the 8th District because I caught him in a lie. In that column I referred to John Kerry by his middle name and called him "Forbesy"—but it was all tongue in cheek and hardly malicious although Tom Vallely, the subject of that column, might disagree.

In 1988 I covered the Democratic Convention in Atlanta and did a couple of stints on the Jerry Williams WRKO talk show. In Boston over the years I had guested on his talk show on many occasions. In Atlanta I stayed in the same motel as Jerry, the most successful and talented talk show host in Boston radio, who had become a buddy of mine. One night Williams and I were having a drink together in a hotel bar when Larry King walked up to Jerry to say hello. Jerry introduced me to King who told me the story of how he actually owed his amazing career to the good advice of his pal Jerry Williams. After an amazing talk radio run in many of the major markets of America (Philadelphia, Miami, Chicago and Boston) Jerry was summarily dismissed from his slot at WRKO-AM without so much as a fare-thee-well and he died in 2003. Some say of a broken heart. He was succeeded by *Boston Herald* columnist Howie Carr who, still on the air, owes more than he could ever admit to Jerry Williams. You want to hear the best voice that ever burned up the airwaves? Listen to a tape of Jerry Williams reading *A Child's Christmas in Wales* by Dylan Thomas. Or read *Burning up the Air: Jerry Williams, Talk Radio, and the Life in Between* by Jerry's old producers Alan Tolz and Steve Elman. Jerry Williams was *sui generis*.

I broke a fairly big story for *The Ledger* during the convention about the return of John Sasso (who had been fired a year before over his releasing a video tape dealing with Joe Biden) to the disheveled Dukakis campaign. I dictated the story to one of our reporters over the phone and came back unhappily convinced that Governor Michael Dukakis would somehow squander a 17 point lead over his opponent Vice-President George H. W. Bush. In fact, shortly after the Georgia Convention I wrote a column blasting the Vice-President that was picked up and covered by Chris Black of *The Boston Globe* and circulated by Senator John Kerry's D.C. office who called requesting my column in the overnight mail before it hit the street so they could help circulate it. Of course, I sent the Kerry people my column giving them a day or so heads up before publication. In my *Bostonia* column I had predicted a Dukakis nomination during the primaries; and a Dukakis loss in the general election. I had an excellent source in the Dukakis campaign constantly filling me in on the daily disarray that the campaign suffered almost to the day of the election.

While I had my political differences over the years with Mike Dukakis, I always liked him personally. And one thing I knew without a shadow of a doubt: Michael Dukakis was one of the most decent politicians and honorable men I had ever met in public life. If every political leader was like Mike Dukakis the United States would be a far better country. I actually endorsed Dukakis in 1988 in a column to which Dukakis kindly responded a day or so after his crushing loss to George Bush. I have always wondered what kind of president Mike Dukakis would have made. The bottom line is that if the Duke had beaten George Bush in 1988 the country might well have been spared the despicable years of creeping and creepy Clintonism. My late brother-in-law Alvin Brown always described both Clintons as an "affliction" on the body politic. I felt, from the moment Bill and Hillary entered the White House in 1993, that they brought a dictionary with them where the word "truth" had been deleted. The Clintons have sullied American political life in ways that are irreparable. And the worst thing is that they both got away with it. The Clintons are both living proof that sometimes the good guys just don't win.

At any rate aside from my "Forbesy" throwaway, I never once wrote anything that could even be considered remotely negative about Senator John Kerry. I had no axes to grind with the senator or anyone remotely related to his work in Washington.

By 1990 Citizen Group Publications had hit difficult times. In the late eighties and nineties newspapers, giving way to new technological modes of communication, were folding in record numbers. Our biggest competition wasn't *The Boston Phoenix. The Ledger* was taking its major lumps from *The Tabs,* another group of Boston weeklies founded and owned by a very creative publisher Russell Pergament and a few of his buddies. Our advertising base was shrinking and Fred Phinney attempted to make cuts in every way possible. He decided to shrink *This Week,* which I still continued to edit, down into four-page insert as opposed to a separately published section. I had to fire a few freelancers which I found difficult. But nothing Fred seemed to do could ultimately prevent the tragic financial freefall of his five weekly publications.

One day over a difficult luncheon Fred told me he had to let me go since I was the highest paid journalist on his staff. He sweetened the impact by promising to continue to run my weekly column at a more than generous free lance number. However, with no benefits and a shrunken salary I was forced to quickly look elsewhere for work. And the party didn't last long. By summer 1990 Citizen Group Publications had become part of Boston's journalistic history.

Luckily I had met up with an ambitious and creative young Russian émigré by the named of Alex Teperman. Teperman and his wife had just started a local magazine, *Boston Woman.* Alex had heard of my departure from Citizen Group and over lunch offered me a fairly decent contract to write monthly features for *Boston Woman.* I had written many features over the years at Citizen Group so there did not seem to be a major problem. I was still teaching two courses at Boston University; I was still the bi-monthly political columnist for *Bostonia,* (I was summarily fired in mid-1990 when John Silber, Boston University's very capable president, ran for Governor and I turned in a column describing why Silber's campaign was a political disaster. *The Boston Globe* ran the story of my dismissal as did Channel 5's TV magazine *Chronicle.* John Silber went on to lose the election to Republican William Weld) the Boston University alumni magazine that John Silber and his editor Laura Fried (Laura was not the editor when one of BU's lickspittles canned me!) had decided to take nationally; and so with my weekly column still running for Citizen

Group and the money from *Boston Woman* I was actually doing better financially than when I was tied down to a fulltime job for over forty hours a week.

My first piece for *Boston Woman* was a very long article on Jonathan Pollard, the jailed Jewish spy who had been James Bonding for the Israelis, and his wife Anne. I interviewed both Alan Dershowitz and his brother Nathan who, at the time, both represented Pollard (who, at this writing over twenty years later, still sits in a federal prison). The article was published and there was little response. I attributed it to the fact that the magazine was still experiencing the pangs of being newly born or the fact that no one gave much of a shit about the plight of the infamous Pollards!

The editor of *Boston Woman,* Nancy Roosa, a bright young woman from Cincinatti, then asked me to do an article on sex and politics. No problem. A few weeks later I turned my manuscript in. It was about Abraham and Mary Lincoln, Andrew and Rachel Jackson, Franklin and Eleanor Roosevelt and John and Jacqueline Kennedy among others. Nancy called me at home. Sensitive to my fragile scribbler's ego, she noted that the article was very well written and that its historical accuracy could hardly be questioned. But, Nancy noted, the damn thing bored her to tears. Couldn't I spice it up with a few more current examples of political relationships that might hit her readers a little more firmly in the solar plexus? Nancy wanted a full-scale rewrite and, she made it clear, she wanted some real dirt dug up if I could possibly find it. Did I know anyone who might go on the record about their relationship with a local prominent pol?

As a matter of fact, I did.

CHAPTER 60

"I think that when the lies are all told and forgot the truth will be there yet. It don't move about from place to place and it don't change from time to time."
  No Country for Old Men
  Cormac McCarthy

"...you probably can't figure out the truth, if you think you know ahead of time what the truth is supposed to be."
  Robert B. Parker
  School Days

The rumor around Boston in late 1989 and early 1990 was that Senator John Kerry had unceremoniously broken up with his longtime paramour. I had heard it but John Kerry's love life held precious little interest for me. The story I had heard and which was confirmed after a few phone calls was that he had been romantically involved with a number of Hollywood types like Morgan Fairchild and Michelle Phillips from the Mamas and Papas (surprise! surprise!) and that his girlfriend of long standing had simply tired of reading about his amorous antics in the newspapers. As I said, I knew little of Kerry's private life and could have cared less.

Over a conversation with a former Kerry staffer I was filled in with some of the more gory details. Kerry, by 1990 was divorced or in the process, was a lying and philandering no-good bastard (according to another source, a friend of Kerry's former girlfriend). He had, I was told, cheated on her for years and she finally, in devastated frustration, had given the senator his walking papers. It has always amazed me that many women, who engage in an affair with a married man, don't seem overly concerned that he would ultimately do to her just what he had done to his wife—cheat like a bandit! After all, John Kerry had cheated on his wife Julia with Nora Flax (the name I used for the girlfriend in the article) for years.

However, according to my source, even though she was heartbroken and very angry, the girlfriend would never go public with the season of her discontent. What did I have to lose? I picked up the phone and called the girlfriend. To my great surprise, she was delightfully receptive, friendly and seemed desirous of unburdening herself to somebody she knew and trusted. That somebody would be me! We made a date to meet for drinks at the Lafayette Hotel bar in Downtown Crossing in center city Boston.

Over the years when I interviewed a celebrity (like Judy Collins, Jane Russell or Roddy McDowell) I usually used a tape recorder and then returned to my office where I painstakingly transcribed the interview verbatim into my computer. Then I printed it out, pasted it up and, with an accompanying photo that is how the interview appeared in print. But this interview was to be different. I was not about to freak out the senator's ex-paramour. So, instead of a tape recorder I took my small Reporter's Notebook and, after a comfortable few minutes of catch-up small-talk, I took out my notebook and began to write down exactly what she said. She didn't blink.

We spent about two hours at the hotel during the interview over drinks and then she asked if I would give her a lift to her nearby apartment not far from the Charles River at Charles River Park, a high-end Boston complex. There were two caveats to which I agreed: one was that I would not use her real name; the second was that, no matter what fallout resulted from the article, she would always deny having spoken to me even though I told her that hardly anyone in Boston journalistic circles would not know the actual identity of the pseudo-anonymous girlfriend. That turned out to be a mistake and I would have to live with that mistake because under our agreement I could never divulge her name. And I never have!

The article "The Politics of Passion" appeared in the February 1989 issue of *Boston Woman* with my byline.

And then all hell broke loose in the Boston media.

I am not going to rehash my article. Suffice it to say that it didn't make the senator in question (I never named him in the article!) look very good.

In the winter of 1989 the Boston media went into feeding frenzy mode: there was a TV show on Channel 5's daily magazine show *Chronicle* about my story.

The Boston Globe predictably joined the fray February 22, 1989 with a piece that said in part:

> *Just last week, the magazine Boston Woman printed a story purportedly about a US Senator and the lover he abandoned after a long relationship. The story, which does not mention Kerry's name, was widely believed to be an account of Kerry's long, fitful relationship with Boston attorney Roanne Sragow, but Kerry called the article fiction. The affair collapsed under the weight of repeated press allegations of simultaneous love affairs Kerry was conducting with Sragow and other women, most notably (Morgan) Fairchild (also mentioned in article: Emma Gilby, Catherine Oxenberg, Susan Sullivan and Michelle Phillips). Kerry was divorced last August from his heiress wife, Julia...Sragow declined comment about her relationship with Kerry, but friends said she was deeply hurt more by Kerry's denial of repeated printed revelations than by the revelations themselves.*

All of this was difficult for me (although more than anyone I certainly should have been aware of the consequences of writing about sexual politics in the pre-Lewinsky era). The most troubling reaction to "The Politics of Passion" came when *the Boston Phoenix* published a long article in their February 24-March 2, 1989 issue by Mark Jurkowitz and Scot Lehigh entitled "Kerry-ed Away" in which the two political reporters eviscerated me. Now I had known Lehigh for a while. I always liked and respected Scot Lehigh (who is now an op-ed columnist for *the Boston Globe*). Scot Lehigh is a political writer who has never been in any pol's pocket. Mark Jurkowitz was another story. He had an axe to grind with me for years ever since I had covered the campaign of James Roosevelt against Joe Kennedy in the 8th District congressional race in 1986. Jurkowitz was the press secretary for Roosevelt's congressional run and, although I liked the great president's grandson personally, after closely following the campaign I came to the judgment that Roosevelt was a lousy candidate and was running a stupid race against Joe Kennedy (he was ultimately crushed in the primary). Of course, I said so on many occasions in print. Jurkowitz actually called me at one point and asked me to let up on his candidate. I told him in no uncertain terms to get stuffed. So Mark Jurkowitz was playing a little game of pay-back.

The brutal article in *the Phoenix* hit me personally both as a writer and columnist and just about accused me of fabricating my *Boston Woman* piece because Kerry's ex-girlfriend when asked to comment, of course, denied having ever talked or met with me. As Lehigh and Jurkowitz wrote, "The major question that lingered was whether well-known Boston attorney Roanne Sragow was the source of the unflattering portrait of her longtime, and now former lover John Kerry. And if she was not, where did former Citizen Group editor Martin S. Goldman get the quotes for his story in *Boston Woman*? Sragow has moved to distance herself from the piece. 'I've read the story that appeared in *Boston Woman* magazine,' she told the *Phoenix*. 'I was not the source for the information that appeared in the article. The story is fiction. It's not about me and I don't want to be associated with it.'" At one point 'Nora Flax' even called me at home to commiserate and apologize for distancing herself from the truth. She asked if I was ultimately going to divulge her name. I told her that, as I had promised, I would not.

Lehigh and Jurkowitz (that's his real name!) went on to question my motives for writing the piece, claiming that I was settling a score with the senator. As they wrote, "...the Kerry forces think he harbors a grudge." To prove their point they brought up my old column in *The Boston Ledger* from 1987 where I joked about "Forbesy." They also quoted Ron Rosenblith, who had been obviously trotted out by the Kerry defense forces. Rosenblith said that he had asked me to leave the Kerry campaign in 1984 because "it wasn't working out." The truth is that after that first morning I never spoke to Ron Rosenblith again. And so the Kerry troops were painting me as a disgruntled employee who had been fired from the great man's quest of 1984. The truth is that I was not even "gruntled."

The straw that broke the camel's back came when Howie Carr The Boston Herald's well-known bad boy interviewed me over the phone and published a column in the Sunday Herald rehashing my writing with a few well-aimed (at Kerry) misquotes and gleefully bashing the junior senator from Massachusetts. As I had told Kerry's girlfriend, everybody in the Boston journalism and political community would instantly know the identity of "Nora Flax." A very bright woman, she should have been aware of that fact. But you know what they say about "a woman scorned!"

Needless to say, it was an uncomfortable few weeks for me. Nobody, who has little in the way of tangible assets beyond their integrity as a writer, enjoys being called a liar in print. But I took my lumps and for the most part kept my own counsel. I don't recall if I responded to the hatchet job by Lehigh and Jurkowitz. If I did, it never made it into print. But, like all things in the ongoing scandals of American political life, the controversy over the Boston Woman article finally passed into obscurity as the Boston media sharks swam off to other blood in the Massachusetts waters.

The following summer in its "Best and Worst" section Boston Magazine named me the worst political columnist in Boston. At first, the choice upset me. But I was in good company. Mike Barnicle of the Boston Globe (now a fixture as a commentator on MSNBC's "Morning Joe") was named worst columnist and so, after a phone call to the magazine's editor John Strahinich, I put it all behind me. Strahinich, another Boston writer I knew and always liked, apologetically informed me that the choice had been made by a Boston political consultant who had been in John Kerry's hip pocket for years. And since I knew the fat pantload in question also had a score to settle with me for a number of reasons, I did not respond to the dubious award. As my then girlfriend Ann tried to cajole me, "At least they spelled your name correctly!"

I didn't think much about John Kerry or his ex-girlfriend for years. On his way out of office in December 1990 Governor Michael Dukakis appointed her a district court judge. Although I wondered if that was partly due to the junior senator's influence for his ex's continued silence, I really never knew. When she ultimately married, the girl just couldn't get away from politics. The man she married, Richard Licht, had been Lieutenant Governor of Rhode Island. When asked if he knew anything about his wife's long attachment to Senator John Kerry it was reported that he responded, "I'm certainly aware of their relationship" said Richard Licht but Sragow, "has only the nicest things to say about John Kerry." Licht should have been sitting with me and "Nora Flax" at the Lafayette Hotel in the winter of 1989!

CHAPTER 61

As everyone knows Senator John Kerry finally achieved his lifelong dream and goal garnering the Democratic nomination for the presidency in Boston in 2004 where he saluted the American people in his lame statement "...reporting for duty." I watched the primaries that political season with bemused ambivalence from afar. I had moved to Southern Maine in 1999 after teaching college for most of the 1990s. George W. Bush, reacting to the national fallout from 9/11, had drawn the country into an unpopular war in Iraq in order to take down Saddam Hussein and was getting kids blown up by IEDs on a daily basis. And the economy had begun to tank. John Kerry should have waltzed into the White House. There is no question that when it came to intellect and knowledge of the troubled world, John Kerry was heads and tails above the amiable but limited Texan who came to power under disputed circumstances in the presidential election of 2000.

But John Kerry was absolutely predictable. More out of touch with mainstream America than most big-foots in D.C., Senator Kerry surrounded himself with the usual cast of liberal Democratic apparatchiks like Bob Shrum who had lost more presidential campaigns than I can count and Kerry was ultimately deep-sixed by the Swift Boat guys who wrote that scathing book *Unfit for Command*. Unfortunately Kerry had learned nothing from Michael Dukakis's failure to respond to the patriotic trashing he took by Bush the Elder in 1988. To question Kerry's Viet Nam record, in my estimation, was a tragic sham. Kerry enlisted and to my knowledge he served honorably. I have a great many friends in Florida who are Viet Nam veterans. They all have one thing in common: none of their combat experiences were similar. Each returned home with a different view of the war. Kerry's later opposition to the war only mirrored the dissatisfaction many vets (including this one) felt about that misbegotten adventure in Southeast Asia. By the time Kerry decided to stop windsurfing off Nantucket and respond to the vicious attacks by the Swift Boaters the election of 2004 was lost along with John Kerry's fondest dream.

When it was apparent that Kerry had the nomination wrapped up I began to worry. Would someone, somehow resurrect "The Politics of Passion?" I didn't have long to wait.

On July 20, 2004 *the Boston Herald* published an article titled "All the senator's women (Gigolo John) and Kerry due for manscaping" by David R. Guarino and Andrew Miga. Don't ask me what that means! The piece read in part:

> *Boston Woman magazine never drew a lot of interest locally, and it eventually folded. But its February 1989 issue had a scorcher of a story that quickly drew in political Massachusetts—mostly with knowing nods of understanding.*
>
> *The piece called "The Politics of Passion," detailed the romance, lengthy "affair" and breakup of a woman and a U.S. senator.*
>
> *The woman, given the assumed name of Nora Flax, talked about the opportunistic, ego-driven pol who went to Washington and quickly developed a love for the televison cameras and Hollywood actresses.*
>
> *"When these guys are elevated to a public position—every day of their life, they have women throwing themselves at them," she was quoted as saying. "It served his ego, this movie-star thing."*
>
> *Most everyone in the reading public assumed the woman was Boston Attorney Roanne Sragow and the senator was John F. Kerry. Kerry called the piece "fiction..."*

Then on August 11, 2004 someone (not me) put the entire article with my byline "U.S. Senator's Mistress: The Politics of Passion: A U.S. Senator's Mistress Tells How Her Powerful Love Was Destroyed By His Love of Power" on the internet without my permission.

I knew it would not be long before my phone would be ring.

The call came from *The National Enquirer.* A representative of the scandal sheet identified himself and then asked if I would allow him to come to Maine for an interview. No I answered. I was not interested in being interviewed by *the National Enquirer*. He persisted. What did I want for an interview? I told him that before I would continue the conversation that I wanted to talk to my lawyer in Boston. The problem was that I really didn't have a lawyer in Boston!

I thought about calling Alan Dershowitz. But this could get really sleazy. And I didn't want to involve Dersh, who was probably still friendly with John Kerry, in anything as tawdry as a negotiation with *the Enquirer*. I called an old friend, Attorney Mark Levinson, who I knew from his time as President of the Board of the American Jewish Committee's New England region in the early 1990s. Mark was with a large law firm, Burns and Levinson, in Boston and had recently visited me in Maine where we had enjoyed a delightful dinner together.

Mark agreed to represent me with *the Enquirer*.

When *the Enquirer* called back I gave them my attorney's Boston phone number, told them that I would have nothing else to say and that all negotiations would have to go through my lawyer. They called Mark and in the first conversation, according to him, they were willing to spend big bucks. Mark, completely aware of the circumstances, wanted to know how much money I wanted him to ask for. I had no idea.

Over the next few days I lost a great deal of sleep. There were a number of conversations between *the Enquirer* and my attorney. The monetary figure was rising. But I was acutely aware of exactly what I was about to get myself involved with. At one point Mark called to inform me that if an accommodation was reached that *the Enquirer* would expect me to sit with them for a press conference and that event would probably lead me to doing the major radio talk shows as well as the cable TV talk shows. I thought about being grilled by Larry King or that blowhard Chris Matthews. And I thought more about what the impact of my article would be on a presidential election. John Kerry was hardly my hero. But whatever his relationship had been with "Nora Flax," it certainly had no bearing whatsoever on whether or not he should become President of the United States. It was, after all, a relationship and I had blown so many of those that I had no right to be the moral arbiter of John Kerry's love life.

On the third day of negotiations Mark called to tell me that he thought the figure was going to rise to $200,000. I told Mark of my misgivings and also told him that my wife was deadset against this thing going forward. It was, my wife believed and I came to feel, just sleazy. And although I have not led a life of moral perfection, I have never done sleazy well. So I finally told Mark to tell *the Enquirer* that we were dropping out of the negotiations and that under no circumstances would I cooperate with any story relating to the Democratic nominee for president.

But *the National Enquirer* didn't give up easily. Their guy called me to ask me to give him a number. Visions of hundred thousand dollar bills danced in my head. A new Grady White cabin cruiser; a Corvette; a long family trip to France! Then reality set in. Even a million dollars would not appreciably change my life which in 2004 was pretty damn good. I had a new home in Maine without a mortgage; two cars; an adequate fishing boat; a new wife, daughters and grandkids; a great Labrador retriever named Gideon. Why mess with all that to do the wrong thing? Who was I to insert myself in such a sleazy fashion into the middle of a presidential election? So, to make a long story short, I didn't. To paraphrase Spike Lee, I did the right thing.

One more thing about John Kerry: Not that it matters much but I didn't vote for him in 2004. I wanted to vote for him because I knew he was a lot brighter than George W. Even Kerry himself, at one moment of maximum frustration during the 2004 race, is alleged to have complained to his campaign consultant Bob Shrum, "I can't believe that this guy is beating me!" My take on Kerry in 2004 was the same as it was in 1984. He just couldn't connect with the average guy on the American street. Oh, Kerry was great with the Springsteens and Streisands in Hollywood. But when it came to connecting with the American people, he couldn't jump the broom and make a marriage. And although my heart told me to vote for Kerry, my head couldn't forget what Nora Flax had said for my *Boston Woman* article in 1989. According to Nora back then, "His number-one priority is himself… The rest, what he told people, was all bullshit…what the public saw. It was all for show…and he is a pathological liar."

For me the ultimate test of John Kerry's abortive attempt for the White House was his choice of John Edwards as his running mate. Kerry's VP pick in itself validated my vote. As I said, I make no moral judgments about John Kerry and his female relationships. However, a president of the United States must be a strong judge of character. And by choosing John Edwards as his running mate in 2004 John Kerry demonstrated a serious lack of good judgment. John Edwards was a fraud and is a superannuated scumbag. And I don't believe for a moment that John Kerry was unaware of his running mate's shortcomings—maybe not his illicit affair but certainly of the fact that John Edwards was and is a phony.

Washington is just too small a town where gossip is coin of the realm and Kerry, whatever his faults, has always been plugged in to that town. If a man like John Edwards didn't give a fig for his ailing wife and children how can anyone have thought he really cared about the poverty-stricken people he was always preaching to America about? The idea that a man like John Edwards could have been our president is not only a sad commentary on our democracy; it is absolutely sickening. And John Kerry would have had that man a heartbeat away from 1600 Pennsylvania Avenue. Like I said, the guy is a poor judge of character (and lacks a bit of character himself).

During the summer of 2010 John Kerry was excoriated in the Boston press for buying a sail boat that cost over $7 million and for trying to beat the state of Massachusetts out of $500,000 in sales tax. Could any elected official be more out of touch with the American electorate? At a time when the American people were suffering massive recession, unprecedented home foreclosures and almost depression level unemployment the senator from Massachusetts now married to Teresa Heinz, one of the richest women in the United States, told all his fellow citizens to eat cake. They ought to rename Kerry, "Senator Antoinette."

In late 2010, to celebrate his 25 years in the Senate, John Kerry rented the 2,000 seat Boston Symphony where Boston Pops conductor Keith Lockhart, singer James Taylor and Ben Affleck were scheduled to fete the country's richest senator whose net worth is an estimated

$239 million. With $2.7 million in his campaign warchest, no re-election fight for four years, and the toughest economy in recent memory, John Kerry was looking to sell tickets for from $75 to $4,800 for this particular fundraising extravaganza. As Boston University political science professor Thomas Whalen noted, "The symbolism really works against him, which is typical of Kerry. It doesn't exactly portray him as a man of the people..."

Kerry is now jockeying for his place in history as he lines up his ducks to leave public life as Secretary of State. Perhaps one day a historian writing a biography of Kerry will hopefully be diligent in their research. In the end perhaps the people get the leaders they deserve. Case closed.

CHAPTER 62

"One of the things you realize about gettin(g) older is that not everybody is goin to get older with you..."
Sheriff Bell
No Country for Old Men
Cormac McCarthy

The 1990s were not nearly as dramatic. I had left Massachusetts during the winter of 1990-91 to stay part of the winter in Florida with my faithful little Terrier Wookie who had, in 1982, followed me into my office at the ADL from the streets of Boston. After almost three months in Florida Wookie and I returned to Massachusetts where I wrote my first book, *Nat Turner and the Southampton Revolt of 1831* under contract to the well-known publisher Franklin Watts in New York. The book was named one of the notable books of that year by the National Council of Social Studies. And the best thing to happen with the publication of the book is one of my most prized and treasured possessions now framed on my office wall in Maine—a personal letter from my favorite American writer, William Styron, praising my work on the rebel slave as "the best possible introduction to the subject imaginable..."

I finally met Styron for the first time in 2003, three years before he died, at a televised C-Span panel at the Boston Public Library where the great writer and some of his works were being feted. I was able to (nervously) read the passage from my book pertaining to Styron and Nat Turner before the large crowd and the TV audience. I could tell that the fragile old man was touched and when, after the TV part was over, we were able to chat he thanked me for my written words about him and signed a couple of copies of his classic book for me.

Styron's youngest daughter Alexandra recently published a memoir, *Reading My Father*, in which she called her father an "asshole."

Undoubtedly, Bill Styron left much to be desired as a father although I believe Alexandra Styron clearly loved him. I have no quarrel with the young Ms. Styron who often felt alienated by growing up in the clutches of her father's hard-earned fame and notoriety not to mention his world famous friends. But I only knew him as one of the most important postwar writers in American life. And as a writer (*Sophie's Choice, Lie Down in Darkness, This Quiet Dust, Tidewater Morning, Darkness Visible* to name a few) he was superb. My grandfather on my mother's side also was an asshole. But when he died he didn't leave a memorable body of work that was worthy of anything. I'll take Bill Styron any day.

In mid-1991 I took a job as Associate Director of the American Jewish Committee in Boston where I would work with one of my closest and dearest friends Larry Lowenthal for over four years. My heart was never heavily into that work but I managed to jump into the middle of a number of controversies by confronting the black bigot Tony Martin on radio and TV. Martin and I did the David Brudnoy radio show for almost four hours where the popular Brudnoy (who died a few years ago) and I pummeled him relentlessly as a Black bigot and Martin and I appeared on one of those local Sunday morning TV shows moderated by Rehema Ellis (now a correspondent for NBC) where I continued my excoriation of Professor Martin as a bigot and an anti-Semite. Martin had been teaching the Nation of Islam's scurrilous tract *The Secret Relationship between Blacks and Jews* at Wellesley College and had jumped on the Nation of Islam bandwagon gleefully convicting Jews as the major culprits of the Slave Trade. The Farrakhan-NOI funded book claimed that the Jews were major players in the African Slave Trade and Tony Martin, a tenured member of the Africana Studies Department at Wellesley, was appearing all over the country garnering large lecture fees to spew out his lopsided views about slavery and Jews. Martin went on to self-immolate when he self-published a book he called *The Jewish Onslaught: Despatches (sic) from the Wellesley Battlefront.* That book managed to finally show his largely silent colleagues on the elite campus that he was a vicious bigot. In the end Tony Martin isolated himself and although the Wellesley College administration took little action his courses were dropped from the History Department curriculum and a majority of his colleagues censured him.

I was able to work with all my former colleagues, my old friend Lenny Zakim (who died in December 1999 at the young age of 46) from the ADL, Sheila Decter at the American Jewish Congress, Nancy Kaufman from the Jewish Community Council and Larry Lowenthal as we formed a rare united Jewish defense agency front in the face of Wellesley's attempt to sweep Tony Martin and his ugly campus antics under their academic robes.

You can read about our conflict with Martin and Wellesley College in Spencer Blakeslee's book, *The Death of American Anti-Semitism* and Mary Lefkowitz's great book, *History Lesson.* Blakeslee got a lot of his history about me dead wrong. But he did get the basic outlines of the Martin-Wellesley College conflagration with the Boston Jewish community. And Mary Lefkowitz and Guy Rodgers, brave professors of classics at the women's college were two of the very few on that campus who dared to stand up to Tony Martin and his classroom distortions as well as his ugly brutalization of a coed that the President and college Deans also had attempted to sweep under the smug rug of proper Wellesley teas and crumpets.

As a result of my year-long conflict with Wellesley College bigotry where I had managed to bring some unwanted and very negative publicity to the college while treading on a naive Hillel rabbi's precious turf, some powerful Wellesley Jewish alumni constantly bad-mouthed me to our New York headquarters and so my four-year tenure at the American Jewish Committee came to an abrupt end by the summer of 1994. New York constantly claimed that I wasn't being fired and that our separation was mutual. But like so much else in organized Jewish life, that was a bit of a stretch. The big givers to the AJC who were also Wellesley alumni wanted my head. And they got it.

Interestingly enough Mark Levinson, who passed away in late 2007 after a heroic battle with cancer, represented me in my separation from the agency. Although my dear friend Larry Lowenthal thrived in his time as director of the Committee, aside from a few lay leaders like Mark who I loved and admired, I found that the stultifyingly bureaucratic Jewish organization talked a great deal but did little of real substance. The AJC, which did practically nothing to save Jews during the Holocaust and had actually opposed the founding of the State of Israel in 1948, thrived on doing as little as possible that could lead to public controversy resulting in real community action. To me the AJC was intellectually and, at times, morally bankrupt. To the AJC executives and leaders in New York the most important thing that could emanate from their field offices was more and more money. And as little noise as possible.

In 1995 I became the founding director of the Center for the Study of Jewish-Christian Relations at Merrimack College in North Andover, Massachusetts. I did my best to administer the Center in a very hostile academic atmosphere. The creative president of the college, Richard Santagati, was always in my corner but others at the small school felt my presence an infringement on their academic territory. I found myself in an unwanted turf war. You may have heard the old question: why are the battles always so fierce in the academic world? Answer: because the stakes are so small.

Merrimack, an Augustinian Catholic college is a sister school to better known Villanova University outside of Philadelphia. Between 1995 and late 1998 I did my best to get an academic foothold at the school where I was able to inaugurate a number of interesting and creative new courses in the Religion Department including The Holocaust (which I taught), the Jew in American Film and Judaism (taught by a local rabbi). I also served as an adjunct professor. I enjoyed the students and many of my Merrimack colleagues but it was always an uphill fight—especially in the ongoing struggle to raise enough money to fund the Center. In 1998 exhausted by the academic infighting and the smaller minds at Merrimack College, after a brief illness and an operation, I sent the president my letter of resignation. I signed on to teach a semester at New England College in Henniker, New Hampshire that fall and then returned to Massachusetts where I sold my house in Sudbury and moved with my 4 year-old Lab Gideon to Southern Maine. I intended to spend the rest of my life fishing, gardening and writing. This is my sixth book including a racial mystery novel, *Affirmative Reaction,* where my alter ego "Michael Gideon" fights the forces of bigotry and evil with extreme prejudice.

We lost Pop in 1999, a week before the millennium, when he was almost 92; Mom hung around for seven more years but a debilitating stroke moved her rapidly into dementia and by mid-2002 she needed care around the clock. She passed away in 2006 also close to 92. So, the mortality charts may be with Ken and me. You could not have asked for better parents. Richer, maybe…but not better; I think my parent's unqualified love and support throughout my life helped to center me and keep me from going over the edge. I have never been able to understand the recent trend in American life of women having children without the presence of a man. To me, a mother and a father are equally important to the successful healthy psychological development of children. A child without the presence of a father is only halfway there when they reach adulthood. The trip through this life is difficult enough. No sense starting a kid off with half a family.

I imagine that if I had had my druthers that I would have preferred to have enjoyed a tranquil life on a small New England liberal arts college campus over all those years where I would have quietly taught American and African American history. But, caught up in the vortex of the tornadic academic forces of blatant stupidity, rank cowardice and reverse racism that tore across the college campuses of America since the late 1960s, combined with the political correctness of the era, playing the role of Mr. Chips was not to be my calling in life.

Somebody once asked me why I had chosen to center my study of American history on Black America. Why didn't I do American Jewish history? The answer is simple: it was what was interesting to me, it was what I cared about (race relations in the United States) what I wanted to do and, in my mind, the central issue of American life. Even the 2008 election of Barack Obama has not changed the issue. To me it is still the one issue that holds America back from being the country it ought to be. Except now the racists include as many Blacks as Whites. In recent years a number of academic simpletons have re-written *Huckleberry Finn* because Mark Twain used the word "nigger" over two hundred times. These intellectual pygmies expunged the "N" word and, of course, destroyed the meaning of an American classic for an entire generation of American students. It just never stops does it? Next these idiots will probably be taking "Jim" out of the book altogether because slavery was such an unmitigated evil and an embarrassment to the nation.

Well, I would happily do it all again knowing that it probably cost me an establishment academic career and a good TIAA-CREF pension. But you have to remember that I have always been from Bohemia. And guys from Bohemia, in the end, just do what they want!

Harper Lee of *To Kill a Mockingbird* fame once said, "People who have made peace with themselves are the people I most admire in the world." In a sentence, I have made peace with myself. As I complete this memoir, I am a few months away from turning 72. As my old friend Stanley, "Benny" Stein recently recently said to me, "We're all in the last quarter; and there are no time outs and no overtime!" My friend the B is a bit of a philosopher. I guess you are waiting for me to say that I wish I had done some things a little differently. I certainy do; but not too many things. Not many of the guys that came out of West Philly with me have seen what I have seen. Thank goodness Ben Shtatman didn't take me into his business! I probably would have made a lousy businessman and run his factories into the ground—itchy wool pants, ties (I hate to wear ties!) and all that.

George Orwell wrote that, "Every life viewed from the inside would be a series of defeats."

As you might surmise, I don't completely agree with the great writer. Sometimes those defeats make you stronger—tougher. I think that is what my defeats have meant to me. I did, at one point long ago feel sorry for myself. So much hard work and study; so much of my educational and teaching talent wasted. But I have never been one to dwell very long in my sadness. When depressed, I usually write or shop. I am that rare guy who isn't gay who loves to shop; to find things that are cheap—bargains. And so, although I might well be a shrink's delight (as my friend Pauline Gerson, herself a shrink, believes), I have assiduously avoided therapy, think it is largely hocum and purchased a lot of crap over the years (and thousands of books).

Since 2008 I have been splitting my time with springs and summers in Maine where I garden, write and fish in the icy dark blue Atlantic from my 18-foot Lund and winters in Central Florida where I play third base with great guys like Cincinatti, Ohio's Terry Victor on Spruce Creek's Community Softball teams and where I am again teaching a variety of history courses (The Holocaust, African American History, The Kennedy Presidency) and a film course on Woody Allen at the College of Central Florida in Ocala. I have happily re-entered the academic world with interesting, knowledgeable and very interested students. And so I am not fading into the woodwork of retirement or riding off into the sunset like John Wayne did a hundred times in his great films. I intend to go out if at all possible kicking and screaming… just like any guy from Bohemia.

And oh yes, one more thing: the lovely little Philly blonde with the pony tail from Woodcrest Avenue in Wynnefield. You remember Arlene Rachman; the great love of my young life between 1956 and 1960. I lost her but never forgot her. Her photo with me was always in my wallet throughout the years.

She called me in May of 2003 in Maine. We had not spoken in almost 35 years and had only seen one another once in 43 years. She was living in Florida and I was still hot for her. She moved to Maine two months later and we were married in 2004. But that, as they say, is another story.